DATE DUE

MAR 2 3 1981		
MAR 2 4 1984		
DEC 4 1985		
FEB		

Jurors and Rape

Jurors and Rape

A Study in Psychology and Law

Hubert S. Feild
Auburn University

Leigh B. Bienen
Department of the
Public Advocate
State of New Jersey

LexingtonBooks
D.C. Heath and Company
Lexington, Massachusetts
Toronto

Library of Congress Cataloging in Publication Data

Feild, Hubert S
   Jurors and rape.

   Includes bibliographical references and index.
   1. Rape—United States. 2. Jury—United States—Decision making. 3. Psychology, Forensic. I. Bienen, Leigh B., joint author. II. Title.
KF9329.F44   345.73'02532'019   76-48473
ISBN 0-669-01148-7

Published simultaneously in Canada

Printed in the United States of America

International Standard Book Number: 0-669-01148-7

Library of Congress Catalog Card Number: 76-48473

To Hubert Spottswood and Bernice Greene Feild, loving parents and friends, and to Henry Bienen, a true feminist, and for Laura, Claire, and Leslie Bienen who hopefully will live in times when some of these changes will simply be taken for granted.

Contents

List of Figures   ix

List of Tables   xi

Acknowledgments   xiii

Part I   *Extra-evidential Influences on Rape Trials*   1

Chapter 1   **Overview of the Study**   3

Chapter 2   **The Study: Sample, Measures, and Procedures**   9

    Sample   9
    Measuring Instruments   12
    Procedure   21
    Summary   21
    Appendix 2A: Measuring Instruments   27

Chapter 3   **Measurement and Correlates of People's Views and Knowledge about Rape**   45

    Attitudes toward Rape   49
    Knowledge about Rape   74
    Summary   88

Chapter 4   **Juror Decision Making in Rape Trials**   95

    Nature and Procedural Aspects of Rape Trials   99
    Characteristics of a Rape Case Brought to Trial   102
    Application of the Legal Rape Case   105
    Effects of Defendant, Victim, and Rape Case
       Characteristics on Juror Decision Making   106
    Background and Attitudinal Correlates of Juror
       Decision Making   119
    Effects of Juror-Rape Case Characteristic
       Interactions on Juror Decision Making   125
    Summary   141

Part II   *Rape Laws: The Accomplishments of Legislative Reform*   151

Chapter 5   **Recent Developments in Rape Reform Legislation**   153

Introduction   153
National Trends in Rape Reform Legislation   154
The Legislative History of Rape Reform
    Legislation in New Jersey   156
The Status of Consent under Reform Statutes   159
Legislative Changes in the Common-Law
    Spousal Exception   163
Changes in Statutory Age Provisions   166
Recent Legislative Developments in the Area
    of Evidence   171
The Effect of Statutory Changes in the Law
    of Evidence   174
The Social Implications of Legislative Changes
    in the Rape Laws   180

Chapter 6   **State-by-State Analysis of the Rape Laws**   207

Chapter 7   **Conclusions and Import of the Research**   459

          Index   467

          About the Authors   475

List of Figures

2A-1   Examples of Victim and Defendant in Legal Rape Case   28

4-1   Mean Juror Recommended Prison Sentence for Rape Defendants as a Function of Race of the Defendant and Race of the Victim   110

4-2   Mean Juror Recommended Prison Sentence for Rape Defendants as a Function of Race of the Defendant, Race of the Victim, and Physical Attractiveness of the Victim   111

4-3   Mean Juror Recommended Prison Sentence for Rape Defendants as a Function of Race of the Defendant, Physical Attractiveness of the Victim, and Sexual Experience of the Victim   112

4-4   Mean Juror Recommended Prison Sentence for Rape Defendants as a Function of Type of Rape and Strength of Evidence in the Case   113

4-5   Mean Juror Recommended Prison Sentence for Rape Defendants as a Function of Type of Rape and Sexual Experience of the Victim   114

4-6   Mean Juror Recommended Prison Sentence for Rape Defendants as a Function of Race of the Defendant, Sexual Experience of the Victim, and Type of Race   115

4-7   Mean Juror Recommended Prison Sentence for Rape Defendants as a Function of Race of the Victim, Sexual Experience of the Victim, and Strength of Evidence in the Case   116

4-8   Mean Juror Recommended Prison Sentence for Rape Defendants as a Function of Race of the Defendant and Race of the Jurors   128

4-9   Mean Juror Recommended Prison Sentence for Rape Defendants as a Function of Race of the Defendant and Jurors' Knowledge of a Rape Victim   129

4-10   Mean Juror Recommended Prison Sentence for Rape Defendants as a Function of Race of the Defendant and Jurors' Belief that Punishment for Rape Should Be Severe   130

4-11   Mean Juror Recommended Prison Sentence for
            Rape Defendants as a Function of Race of the
            Victim and Jurors' Knowledge of a Rape Victim   131

4-12   Mean Juror Recommended Prison Sentence for
            Rape Defendants as a Function of Physical
            Attractiveness of the Victim and Age of Juror   132

4-13   Mean Juror Recommended Prison Sentence for
            Rape Defendants as a Function of Physical
            Attractiveness of the Victim and Jurors' Belief
            that Women Should be Responsible for
            Preventing Their Own Rape   133

4-14   Mean Juror Recommended Prison Sentence for
            Rape Defendants as a Function of Physical
            Attractiveness of the Victim and Jurors' Belief
            that Motivation for Rape Is Power   134

4-15   Mean Juror Recommended Prison Sentence for
            Rape Defendants as a Function of the Type of
            Rape and Jurors' Knowledge of a Rape Victim   135

4-16   Mean Juror Recommended Prison Sentence for
            Rape Defendants as a Function of the Type of
            Rape and Jurors' Belief that Punishment for
            Rape Should Be Severe   136

4-17   Mean Juror Recommended Prison Sentence for
            Rape Defendants as a Function of Sexual
            Experience of Victim and Jurors' Belief that a
            Victim Precipitates Her Rape   137

4-18   Mean Juror Recommended Prison Sentence for
            Rape Defendants as a Function of Strength of
            Evidence in the Case and Race of Jurors   138

4-19   Mean Juror Recommended Prison Sentence for
            Rape Defendants as a Function of Strength of
            Evidence in the Case and Jurors' Belief that
            Women Should Be Responsible for Preventing
            Their Own Rape   139

4-20   Mean Juror Recommended Prison Sentence for
            Rape Defendants as a Function of Strength of
            Evidence in the Case and Jurors' Belief that
            Punishment for Rape Should Be Severe   140

List of Tables

2-1   Summary of Responses of Respondent Groups to Background Variables   10

2-2   Description of Measures Used in the Study   22

3-1   Percentage of Citizens by Sex and Race Agreeing with Items on the Attitude toward Rape Questionnaire   50

3-2   Percentage of Respondent Groups Agreeing with Items on the Attitude toward Rape Questionnaire   52

3-3   Varimax Rotated Factor Structure of Attitudes toward Rape   60

3-4   Intercorrelations among Respondent Characteristics   64

3-5   Product-Moment and Multiple Correlations between Respondent Characteristics and Dimensions of Rape Attitudes   66

3-6   Summary of Means, Univariate-Multivariate ANOVAs, and Discriminant Analysis with Rape Attitudes as Defendant Variables for Respondent Groups   72

3-7   What Proportion of Rapes Are Reported to the Police?   75

3-8   In What Proportion of Rapes Reported to the Police Are Arrests Made?   76

3-9   What Is the Role of Physical Violence when There Is a Close Relationship between the Rapist and the Victim?   77

3-10   What Percentage of Women Who Have Been Raped Know the Rapist?   77

3-11   Where Do Most Reported Rapes Occur?   78

3-12   What Proportion of Reported Rapes Involve Sexual Humiliation of the Victim?   79

3-13   Among Which Racial Combination Do Most Rapes Occur?   80

3-14   What Is the Racial Makeup of Convicted
            Rapists?   81

3-15   In Prosecuting a Rape Case, What Do Most
            States Require?   82

3-16   Of Those Persons Brought to Trial for Rape,
            What Proportion Are Found Innocent or Have
            Their Case Dismissed?   82

3-17   In What Proportion of Rapes Do Brutal
            Beatings of the Victim Occur?   83

3-18   How Old Are Most Rape Victims?   83

3-19   How Old Are Most Rapists?   84

3-20   In What Part of the United States Does the
            Highest Number of Reported Rapes Occur?   85

3-21   Correlations between Respondent Characteristics
            and Knowledge about Rape   86

4-1   Variables Suggested as Having Discriminatory
            Effects in Jury Trials   96

4-2   Disposition of Reported Violent Crimes for
            Adults   99

4-3   Summary of the Effects of Defendant, Victim,
            and Rape Case Characteristics on Jurors'
            Recommended Prison Sentences for a Rape
            Defendant   108

4-4   Correlations between Black and White Juror
            Characteristics and Recommended Prison
            Sentence Length for Rape Defendants   121

4-5   Contribution of Juror Background and Juror
            Attitudinal Variables in Predicting Jurors' Deci-
            sions in Rape Trials   123

4-6   Summary of the Effects of Rape Case
            Characteristics × Juror Characteristics on
            Jurors' Recommended Prison Sentences for a
            Rape Defendant   126

Acknowledgments

Any book based upon extensive library research and detailed empirical findings depends upon the cooperation of many people for success. First, we would like to thank our institutions, Auburn University and the New Jersey State Department of the Public Advocate, for their consistent support. Special thanks is also given to Gloria Levin of the National Center for the Prevention and Control of Rape for bringing the two authors together. Unfortunately for us, we never had as much time as we wanted to work personally together while the book was being written.

In particular, several individuals at Auburn University deserve special recognition and our thanks. We are indebted to George R. Horton and John F. Henry for providing funds and resources for initiating and continuing the project to its completion. Sincere appreciation is also due to William F. Giles who read countless drafts of the manuscript and made numerous suggestions and to Achilles A. Armenakis, Arthur G. Bedeian, and William H. Holley for their personal counsel and guidance which were, in a large way, responsible for the success of the project.

At the Department of the Public Advocate, our long-standing interest in national developments in the area of rape reform was consistently and patiently supported by Commissioner Stanley C. Van Ness, Assistant Commissioner Marcia Richman, and Assistant Public Defender John M. Cannel. Research for chapter 6 was sponsored in part by New Jersey State Law Enforcement and Planning Agency Grants No. A-C: 10-16-78 and A-C: 10-18-79. Gary Mitchell, former editor of the *Women's Rights Law Reporter* and presently with the Department of the Public Advocate, made a number of important substantive suggestions, especially concerning the presentation of the material in chapter 6. On several occasions, the entire project would have ground to a halt without the able assistance of Camille Trotto. Mary Ellen Dickson of the Department of the Public Advocate Library was also very helpful.

The legal research would have been impossible without the excellent historical collections of the New Jersey State Law Library. Robert Hand, librarian, and his knowledgeable staff were invaluable when the task required locating arcane and fugitive compilations of the law. Phyllis Warren helped with the historical research at a critical juncture. Alba Conte of the University of Pennsylvania Law School and the editors and staffmembers of the *Women's Rights Law Reporter* at Rutgers School of Law in Newark provided a great deal of assistance with the state by state summary of the laws.

The authors would also like to extend their thanks to the editorial staff of Lexington Books for their patience when deadlines passed and passed again. A book written by people in two different parts of the country and whose schedules also consist of teaching and practice will necessarily suffer unforeseen delays. Finally, a warning: there can never be a completely up-to-date summary of legislation in an area which is developing so rapidly. Any analysis will inevitably exclude some important law passed yesterday which did not appear in the most recently printed advance sheets. Of course such inadequacies, as well as all other inadequacies and mistakes, are solely the responsibility of the authors.

Lastly, we say thanks to our families, Claire and Taylor Feild and Henry, Laura, Claire, and Leslie Bienen, for their patience, support, and encouragement.

Part I
Extra-Evidential Influences and Rape Trials

1 Overview of the Study

This study examines the relationships between selected demographic and attitudinal characteristics of potential jurors and their reactions to hypothetical rape cases brought to trial. From this perspective such questions as the following become important: what attitudes and what factors make a potential juror more or less likely to vote for a conviction or an acquittal in a rape case? Are attitudes toward rape crucial? Are jurors' responses incident-specific? Or do personal attitudes toward women and sex roles determine willingness to convict?

In addition to considering the effects of juror characteristics on jurors' decisions in rape cases, the study also explores how selected victim, defendant, and case characteristics may influence their decisions. From this view, we are interested in addressing issues such as: does race of the victim or the defendant seem to influence jurors' decisions? What about the physical attractiveness of the victim; is there an effect? Are some victim or defendant characteristics more important than others in determining the outcome of a rape trial?

As the data amply illustrate, attitudes toward rape need to be defined. The prospective jurors' attitudes toward rape turn out, in part, to be a series of misconceptions about rape and the criminal justice system. What does the phrase "attitudes toward rape" mean? Rape itself refers to the crime, the criminal incident, the act of sexual intercourse which society, more particularly the state legislature, has declared to be prohibited. A crime called *rape* no longer exists in many states. States which have passed rape reform legislation no longer include rape in their criminal code. And yet, the absence of a crime called rape from the statutes does not mean that what was formerly rape (sexual intercourse without consent) does not exist. It has simply been called something else. In spite of the trend toward redefining rape as sexual assault or criminal sexual conduct, the phrase "attitudes toward rape" is still descriptive. Universities in those states which have redefined the crime will continue to hold seminars on rape, and rape crisis centers in those states are not expected to go out of existence for want of clients. Even without the semantic redefinition of the crime, however, it is apparent from a cursory glance at the literature that people do not hold the same opinions as to what constitutes rape, irrespective of what the state legislature at a particular time will define as prohibited sexual conduct of rape. For some, rape will only be encounters at gunpoint in a dark alley. For

3

others, a husband will never be able to rape his wife. For still others, the existence of a social relationship or acquaintanceship between the rapist and victim will mean that sexual conduct cannot be criminal. When we ask people—potential jurors, police officers, rape crisis counselors—about their attitudes toward rape, we will get responses which are based upon many different conceptions of rape.

From a methodological view, the present study attempts to control the unpredictable aspects of individuality by asking potential jurors and others to respond to a series of hypothetical rape cases. Potential jurors are asked to respond to hypothetical cases in which distracting elements such as trial publicity or selected individual characteristics of the witness or defendant have been manipulated in such a way so that the effect of prejudical elements on decision-making mechanisms can be examined. Thus the hypothetical cases involve "constructed" victims and "constructed" defendants; yet, they are written to seem realistic. The attempt in using a written, case approach is to screen out those aspects of a real case which are idiosyncratic, even if they are outcome-determinative, and to include those factors which some writers have felt are important in determining the outcome of a rape case. Thus the potential jurors in this study are not responding to a true-to-life rape situation as such, and the research makes an assumption that behavior in a constructed, sanitized rape situation will resemble behavior which that same person would have engaged in were he or she sitting as a juror in an actual case. Although this methodology may raise some questions, the only suitable alternative is to ask actual jurors why they voted as they did in an individual case. Yet the responses in this kind of research will be highly specific to the individual case, and many questions will remain unanswered. For example, was the particular witness or defendant personally appealing? What was the social or economic background of the juror or the jury foreman? How do such variables affect jurors' decisions? Both strategies for research must be pursued if any sort of understanding of the way in which jurors decide is to be understood. Each type of study must serve as a corrective for the biases inherent in the other. One bias in the present study is that responses to a hypothetical case may not be an accurate predictor of potential jurors' responses to an actual case because the hypothetical case is by necessity so spare in its information, in comparison to what an actual juror would take in during an actual trial, that responses to the hypothetical case indicate little about responses to an actual case. One bias of studies of actual jurors is that the explanations in one case may not have any application to a set of facts in another case. Further, if interviewing of jurors is used, the question of determining what factor determined (caused) a specific decision still remains open.

Another source of bias in studies of actual jurors is that those jurors have, at least to some extent, adopted the norms of expected juror behavior.

Actual jurors when interviewed use legal terminology such as "beyond a reasonable doubt" to explain their votes, whereas the point of studying jury behavior is to find out what are the components of the reasonable doubt whose social function is to excuse and exonerate. The circumstances of the hypothetical cases are varied in significant aspects so that the potential jurors' responses will indicate whether or not he or she thinks the incident described is rape. The decision to convict or acquit is a decision as to whether or not the conduct described is criminal, whether or not the incident constitutes rape.

The reason why this study includes a summary of state laws is because jurors will be instructed by the judge on what the law is defining rape. The judge will tell the jury what the prosecution must prove in order to document the crime. The judge will describe the elements of the crime. The jury may or may not be significantly influenced by what the judge says. Appellate courts and the legal system as a whole operate on the assumption that jurors are influenced by what the judge tells them. Most criminal cases are reversed on the basis of an error in the judge's instructions to the jury. That is in part because the judge's error in an instruction appears clearly on the record whereas other more subtle sources of prejudice, the suggestive tone of a prosecutor's attorney's comments, for example, are difficult to detect from a typed transcript.

The hypothetical case approach as used here controls additional considerations which might impact upon the decision to convict or acquit: the identity of the defendant; the social and economic status of the victim and defendant, except in the crudest terms of race; the quality of counsel; and the personality of the judge. In a real trial, all these factors and a great many others may influence the decision to convict or acquit. For example, no attempt in this study was made, or could have been made, to measure the credibility of the complaining witness on the stand. The legal term *credibility* is not defined. Nonetheless, attorneys make a rapid, intuitive assessment of the credibility of a witness and make strategic decisions accordingly. For example, a prosecutor may have two honest and sincere victims of similar rape incidents who present totally different aspects to the jury. The following examples illustrate how this could happen.

Two victims report rape on the same day to the same prosecutor in the same county of approximately 500,000 people where the largest town has about 25,000 inhabitants. Both victims live in the town, both were raped by an unknown burglar who entered by an unlocked back door, robbed the house of a television and then raped the victim at knife point. The first victim is 25 years old and lives in a duplex apartment which she shares with three roommates, all of whom were out at 2:00 A.M., the time of the incident. She had previously complained of robbery of the apartment to the police. The previous robbery incident involved the theft of cash and a radio after a party. Though she has no regular job, she works as a part-time waitress at an all-night diner on a nearby highway. She is a high school graduate, inarticulate and shy, with an untidy physical appearance. Although she comes to court in a skirt, it is a blue-jeans skirt and her hair is uncombed. She lookd distracted, vague, and helpless.

Victim number two is a housewife aged 42 who lives in the same town with her husband and two sons, both of whom are away at college. She is a professional: a teacher, a nurse, or a computer analyst. There was no one else in the house at 2:00 A.M. because the husband was away on a business trip. In both cases, the back door was unlocked because the victim forgot to lock it before going to bed. In court, victim number two wears a tailored suit, expensive shoes, jewelry, and a hat. When she walks to the witness stand it is with a precision of gait and an authority which communicates to the jury she usually knows what she is doing and why.

Most prosecutors would go to trial and expect to win with victim number two and be more receptive to a plea with victim number one. Why? It is simply factors of social class. That is certainly part of the answer, as are the psychological and social dynamics of the courtroom, a subject which is just beginning to receive attention from scholars. Practicing attorneys have always claimed to understand those intangible, immeasurable, circumstantial, or unpredictable factors which are crucial to the outcome of a criminal case.

In the previous example, consider the consequences of introducing the following facts. In the case of victim number one, the television has been identified and recovered. In the case of victim number two, there has been no recovery or identification of stolen items. This fact, which has nothing to do with the rape incident or the individual victim, may have a significant influence upon the jury, as would the fact that the defendant had previously been convicted of similar crimes. Facts which may or may not be crucial to disposition in a particular case can be endlessly varied. The attempt in this study is to vary only crucial facts concerning the rape offense, the rape victim, and the rape offender. But no rape case can divorce itself from a myriad of influences and distractions present in any criminal case. In our previous example, what if the young victim in the duplex was one of four medical interns living in a "bad" area because it was near the hospital? What if all the other roommates were absent because they were on duty at the hospital at 2:00 A.M.? What if the professional with the aggressive personality had just lost her job or was "between jobs"; or if she was recently spearated from her husband, and the man she lived with was twenty years her junior and unaccountably absent at 2:00 A.M.? What if the incident occurred at 2:00 P.M.? In both cases what if the defendant was the pharmacist's clerk at the local drugstore where the victim was a frequent customer? What if the defendant was a delivery boy at the same drugstore and had previously come to the victim's home on several occasions to deliver prescriptions?

Introducing variations in circumstances or fact patterns point out that a criminal case always asks the jury to make a judgment far more complicated than the judgment defined as: did this person do the act defined as criminal? And it is a recognition of the subtlety of the jury's social role which prompts this study and the other interdisciplinary work. A jury punishes, excuses, exonerates, ignores, or selects from a hodgepodge of social and psychological information received in the courtroom. Only a small part of that information will relate to the actual criminal incident. The theory of our system is that jurors can separate out the facts which legally determine guilt in a particular incident. The reality may be that human beings cannot suppress or sort out the social and psychological information which is received and processed constantly during a criminal trial. Rape cases are a particularly fruitful area of interdisciplinary study because attitudes toward sexual behavior are blatantly personal, social, idiosyncratic, and emotional. Most members of the public probably do not have strong opinions about whether or not the government should pay damages to a railway trainman injured on the tracks. Most members of the public have very definite opinions as to whether or not a particular circumstance involving sexual intercourse should be classified as criminal. The opinions will vary enormously or may be self-contradictory, but most people will have an opinion about what is rape, what is statutory rape, and whether or not the police and courts should punish or excuse.

The authors hope the information in this study will help others understand why sexual conduct will be excused in one circumstance, condoned in another, and result in the imposition of criminal penalties, a jail sentence, in another case. Changes in the law may be relevant. Individual characteristics of jurors may be part of the explanation. A juror's personal attitudes toward women may be determinative. This study assumes that changes in the law and defendant, victim, and juror characteristics must be among the most important factors. Determining the exact relationship among these factors is the basis for another study.

To study jurors, or potential jurors, we assume that the jury carries out the wishes of the society at large. Therefore, if jurors acquit or excuse men charged with sexual assault or rape, those jurors are probably expressing the collective view of the society in some sense. The expressions of outrage expressed over the antiquated state of the rape laws in every American jurisdiction usually neglect one fact: the fact that the rape laws did not result in convicting men of rape was not a mistake or an oversight. Juries are not atypical of the rest of society. When juries refuse to convict for rape, when judges acquit in cases of brutal attacks and cite ambiguity on the issue of consent, the law alone is not what needs to be changed. An analysis of juror attitudes assumes that instructing jurors will solve the problem. But insofar as jurors carry out the mandate of the society at large, instructions will be relatively ineffective. A wholesale change in attitudes may have to wait for another generation. The changes in the law by themselves, however, serve an educative function. As women lobby legal change through the legislatures, legislators at least come to realize that voters think this is an important issue. When women start an impeachment action against a judge, even if the action fails, the community has been told that this is an issue for which women will marshal political support. When the newspaper prints a story about a contemplated change in the evidence rules in rape cases, readers who understand nothing of the technical question understand that someone thinks change is necessary.

This study demonstrates two very different expressions of changed social attitudes toward rape. In the past five years, a wholesale revision of the rape laws has taken place in response to a coordinated political effect at the national and state level. This collective effort could never have succeeded, however, unless individual attitudes toward rape, as measured by the responses in this study, had not already changed significantly. Although individuals often express a lack of sympathy for victims and a lack of understanding of the crime, the movement for legislative reform did not in most states encounter popular opposition. The passage of some sort of legislation in the majority of states is as much an index of opinion as the tabulated responses to the questionnaire.

The book is organized into two sections, which consist of seven chapters. Chapter 1 provides an overview of the study by detailing the interrelation between jury trials and rape and the problems encountered in studying this subject. Chapter 2 describes the survey sample on which the empirical portion of the book is based. In addition, detailed information is presented on the measuring instruments and data analytic procedures used. The measurement and correlates of people's views and knowledge about rape are detailed in chapter 3. In chapter 4, the nature of juror decision making in rape trials is presented. We discuss such issues as the nature and procedural aspects of rape trials and the effects of defendant, victim, and rape case characteristics on juror decision making as well as the relationship of selected juror characteristics to their decisions in rape cases.

Then we introduce a new section of the book. Chapter 5 in combination with chapter 6 provides one of the most up-to-date accounts of the rape laws and statutes as they are currently written in the United States. Chapter 6 simply details the laws and statutes on a state-by-state basis. Finally, we present the conclusions of our research in chapter 7. Here, we also attempt to forecast the implications of our work on the administration of justice as it applies to rape.

The Study: Sample, Measures, and Procedures

In answering the research questions posed in chapter 1, the collection of the necessary data required the selection of a sample, the development of special measuring instruments, and the application of these measures to selected participants in the study. This chapter describes the various phases of the data collection.

Sample

The subjects for the study were 1,448 adults (19 years of age or older) from a wide variety of socioeconomic backgrounds. In general, the participants in the study came from the four respondent groups: citizens of a medium-sized southeastern community ($n = 1,056$); patrol police officers of two urban and two rural southeastern communities ($n = 254$); female counselors from rape crisis centers located in twelve major metropolitan areas across the country ($n = 118$); and committed rapists at a southeastern state mental hospital ($n = 20$). Table 2-1 summarizes the major background characteristics of the subjects in the four respondent groups.

Of the total sample, 47 percent of the subjects were women and 53 percent were men; 14 percent were black and 86 percent were white. The average age of the respondents was 33 (SD = 11.66), and they had an average of 15 years (*SD* = 2.75) of education.[1] Approximately one-third (35 percent) indicated they knew personally a woman who had been raped.

Citizens

Each of the 1,056 citizens included in the research resided in a southeastern city of approximately 50,000 population. Half of this group was male and half female; 15 percent were black and 85 percent white. Most (78 percent) were or had been married.

In terms of age, the citizens were approximately 34 (*SD* = 12.66). They had an average of fifteen years of education. Over fifty different occupations ranging from auto mechanic to university professor were represented in the sample.[2] As can be seen, this diversity of occupations points to the wide variety of citizens included in the sample. Finally, almost one out of four citizens (24 percent) said they knew a woman who had been raped.

Table 2-1
Summary of Responses of Respondent Groups to Background Variables

Background Variable	Citizens N	M	SD	%	Rape Crisis Counselors N	M	SD	%	Patrol Police Officers N	M	SD	%	Rapists N	M	SD	%	All Respondents N	M	SD	%
Sex																				
Female	528			50	118			100	18			7	0			0	664			47
Male	528			50	0			0	236			93	20			100	784			53
Race																				
Black	160			15	11			9	28			11	4			20	203			14
White	896			85	107			91	226			89	16			80	1245			86
Marital status																				
Single	232			22	53			45	25			10	3			15	313			21
Married	824			78	65			55	229			90	17			85	1135			79
Age	1056	33.91	12.66		118	29.20	7.27		254	31.61	8.20		20	30.85	7.24		1448	33.06	11.66	
Education	1056	15.35	2.89		118	15.84	2.01		254	14.06	1.72		20	10.55	2.44		1448	15.10	2.75	
Personally know a raped woman?																				
Yes	253			24	92			78	150			59					495			35
No	813			76	26			22	104			41					943			65
Testified at a rape trial?		—[c]												—[c]				—[c]		
Yes					12			8	64			25								
No					106			92	190			75								
Interviewed Rape Victims About Their Rape?[a]		—[c]			118	4.23	2.04		254	3.29	2.06			—[c]				—[c]		
Contact with Rape Victims[b]		—[c]			118	3.95	1.57		254	3.08	1.53			—[c]				—[c]		
Contact with Rapists[b]		—[c]			118	1.48	0.82		254	2.58	1.43			—[c]				—[c]		
Received Rape Training?		—[c]																—[c]		
Yes					106			90	99			39								
No					2			10	155			61								
Served on a Jury?						—[c]				—[c]				—[c]				—[c]		
Yes	180			17																
No	876			83																

[a]Based on a six-point rating scale ranging from 1 = never; 6 = 5 or more times.
[b]Based on a six-point rating scale ranging from 1 = no contact at all to 6 = very much contact.
[c]Dashes (—) indicate that these data were not collected.

Patrol Police Officers

Patrol police officers were also included since a patrol officer may well be one of the first law-enforcement members to come into contact with a rape victim. The vast majority (93 percent) of the 254 patrol police officers were male, white (89 percent), and had been or were currently married (90 percent). The average age of the police officers was 32 ($SD = 8.20$), and they had an average of fourteen years of education.

Over half the officers surveyed (59 percent) knew a raped woman, and one out of four had testified perviously at a rape trial. The officers reported having had some contact with rape victims and rapists. However, they had interviewed rape victims less frequently ($p < .001$) and, in general, had less contact ($p < .001$) with victims than had the counselors. On the other hand, they reported more contact ($p < .001$) with offenders than did the counselors. Fewer than 40 percent had received some form of training focusing primarily on rape.

Rape Crisis Counselors

Although the specific tasks of a rape crisis counselor may vary from one organization to another as well as from one individual to another, their prime responsibility is to serve as a counselor to a victim of rape. The services extended may include such activities as listening and talking with victims to reduce the emotional trauma of rape; recommending specific steps of physical care to victims; suggesting steps to be taken by victims to preserve evidence of an assault; accompanying victims to a hospital, police station, or a court hearing; and counseling relatives of victims about rape and its effects on victims.

Since only large metropolitan areas typically have such centers and these are staffed by relatively small numbers of counselors, it was necessary to collect data from crisis centers in a variety of cities. Data reported in the study were obtained from 118 counselors in twelve metropolitan areas.[3] Each of these individuals had had prior contact with rape victims.

As might be expected, the 118 counselors were women; 9 percent were black and 91 percent white. Almost half (45 percent) were single and approximately 29 years of age ($SD = 7.27$), and they had just over fourteen years of education.

Contrary to the citizens, the vast majority (78 percent) knew a woman who had been raped. All had interviewed at least one rape victim about her rape and reported little contact with rapists. Nine of ten counselors had received some kind of formalized training concerning rape.

Rapists

Twenty rapists who had been convicted of rape and committed to a southeastern state mental hospital served as the fourth group of respondents.[4] As a group, they average about 31 years of age and had about eleven years of education. Their tenure at the hospital ranged from two to fourty-five months with an average of 14.9 months (SD = 12.6). Eighty percent of the group was white and most had been married.[5] With the exception of one individual, an accountant, they had held a blue-collar job (for example, bricklayer, truck driver) prior to their commitment.

Respondent Group Comparisons

To see if the respondent groups might differ with respect to major individual difference characteristics, statistical tests were made among the groups for key background variables.[6]

For age, it was found that the citizens tended to be older (p < .05) than the counselors; no other differences were found in the group comparisons. Although there were no differences among these same two groups for level of education, both had more (p < .05) years of education than the police or the rapists. The police, however, reported more (p < 05) years of education than the rapists.

There were no differences in the proportion of males in the rapist and police officer respondent groups. Significant (p < .05) differences were found, however, in the proportion of males composing the remaining groups. In terms of race, the citizens had a greater (p < .05) proportion of blacks than did the couselors or police officers. No difference in the proportion of blacks was found between these latter two groups.

Finally, a smaller proportion of the citizens personally knew a raped woman than did the counselors or police officers. Compared with the police, a greater portion of the counselors knew a woman who had been raped.

Measuring Instruments

Given the research questions described in chapter 1, it was necessary to use specially designed instruments to collect the needed data. For these purposes, five basic measures were used: Legal Rape Case (LRC), Attitudes toward Rape (ATR) questionaire, Attitudes Toward Women (ATW) scale, Rape Knowledge Test (RKT), and Personal Data Sheet (PDS). This section describes the nature of these instruments and their application. A copy of each questionnaire is shown in Appendix 2A.

Legal Rape Case

One important objective of the study was to examine the effects of selected victim, defendant, crime, and juror characteristics on jurors' decisions in a rape case. The Legal Rape Case (LRC), a six-page, written narrative incorporating various combinations of variables suggested by the rape literature as being important in determining the outcome of rape trials was developed to make this assessment.

The first page of the LRC contained a set of instructions for completing the case. The second page provided each respondent or juror with a general description of a rape attack. On page three, photographs of the victim, Mary Harrington, and the defendant, David Willoughby, were shown. Page four then presented the prosecuting attorney's remarks to the jury, and page five summarized the defense's case. The final page asked the juror to render a decision on the case given the information presented.

Independent Variables. Based upon previous research, the following six variables were systematically manipulated in the LRC to study their effects on jurors' decisions: race of the victim, physical attractiveness of the victim, moral character of the victim, race of the defendant, type of rape, and strength of evidence presented in the case. These variables were defined in the LRC as described below.

Victim Characteristics. As to race, two different races of the victim were presented to the jurors: black and white. Race of the victim was shown to the jurors through a 3″ × 5″ black-and-white photograph included in the LRC.[7]

In conjunction with race, physical attractiveness of the victim was also manipulated through the photographs. Two categories of victim attractiveness were presented, that is, physically attractive and physically unattractive for the black and white victims. To check our manipulation of the victims' race and attractiveness, eighty judges (half female, half male) were asked to independently rate the physical attractiveness of the victim shown in the four photographs (that is, black-attractive, black-unattractive, white-attractive, white-unattractive). Thus each photograph was randomly presented to and rated by a single judge; in all, twenty judges rated each picture in terms of physical attractiveness.

The judges were presented with the following set of instructions in making their attractiveness ratings:

This is a research study which deals with how people see the *physical attractiveness* of a person. On the other side of this page is a picture and the name of a person. Please turn the page and do the following:

1. Look at the picture.
2. Ask yourself: How physically attractive or unattractive is this person to me?
3. Then, rate the person with a number between 1 and 15 to show how attractive or unattractive the individual is to you where: 1 = physically unattractive and 15 = physically attractive.

I would give the person an attractiveness rating of ____ .

An analysis of variance among the four mean attractiveness ratings showed that there were differences in perceived physical attractiveness of the women ($F = 15.28$, $df = 3,76$, $p < .0001$).[8] Further, it was found that these ratings agreed with our expectations. That is, our attractive women were judged to be more physically attractive than the unattractive women. In addition, there were no racial differences in these ratings; the white-attractive victim was viewed just as physically attractive as the black-attractive one. Also there was no significant difference in the average attractiveness ratings given to the black-unattractive and the white-unattractive victims.

For the purposes of the study, moral character of the victim (unmarried) referred to the victim's sexual history, that is, whether she had had any sexual experiences prior to the assault.[9] Two kinds of moral character were described in the LRC: sexually inexperienced and sexually experienced. For the sexually inexperienced victim, it was pointed out in the prosecuting attorney's case that "while being questioned, it was established by the prosecuting attorney that Mary Harrington lived alone and had no previous sexual experiences." In the case of the sexually experienced victim, it was established by the defense attorney that "Mary Harrington had previously lived with a man to whom she was not married, and she admitted having had sexual relations with several men."

Defendant Characteristics. Like the variable race of the victim, two races of the defendant were incorporated in the LRC; one defendant was black, the other white. The race of the defendant was also presented to the jurors in the form of a photograph. Ratings of the physical attractiveness of the black and white defendants by forty independent judges (half female, half male) showed no significant differences ($p > .05$)[10]

Crime Characteristics. Two different kinds of rape were described in the LRC and presented to the jurors: precipitory and nonprecipitory rape. Precipitory rape can be characterized as an assault resulting from a victim's appearance or behavior that could be perceived as being "suggestive." Nonprecipitory rape, on the other hand, refers to an assault on a woman which cannot be attributed to her appearance or behavior.

On the general description page, the nonprecipitory rape was described as follows:

On Friday, August 12, at 10:00 P.M., Mary Harrington answered a knock at her apartment door. Harrington was confronted by a black male who explained that he had had some car trouble and asked if he could make a telephone call to a service station for help. Harrington said she would make the call for him. At this time, the man pushed the door open, dragged her into the bedroom, and then raped her.

The precipitory rape was characterized as follows:

On Friday, August 12, at 10:00 P.M., Mary Harrington answered a knock at her apartment door. Harrington was confronted by a black male who explained that he had had some car trouble and asked if he could make a telephone call to a service station for help. Harrington let him in to use her telephone. The service station indicated that it would be about two hours before a truck could be sent due to a shortage of station attendants. While waiting for the service truck, Harrington asked him if he would care to wait in her apartment and to have a cup of coffee. Approximately an hour and a half after Willoughby called the station, sexual relations occurred between the two individuals.

In both cases, the specific details of the case were presented in the prosecuting and defense attorneys' arguments.

Strength of Evidence. The strength of evidence given in the LRC was either strong or weak. For this particular variable, the specific manipulation was made by the presence or absence of incriminating evidence in the prosecution's case. For example, in the strong, nonprecipitory case, the prosecution's case read as follows:

The trial started after David Willoughby, the defendant, had entered an initial plea of innocent. The prosecution immediately presented its case against the defendant. Arguments by the prosecution were prefaced by the comment that the crime was 'one of the most vicious and senseless acts that could be committed against women.'

Mary Harrington was called to the stand. She told how Willoughby had forced his way into her apartment and raped her. She noted that he had verbally threatened her with physical violence if she did not comply. However, she had attempted to offer some resistance to him by fighting him. As she pointed out, her efforts were evidenced by the fact that his shirt was torn with a button ripped loose during the struggle, and by scratches on his face and back. While being questioned, it was established by the prosecuting attorney that Mary Harrington lived alone and had no previous sexual experiences.

The prosecuting attorney noted that a button was found in Harrington's apartment. An examination of Willoughby's shirt at the time of his arrest revealed that a button was missing. The button located in Harrington's apartment matched those on Willoughby's shirt. Further, the prosecuting attorney pointed out that Willoughby fit the description given by Harrington to the police. In addition, she had positively identified him.

Dr. Charles Hall, Harrington's attending physician, was asked to take the stand. Hall testified that he had examined Harrington the night of August 12. According to Hall, the results of his examination revealed that sexual intercourse had occurred and that she had some red marks on her chest and neck.

The prosecuting attorney called for a conviction. As the attorney noted, "Willoughby is guilty."

In contrast, the defense's case read as follows:

David Willoughby, the defendant, took the stand and stated that he was innocent of the charges. He explained that the scratches on his face and back as well as his torn shirt had occurred when he was assaulted by two unidentified youths while walking alone through a park earlier in the evening. When asked if he had reported the incident to the police, Willoughy said "No, they didn't get my money, and the police probably wouldn't have caught them anyway." The defense attorney insisted that the fact that the button found in Harrington's apartment matched Willoughby's shirt and his resemblance to her assailant were mere coincidences. Willoughby maintained that he was watching television alone in his apartment at the time of the rape of Mary Harrington.

The defense attorney demanded acquittal; the attorney maintained that his client was innocent. As the attorney noted, the evidence was clearly circumstantial, and David Willoughby was being framed as a victim of the circumstances.

It is important to note that in the "strong" evidence case, there were several elements of evidence presented: verbal threat by the offender, resistance by the victim, torn shirt of the assailant matching that of the defendant, missing shirt button of the assailant found in the victim's residence matching that of the defendant, scratches on the face and back of the defendant, positive identification by the victim of the defendant as the offender, and testimony of an attending physician regarding the attack.

In the "weak" evidence case, however, the amount of evidence was reduced. For example, the prosecution's case in the weak, nonprecipitory condition was presented as follows:

The trial started after David Willoughby, the defendant, had entered an initial plea of innocent. The prosecution immediately presented its case against the defendant. Arguments by the prosecution were prefaced by the comment that the crime was "one of the most vicious and senseless acts that could be committed against women."

Mary Harrington was called to the stand. She told how Willoughby had forced his way into her apartment and raped her. She noted that he had verbally threatened her with physical violence if she did not comply. While being questioned, it was established by the prosecuting attorney that Mary Harrington lived alone and had no previous sexual experiences.

Further, the prosecuting attorney pointed out that Willoughby fit the description given by Harrington to the police. In addition, she had identified him.

Dr. Charles Hall, Harrington's attending physician, was asked to take the stand. Hall testified that he had examined Harrington the night of August 12. According to Hall, the results of his examination revealed that sexual intercourse had occurred and that she had some red marks on her chest and neck.

The prosecuting attorney called for a conviction. As the attorney noted, "Willoughby is guilty."

On the other hand, the defense's case was as follows:

David Willoughby, the defendant, took the stand and stated that he was innocent of the charges. He told the jury that he had never seen Mary Harrington before his arrest and had not forced his way into her apartment. Willoughby maintained that he was watching television alone in his apartment at the time of the rape of Mary Harrington.

The defense attorney demanded acquittal; the attorney maintained that his client was innocent. As the attorney noted, the evidence was clearly circumstantial, and David Willoughby was being framed as a victim of the circumstances.

Dependent Variables. Three dependent variables were also obtained from the jurors. After reading the case, they were asked to read the following instructions:

Assume that the judge has asked you to make a decision concerning the charge of rape brought by Mary Harrington against David Willoughby. The judge has instructed you to consider the following legal definition of rape in making your decision.

Rape is an act of sexual intercourse with a female, not one's wife, against her will and consent, whether her will is overcome by force or fear resulting from the threat of force.

Now, think of the information you read in the previous case. Based on this information, answer the three questions below. Please feel free to review the case.

1. As a juror, I find David Willoughby, the defendant, (check one):
   ___ (1) Guilty
   ___ (2) Not guilty

2. How confident are you that your judgment given in Question 1 is correct? Indicate your *degree of confidence* by checking how you feel on the
   following scale (check one):
   ___ (1) Extremely confident of my verdict
   ___ (2) Strongly confident of my verdict
   ___ (3) Moderately confident of my verdict
   ___ (4) Slightly confident of my verdict
   ___ (5) Unsure of my verdict

3. *If you voted guilty in Question 1 above*, what would your sentence be?
   Assume that probation is beyond your control. The maximum sentence
   for rape is 99 years. Using your own judgment, *write in the length of
   prison sentence* you would give to David Willoughby, the defendant.

   I hereby sentence David Willoughby, the defendant, to ___ year(s) in
   prison.

Since it was important to consider how the six independent variables,
both singly and in combination, influenced the jurors' decisions, it was
necessary to have all possible combinations of these variables represented in
the cases. Given the independent variables of race of victim (black and
white), physical attractiveness of th victim (attractive and unattractive),
moral character of the victim (sexually inexperienced and sexually experienced), race of the defendant (black and white), type of rape
(precipitory and nonprecipitory), and strength of evidence (strong and
weak), sixty-four different versions of the LRC were developed and randomly presented to the jurors in the study.[11]

Attitudes toward Rape Questionnaire

As discussed in chapter 3, a consideration of people's attitudes toward rape
are important when conducting research on rape. For this reason, and for
many others that will become more apparent later, the Attitudes toward
Rape (ATR) questionnaire was developed.

Initially, the literature, including popular as well as scholarly publica-
tions (Feild and Barnett 1977), was searched for statements that would be
useful for characterizing people's attitudes toward the following broad do-
mains of rape: the act of rape, the rape victim, and the rapist. From this
review, thirty-seven items representing affective (feelings of liking-
disliking), cognitive (beliefs, expectations), and conative (action orientation) components of rape attitudes were then written. These statements

were subsequently placed into a questionnaire with a six-point agreement-disagreement response scale and administered to a random, developmental sample of 200 female and 200 male students at a large, southeastern university. Using the attitude statements as dependent variables, a discriminant analysis followed by univariate analyses of variance were performed between the two sex groups to determine how well the items might differentiate the groups (Barnett and Feild 1977). The discriminant function was significant ($p < .001$), as were eighteen of the analyses of variance, suggesting that the items could identify sex differences with respect to attitudes toward rape. Further, analyses of the item distributions and item content as well as interviews with selected respondents resulted in the revision of four items and the removal of five statements due to a lack of clarity in meaning. Based on these modifications, the final form of the instrument consisted of thirty-two items (half positively phrased, half negatively) which respondents were asked to respond to using a six-point Likert scale ranging from strongly agree (scored 1) to strongly disagree (scored 6).

Attitudes toward Women Scale

A third instrument used in the study concerned the measurement of respondents' attitudes toward women. To make this assessment, the short form of Spence and Helmreich's (1972) Attitudes toward Women Scale (AWS) was also used to provide a measure of the subjects' attitudes regarding the rights and roles of women in contemporary society. The AWS consists of twenty-five items with a four-point response scale ranging from agree strongly (scored 0) to disagree strongly (scored 3). Scores on the AWS are obtained by summing across each of the twenty-five items, with possible scores ranging from 0 to 75. The higher the score, the more liberal the view of women and their roles. For the sample as a whole, the average score was 48.18 ($SD = 12.52$). Split-half reliability (Spearman-Brown corrected) of the scale was .78, which compares quite favorably with previously reported estimates (Spence and Helmreich 1972). Examples of items appearing on the AWS are:

> There are many jobs in which men should be given preference over women in being hired or promoted. (negatively phrased)

> Women should take increasing responsibility for leadership in solving the intellectual and social problems of the day. (positively phrased)

Rape Knowledge Test

The Rape Knowledge Test (RKT) was developed to measure people's factual knowledge about rape. Using thirty-three multiple-choice items, an initial version of the RKT was administered to a sample of 400 college students (200 females and 200 males). Based upon item analyses (including item-total test score correlations and item difficulty indexes) of the responses, fourteen items were selected for inclusion in a revised form of the RKT. This revised form was then administered to the subjects in the study. The following item is illustrative of questions contained in the test:

> Most reported rapes occur in:
> 1. Automobiles
> 2. Open spaces such as alleys, parks, and streets
> 3. The victim's residence
> 4. The rapist's residence
> 5. Abandoned or unoccupied buildings

Other questions in the RKT dealt with the percentage of rapes reported to the police, typical age of rape victims, typical age of rapists, percentage of accused rapists who are found innocent or who have their case dismissed when brought to trial, racial composition of victim and offender in reported rapes, racial composition of convicted rapists, geographical location in the United States of the highest number of reported rapes, percentage of rapes reported to the police in which arrests are made, percentage of raped women who know their rapist, percentage of reported rapes involving brutal beatings of the victim, relationship between degree of physical violence in a rape and knowledge of the rapist by the victim, percentage of reported rapes involving sexual humiliation of the victim through practices described as sexually deviant, and type of evidence required of the prosecution in a rape case by most states. Answers to the items were keyed to sources involving the collection or reporting of empirical data on rape (Amir 1971; *National Commission on Causes and Prevention of Violence*1969; *Uniform Crime Reports* 1975)[12]

Scores on the RKT were based on the total number of items answered correctly. Thus possible scores could range from 0 to 14 with the higher the score, the more the knowledge of rape. For the sample as a whole, the average score was 4.59 (SD = 1.67). Split-half reliability (Spearman-Brown corrected) of the measure was .70.

Personal Data Sheet

The Personal Data Sheet (PDS) provided background information on each of the respondents. Although some unique information was obtained for each respondent group, the following personal data were obtained from a personal data sheet given to all subjects: age, sex (scored 1 = female; 2 = male), race (scored 1 = black; 2 = white), years of education, and marital status (scored 1 = single; 2 = married).

In addition to these variables, the following questions were asked of specific respondent groups: Have you personally known a woman who was raped? (scored 1 = yes; 2 = no; citizens, police, and counselors). Have you ever testified in court during a rape trial? (scored 1 = yes; 2 = no; police and counselors). How many times have you interviewed rape victims about their rape? (scored 1 = never to 6 = 5 or more times; police and counselors. How much contact have you had with accused or convicted rapists? (scored 1 = no contact at all with rapists to 6 = very much contact with rapists; police and counselors). How much contact have you had with rape victims? (scored 1 = no contact at all with rape victims to 6 = very much contact with rape victims; police and counselors). As part of your job, have you ever received any special training dealing with rape? (scored 1 = yes; 2 = no; police and counselors).

Table 2-2 was developed to summarize the various measures applied in the study. By examining the table, the specific measures, their purposes, and their use with a specific group can be determined.

Procedure

Research by Abramson, Goldberg, Mosher, Abramson, and Gottesdiener (1975) indicates that the sex, status, and style of interacting of an experimenter may have a significant effect on a subject's response to sexually oriented material. Following the suggestions of Abramson and Mosher (1975), black and white experimenters of both sexes with various levels of status (professor to undergraduate student) were used in administering the instruments. Prior to distribution, all experimenters were trained in the administration of the instruments.

Due to the nature of the participant groups, the conditions of instrument administration could not be controlled. The citizen group completed the questionnaires alone which was later collected by one of the experimenters. The police officers, committed rapists, and rape crisis counselors worked in small groups, supervised by an experimenter, at their respective organizations. In all cases, the questionnaires were administered anonymously.

Summary

The sample for the study included 1,448 respondents. Of this number, four major respondent groups were represented: citizens (n = 1,056); patrol police officers (n = 254); rape crisis counselors (n = 118); and convicted rapists (n = 20).

Table 2-2
Description of Measures Used in the Study

Measure Used	Purpose and Description	Respondent Group Receiving Measure	N
Legal Rape Case (LRC)	To assess the effects of race of victim, physical attractiveness of the victim, moral character of the victim, race of the defendant, type of rape, and strength of evidence on jurors' decisions in a rape case. Consists of a general description of a rape, prosecuting and defense attorney's cases. Jurors are asked to judge the guilt or innocence of the accused, to rate how confident they are of their verdict, and to sentence the defendant to prison from 0 to 99 years.	Citizens	1,0?
Attitudes toward Rape (ATR) questionnaire	To assess respondents' attitudes or perceptions of rape. Consists of 32 attitudinal statements to which respondents indicate their agreement or disagreement with the items using a six-point scale ranging from strongly agree (scored 1) to strongly disagree (scored 6).	Citizens, police officers, rape crisis counselors, rapists	1,4
Attitudes toward Women Scale (AWS)	To measure respondents' attitudes toward the rights and roles of women in contemporary society. Consists of 25 statements to which respondents indicate their agreement or disagreement with the statements using a four-point scale ranging from agree strongly (scored 0) to disagree strongly (scored 3). The higher the score, the more liberal the view of women.	Citizens, rapists	1,0
Rape Knowledge Test (RKT)	To measure respondents' factual knowledge of rape. Consists of 14 multiple-choice items where respondents are asked to select the correct answer from three to five options. The higher the total number of items answered correctly, the greater the knowledge about rape.	Citizens, police officers, rape crisis counselors, rapists	1,4
Personal Data Sheet (PDS)	To obtain background data for classifying and describing the respondents. Different versions are used for specific respondent groups.	Citizens, police officers, rape crisis counselors, rapists	1,

To accomplish the objectives of the study, five survey instruments were developed.

1. Legal Rape Case: A six-page, written narrative of a rape trial designed

to assess the effects of race of victim, race of defendant, physical attractiveness of the victim, moral character of the victim, type of rape, and strength of evidence on jurors' deliberations. Sixty-four different versions of the LRC, involving all possible combinations of the variables, were used in the study.

2. Attitudes toward Rape questionnaire: A thirty-two-item questionnaire containing statements reflecting various perceptions people may have about rape. Respondents use a six-point Likert scale ranging from strongly agree to strongly disagree to answer the questionnaire.

3. Attitudes toward Women scale: A twenty-five-item questionnaire measuring people's attitudes toward the rights and roles of women in society. Respondents use a four-point Likert scale ranging from agree strongly to disagree strongly to respond to the instrument.

4. Rape Knowledge Test: A fourteen-item, multiple-choice test was developed to measure respondents' factual knowledge of rape.

5. Personal Data Sheet: A questionnaire designed to obtain limited demographic data from the respondents to be used for classifying and describing their responses to the other instruments. Four different versions of the instrument were incorporated in the study.

The instruments were administered by a team of trained survey administrators. All instruments were completed anonymously.

Notes

1. The variable "years of education" includes any time spent in a trade school as well as time spent in elementary, junior high, high school, and two- and four-year colleges.

2. Using the Hodge-Siegel-Rossi Occupational Prestige scores (Social Science Research Council 1975), the employed citizens had a mean occupational prestige score of 41.33 ($SD = 24.49$). Such jobs as typists, sales persons, mail carriers, and plumbers would have a similar score. These citizens would be characterized as being from the lower-middle and middle classes.

3. The counselors included in the study were located in the following cities: Atlanta, Georgia; Jacksonville, Florida; Detroit, Michigan; Venice, California; Baltimore, Maryland; Memphis, Tennessee; San Francisco, California; Tampa, Florida; Houston, Texas; Philadelphia, Pennsylvania; Jackson, Mississippi; and Gainesville, Florida.

4. Of the thirty rapists available, twenty volunteered to participate in the study. Each person signed a statement to the effect that his participation was voluntary.

5. It is interesting to note that the rapists had a high divorce rate relative to the other respondent groups. Of the twenty rapists interviewed, 60 percent of them had been divorced.

6. Differences among the respondent groups were tested using chi-square for frequencies and analysis of variance in the remaining instances.

7. Each of the six individuals volunteering to pose in a photograph as a defendant or as a victim was paid $5.00 for their participation. In addition, each one signed a statement giving permission for the use of their photograph in the research.

8. The mean attractiveness ratings (where 1 = physically unattractive to 15 = physically attractive) for the four females were: black, attractive (M = 8.35); black, unattractive (M = 7.10); white, attractive (M = 9.90); white, unattractive (M = 4.85).

9. The term *moral character* is not used to place a value judgment on another individual. It simply refers to the kind of stereotyping processes made by some jurors about some victims who are thought to be promiscuous.

10. The mean attractiveness ratings (where 1 = physically unattractive to 15 = physically attractive) for the two male defendants were: black (M = 5.75) and white (M = 1.80).

11. More specific details with regard to the application of the LRC are given in chapter 4.

12. The problems encountered in identifying the "facts" of rape are described more fully in chapter 4.

References

Abramson, P.; Goldberg, P.; Mosher, D.; Abramson, L.; and Gottesdiener, M. Experimenter effects on responses to explicitly erotic stimuli. *Journal of Research in Personality* 9 (1975):136-146.

Abramson, P., and Mosher, D. Development of a measure of negative attitudes toward masturbation. *Journal of Consulting and Clinical Psychology* 43 (1975):485-490.

Amir, M. *Patterns of forcible rape.* Chicago: University of Chicago Press, 1971.

Barnett, N., and Feild, H. Sex differences in university students' attitudes toward rape. *Journal of College Student Personnel* 18 (1977):93-96.

Feild, H., and Barnett, N. Forcible rape: An up-dated bibliography. *Journal of Criminal Law and Criminology* 67 (1977):146-159.

National commission on the causes and prevention of violence. Washington: U.S. Government Printing Office, 1969.

Social Science Research Council. *Basic background items for U.S. household surveys.* New York: Social Science Research Council, 1975.

Spence, J., and Helmreich, R. The Attitudes toward Women Scale: An objective instrument to measure attitudes toward the rights and roles of women in contemporary society. *JSAS Catalog of Selected Documents in Psychology* 2 (1972):66.

Uniform crime reports for the U.S. Federal Bureau of Investigation, Department of Justice. Washington: U.S. Government Printing Office, 1975.

Appendix 2A:
Measuring Instruments

The five basic instruments used in this study were Legal Rape Case, Attitudes toward Rape questionnaire, Attitudes toward Women scale, Rape Knowledge Test, and, Personal Data Sheet.

In reviewing the Legal Rape Case (LRC), it should be kept in mind that there were sixty-four different versions used in the study. Only one of these sixty-four versions is presented here. This particular one involved the following combination of six independent variables: white female victim; physically attractive victim; sexually experienced victim; black, male defendant; nonprecipitory rape; and strong evidence in the case. The remaining sixty-three versions involved various combinations of these variables.

Legal Rape Case

Directions

Here is a summary of an actual trial involving an allegation of rape by Mary Harrington against David Willoughby, the defendant. We would like you to put yourself in the role of a juror and imagine that you are serving on the jury in this trial. After reading a general description of the crime, you will see photographs of the complainant and the defendant. Then you will be given both the prosecution and defense's case. After this information, you will be asked to give your decisions, be as realistic as you would be if you had actually been a juror at the trial. Finally, we have attached several questionnaires for research purposes. We would appreciate your completing these also. Thank you for your time and help with our research.

General Description of the Crime

On Friday, August 12, at 10:00 P.M., Mary Harrington answered a knock at her apartment door. Harrington was confronted by a black male who explained that he had had some car trouble and asked if he could make a telephone call to a service station for help. Harrington said she would make the call for him. At this time, the man pushed the door open, knocking Harrington to the floor. He closed and locked the door, dragged her into the bedroom, and then raped her.

After the act, he left, and Harrington called the police stating she had been raped. Following medical treatment, the police took her story, and an all-points bulletin was released for a black male, approximately 6 feet tall weighing 170 pounds, in his early twenties, wearing dark-blue pants, and a light-blue striped shirt.

Three hours later, the police arrested a suspect named David Willoughby who fit the description given by Harrington. Willoughby was read his rights and charged with rape. A trial date was set for November 1. Figure 2A-1 shows photographs of Mary Harrington, the victim, and David Willoughby, the defendant.

The Prosecution's Case

The trial started after David Willoughby, the defendant, had entered an initial plea of innocent. The prosecution immediately presented its case against the defendant. Arguments by the prosecution were prefaced by the comment that the crime was "one of the most vicious and senseless acts that could be committed against women."

Mary Harrington was called to the stand. She told how Willoughby had forced his way into her apartment and raped her. She noted that he had verbally threatened her with physical violence if she did not comply. However, she had attempted to offer some resistance by fighting him. As she pointed out, her efforts were evidenced by the fact that his shirt was torn with a button ripped loose during the struggle, and by scratches on his face and back.

Mary Harrington   David Willoughby

Figure 2A-1. Examples of Victim and Defendant in Legal Rape Case

The prosecuting attorney noted that a button was found in Harrington's apartment. An examination of Willoughby's shirt at the time of his arrest revealed that a button was missing. The button located in Harrington's apartment matched those on Willoughby's shirt. Further, the prosecuting attorney pointed out that Willoughby fit the description given by Harrington to the police. In addition, she had positively identified him.

Dr. Charles Hall, Harrington's attending physician, was asked to take the stand. Hall testified that he had examined Harrington the night of August 12. According to Hall, the results of his examination revealed that sexual intercourse had occurred and that she had some red marks on her chest and neck.

The prosecuting attorney called for a conviction. As the attorney noted, "Willoughby is guilty."

The Defense's Case

David Willoughby, the defendant, took the stand and stated that he was innocent of the charges. He explained that the scratches on his face and back as well as his torn shirt had occurred when he was assaulted by two unidentified youths while walking alone through a park earlier in the evening. When asked if he had reported the incident to the police, Willoughby said "no, they didn't get my money, and the police probably wouldn't have caught them anyway." The defense attorney insisted that the fact that the button found in Harrington's apartment matched those on Willoughby's shirt and his resemblance to her assailant were mere coincidences. Willoughby maintained that he was watching television alone in his apartment at the time of the rape of Mary Harrington.

Mary Harrington was called to the stand for cross-examination. While being examined, it was established by the defense attorney that she had previously lived with a man to whom she was not married, and she admitted having sexual relations with several men.

The defense attorney demanded acquittal; the attorney maintained that his client was innocent. As the attorney noted, the evidence was clearly circumstantial, and David Willougyby was being framed as a victim of the circumstances.

Juror's Decisions

Assume that the judge has asked you to make a decision concerning the charge of rape brought by Mary Harrington against David Willoughby. The judge has instructed you to consider the following legal definition of rape in making your decision:

Rape is an act of sexual intercourse with a female, not one's wife, against her will and consent, whether her will is overcome by force or fear resulting from the threat of force.

Now, think of the information you read in the previous case. Based on this information, answer the three questions below. Please feel free to review the case.

1. As a juror, I find David Willoughby, the defendant (check one):

   ____ (1) Guilty

   ____ (2) Not guilty

2. How confident are you that your judgment given in Question 1 is correct? Indicate your degree of confidence by checking how you feel on the following scale (check one):

   ____ (1) Extremely confident of my verdict

   ____ (2) Strongly confident of my verdict

   ____ (3) Moderately confident of my verdict

   ____ (4) Slightly confident of my verdict

   ____ (5) Unsure of my verdict

3. If you voted guilty in Question 1 above, what would your sentence be? Assume that probation is beyond your control. The maximum sentence for rape is 99 years. Using your own judgment, write in the length of prison sentence you would give to David Willoughby, the defendant.

   I hereby sentence David Willoughby, the defendant, to ____ year(s) in prison.

Attitudes toward Rape

Directions

This questionnaire deals with people's attitudes toward rape. Below is a list of statements concerned with various attitudes people may have toward rape. For each of the statements, do the following:

1. Read each statement carefully.
2. Ask yourself: "How much do I agree or disagree with this statement?
3. Using the rating scale below, select the number which best represents your feeling?
4. Then, place the number in the blank space to the left of the statement.
5. Please answer all items. Do not leave any items blank.

Rating Scale

```
1 = Strongly agree
2 = Agree
3 = Slightly agree
4 = Slightly disagree
5 = Disagree
6 = Strongly disagree
```

_____ 1. A woman can be raped against her will.
_____ 2. The reason most rapists commit rape is for the thrill of physical violence.
_____ 3. Rapists are "normal" men.
_____ 4. In forcible rape, the victim never causes the crime.
_____ 5. All rapists are mentally sick.
_____ 6. A charge of rape two days after the act has occurred is probably not rape.
_____ 7. A woman should be responsible for preventing her own rape.
_____ 8. A man who has committed rape should be given at least 30 years in prison.
_____ 9. Women are trained by society to be rape victims.
_____ 10. A raped woman is a less desirable woman.
_____ 11. If a woman is going to be raped, she might as well relax and enjoy it.
_____ 12. Rape provides the opportunity for many rapists to show their manhood.
_____ 13. Most women secretly desire to be raped.
_____ 14. It would do some women some good to get raped.
_____ 15. Women provoke rape by their appearance or behavior.
_____ 16. "Nice" women do not get raped.
_____ 17. Most charges of rape are unfounded.
_____ 18. In order to protect the male, it should be difficult to prove that a rape has occurred.

_____ 19. Rape is the expression of an uncontrollable desire for sex.
_____ 20. Rape is the worst crime that can be committed.
_____ 21. Rape is a sex crime.
_____ 22. All rape is a male exercise in power over women.
_____ 23. During a rape, a woman should do everything she can do to resist.
_____ 24. Rapists are sexually frustrated individuals.
_____ 25. In most cases when a woman was raped, she was asking for it.
_____ 26. The reason most rapists commit rape is for sex.
_____ 27. Rape of a woman by a man she knows can be defined as a "woman who changed her mind afterward."
_____ 28. A convicted rapist should be castrated.
_____ 29. A woman should not feel guilty following a rape.
_____ 30. The degree of a woman's resistance should be the major factor in determining if a rape has occurred.
_____ 31. A raped woman is a responsible victim, not an innocent one.
_____ 32. Rape serves as a way to put or keep women in their "place."

Attitudes toward Women

Directions

The statements listed below describe attitudes toward the role of women in society which different people have. There are no right or wrong answers, only opinions. For each of the statements, do the following:

1. Read each statement carefully.
2. Ask yourself: "How much do I agree or disagree with this statement?"
3. Using the rating scale below, select the number which best represents your feeling.
4. Then, place the number in the blank space to the left of the statement.
5. Please answer all items. Do not leave any items blank.

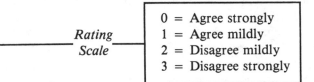

Rating Scale

```
0 = Agree strongly
1 = Agree mildly
2 = Disagree mildly
3 = Disagree strongly
```

_____ 1. Swearing and obscenity is more repulsive in the speech of a woman than a man.

_____ 2. Women should take increasing responsibility for leadership in solving the intellectual and social problems of the day.

_____ 3. Both husband and wife should be allowed the same grounds for divorce.

_____ 4. Telling dirty jokes should be mostly a masculine prerogative.

_____ 5. Intoxication among women is worse than intoxication among men.

_____ 6. Under modern economic conditions with women being active outside the home, men should share in household tasks such as washing dishes and doing the laundry.

_____ 7. It is insulting to women to have the "obey" clause remain in the marriage service.

_____ 8. There should be a strict merit system in job appointment and promotion without regard to sex.

_____ 9. A woman should be as free as a man to propose marriage.

_____ 10. Women should worry less about their rights and more about becoming good wives and mothers.

_____ 11. Women earning as much as their dates should bear equally the expense when they go out together.

_____ 12. Women should assume their rightful place in business and all the professions along with men.

_____ 13. A woman should not expect to go to exactly the same places or to have quite the same freedom of action as a man.

_____ 14. Sons in a family should be given more encouragement to go to college than daughters.

_____ 15. It is ridiculous for a woman to run a locomotive and for a man to darn socks.

_____ 16. In general, the father should have greater authority than the mother in the bringing up of children.

_____ 17. Women should be encouraged not to become sexually intimate with anyone before marriage, even their fiances.

_____ 18. The husband should not be favored by law over the wife in the disposal of family property or income.

_____ 19. Women should be concerned with their duties of childrearing and housetending, rather than with desires for professional and business careers.

_____ 20. The intellectual leadership of a community should be largely in the hands of men.

_____ 21. Economic and social freedom is worth far more to women than acceptance of the ideal of femininity which has been set by men.

_____ 22. On the average, women should be regarded as less capable of contribution to economic production than are men.

_____ 23. There are many jobs in which men should be given preference over women in being hired or promoted.

_____ 24. Women should be given equal opportunity with men for apprenticeship in the various trades.

_____ 25. The modern girl is entitled to the same freedom from regulation and control that is given the modern boy.

Rape Knowledge Test

Directions

This is a test designed to measure your knowledge of rape. There are right and wrong answers for each of the questions. In taking the test do the following:

1. Read each question and each of its alternatives or answers.
2. Choose the number of the alternative which best represents your answer.
3. Then, place the number in the blank space to the left of the question.
4. Please answer all items. Do not leave any items blank.

_____ 1. Approximately what percentage of all rapes are actually reported to the police?
   1. 10%
   2. 30%
   3. 50%
   4. 70%
   5. 90%

_____ 2. When there is a close relationship between the rapist and the victim:
   1. Physical violence used against the victim tends to be greater than in rapes where they do not know each other.
   2. Physical violence used against the victim tends to be less than in rapes where they do not know each other.
   3. Physical violence seldom occurs in this type of rape.

_____ 3. Most states require the prosecution in a rape case to:
   1. Prove that force was used to commit the rape
   2. Prove that there was penetration of the man into the woman
   3. Produce a witness who will connect the defendant with the rape offense
   4. Only 1 and 2 above
   5. All of the above

_____ 4. About what proportion of reported rapes involve sexual humiliation of the victim through the use of practices usually referred to as "sexually deviant"?
   1. 10%
   2. 30%
   3. 50%
   4. 70%
   5. 90%

_____ 5.   The largest number of rape victims are between the ages of:
           1. 15 to 19
           2. 20 to 24
           3. 25 to 29
           4. 30 to 34
           5. 35 to 49

_____ 6.   Most reported rapes occur in:
           1. Automobiles
           2. Open spaces such as alleys, parks, and streets
           3. The victim's residence
           4. The rapist's residence
           5. Abandoned or unoccupied buildings

_____ 7.   Of those persons brought to trial for rape, approximately what
           percentage are found innocent or have their case dismissed?
           1. 10%
           2. 30%
           3. 50%
           4. 70%
           5. 90%

_____ 8.   In about what proportion of rapes do brutal beatings of the victim
           occur?
           1. 5%
           2. 15%
           3. 20%
           4. 30%
           5. 45%

_____ 9.   About what percentage of women who have been raped know the
           rapist?
           1. 5%
           2. 25%
           3. 45%
           4. 65%
           5. 85%

_____ 10. In approximately what percentage of the rapes reported to the police
           are arrests made?
           1. 10%
           2. 30%
           3. 50%
           4. 70%
           5. 90%

_____ 11. The racial makeup of convicted rapists is approximately:
1. 80% black and 20% white
2. 60% black and 40% white
3. 50% black and 50% white
4. 40% black and 60% white
5. 20% black and 80% white

_____ 12. In which part of the United States does the highest number of reported rapes per capita occur?
1. Northcentral states
2. Southern states
3. Northeastern states
4. Western states

_____ 13. Most reported rapes occur between:
1. black males and black females
2. black males and white females
3. white males and white females
4. white males and black females

_____ 14. The largest number of rapists are between the ages of:
1. 15 to 19
2. 20 to 24
3. 25 to 29
4. 30 to 34
5. 35 to 39

Personal Data Sheet: Citizens

Please answer the following questions. The answers will be used to classify your responses to this questionnaire.

1. What is your sex (check one)?

    ____ (1) Female

    ____ (2) Male

2. What is your race (check one)?

    ____ (1) Black

    ____ (2) White

    ____ (3) Other

3. What is your present marital status (check one)?

    ____ (1) Single

    ____ (2) Married

    ____ (3) Divorced

4. What is your present age? (fill in) ____ years of age.

5. How many total years of formal education (include elementary, junior high, high school, trade school, and college) have you had? (fill in) ____ years.

6. Have you personally known a woman who was raped (check one)?

    ____ (1) Yes

    ____ (2) No

7. Have you ever served on a jury (check one)?

    ____ (1) Yes

    ____ (2) No

8. What is your present occupation (for example, housewife, carpenter, teacher)? _____

Personal Data Sheet: Patrol Police Officers

Please answer the following questions. The answers will be used to classify your responses to this questionnaire.

1. What is your sex (check one)?
   ____ (1) Female
   ____ (2) Male

2. What is your race (check one)?
   ____ (1) Black
   ____ (2) White
   ____ (3) Other

3. What is your present marital status (check one)?
   ____ (1) Single
   ____ (2) Married
   ____ (3) Divorced

4. What is your present age? (fill in) ____ years of age.

5. How many total years of formal education (include elementary, junior high school, trade school, and college) have you had? (fill in) ____ years of formal education.

6. Have you personally known a woman who was raped (check one)?
   ____ (1) Yes
   ____ (2) No

7. As part of your job, have you ever testified in court during a rape trial (check one)?
   ____ (1) Yes
   ____ (2) No

8. As part of your job, how many times have you interviewed rape victims about their rape (check one)?
   ____ (1) Never
   ____ (2) 1 time
   ____ (3) 2 times
   ____ (4) 3 times
   ____ (5) 4 times
   ____ (6) 5 or more times

9. As part of your job, how much contact have you had with rape victims (check one)?

_____ (1) No contact at all with rape victims

_____ (2) Very little contact

_____ (3) A little contact

_____ (4) Some contact

_____ (5) Much contact

_____ (6) Very much contact with rapists

10. As part of your job, how much contact have you had with convicted *or* accused rapists (check one)?

_____ (1) No contact at all with rapists

_____ (2) Very little contact

_____ (3) A little contact

_____ (4) Some contact

_____ (5) Much contact

_____ (6) Very much contact with rapists

11. As part of your job, have you ever received any special training dealing with rape?

_____ (1) Yes

_____ (2) No

12. What is your present job title (please be specific)?

_____

13. How long have you worked in your present job?

_____ years _____ months

14. How long have you worked for your present employer?

_____ years _____ months

Personal Data Sheet: Rape Crisis Counselors

Please answer the following questions. The answers will be used to classify your responses to this questionnaire.

1. What is your sex (check one)?
   ____ (1) Female
   ____ (2) Male

2. What is your race (check one)?
   ____ (1) Black
   ____ (2) White
   ____ (3) Other

3. What is your present marital status (check one)?
   ____ (1) Single
   ____ (2) Married
   ____ (3) Divorced

4. What is your present age? (fill in) ____ years of age.

5. How many total years of formal education (include elementary, junior high school, trade school, and college) have you had? (fill in) ____ years of formal education.

6. Have you personally known a woman who was raped (check one)?
   ____ (1) Yes
   ____ (2) No

7. Have you ever testified in court during a rape trial (check one)?
   ____ (1) Yes
   ____ (2) No

8. How many times have you interviewed rape victims about their rape (check one)?
   ____ (1) Never
   ____ (2) 1 time
   ____ (3) 2 times
   ____ (4) 3 times
   ____ (5) 4 times
   ____ (6) 5 or more times

9. How much contact have you had with rape victims (check one)?

_____ (1) No contact at all with rape victims

_____ (2) Very little contact

_____ (3) A little contact

_____ (4) Some contact

_____ (5) Much contact

_____ (6) Very much contact with rape victims

10. How much contact have you had with convicted or accused rapists (check one)?

_____ (1) No contact at all with rapists

_____ (2) Very little contact

_____ (3) A little contact

_____ (4) Some contact

_____ (5) Much contact

_____ (6) Very much contact with rapists

11. Have you ever received any special training dealing with rape?

_____ (1) Yes

_____ (2) No

12. What is your present job title (please be specific)?

_____

13 How long have you worked in your present job?

_____ years _____ months

14. How long have you worked for your present organization?

_____ years _____ months

Personal Data Sheet: Rapists

Please answer the following questions. The answers will be used to classify your answers to the questionnaires.

1. What is your race (check one)?

    ___ (1) Black

    ___ (2) White

    ___ (3) Other

2. What is your present marital status (check one)?

    ___ (1) Single

    ___ (2) Married

    ___ (3) Divorced

3. What is your present age? (fill in) ___ years of age.

4. How many total years of formal education (include elementary, junior high school, high school, trade school, and college) have you had? (fill in) ___ years

5. How long have you been at the hospital?

    ___ years ___ months

6. What was your occupation (for example, carpenter, teacher) before you entered the hospital? _____

Measurement and Correlates of People's Views and Knowledge about Rape

Few issues elicit such a wide variety of opinions and beliefs among the general populace as does the topic of rape. Rape can and does mean many different things to many people, and sometimes it means many contradictory things. Evidence regarding the diversity of people's perceptions of rape is readily apparent by reviewing any number of popular magazines (Calvert 1974; Medea and Thompson 1974; Salerno 1975) or best-selling books (Brownmiller 1975a).

Recently, it has been suggested that the perceptions or attitudes of people toward rape are important for understanding not only their reactions to the act itself but their behavior concerning the victim or offender as well (Brownmiller 1975b). Various researchers have proposed that it is these attitudinal sets which have been influential in the reporting of rape by rape victims (Schwendinger and Schwendinger 1974); the treatment of rape victims by judges (Bohmer 1974; Bohmer and Blumberg 1975), by juries (Barber 1974; Brownmiller 1975a, pp. 373-374), and by attorneys (Chappell 1975a; Holmstrom and Burgess 1975; Landau 1974); the writing of rape laws and rape legislation (Heinz 1974; Leurs 1974; Sasko and Sesck 1975); the processing of rape complaints by police (Chappell 1975b; Keefe and O'Reilly 1976); and the physical and psychological care administered by medical personnel to rape victims (Burgess and Holmstrom 1976; LeBourdais 1976; McGuire and Stern 1976).

Some specific illustrations of the effects of rape attitudes may help to clarify their importance in studying rape. From the perspective of the victim, if she perceives rape as being "sex" outside marriage or precipitated by a woman, or if she perceives it as resulting in "damaged goods" and as affecting her desirability, she will certainly be less likely to report a rape to the police. From such beliefs, feelings of shame, guilt, and embarrassment and a desire to protect her reputation are likely to be heightened. Although many other reasons such as fear of offender retaliation, protection of her family from embarrassment, and protection of the offender where a special relationship existed (for example, supervisor, lover, date, friend, relative), and perceived punitive treatment and humiliation by police, medical personnel, or the courts as they attempt to determine if she was "really raped" may account for nonreporting, the significance of a victim's perceptions of rape and its impact on her should not be underestimated.

The treatment of rape patients by medical personnel may be influenced by the way in which they view rape and its victims. Attitudes expressed through insensitive, inhumane statements or behavior by staff members of hospitals and other physical care institutions will likely accentuate the victim's emotional reactions to the physical and psychological trauma of rape. Comments such as "He must have really enjoyed you since you have such a tight vagina," reportedly made by an examining physician of a rape victim, can only lead to further distress to the patient.

In many jurisdictions, the ultimate disposition of a rape complaint, that is, whether the complaint will or will not be investigated, is frequently determined by police investigators. Galton (1976) pointed out that investigators' attitudes toward rape complaints affect their analysis of the elements of a rape offense. Since rape tends to be a private crime where there are no witnesses, quite frequently it turns out that it is the victim's word against the defendant's. Thus police tend to be more skeptical of a rape victim's accusations than those of a victim of an assault or a robbery (Curtis 1974, p. 601). Factors such as evidence of breaking and entering, type and condition of a victim's clothing, physical condition such as bruises and scratches on a victim, emotional condition and reputation of a victim, location and time of the rape, race of the victim, promptness of the complaint, evidence of a weapon, submission to medical examination, and use of drugs or alcohol by the victim play a major role in officers' decisions whether to investigate a rape (Brownmiller 1975a; Chappell 1975b). Certainly, these factors, in combination with police officers' perceptions of rape, may explain why some officers in their investigations have asked victims such questions as "Did you enjoy it? Did you have an orgasm?" Lake (1974, p. 137) noted that police officers told a task force investigating rape in Maryland in 1972 that they habitually yelled at rape victims while questioning them since they believed this was the best way to find the truth in the "large" number of "unfounded" rape charges. These procedures have been used apparently by some investigating officers even though rape victims appear to lie no more frequently than victims of other crimes (Curtis 1974, p. 601).

Within a legal context, jury members' attitudes toward rape may influence their verdicts as well as the outcome of rape trials. Wood (1973) noted that because of the assumption that jurors may feel sympathy for the victim and convict the defendant without adequate proof, many state laws have more stringent proof requirements for rape than for other crimes. In many cases, these laws appear to have been developed from traditional moral and social attitudes about rape and rape victims (Mathiasen 1974, p. 43). The effects of such attitudes on the legal processes in some rape trials are clearly evident in the cautionary instructions given by judges to jurors of rape cases in some jurisdictions. (More will be said about the impact of the judge's instructions in chapter 5.)

Although many women are sexually active with partners of their own choosing, some jurisdictions also note that consent of the victim in a rape charge may be inferred from unchastity (Aitken 1974, p. 197). Due to their perceptions of women and rape, jurors tend to think of the victim in terms of assumption of risk and victim precipitation. The law recognizes only one issue other than penetration of intercourse, that is, consent. However, many juries may carefully scrutinize the victim and choose to be lenient with the accused if there are indications of victim contributory behavior (Kalven and Zeisel 1966, p. 249). Thus jurors may conclude that the victim consented when in fact consent was not given; that a rape victim, particularly one with a "bad" moral character, is less credible than other witnesses; and that lack of evidence other than a victim's testimony suggests that a rape did not occur.

It is no wonder then that among many jurors, there is the belief that women cannot be trusted to tell the truth even under oath (see comments of a New York Appellate Court judge cited in Lake 1974, p. 134). Thus unless the victim is physically harmed, there is the suspicion among some jurors that she consented to intercourse (see comments of juror of a rape case cited in Lake 1974, p. 134).

Since many juries are composed of citizens who believe many of the myths surrounding rape (for example: women want to be raped, women falsely accuse innocent men of rape, women provoke rape by their physical appearance), jurors may judge the complainant and ultimately determine the outcome of a trial according to these myths (Brownmiller 1975a, p. 373). Two recent cases will illustrate the point. In one case, a 19-year-old secretary was raped in broad daylight in a parking lot. A witness to the crime made a positive identification of the offender. The district attorney in the case noted that contrary to some rape cases, this was a solid one. However, the jury acquitted the defendant. Following the trial, one of the jurors was found to reason that since a plain-looking girl was the victim, she (the juror) found it hard to believe anyone would want to rape her. Although such evidence was not introduced at the trial, the defendant had also been acquitted on a charge of assault with intent to rape nine days previously (Rape: Does justice turn its head? 1972).

Jurors' interpretations of resistance appeared to play a major role in the acquittal of a defendant charged with raping a George Washington University student and forcing her and another student to commit sodomy. The accused admitted that he had comitted the crimes, but due to technicalities the admission was not admitted during the trial. After the verdict, one juror stated that the defendant had been found innocent because the victims neither resisted enough nor tried to escape. Testimony at the trial revealed that both women were hysterical after the incident, and one woman was described by a physician as having at least ten bruises on her body. Further, one of the women who had been beaten on the head testified that she was afraid the defendant was armed with a gun. A witness also testified that she had seen him and one of the victims, bruised and disheveled, leaving a restroom where the assault had occurred. Yet jurors may interpret the absence of "enough" resistance as implying consent (Barker 1972, p. E1).

Outcomes such as those described have led some writers such as Brownmiller (1975a) to argue that societal beliefs about rape and about women and their roles as interpreted through rape laws have caused the victimization of women. Similarly, from a legal perspective, LeGrand (1973) has proposed that there is an intimate interrelationship between the subjugation and repression of women through current rape laws and societal attitudes concerning rape. She has noted that not only are attitudes important in determining the construction of the rape laws, but in turn it is these same attitudes which reenforce the laws (LeGrand 1973, p. 919).

Even though rape is one of the most rapidly increasing, hotly debated, and newly researched crimes in America (Goldner 1972) and even though it appears generally accepted that attitudes are important in studying rape, little empirical research has been undertaken in this area. For the most part, when rape attitudes have been studied, the data base has been restricted to anecdotal events or case histories (MacKellar 1975). Of course, these data are useful, but such information is not readily susceptible to quantitative analysis and provides little objective evidence on the generality or magnitude of the problem. In particular, when rape attitudes have been discussed, they have been characterized as being unidimensional in nature. Few investigations, or propositions for that matter, appear to have been made which identify what *specific* dimensions of rape attitudes exist or are important in rape research.

Recognizing the importance of rape attitudes, members of the criminal justice system, rape crisis counselors, and the general public are beginning to ask such questions as the following:

1. How do people perceive rape? That is, are there different categories or dimensions of rape attitudes which people hold?
2. Are selected characteristics (for example, sex and race) of people in these groups predictive of their attitudes toward rape? If so, which characteristics seem to be most important in predicting these attitudes?
3. Are there differences in attitudes toward rape among police officers, rape crisis counselors, the general public, and other groups?
4. Are jury members' attitudes toward rape predictive of their verdicts in rape trials?
5. How much do people know about rape?
6. Does this knowledge about rape relate to jury members' verdicts in rape trials?

The purpose of the present chapter is to examine these and other questions, drawing upon data collected from patrol police officers, rape crisis counselors, rapists, and citizens. Relationships between jury members' attitudes toward and knowledge about rape and their verdicts in rape trials will be studied in chapter 4.

Attitudes toward Rape

How People View Rape

The ways in which the subjects in the study perceived rape could be characterized in any number of ways. Initially, percentages were used to describe how various types or groups of people responded to each of the items on the Attitudes toward Rape (ATR). However, the sheer bulk of data consisting of 46,336 ratings (32 items × 1,448 respondents) from the ATR alone necessarily limits this method as the sole alternative. For this reason, factor analysis, a more complex but more illuminating and informative technique, was also employed to depict people's perceptions of rape. Essentially, this technique serves as a means for reducing a large number of items to a smaller set of factors or dimensions composed of items having similar themes. By focusing on the interrelations among the ATR items, factor analysis enables us to determine what the categories or dimensions of people's views of rape are and to describe their views according to these underlying attitudinal dimensions.

In addition to identifying various dimensions of rape attitudes, factor analysis also permits the respondents to be scored on these derived dimensions. Then, rather than having to deal with scores on thirty-two items concerned with various aspects of rape, the technique will permit us to score and describe the respondents' views on a reduced number of measures. Before turning to these attitudinal dimensions of rape, however, let us first take a look at the respondents' answers to the individual items of the ATR.

Description of Rape Attitudes. If one were to carefully study the literature discussing rape attitudes, it would quickly become apparent that much of the writing has speculated on the nature of sex and race differences as well as group differences (for example, police or citizens) in regard to attitudes toward rape. Given these concerns and using data collected through the ATR, the proportions (percentages) of women, men, black and white citizens as well as the four respondent groups agreeing with the ATR items were calculated.[1] Tables 3-1 and 3-2 were prepared to show the proportions of citizens by sex and race as well as by type of respondent agreeing with each of the attitude statements. Significance tests were also made between

Table 3-1

Percentage of Citizens by Sex and Race Agreeing with Items on the Attitude toward Rape Questionnaire

Item	Citizens (n = 1,056)	Sex		Race	
		Women (n = 528)	Men (n = 528)	Black (n = 160)	White (n = 896)
1. A woman can be raped against her will.	96	98	94	86	98
2. The reason most rapists commit rape is for the thrill of physical violence.	55	60	50	48	56
3. Rapists are "normal" men.	15	12	18	23	13
4. In forcible rape, the victim never causes the crime.	37	44	31	45	36
5. All rapists are mentally sick.	57	60	54	48	58
6. A charge of rape two days after the act has occurred is probably not rape.	41	42	39	58	37
7. A woman should be responsible for preventing her own rape.	34	32	36	54	30
8. A man who has committed rape should be given at least 30 years in prison.	39	41	38	51	37
9. Women are trained by society to be rape victims.	27	30	24	30	26
10. A raped woman is a less desirable woman.	14	15	13	24	12
11. If a woman is going to be raped, she might as well relax and enjoy it.	12	8	16	24	10
12. Rape provides the opportunity for many rapists to show their manhood.	49	52	46	36	52
13. Most women secretly desire to be raped.	13	10	15	34	9
14. It would do some women some good to get raped.	16	12	20	30	14
15. Women provoke rape by their appearance or behavior.	66	61	71	69	65
16. "Nice" women do not get raped.	4	3	4	7	3
17. Most charges of rape are unfounded.	29	28	31	60	24

	Statement					
18.	In order to protect the male, it should be difficult to prove that rape has occurred.	34	25	43	36	34
19.	Rape is the expression of an uncontrollable desire for sex.	45	41	49	68	41
20.	Rape is the worst crime that can be committed.	23	26	21	36	21
21.	Rape is a sex crime.	83	84	82	84	83
22.	All rape is a male exercise in power over women.	44	53	34	46	43
23.	During a rape, a woman should do everything she can do to resist.	59	52	55	64	57
24.	Rapists are sexually frustrated individuals.	75	74	76	81	73
25.	In most cases when a woman was raped, she was asking for it.	11	11	11	23	9
26.	The reason most rapists commit rape is for sex.	45	41	49	61	42
27.	Rape of a woman by a man she knows can be defined as a "woman who changed her mind afterward."	29	21	31	46	26
28.	A convicted rapist should be castrated.	23	23	23	29	22
29.	A woman should not feel guilty following a rape.	89	91	87	78	91
30.	The degree of a woman's resistance should be the major factor in determining if a rape has occurred.	32	29	35	49	29
31.	A raped woman is a responsible victim, not an innocent one.	16	11	21	27	14
32.	Rape serves as a way to put or keep women in their "place."	6	7	5	15	4

Note: Pairs of italicized percentages are significantly ($p < .01$) different. The percentages have been rounded to the nearest whole percent.

Table 3-2
Percentage of Respondent Groups Agreeing with Items on the Attitude toward Rape Questionnaire

Item	Respondent Group			
	Citizens (n = 1,056)	Rapists (n = 20)	Patrol Police Officers (n = 254)	Rape Crisis Counselors (n = 118)
1. A woman can be raped against her will.	96	70	96	99
2. The reason most rapists commit rape is for the thrill of physical violence.	55	35	65	75
3. Rapists are "normal" men.	15	25	13	48
4. In forcible rape, the victim never causes the crime.	37	50	23	75
5. All rapists are mentally sick.	57	70	53	37
6. A charge of rape two days after the act has occurred is probably not rape.	41	20	28	4
7. A woman should be responsible for preventing her own rape.	34	50	45	25
8. A man who has committed rape should be given at least 30 years in prison.	39	5	70	39
9. Women are trained by society to be rape victims.	27	30	37	64
10. A raped woman is a less desirable woman.	14	15	14	4
11. If a woman is going to be raped, she might as well relax and enjoy it.	12	30	10	3
12. Rape provides the opportunity for many rapists to show their manhood.	49	60	51	51
13. Most women secretly desire to be raped.	13	50	11	1
14. It would do some women some good to get raped.	16	25	19	1
15. Women provoke rape by their appearance or behavior.	66	65	78	10
16. "Nice" women do not get raped.	4	5	4	1
17. Most charges of rape are unfounded.	29	55	34	6

18.	In order to protect the male, it should be difficult to prove that a rape has occurred.	*34*	50	38	*8*
19.	Rape is the expression of an uncontrollable desire for sex.	*45*	60	47	*9*
20.	Rape is the worst crime that can be committed.	*23*	15	24	*44*
21.	Rape is a sex crime.	*83*	90	89	*33*
22.	All rape is a male exercise in power over women.	*44*	45	37	*64*
23.	During a rape, a woman should do everything she can do to resist.	*59*	65	63	*56*
24.	Rapists are sexually frustrated individuals.	*75*	75	76	*28*
25.	In most cases when a woman was raped, she was asking for it.	*11*	10	19	*1*
26.	The reason most rapists commit rape is for sex.	*45*	40	45	*9*
27.	Rape of a woman by a man she knows can be defined as a "woman who changed her mind afterward."	*29*	45	31	*4*
28.	A convicted rapist should be castrated.	*23*	10	39	*22*
29.	A woman should not feel guilty following a rape.	*89*	70	84	*97*
30.	The degree of a woman's resistance should be the major factor in determining if a rape has occurred.	*32*	35	34	*2*
31.	A raped woman is a responsible victim, not an innocent one.	*16*	15	21	*3*
32.	Rape serves as a way to put or keep women in their "place."	*6*	10	3	*39*

Note: Pairs of italicized percentages between the citizen respondent group and each of the other respondent groups are significantly ($p < .01$) different. The percentages have been rounded to the nearest whole percent.

pairs of percentages (significantly different percentages are indicated by values in italics) to test for statistically significant ($p < .01$) differences in the proportions of various combinations (such as women versus men) or types of respondents (such as citizens versus rape crisis counselors) agreeing with an item. No attempt will be made to describe the responses of the various groupings to each of the items; however, several of the more interesting trends for the citizen sample as it relates to other respondent groups will be highlighted. Many of the major differences observed for the sex, race, and respondent groups (table 3-2) will be discussed in the two subsequent sections of the chapter.

Looking first at table 3-1, it can be seen that most of the 1,056 citizens (96 percent) believed a woman can be raped against her will. Somewhat surprisingly, however, many appeared to attribute a rape attack to the woman. Rape was seen by the majority of (66 percent) of the citizens as being provoked by women's behavior or appearance; a substantial number (34 percent) felt that women should be held responsible for preventing their own rape. Eleven percent placed the blame for rape on women as they indicated that if a woman was raped, she was asking for it.

Although 89 percent felt that a woman should not feel guilty following a rape, 14 percent of the respondents stated that she would be a less desirable person after the offense. One might wonder how citizens could hold such attitudes toward an individual who has experienced the trauma of rape. In part, these reactions may be the product of a belief that the "property or goods" are now damaged and thus have lost their value. Additionally, according to Symonds' (1975) conceptions, there is a reluctance on the part of people to accept the idea that a crime victim is blameless. Violent, senseless, and irrational crimes make people feel insecure and vulnerable, especially if these people or their friends may be exposed to these offenses anytime, anywhere, or anyplace. For these people, it is both a relief and a comfort to feel that the victim, through appearance or behavior, may have done something to contribute to or precipitate the act. They no longer feel as helpless or as vulnerable. Thus, as with many of the citizens in the study, causes for rape may be sought in the victim rather than in the offender since he is not likely to be accessible for their examination.

If the trends in our set of data can be extrapolated to other populations, it would appear that rather substantial numbers of people attribute rape primarily to women, not to men. In reality, however, reported rape cases appear to involve relatively few instances of victim precipitory acts. A national survey by the Federal Commission on Crimes of Violence reported that at the national level only 4 percent of the clearances of rape charges and 6 percent of nonclearances involved victim precipitation (Curtis 1974). Amir (1971), in a comprehensive study of 646 Philadelphia rape cases in the 1958-1960 period, estimated the rate at 19 percent.

It has been noted that citizens view rape as being victim-precipitated, but a key issue is whether such perceptions may have a bearing on jurors' verdicts in rape trials. Survey research conducted by Kalven and Zeisel (1966) sheds some light on the possible effects of factors such as victim precipitation or reputation in juror deliberations. In their research they were interested in, among other things, determining if there were discrepancies between jurors' and judges' verdicts of trials and, if so, what factors may account for these discrepancies. For each of 3,576 trials, including rape and other issues, a questionnaire was sent to the presiding judge which asked about the verdict of the jury, the fact pattern in the case, and how the judge would have ruled in the case without the jury. They examined the effects of jurors' perspectives of victim precipitation on the outcome of rape trials by splitting the rape cases into two types: aggravated and simple rape. Aggravated rape was characterized by extrinsic violence, two or more offenders, or no prior acquaintance between the two parties; simple rape included all other cases. They felt there would be less chance of victim contributory behavior in aggravated than in simple rape cases. It was found that in 12 percent of the aggravated rape cases the jury acquitted when the judge convicted, but in simple rape the rate of disagreement was 60 percent. Certainly, it would appear that jurors' beliefs regarding victim precipitation of rape may play a significant role in rape trials.

Due to the predominant role of physical violence in many rapes, several writers have argued that rape should not be treated as a sex crime but as a form of assault against the person with sex as the weapon. Almost half (45 percent) of the citizens felt that the reason most rapists commit it is for sex; therefore, many concluded that rape is a sex crime (83 percent) committed by sexually frustrated individuals. It would seem that the perceptions of rape as a sex crime might be tied to the views of the roles of women in rape and sexual activities. Historically, men have been viewed and even encouraged to be aggressors in sexual encounters while women have been characterized as being passive, disinterested receivers of these attentions. Once stimulated by women, however, men have been depicted as being victims of uncontrollable sexual desires and passionate emotions, thus placing the responsibility on a woman for determining how far sexual relations with a man will go. When such relations have gone "too far," society has been quick to blame the woman while her aggressor has been excused for "just being a man." Due to some individuals' conceptions of woman's monitoring role in sexual activities and their views of rape as a sex crime, it would seem these same individuals would likely hold a woman responsible in a rape, particularly if it is believed she "encouraged" the attack. Also the logic that "rape is sex, sex is fun; therefore, rape is fun" may subconsciously be used by some in perceiving rape.

Rather than a need for sex, several feminist writers, most notably Brownmiller (1975*a*), have suggested that men rape out of a desire for power over women and use rape as a fear tactic to keep women in their "place." Most of the respondents did not have the same opinion. Less than one out of ten (6 percent) felt rape serves as a way to put or keep women in their place. Since many of the respondents perceived rape as resulting from an offender's drive for sex, it is understandable why very few saw rape as a desire for power over women.

In general, the citizens tended to see rapists as being "sick," sexually frustrated individuals. Eighty-five percent of the citizens concluded that rapists are not "normal" men. Over half (57 percent) tended to view such individuals as being mentally sick. Although viewing rapists as mentally ill, more than one out of five believed that a convicted rapist should be castrated or given at least thirty years in prison. Data regarding the normality of rapists are somewhat contradictory (Sherman 1975). Brownmiller (1975*a*) has suggested that many rapists are much like normal men. LeGrand (1973, p. 922) concluded that, based on a series of psychological studies, rapists appear to have basically normal personality profiles, though they do seem to be somewhat more impulsive, aggressive, and violent. Assuming that rapists appear on the surface to be normal and thus do not conform to many jurors' expectations, the severity of punishment required by many state rape laws may actually work in favor of the defendant. For example, if jurors think of a stereotypic rapist as being a psychopathic degenerate, when confronted with an individual who does not look like their conceptions, the jury may acquit because they perceive the mandatory penalty as too severe for the individual given the offense.

The question of victim consent in rape is typically judged to be a critical factor in deciding whether a rape has occurred. In many rape cases, this issue has been settled through an assessment of the degree of resistance used by the victim in the attack. Almost one-third (32 percent) of the respondents indicated that the degree of a woman's resistance should be the major factor in determining if a rape has taken place; 59 percent noted that during a rape, a woman should do everything she can to resist.

The law does not require complete and total resistance; yet based on these percentages, one wonders if some jurors do not "write their own laws" regarding the degree of victim resistance required to prove a rape. Further, 34 percent of the citizens tended to support the sexist logic behind many of the rape laws as they said it should be difficult to prove a rape in order to protect the male. Such reasoning is apparently based on the idea that rape is a charge easy to make but difficult to defend against even though the defendant is innocent (Hale 1847). More than likely, as evidenced by the low conviction rates in rape trials, guilty assailants will probably avoid prosecution due to juries' reluctance to convict, victims' unwillingness to report the crime, and the writing of current rape laws (Wood 1973).

In deciding rape cases, jurors typically look for corroborating evidence as an indication that a rape has occurred. One form of proof frequently considered as evidence of forcible rape is the physical condition of the victim. The presence of bruises, scratches, or cuts is taken as one form of proof that the victim did not consent to intercourse. Their absence, however, may suggest to some jurors that a rape did not take place. The insistence of active victim resistance by jurors, the courts, or the police may produce a conflict situation for her. On the one hand, she may be told by the police or experts in victimology to do as her attacker directs; compliance is the best course for self-protection. Society as well as the criminal justice system, however, typically insists upon resistance as proof of rape. Our data confirm this insistence among many of the citizens in the sample.

Dimensionality of Rape Attitudes. Prior to conducting the factor analysis of the ATR items, it was decided to include the responses from all 1,448 subjects in the analysis. Their inclusion was considered important since scores on the derived factors for each individual in the study would be necessary in later analyses. However, it might be argued that individuals in the different respondent groups, due to their differences in dealing with rape, its victims, and offenders, may perceive rape in different ways. To test the possibility that the ways or dimensions people use in perceiving rape may differ among the various subgroups of respondents, separate principal components factor analyses of the ATR responses, followed by varimax rotations (Kaiser 1958), were performed for the following groups: citizens ($n = 1,056$), patrol police officers ($n = 254$), and rape crisis counselors ($n = 118$). Due to the small number of rapists in the sample ($n = 20$), a separate factor analysis of the ATR could not be performed for this group.

Using Cattell's (1966) screen test, a plot of the eigenvalues indicated that for each of the analyses eight factors (all with eigenvalues greater than 1) should be extracted. The eight factors for each combination of the three groups were then paired and coefficients of congruence (Harman 1967) computed for each of the pairings to determine the degree of similarity between the rotated factors of each pair of subgroups. The congruence coefficients indicated that the derived factor structures were highly similar as the congruence indexes ranged from .81 to .89 with a mean of .87.

Since the respondent subgroups were quite similar in their attitudinal sets of rape, all subjects were combined and their ATR responses factor-analyzed using a principal components solution with varimax rotation to orthogonality. Based on a plot of the eigenvalues, eight factors (all with eigenvalues greater than 1) were extracted from the 32 × 32 item intercorrelation matrix. The eight factors accounted for 50 percent of the total common variation among the items. All eight factors were found to be interpretable as well as to possess an adequate number of variables with loadings of sufficient magnitude ($\geq \pm$ .30) to warrant interpretation and subsequent scoring (Comrey 1973, p. 209). Table 3-3 presents the varimax rotated factor loadings for the eight major factors extracted from the factor analysis on the total sample. Along with each factor is the percentage of common variance accounted for by each factor as an index of relative factor importance. (In interpreting the direction of scoring of a factor, it should be kept in mind that a high score indicates that a greater amount of a dimension is represented by a factor.)

Factor I is principally defined by items dealing with a woman's responsibility in preventing rape, for example, a woman should be responsible for preventing her own rape, and a raped woman is a responsible victim, not an innocent one. A clear theme among these items is the notion of victim responsiblity. Thus this factor was named *woman's responsibility in rape prevention*. High-scoring individuals on this factor would be ones who feel that women should be held responsible for preventing their own rape (pro-rape attitude).

Factor II tends to be saturated with items dealing with sex and its relation to rape. Themes such as the reason most rapists commit rape is for sex, rape is the expression of an uncontrollable desire for sex, and rape is a sex crime are most characteristic of this factor. As such, this factor was labeled *sex as motivation for rape*. A high score on this factor would characterize individuals who believe that the motivation for rape is sex.

Items dealing with the punishment of a rapist readily characterize factor III. For instance, items like a convicted rapist should be castrated, and a man who has committed rape should be given at least thirty years in prison tend to reflect the respondents' notions of retribution for rape. Based on these items, the factor was named *severe punishment for rape*. Individuals who feel rapists should be severely punished would score low on this factor (antirape attitude).

On the whole, factor IV reflects the perceived role of women in precipitating or causing rape. High loadings of items like in forcible rape, the victim never causes the crime, and women provoke rape by their appearance or behavior suggest that this factor be called *victim precipitation of rape*. A high score on factor IV indicates a belief that women cause rape through their appearance or behavior (prorape attitude).

Factor V is defined by the loadings of items dealing with the perceived "normality" or mental well-being of rapists. High-loading items on this factor are rapists are normal men, and all rapists are mentally sick. This factor was labeled *normality of rapists*, with a high score suggesting that rapists are normal.

Like factor II, factor VI centers on the motivation for rape. In this case, however, the focus is on power rather than sex as shown by such items as women are trained by society to be rape victims, rape provides the opportunity for many rapists to show their manhood, and all rape is a male exercise in power over women; therefore, the title of *power as motivation for rape* was given to this dimension. A high score would depict individuals who feel that the basic motivation for rape is power.

Factor VII concerns the perceived attractiveness of a woman following her rape, for example, a woman should not feel guilty following a rape, and a raped woman is a less desirable woman. This factor was called *favorable perception of a woman after rape*. High-scoring persons would be those who perceive a raped woman in a favorable manner (antirape attitude).

Finally, factor VIII tends to deal with those items which seem to reflect the expected behavior of a woman *during* a rape. The high-loading items were: during a rape, a woman should do everything she can do to resist, and if a woman is going to be raped, she might as well relax and enjoy it. This final factor was named *resistance as woman's role during rape*. A high score would indicate a belief that a woman should attempt to resist during a rape attack.

Following the derivation of the eight factors, factor scores for the subjects were calculated using a procedure developed by Kaiser (see Nie, Hull, Jenkins, Steinbrenner, and Bent 1975, pp. 487-490, for details). This procedure produced uncorrelated, standardized scores on the factors with a mean of zero and a standard deviation of one.

In terms of factor reliability, no data were collected from the same respondents at a second point in time, so the stability of the factors through test-retest methods could not be ascertained. However, data are available which provide some information relative to the internal consistency of the dimensions of rape attitudes. First, the separate factor analyses showed a high degree of similarity in factor structures of rape attitudes across the various respondent subgroups. Second, the square root of the estimated communalities of the ATR factors, the theoretical lower bound of reliability (Taylor and Parker 1964, p. 39), had a mean value of .62. Although somewhat low, this value seems acceptable, given the heterogeneity of the items and the number of factors extracted, and the number of items loading greater than .30 on the factors.

In summary, the factor analysis of the ATR reduced the content from thirty-two items to eight identifiable, meaningful dimensions of rape attitudes. On the whole, half of these factors centered on issues concerned with the victim while the remainder dealt with various aspects of the offender. Limited data reported earlier also suggest reasonable reliability of these dimensions. These scales also "make sense" implying face validity and, although not confirmed empirically elsewhere, these dimensions have been discussed in the literature (Brownmiller 1975a; MacKellar 1975; Schwendinger and Schwendinger 1974). (Data relating to the construct validity of the dimensions are presented in the next section.) The scales of

Table 3-3
Varimax Rotated Factor Structure of Attitudes toward Rape

Item	I	II	III	IV	V	VI	VII	VIII	M	SD
1. A woman can be raped against her will.	.51						-.17	-.17	1.47	0.94
2. The reason most rapists commit rape is for the thrill of physical violence.			-.45	-.12		-.29	-.32		3.36	1.46
3. Rapists are "normal" men.	-.16			.23	-.76	-.19			4.75	1.36
4. In forcible rape, the victim never causes the crime.	.14			.76		-.10			3.73	1.54
5. All rapists are mentally sick.			-.10	.29	.75				3.38	1.56
6. A charge of rape two days after the act has occurred is probably not rape.	-.58	-.27			-.10		-.18		4.11	1.56
7. A woman should be responsible for preventing her own rape.	-.64						-.18		4.24	1.50
8. A man who has committed rape should be given at least 30 years in prison.		-.11	-.70				.11	-.16	3.54	1.71
9. Women are trained by society to be rape victims.	-.17	.24				-.65			4.31	1.52
10. A raped woman is a less desirable woman.	-.21	-.15			.10	-.32	.60		5.04	1.23
11. If a woman is going to be raped, she might as well relax and enjoy it.	-.33	-.13				-.12		.63	5.16	1.20
12. Rape provides the opportunity for many rapists to show their manhood.	.16	-.22		-.16		-.63	.28		3.75	1.72
13. Most women secretly desire to be raped.	-.45	-.13		-.11	-.14	-.15		.40	5.07	1.15
14. It would do some women some good to get raped.	-.44	-.13		-.16			.25	.36	5.04	1.31
15. Women provoke rape by their appearance or behavior.	-.36	-.27		-.58					3.37	1.41
16. "Nice" women do not get raped.	-.50					-.11	.35		5.44	0.81
17. Most charges of rape are unfounded.	-.46	-.35	-.11		-.11		.11	.10	4.25	1.41
18. In order to protect the male, it should be difficult to prove that a rape has occurred.	-.30	-.28	.15	-.32		-.22			4.22	1.47
19. Rape is the expression of an uncontrollable desire for sex.	-.20	-.72	-.11				.17		3.85	1.55

	I	II	III	IV	V	VI	VII	VIII	Mean	SD
20. Rape is the worst crime that can be committed.	-.11	-.11	-.62	.40	-.16				4.42	1.44
21. Rape is a sex crime.		-.66	-.10	-.14	.11		-.10		2.43	1.42
22. All rape is a male exercise in power over women.		-.14	-.23	.37		-.48	-.10		3.76	1.47
23. During a rape, a woman should do everything she can do to resist.	-.16	-.14	-.12				.10	-.72	3.13	1.54
24. Rapists are sexually frustrated individuals.	-.11	-.61			.32	-.14			2.96	1.38
25. In most cases when a woman was raped, she was asking for it.	-.61	-.18	-.12	-.10	-.11		.26	.10	4.92	1.08
26. The reason most rapists commit rape is for sex.	-.18	-.73			-.11		.19		3.85	1.45
27. Rape of a woman by a man she knows can be defined as a "woman who changed her mind afterward."	-.57	-.37			-.11		.12		4.32	1.33
28. A convicted rapist should be castrated.			-.72						4.43	1.55
29. A woman should feel guilty following a rape.	.16		.10		.13	-.20	-.65		2.05	1.19
30. The degree of a woman's resistance should be the major factor in determining if a rape has occurred.	-.51	-.27		-.14		-.11	.19	-.32	4.36	1.50
31. A raped woman is a responsible victim, not an innocent one.	-.62			-.20			.14		4.77	1.20
32. Rape serves as a way to put or keep women in their "place."	-.20	.33		.29	-.19	-.38	.14	.10	5.37	1.14
Percentage of common variance	17.6	7.6	7.0	4.4	3.9	3.7	3.5	3.3		

Note: $N = 1,445$. For clarity, only those loadings greater than $\pm.09$ are reported. Definition of factors: I = woman's responsibility in rape prevention; II = sex as motivation for rape; III = severe punishment for rape; IV = victim precipitation of rape; V = normality of rapists; VI = power as motivation for rape; VII = favorable perception of a woman after rape; VIII = resistance as woman's role during rape.

the ATR are useful, not because they describe previously unknown aspects of rape attitudes but because they provide a systematic, relatively objective way for measuring concepts not previously well-operationalized.

It is interesting to note that the citizens, patrol police officers, and rape crisis counselors did *not* differ in terms of the dimensionality or structure of their perceptions of rape. Of course, this does not necessarily mean that there are no differences among the respondent groups on these underlying attitudinal dimensions. Such group differences are studied later.

Correlates of Rape Attitudes

Another purpose of the study was to investigate how predictable rape attitudes were from personal characteristics (for example, sex, race) of the respondents. To accomplish this task, several different correlational procedures were utilized.[2] Using data collected from the personal information sheets, product-moment (simple and point-biserial) as well as multiple correlations were computed between the respondent characteristics and the eight attitudinal dimensions of rape measured by the ATR. These correlations were generated for each of the respondent subgroups as well as for the sample as a whole. The purposes of this type of analysis were twofold. First, it was central to the investigation to see how various respondent characteristics might *singly* predict or correlate with rape attitudes. This was accomplished, in part, by computing simple correlations (r) between the relevant variables under consideration. Where categorical characteristics (for example, sex, race, marital status) were involved, the variables were dummy-coded (for instance, 1 = female; 2 = male) and point-biserial correlations calculated. As Welkowitz, Ewen, and Cohen (1971) noted, the point-biserial is an appropriate test of the difference between the means of two groups, providing an index of the strength of the relationship as well as the level of significance.

While it was important to describe the degree of association between single respondent characteristics and the dimensions of rape attitudes, it was also of interest to determine how predictable each of the attitudes might be when considering more than one or sets of these characteristics. For example, taken separately, sex and race of respondents may be useful in predicting how people view rape. However, our ability to predict these perceptions may be enhanced by considering both sex and race of the respondent simultaneously rather than simply by themselves. To address this issue, multiple correlations (R) were used to locate sets of respondent characteristics having significant correlations with rape attitudes. The use of multiple correlations would help us to determine how useful groups or sets of respondent characteristics would be in explaining or predicting rape attitudes.

To assess the degree of interrelationship among the thirteen respondent characteristics, intercorrelations were computed among the variables. The resulting significant ($p < .05$) correlations are shown in table 3-4. As may be seen in the table, the correlations ranged from .00 to .78 with a mean of .17. Of the correlations computed, 40 percent were less than .10 and 73 percent less than .20, suggesting that the characteristics were relatively independent.

Citizens. With the exception of the factor *power as motivation for rape*, the multiple correlations between the respondent characteristics and rape attitudes were highly significant ($p < .0001$) with the multiple correlations ranging from .19 to .42. A closer inspection of the product-moment correlations shows that the respondents' sex, race, and attitudes toward women were the most consistent predictors as sex was correlated with seven factors, attitudes toward women with six of the factors, and race was related to four.[3] Interestingly, personal knowledge of a raped woman was found to be uncorrelated with the factors.

A number of sex differences with respect to attitudes toward rape are evident in table 3-5. As contrasted to women (scored 1), men (scored 2) tended to indicate to a greater extent that it was a woman's responsibility in preventing rape ($r = .17, p < .001$), punishment for rape should be harsh ($r = .09, p < .01$), victims precipitate rape through their appearance or behavior ($r = .16, p < .001$), rapists are mentally normal ($r = .08, p < .01$), rapists are not motivated by a need for power over women ($r = -.07, p < .05$), a woman is less attractive after rape ($r = -.11, p < .001$), and women should resist during rape ($r = -.17, p < .001$).

In terms of race, blacks (scored 1) in comparison to whites (scored 2) felt that women are primarily responsible in rape prevention ($r = -.30, p < .001$), a victim's appearance or behavior is less likely to precipitate rape ($r = .13, p < .001$), rapists are likely to be mentally normal ($r = -.16, p < .001$), and a woman is less attractive following her rape ($r = .17, p < .001$). Race was selected by two of the stepwise regressions as being the most important respondent characteristic for the factors of *woman's responsibility in rape prevention* and *normality of rapists*.

As might be expected, attitudes toward women exhibited a pattern of correlations with rape attitudes similar to that of sex of respondent. Two exceptions are worth noting, however. Liberal views of women's roles in society were associated with the beliefs that the motivation for rape is not sex ($r = -.20, p < .001$) and a woman is a desirable person following her rape ($r = .25, p < .001$).

Rapists. Only three correlations between characteristics of rapists and attitudes toward rape were found to be significant for the rapists. Marital

Table 3-4
Intercorrelations among Respondent Characteristics

Respondent Characteristic	Respondent Characteristic												
	1	2	3	4	5	6	7	8	9	10	11	12	13
1. Sex (1 = female; 2 = male)	—	.13	.19	.12	-.10			-.17	-.20	.40	.45	.06	-.27
2. Race (1 = black; 2 = white)		—	.25	.19	.28					.14		.10	.13
3. Marital status (1 = single; 2 = married)			—	.19	.08					.23			
4. Age				—	.21	-.10		.18	.16	.22	.11	.19	-.14
5. Years of education					—	.08	-.22	.17	.20	.11	-.15	.16	.18
6. Personally know a raped woman[a]						—	.30	-.34			.08		
7. Testified at a rape trial[a]							—	-.41	-.32	-.51			—[b]
8. Interviewed rape victims about their rape[a]								—	.78	.40	-.31	.13	—[b]
9. Contact with rape victims									—		-.34	.12	—[b]
10. Contact with rapists										—			—[b]
11. Received rape training[a]											—	-.13	—[b]
12. Knowledge about rape												—	.16
13. Attitudes toward women													—

Note: Since different sets of data were collected from the respondents ($N = 1,448$), the degrees of freedom varied for the reported correlations. Only those correlations significant at $p < .05$ are reported.

[a]The variables were coded where 1 = yes; 2 = no.

[b]Pairs of data were not collected for these variables.

status, age, and knowledge about rape were significantly ($p < .05$) related to three of the ATR factors. However, given the number of significant results relative to the number of correlations computed, it is quite possible that at least two of these could have occurred due to chance.

Patrol Police Officers. *Victim precipitation of rape* was the one attitudinal variable which could be predicted best by selected characteristics of police officers ($R = .28$, $p < .0001$). For this particular dimension, sex and race were the two characteristics which were significantly ($p < .01$) related, with race being the most important. As was true for the citizen sample, white officers were more likely than black officers to perceive rape as being caused by the victim's appearance or behavior. Similar to the citizen sample, race was negatively related to perceived *normality of rapists* ($r = -.14$, $p < .05$) and positively related to *favorable perception of a woman after rape* ($r = .13$, $p < .05$), though the magnitude of these correlations was higher in the citizen sample.

Contact with rapists, contact with rape victims, interviews with rape victims about their rape, and personal knowledge of a raped woman were not significantly correlated with rape attitudes. Participation in rape training programs was associated with the perception of a woman's behavior during rape. More specifically, officers who had not participated (scored 2) in these training programs (versus those who had, scored 1) were inclined to feel that one of the victim's prime responsibilities was resistance ($r = .20$, $p < .001$).

On the whole, police officers' perceptions of rape appeared to be less predictable than those of the citizen sample. Only eleven correlations were found to be significant with only one (race) of twelve variables related with as many as three of the ATR factors.

Rape Crisis Counselors. Two factors were highly predictable from the personal data collected from the counselors. The factors dealing with perceived motivation for rape, that is, sex and power, showed the highest multiple correlations—.55 ($p < .0001$) and .45 ($p < .0001$) for sex and power, respectively. With regard to these two factors, contact with rape victims seemed to account for more of the variance in these attitudes than any other single respondent characteristic. An examination of the simple correlations ($r = -.32$, $p < .001$ and $r = .31$, $p < .001$) suggests that as contact with rape victims increased, the counselors were more likely to view rape as being motivated by a desire for power over women rather than simply as a desire for sex.

Further examination of table 3-5 points up the importance of rape training for counselors and its relation to perceptions of rape. As shown, participation in training programs (scored 1) was related to the factors of *woman's responsibility in rape prevention* ($r = .23$, $p < .05$), *victim precipi-*

Table 3-5
Product-Moment and Multiple Correlations between Respondent-Characteristics and Dimensions of Rape Attitudes

Respondent Characteristic	Woman's Responsibility in Rape Prevention	Sex as Motivation for Rape	Severe Punishment for Rape	Victim Precipitation of Rape	Normality of Rapists	Power as Motivation for Rape	Favorable Perception of a Woman after Rape	Resistance as Woman's Role during Rape
All Respondents (N = 1,448)								
Sex[a] (1 = female; 2 = male)	.18***	.12***		.29***		-.11**	-.12***	-.13***
Race[a] (1 = black; 2 = white)	-.26***			.12***	-.12***	.06*	.15***	
Marital status[a] (1 = single; 2 = married)				.19***	-.11**	-.06*		.10***
Age	.06*			-.06*				
Years of education	-.16***	-.16***	.20***					
Knowledge about rape	-.08**	-.18***	.20****				.07**	
R	.36****	.27****	.20****	.35****	.16****	.15****	.20****	.18****
Citizens (n = 1,056)								
Sex[a] (1 = female; 2 = male)	.17***		.09**	.16***	.08**	-.07*	-.11**	-.17***
Race[a] (1 = black; 2 = white)	-.30***			.13***	-.16***		.17***	
Marital status[a] (1 = single; 2 = married)		-.13***						.12***
Age	.07*							.07*
Years of education	-.15***	-.14***	.23***					
Attitudes toward women	-.30***	-.20***	.19***		-.10**		.25***	-.07*
Knowledge about rape		-.13***	.13***					
Personally know a raped woman[a] (1 = yes; 2 = no)								
R	.42****	.30****	.31****	.21****	.19****	.13*	.29****	.25****

Rapists (n = 20)

Race[a] (1 = black; 2 = white)					
Marital status[a] (1 = single; 2 = married)	-.51*	-.52*			
Age					
Years of education					
Attitudes toward women	.57*				
Knowledge about rape	.57*	.51*	.52*		
R	.32	.38	.38	.33	.29

Patrol Police Officers (n = 254)

Sex[a] (1 = female; 2 = male)	.16**					
Race[a] (1 = black; 2 = white)	-.13*	.23***	-.14*	.13*		
Marital status[a] (1 = single; 2 = married)						
Age	.14*		-.15*	.15*		
Years of education	-.14*					
Knowledge about rape	-.18**					
Testified at a rape trial[a] (1 = yes; 2 = no)						
Interviewed rape victims about their rape						
Contact with rape victims						
Contact with rapists						
Received rape training[a] (1 = yes; 2 = no)	.20***					
Personally know a raped woman[a] (1 = yes; 2 = no)	.29**					
R	.20	.27**	.27**	.26**	.30*	.32*	.33****

Table 3-5 *(continued)*

Rape Crisis Counselors (n = 118)

Respondent Characteristic	Woman's Responsibility in Rape Prevention	Sex as Motivation for Rape	Severe Punishment for Rape	Victim Precipitation of Rape	Normality of Rapists	Power as Motivation for Rape	Favorable Perception of a Woman after Rape	Resistance as Woman's Role during Rape
Race[a] (1 = black; 2 = white)		−.28**						
Marital status[a] (1 = single; 2 = married)			.18*					
Age				.31***	−.17*	−.31***		
Years of education		−.26**						
Knowledge about rape							.19*	
Interviewed rape victims about their rape								
Contact with rape victims		−.32***				.31***		
Received rape training[a] (1 = yes; 2 = no)	.23*			.22*				
Personally know a raped woman[a] (1 = yes; 2 = no)								.26**
R	.23**	.55****	.26**	.38***	.26**	.45****	.29**	.26**

Note: Only those correlations that are statistically significant are reported.

[a]point-biserial correlation.

* $p < .05$. ** $p < .01$. *** $p < .001$. **** $p < .0001$.

tation of rape ($r = .22, p < .05$), and *resistance as woman's role during rape* ($r = .26, p < .01$). Interestingly, as with the police officers, training was correlated with the belief that women should not necessarily resist in a rape attack ($r = .26, p < .01$).

Generally speaking, the correlations between the respondent characteristics and attitudes toward rape ranged from low to moderate. For the sample as a whole, the demographic characteristics of sex, race, and marital status seemed to be most useful in predicting the dimensions of the ATR.

Within the citizen sample, the correlations between the respondent characteristics and the dimensions of the ATR quite readily point to the importance of sex and attitudes toward women when studying attitudes toward rape.[4] In terms of the ideological and historical development of people's perceptions of rape, Brownmiller (1975a) has provided perhaps the most complete account of the ideology of rape and its relation to men and women. With respect to sex differences, she noted that men tend to perceive rape quite differently than do women. For example, ideas such as "no woman can be raped against her will, and if you're going to be raped, you might as well relax and enjoy it" have been characterized by her as being male views of rape which most men believe (Brownmiller 1975a, p. 312).

The correlations between sex of respondent and attitudes toward rape support her thesis regarding sex differences; significant differences on seven of the eight dimensions show that sex is important in understanding or predicting rape attitudes. However, given the significant correlation between sex and attitudes toward women ($r = -.27, p < .001$), it might be argued that sex differences in attitudes toward rape may be attributed to respondents' views of women and their roles in society rather than just respondents' sex. To test this possibility, partial correlations, controlling for attitudes toward women, were computed between sex and the ATR factors. With the exception of the factor *favorable perception of a woman after rape*, sex was still found to be significantly related to the remaining six factors. Seemingly, these sex differences in rape attitudes may be attributed, in part, to the role of men as potential *offenders* versus the role of women as potential *victims* in rape as well as, in part, to people's views of women and their roles.

With respect to attitudes toward women, feminists suggest that there are interrelationships between perceptions of women and those of rape. They argue that rape has served to "keep women in their place" (Sherman 1975; Steinem 1975). Support for the supposition that attitudes toward women and rape are related can be found in table 3-5 as, within the citizen sample, attitudes toward women was correlated with six of the dimensions of rape attitudes. The magnitude and direction of these correlations support the contention that people who view women in traditional roles are likely to see rape as being the woman's fault, motivated by a need for sex, where punishment for rape should be harsh since the "property is now used," and because of the act, a raped woman is a less attractive individual. Following the logic of Medea and Thompson (1974), these results point to the need for examining people's views of rape as something more than simply an act of sex; their perceptions of rape tend to be intimately tied to their views of women.

Race was also found to be significant in both the citizen and the police samples; the reasons for such differences are not entirely clear, however.[5] One possible explanation may be due to racial differences in perceptions of women's roles. Earlier it was pointed out that attitudes toward women was an especially important variable in understanding rape attitudes. In studying black versus white women's sex-role attitudes, Gump (1975) reported that black women were more traditional (in terms of submissiveness, orientation toward the home, and personal development) in their sex-role perceptions than were white women. Based upon her research and drawing upon the findings of the present investigation concerning the relationships between attitudes toward women and rape, it might be hypothesized that the reported racial differences in rape attitudes may be due to the respondents' views of women. To explore this possibility, partial correlations, controlling for attitudes toward women, were computed between race and the eight ATR dimensions for each sex group in the citizen sample. For males, attitudes toward women had no effect on the relationships between attitudes toward rape and race of respondent. Conversely, for women, attitudes toward women were found to have an effect. Of five correlations found to be significant, only two were significant after partialling out the effects of attitudes toward women. These results tended to show that for male citizens, there appeared to be significant relationships between their race and their rape attitudes. However, for women, attitudes toward the female role tended to explain more of their attitudes toward rape than did their race.[6]

How Respondent Groups View Rape

Various writers and researchers writing about rape have implicitly assumed that different groups of people, having contrasting points of contact with the crime, differ in their perspectives on rape. We wanted to test this assumption by seeing whether the groups of respondents incorporated in the present study (that is, citizens, patrol police officers, rape crisis counselors, and rapists) would differ in their attitudes toward rape. Given the diversity of the groups' experiences with rape, we felt the hypothesized differences would exist. For instance, with regard to rape prevention, it has been suggested that some people feel that the prevention of rape is primarily the responsibility of women. We anticipated that the police officers in the study would more likely believe that rape prevention was women's responsibility than would the rape counselors.

Rather than use percentages of people responding to the ATR items (table 3-2), we decided to use more powerful statistical techniques such as analysis of variance and multiple discriminant analysis which would provide a more sensitive test of respondent group differences on the eight factors. In essence the purpose of these analyses was to determine *if* there were differences among these groups and, if so, *how* these groups varied with respect to their perceptions of rape. Basically, the analyses used involved the comparison of the variation in rape attitudes among individuals *within* the groups to the variation in attitudes toward rape *between* the groups. For statistically significant differences to be identified, the variation of people's ATR scores in different groups would have to exceed the variation in scores within these groups.

Since there were eight attitude dimensions on which it was of interest to compare the four groups, a multivariate analysis of variance (MANOVA) was initially calculated to see if there were such differences. The MANOVA was significant ($F = 44.30$, $df = 24,4159$, $p < .0001$), which supported our belief that the groups were different in the ways in which they saw rape. Next, since we wanted to know how the groups varied with respect to these eight dimensions, we applied multiple discriminant analysis along with univariate analyses of variance to make these determinations. The results of these analyses are summarized in table 3-6.

Each of the analyses of variance was statistically significant ($p < .01$) as were three discriminant functions. The standardized weights of the ATR factors on the functions (see table 3-6) indicate the relative contribution or importance of the attitudinal dimensions in explaining differences among the groups. Function I ($\chi^2 = 949.28$, $df = 24$, $p < .0001$) explained most (82 percent) of the variation in attitude scores among the groups. This function was primarily defined by the attitudes of *sex as motivation for rape* and *victim precipitation of rape*. Functions II ($\chi^2 = 202.36$, $df = 14$, $p < .0001$) and III ($\chi^2 = 24.86$, $df = 6$, $p < .0001$), accounting for 16 percent and 2 percent of the variation in the groups' attitudes, were generally defined by *severe punishment for rape* and *resistance as woman's role during rape*.

An inspection of the Newman-Keuls' (Winer 1971) results, also shown in table 3-6, indicated that the rapists significantly ($p < .05$) differed from the rape crisis counselors on each of the factors. In comparison to the counselors, rapists were more likely to have the following views: rape prevention is primarily women's responsibility, rape is motivated by a desire for sex, punishment for rape should not be severe, victims are likely to precipitate rape through their appearance or behavior, rapists are not mentally normal, rape is not motivated by a need for power, a raped woman is a

Table 3-6
Summary of Means, Univariate-Multivariate ANOVAs, and Discriminant Analysis with Rape Attitudes as Dependent Variables for Respondent Groups

Rape Attitude Dimension	Mean Standardized Factor Scores for Respondent Groups				Univariate F (df = 3,1441)	ω^{2a}	Standardized Weights on Discriminant Functions		
	Citizens (n = 1,056)	Rapists (n = 20)	Patrol Police Officers (n = 254)	Rape Crisis Counselors (n = 118)			I	II	III
Woman's responsibility in rape prevention	0.03[a]	0.69[b]	0.14[a]	−0.73[c]	26.81****	.06	.35	.05	.49
Sex as motivation for rape	0.14[a]	0.27[a]	0.03[a]	−1.35[b]	94.36****	.16	.62	.29	−.17
Severe punishment for rape	−0.13[a]	−0.92[b]	0.57[c]	0.10[d]	42.57****	.08	.01	−.84	.01
Victim precipitation of rape	0.01[a]	−0.48[b]	0.49[c]	−1.07[d]	77.71****	.14	.54	−.44	−.10
Normality of Rapists	−0.07[a]	0.06[a]	−0.04[a]	0.72[b]	23.08****	.05	−.33	−.10	.22
Power as motivation for rape	−0.06[a]	0.04[a]	−0.04[a]	0.61[b]	16.67****	.03	−.28	−.08	.17
Favorable perception of a woman after rape	0.01[a]	−0.60[b]	−0.12[a,b]	0.28[c]	6.58****	.01	−.14	.04	−.54
Resistance as woman's role during rape	0.01[a]	−0.75[b]	−0.02[a]	0.11[a]	3.75**	.01	−.06	−.07	−.59
Multivariate F (df = 24, 4159)					44.30****				

Note: For a specific dimension of rape attitudes, respondent groups which do *not* have a common superscript are significantly ($p < .05$) different. Each of the discriminant functions were significant at $p < .0001$.

[a] ω^2 indicates the proportion of variance in each rape attitude dimension accounted for by the respondent groups.

*$p < .05$.   **$p < .01$.   ***$p < .001$.   ****$p < .0001$.

less desirable woman, and women should not resist during rape. No differences were found between patrol police officers and rapists in their perceptions of the basic motivation for rape, normality of a rapist, or the attractiveness of a rape victim following rape. With the exception of perceived punishment for rape and the victim's role in causing rape, the citizen group was quite similar to the patrol officers in their view of rape.

The use of contrasted groups represents one means for examining the construct validity of attitude scales (Dawes 1972). As such, the discriminant validity of a scale can be assessed by its ability to differentiate known groups who are thought to vary with respect to a variable under consideration. The present research setting afforded an unusually pure naturalistic behavioral situation for validating the dimensions of rape attitudes since four diverse groups dealing with rape from different perspectives were included in the study. The utility of the eight ATR factors is demonstrated by their ability to differentiate known subgroups of people in meaningful, definable ways. The multivariate and univariate analyses indicated that the dimensions of the ATR were especially powerful in assessing group differences in regard to attitudes toward rape. The findings showed that the four respondent groups tended to perceive and cognize rape in markedly different ways. As compared to citizens, patrol police officers, and rapists, the rape crisis counselors were quite different in their reported views of rape. In terms of group similarity, citizens and police were most similar as there were no group differences on six of the eight dimensions of rape attitudes.

There are several possible explanations why rape crisis counselors perceived rape so differently from the other respondent groups. First, the rape crisis counselors were women while the other groups were composed predominantly of men. As discussed previously, sex of the respondent appears to be a key variable in explaining differences in perceptions of rape. Referring to such differences, Brownmiller (1975a) has contended that there is a huge disparity between male versus female logic concerning rape. Thus it seems quite likely that the sex composition of the groups is one reason for the observed differences.

In addition, interviews with selected directors and counselors of the crisis centers also revealed that many women who had become counselors were associated with the women's movement and labeled themselves as feminists. Feminists are quite likely to use a broad definition of rape; a violent crime which may occur through one or more avenues and by one or more of several methods (Brownmiller 1975a, p. 376). Such a definition is quite different from the one used by several rapists also interviewed. Two rapists, for instance, characterized rape as being "assault with a 'friendly' weapon" while another considered it as being "Much ado about nothing." Such definitional differences are also likely to explain many of the group differences.

Finally, individuals who have liberal perceptions of women and their roles tend to see rape differently from those who have conservative views of women. Data were not available to test the idea, but it seems that the respondents' attitudes toward women were also likely to account for differences among the respondent groups in terms of rape attitudes.

Even though no empirical evidence seems to be available, several authors have stated that police officers often treat the rape victim as if she were the offender (Chappell 1975*b*; Galton 1976). Here again, no data are available on the treatment of rape victims by police, but it is interesting to compare police officers' attitudes toward rape with those of the rapists and the rape crisis counselors. The officers did not differ from the rapists on four of the attitudinal dimensions while perceptions similar to the counselors were found on only one of the dimensions. Accusations concerning police insensitivity to the plight of rape victims cannot be assessed through the present data; the results do suggest, however, a need for systematically evaluating the interrelations, if any, between police officers' attitudes toward rape and their behavior toward a rape victim.

Knowledge about Rape

Clearly, an examination of people's attitudes toward rape is important for understanding how they perceive rape. However, the sole focus on rape attitudes alone presents an incomplete picture of their perceptions of the offense. To provide a more complete account, the cognitive component of their views, that is, their knowledge of the facts concerning the crime of rape, needs to be examined. (As used here, knowledge simply refers to the right and wrong information people possess about rape.) Caution should be taken, however, in deciding what exactly are the facts regarding rape. A number of empirical studies have been conducted addressing rape (Amir 1971; Brown 1974; *Uniform Crime Reports* 1975), yet the facts are still open to question. Due to differences in the samples studied and the use of different data-collection devices, methods, and statistical techniques, what may appear to be "true" in one study is not necessarily "true" in another. In addition, there are other reasons for the lack of and questionable validity of data on rape; to mention a few: (1) the underreporting of sexual assaults by women; (2) the lack of a standardized, comprehensive reporting device for recording the details of rape attacks; (3) the legal, ethical, and methodological difficulties involved in conducting an intensive, large-scale study of rape; and (4) the inaccessibility of victims and offenders. Even with these limitations, the Rape Knowledge Test (RKT) in the present study, as a cognitive measure of knowledge about rape, was developed and scored based upon data collected through and reported in major research studies. Thus an attempt was made to incorporate questions in the RKT on which (1) empirical data have been collected relative to each question and (2) where possible, at least two studies have agreed in their findings with respect to each question.

Using data collected primarily from the RKT, the respondents' knowledge about rape was studied with respect to two concerns: respondent group differences with respect to knowledge about rape, and correlates of people's knowledge.

Respondent Group Differences
in Knowledge about Rape

In the sections below, information relative to the respondents' knowledge about rape is made by determining the proportion (percentage) of people in the four respondent groups who answered each of the alternatives to the questions on the RKT. Then the correct answer to each of the fourteen questions is discussed relative to data collected in previous investigations. The discussion is organized around the content of the items appearing on the RKT.

Reporting of Rape. Rape represents one of the most underreported criminal offenses (*Uniform Crime Reports* 1975). Due to reasons such as fear or embarrassment, many women victims have been hesitant to report the crime to the police. Although the estimates vary depending upon the source referenced, most authorities agree that between 10 and 30 percent of all committed rapes are actually reported to the police (Amir 1971; Brownmiller 1975b; Curtis 1974). Looking at the data summarized in table 3-7, the majority of the respondents perceived rape as being a crime underreported to this degree. As a group, the counselors were most accurate in their responses as 94 percent gave the correct answer.

Table 3-7
What Proportion of Rapes Are Reported to the Police?

	Respondent Group (%)			
Option	Citizens (n = 1,056)	Rape Crisis Counselors (n = 118)	Patrol Police Officers (n = 254)	Rapists (n = 20)
*A. 10%	31 ⎱ 76	57 ⎱ 94	42 ⎱ 79	35 ⎱ 55
*B. 30%	45 ⎰	37 ⎰	37 ⎰	20 ⎰
C. 50%	17	5	16	15
D. 70%	6	1	4	30
E. 90%	1	0	1	0

Note: An * indicates the correct answers to the question on the Rape Knowledge Test. The percentage of respondents answering each alternative has been rounded to the nearest whole percent.

When asked what percentage of the rapes reported to the police resulted in an arrest, most of the respondents underestimated the proportion arrested (table 3-8). The *Uniform Crime Reports* (1975, p. 24) noted that of the total rapes reported to the police in 1975, 51 percent resulted in an arrest. Rural areas had the highest clearance rate as 68 percent of the reported rapes resulted in an arrest as compared to 51 percent in urban areas.

Violence and Acquaintance Rape. It may be expected that the closer the relationship between the victim and the offender, the less violent would be a rape. However, data provided by Amir (1971, p. 245) imply that physical violence may increase as the closeness of the relationship between the victim and the offender increases. He suggested that neighbors and acquaintances represent the most dangerous group of people as far as physical violence in rape is concerned. The offender who has a relationship with a victim may attempt to subdue the victim through seduction. When seduction or coercion fails, violence is often seen as necessary by the offender. As far as the respondents in the present study are concerned, the counselors were the most accurate with regard to this question (see table 3-9).

Stranger-Victim Rape. Contrary to the expectations of many of the respondents (table 3-10), a significant proportion of reported rapes involve an assailant known by the victim. The *National Commission on the Causes and Prevention of Violence* (1969) reported that in 47 percent of the rape cases studied, the victim had some acquaintance with the rapist. Amir's (1971, p. 234) data confirm these results. Approximately 48 percent of the victims in his study had at least some degree of acquaintance with their offender. (The term "acquaintance" means that the offender is known by the

Table 3-8
In What Proportion of Rapes Reported to the Police Are Arrests Made?

		Respondent Group (%)			
Option		Citizens (n = 1,056)	Rape Crisis Counselors (n = 118)	Patrol Police Officers (n = 254)	Rapists (n = 20)
A.	10%	19	28	24	10
B.	30%	40	48	39	25
*C.	50%	24	14	18	30
D.	70%	13	8	16	15
E.	90%	4	2	3	20

Note: An * indicates the correct answer to the question on the Rape Knowledge Test. The percentage of respondents answering each alternative has been rounded to the nearest whole percent.

Table 3-9
What Is the Role of Physical Violence when There Is a Close Relationship between the Rapist and the Victim?

| | Respondent Group (%) | | | |
| | Citizens | Rape Crisis Counselors | Patrol Police Officers | Rapists |
Option	(n = 1,056)	(n = 118)	(n = 254)	(n = 20)
*A. Physical violence against the victim tends to *increase*	36	43	35	15
B. Physical violence against the victim tends to *decrease*	40	48	42	35
C. Physical violence seldom occurs in this type of rape	24	9	23	50

Note: An * indicates the correct answer to the question on the Rape Knowledge Test. The percentage of respondents answering each alternative has been rounded to the nearest whole percent.

victim prior to the attack or the victim knows some personal data about him, for example, his name or residence.)

Brownmiller (1975a, pp. 351-352) proposed that the police are more likely to believe a woman was raped when she accuses a stranger than when she indicates some prior acquaintance with the offender. (It is interesting to note in table 3-10 that when compared to the rape crisis counselors, the police appeared to believe that relatively few victims know the rapists.) As a result, crime statistics regarding rape which are derived from police reports

Table 3-10
What Percentage of Women Who Have Been Raped Know the Rapist?

| | Respondent Group (%) | | | |
| | Citizens | Rape Crisis Counselors | Patrol Police Officers | Rapists |
Option	(n = 1,056)	(n = 118)	(n = 254)	(n = 20)
A. 5%	33	9	23	45
B. 25%	37	18	40	30
*C. 45%	15	37	14	10
D. 65%	10	30	15	15
E. 85%	5	6	8	0

Note: An * indicates the correct answer to the question on the Rape Knowledge Test. The percentage of respondents answering each alternative has been rounded to the nearest whole percent.

may be an underestimate of rapes committed by acquaintances. However, Brownmiller also suggested that as the general public and the police gain a greater understanding of the crime of rape, women may feel less reluctance to report an assault by men they know.

Location of Rape. Three studies have been reported which provide some information relative to the location of rape assaults. In each one, the victim's residence was found to be the most frequent place of reported rapes. Brown (1974) reported in a study of rape in Memphis that 34 percent of the rapes happened in the victim's home, 22 percent in automobiles, 26 percent in open places (such as alleys, parks, bushes), 9 percent in the offender's residence, and 9 percent in other places. The *National Commission on the Causes and Prevention of Violence* (1969) found that over half (52 percent) of the reported rapes in a seventeen-city survey occurred at home, 23 percent outside the home, 14 percent in commercial buildings, and 11 percent in automobiles. Finally, Amir (1971) noted that 56 percent of the reported rapes in Philadelphia took place in the victim's home, 18 percent in open spaces, 15 percent in automobiles, and the remainder in miscellaneous locations.

Almost half of the citizens (table 3-11) believed that rape occurs primarily in open spaces. This idea is probably related to the belief that rape is also committed by strangers. However, contrary to these popular ideas, rape is likely to be committed in the victim's home. Further, it may very well be committed by an acquaintance. It should be pointed out that rape in victims' residences does not mean that the offender was "invited." He may be a burglar who commits the offense during a break-in.

Table 3-11
Where Do Most Reported Rapes Occur?

| | | Respondent Group (%) | | | |
Option		Citizens (n = 1,056)	Rape Crisis Counselors (n = 118)	Patrol Police Officers (n = 254)	Rapists (n = 20)
A.	Automobiles	8	7	12	15
B.	Open spaces such as alleys, parks, streets	47	20	49	35
*C.	The victim's residence	41	64	36	35
D.	The rapist's residence	2	2	1	5
E.	Abandoned or unoccupied buildings	2	7	2	10

Note: An * indicates the correct answers to the question on the Rape Knowledge Test. The percentage of respondents answering each alternative has been rounded to the nearest whole percent.

Sexual Humiliation. As categorized by Amir (1971, p. 159), sexually humiliating practices in rape include fellatio, cunnilingus, pederasty, use of prophylactics, and repeated intercourse.[7] The first three categories, according to Amir, have typically been regarded as deviate sexual practices in the deviancy literature. In the fourth category, the offender attempts to construct the rape into a regular love relationship or, due to the perceived possibility of venereal disease, he sees the act as potentially dangerous. He is oblivious to the rape situation. The final category, repeated intercourse, involves a longer, captive relationship with the victim and thus results in more physical harm, particularly to those who are sexually inexperienced.

Based upon Amir's analysis of 646 rapes in Philadelphia, 27 percent of the rapes involved one of the above five practices. In terms of race, white victims suffered humiliating experiences more frequently than black victims, 34 percent versus 25 percent. In addition, the use of alcohol by the offender and the number of offenders participating in the rape were also found to be positively associated with the presence of humiliating practices.

As evidenced in table 3-12, significant proportions of the police and the citizens underestimated the extent of humiliating practices occurring during rape. Here again, the counselors tended to be more accurate in their answers.

Race and Rape. It was pointed out earlier that race has been intimately tied to the crime of rape in many people's minds. Various writers have noted that people, in general, seem to believe most rapes involve a black offender

Table 3-12
What Proportion of Reported Rapes Involve Sexual Humiliation of the Victim?

| | Respondent Group (%) | | | |
| | Citizens (n = 1,056) | Rape Crisis Counselors (n = 118) | Patrol Police Officers (n = 254) | Rapists (n = 20) |
Option				
A. 10%	37	15	29	20
*B. 30%	29	31	30	35
C. 50%	21	27	26	30
D. 70%	9	20	11	10
E. 90%	4	7	4	5

Note: An * indicates the correct answer to the question on the Rape Knowledge Test. The percentage of respondents answering each alternative has been rounded to the nearest whole percent.

Sexual humiliation of the victim includes the following practices, fellatio, cunnilingus, pederasty, use of prophylactics, and repeated intercourse (Amir 1971, p. 159).

and a white victim. The data from the present study tend to substantiate these ideas. Tables 3-13 and 3-14 show that a large portion of the citizens (48 percent) viewed reported rapes as occurring primarily between black males and white females; however, only 14 percent of the rape crisis counselors had such a belief. Further, 48 percent of the citizens felt that the race of most convicted rapists was black. Data collected by Amir (1971, p. 44) contradict these perceptions. Amir reported in his research that over three out of four (77 percent) rapes involved a black victim with a black offender, whereas only 4 percent involved a white victim and a black offender. Thus, rape, based on those reported, tends to be an intraracial crime rather than an interracial one.

Approximately half of the offenders are black and half are white (*Uniform Crime Reports* 1975). Relative to their representation in the population, it seems that rape is primarily committed by black males, yet the vast majority of these attacks are aimed toward black women.

Prosecution Requirements in a Rape Case. Given the issues typically addressed in a rape trial, a rape case requires the consideration of three major factors: identification of the accused as the offender, evidence corroborating the penetration of the victim by the defendant,[8] and evidence regarding the possible consent of the victim. In the identification of the offender, it is significant to note that eyewitness testimony of the act or of conditions surrounding the attack is not necessary. Identification may be established through other means such as a court-ordered lineup and photographic identification, or through extrinsic evidence such as fingerprints, shoe prints,

Table 3-13
Among Which Racial Combination Do Most Rapes Occur?

	Respondent Group (%)			
Option	Citizens (n = 1,056)	Rape Crisis Counselors (n = 118)	Patrol Police Officers (n = 254)	Rapists (n = 20)
*A. Black males and black females	16	49	39	15
B. Black males and white females	48	14	36	15
C. White males and white females	33	36	25	60
D. White males and black females	3	1	0	10

Note: An * indicates the correct answer to the question on the Rape Knowledge Test. The percentage of respondents answering each alternative has been rounded to the nearest whole percent.

Table 3-14
What Is the Racial Makeup of Convicted Rapists?

| | Respondent Group (%) | | | |
| | Citizens | Rape Crisis Counselors | Patrol Police Officers | Rapists |
Option	(n = 1,056)	(n = 118)	(n = 254)	(n = 20)
A. 80% black, 20% white	18	24	31	10
B. 60% black, 40% white	48	53	43	25
*C. 50% black, 50% white	18	10	13	5
D. 40% black, 60% white	11	8	11	25
E. 20% black, 80% white	5	5	2	35

Note: An * indicates the correct answer to the question on the Rape Knowledge Test. The percentage of respondents answering each alternative has been rounded to the nearest whole percent.

tire tracks, hair, blood, or other body fluids (Hibey 1973). However, it should be emphasized that the admissibility of identifying evidence provided by the victim will depend upon the conditions surrounding the victim's observation, her physical ability to observe, and the description given of the assailant. When penetration and force have been proven and where the only issue in the case is identification, then evidence indicating that she had an opportunity to observe is all that is needed (Hibey 1973, p. 314). Where consent or penetration are at issue, additional proof of identification will be required. More will be said later about the legal issues involved in prosecuting a rape case.

By common-law definition, rape requires the forcible penetration of a woman without her consent. Therefore, evidence such as that provided by medical examination and testimony as well as the physical and emotional condition of the vicitm are frequently introduced in trials to prove penetration and lack of victim consent.

With the exception of the rapists, the majority of the respondents gave the correct answer to the question. It is interesting to note that eight of the twenty rapists (table 3-15) believed that eyewitness testimony in addition to proof of force and penetration was a prerequisite in the prosecution's case.

The prosecution of a rape case is not an easy task. For instance, of the defendants brought to trial for rape in 1975, 46 percent of the cases resulted in acquittal or dismissal (*Uniform Crime Reports* 1975, p. 24). Of the 54 percent prosecuted, 12 percent of the individuals were convicted of a lesser offense. Table 3-16 shows that, in general, the groups were relatively accurate in their perceptions of the percentage of defendants that were found innocent or had their case dismissed. The rape crisis counselors in contrast to the other groups were inclined to overestimate this proportion.

Table 3-15
In Prosecuting a Rape Case, What Do Most States Require?

| Option | Respondent Group (%) | | | |
	Citizens (n = 1,056)	Rape Crisis Counselors (n = 118)	Patrol Police Officers (n = 254)	Rapists (n = 20)
A. Prove that force was used to commit the rape	15	4	4	0
B. Prove the penetration of the woman by the man	10	6	22	20
C. Produce a witness who will connect the defendant with the rape	3	1	0	5
*D. Only A and B above	54	54	65	35
E. All the above	18	35	9	40

Note: An * indicates the correct answer to the question on the Rape Knowledge Test. The percentage of respondents answering each alternative has been rounded to the nearest whole percent.

Brutality of Rape. Although some have viewed the events occurring during rape as consisting of a "few moments of unpleasantness," rape is a violent crime. In many cases, violence is manifested through physical means. As can be seen in table 3-17, approximately one out of five respondents correctly noted that about one of every five rapes involves some aspect of a brutal beating (Amir 1971, p. 155).[9] Looking further at Amir's data, it appears that brutal beatings were more likely to take place when (1) a black offender was involved in the crime, (2) the victim was much older (at least

Table 3-16
Of Those Persons Brought to Trial for Rape, What Proportion Are Found Innocent or Have Their Case Dismissed?

| Option | Respondent Group (%) | | | |
	Citizens (n = 1,056)	Rape Crisis Counselors (n = 118)	Patrol Police Officers (n = 254)	Rapists (n = 20)
A. 10%	13	9	18	20
B. 30%	23	12	19	20
*C. 50%	30	11	28	40
D. 70%	26	34	25	10
E. 90%	8	34	10	10

Note: An * indicates the correct answer to the question on the Rape Knowledge Test. The percentage of respondents answering each alternative has been rounded to the nearest whole percent.

Table 3-17
In What Proportion of Rapes Do Brutal Beatings of the Victim Occur?

	Respondent Group (%)			
Option	Citizens (n = 1,056)	Rape Crisis Counselors (n = 118)	Patrol Police Officers (n = 254)	Rapists (n = 20)
A. 5%	19	20	19	30
B. 15%	28	24	26	30
*C. 20%	22	23	20	20
D. 30%	20	27	20	15
E. 45%	11	6	15	5

Note: An * indicates the correct answer to the question on the Rape Knowledge Test. The percentage of respondents answering each alternative has been rounded to the nearest whole percent.

   Brutal beatings of the victim include such forms of physical violence as kicking or hitting with a closed fist or a weapon (Amir 1971, p. 155).

ten years) than the offender, (3) group rape versus single rape had occurred, and (4) rape had taken place outdoors rather than in the victim's or offender's home.

Age and Rape. Most of the respondents believed that the majority of rape victims and rapists are between the ages of 20 and 24 (tables 3-18 and 3-19). Their answers appear to be accurate for the offenders but seem to be an overestimate for victims' ages. Generally, victims are somewhat younger than their assailants. Amir (1971, p. 55), for example, noted that the median age for the offenders was 21.6; for the victims, 19.6. At least for the

Table 3-18
How Old Are Most Rape Victims?

	Respondent Group (%)			
Option	Citizens (n = 1,056)	Rape Crisis Counselors (n = 118)	Patrol Police Officers (n = 254)	Rapists (n = 20)
*A. 15 to 19 years of age	22	33	32	30
B. 20 to 24	48	45	38	40
C. 25 to 29	23	19	22	20
D. 30 to 34	6	3	5	5
E. 35 to 39	1	0	3	5

Note: An * indicates the correct answers to the question on the Rape Knowledge Test. The percentage of respondents answering each alternative has been rounded to the nearest whole percent.

Table 3-19
How Old Are Most Rapists?

	Respondent Group (%)			
		Rape Crisis	Patrol Police	
	Citizens	Counselors	Officers	Rapists
Option	(n = 1,056)	(n = 118)	(n = 254)	(n = 20)
A. 15 to 19 years of age	8	11	7	10
*B. 20 to 24	46	38	45	45
C. 25 to 29	35	36	35	40
D. 30 to 34	9	10	10	0
E. 35 to 39	2	5	3	5

Note: An * indicates the correct answer to the question on the Rape Knowledge Test. The percentage of respondents answering each alternative has been rounded to the nearest whole percent.

offenders, these data appear consistent with those of the *Uniform Crime Reports* (1975, p. 189). The 20 to 24 age range accounted for more of the 21,963 arrests for rape in 1975 than any of the other age groupings.

Geographical Location of Rape. The majority of the respondents (table 3-20) believed that the data collected from northeastern states accounted for the greatest proportion of the 56,090 rapes reported in 1975. However, as reported by the *Uniform Crime Reports* (1975, p. 22), the southern states recorded 31 percent of the rapes; the north central and western states, 25 percent; and the northeastern states, 19 percent.

Overall Knowledge about Rape. Since one of the questions of interest was to determine how much people know about rape, the 1,448 individuals were scored on the RKT using the answers to the fourteen items given previously. It was assumed that the total score would represent one measure of knowledge about rape.

The average RKT scores for each of the four groups were citizens = 4.47 (SD = 1.64); patrol police officers = 4.82 (SD = 1.64); rape crisis counselors = 5.30 (SD = 1.82); and rapists = 3.50 (SD = 1.43). An analysis of variance among these means showed that there were significant respondent group differences in knowledge about rape (F = 11.03, df = 3, 1,447, $p < .0001$). Newman-Keuls' tests revealed further that there were no significant differences between the citizens and the police officers. However, significant differences were found between the rapists and these two groups, with the rapists scoring significantly lower. Conversely, the rape crisis counselors scored significantly higher than any of the other groups.

In terms of absolute scores, a police officer had the highest test score with a score of 13. Twenty-one citizens, one rapist, and five police officers

Table 3-20

In What Part of the United States Does the Highest Number of Reported Rapes Occur?

| | Respondent Group (%) | | | |
Option	Citizens (n = 1,056)	Rape Crisis Counselors (n = 118)	Patrol Police Officers (n = 254)	Rapists (n = 20)
A. Northcentral states	15	5	12	10
*B. Southern states	18	35	31	45
C. Northeastern states	62	51	50	40
D. Western states	5	9	6	5

Note: An * indicates the correct answer to the question on the Rape Knowledge Test. The percentage of respondents answering each alternative has been rounded to the nearest whole percent.

did not get any of the items correct. On the basis of chance alone, it would be expected that one item would be answered correctly. Almost 60 percent of the citizens (624) got three or fewer items correct.

So what do citizens know about rape? As a whole, they know very little. Most of the citizens fared only slightly better on the RKT than if they had simply guessed on the fourteen questions. Yet it is this lack of knowledge that has been attributed to the development of such attitudes concerning rape as those discussed earlier in the chapter. In this vein, MacKellar (1975, pp. v-vi) suggested that the myths surrounding rape seem to perpetuate the attitudes toward it which ultimately contribute to the offense. Using her logic, knowledge about rape serves to disprove the myths, providing the means for understanding the causes of rape as well as a basis for reducing the extent of the crime.

Correlates of People's Knowledge about Rape

To see what respondent characteristics may relate to people's knowledge about rape, correlations were computed between relevant characteristics of respondents (that is, background and attitudinal variables) and their knowledge about rape. Data on respondent characteristics were obtained from the classification information sheets and knowledge of rape was determined from the total number of items answered correctly on the RKT.

Table 3-21 summarizes the correlations between the various respondent characteristics and the rape knowledge scores. Looking at the respondents as a whole, three demographic variables (sex, race, and years of education) were predictive of rape knowledge. Specifically, males tended to score higher on knowledge about rape than women ($r = .06$, $p < .05$), whites

Table 3-21
Correlations between Respondent Characteristics and Knowledge about Rape

Respondent Characteristic		Respondent Group			
	Citizens (n = 1,056)	Rape Crisis Counselors (n = 118)	Patrol Police Officers (n = 254)	Rapists (n = 20)	All Respondents (N = 1,448)
Background variables					
Sex (1 = female; 2 = male)[a]	.09**				.06*
Race (1 = black; 2 = white)[a]	.10***				.10***
Marital status (1 = single; 2 = married)[a]					
Age					
Years of education	.20***				.16***
Personally know a raped woman[a] (1 = yes; 2 = no)	—[b]			—[b]	—[b]
Testified at a rape trial (1 = yes; 2 = no)[a]				—[b]	—[b]
Interviewed rape victims about their rape[a] (1 = yes; 2 = no)	—[b]			—[b]	—[b]
Contact with rape victims	—[b]			—[b]	—[b]
Contact with rapists	—[b]			—[b]	—[b]
Received rape training (1 = yes; 2 = no)[a]	—[b]			—[b]	—[b]
Attitudinal variables					
Attitudes toward women	.16***	—[b]	—[b]		
Woman's responsibility in rape prevention	.09**	.18*	.18*	-.57*	.08**
Sex as motivation for rape	.13***				.18***
Severe punishment for rape	.13***				
Victim precipitation of rape	.06*				
Normality of rapists					
Power as motivation for rape					
Favorable perception of a woman after rape	.08**				.07*
Resistance as woman's role during rape					

Note: Knowledge about rape was measured by the total number of items on the Rape Knowledge Test. Since different sets of data were collected from the respondents, the degrees of freedom varied for the reported correlations. Only those correlations that are statistically significant are reported.
[a]Point-biserial correlation.
[b]Pairs of data were not collected for these variables.
*p < .05.   **p < .01.   ***p < .001.

knew more about rape than blacks ($r = .10$, $p < .01$), and individuals with more years of education did better than those having fewer years of education ($r = .16$, $p < .001$). After controlling for education, however, there were no significant relationships between rape knowledge and the demographic variables of sex and race. Thus apparent race and sex differences in rape knowledge should be attributed to differences in educational level.

Three of the eight dimensions of rape attitudes were significantly related with knowledge about rape. Individuals who scored high on the RKT tended to believe women should not be held responsible for preventing their own rape, the motivation for rape is not sex, and a raped woman is a desirable person after a rape.

For the rape crisis counselors, police officers, and rapists, few correlates of rape knowledge were found. However, with respect to the citizen sample, five of the eight attitudinal variables were found to relate to rape knowledge. Earlier it was noted that several writers, principally Brownmiller (1975a), MacKellar (1975), and Medea and Thompson (1974), suggested that the education of the general public through rape awareness programs may serve to alter the myths regarding rape. Although a longitudinal, experimental study would be needed to adequately test this causal hypothesis, data from the present research provide some evidence on the problem. Assuming that the RKT is an index of people's sensitivity to rape and that the eight dimensions of the ATR represent myths surrounding rape, significant correlations between these variables would be expected if rape knowledge has an influence on rape myths. As can be seen in table 3-21, these relationships were found for five of these attitudinal variables. Certainly, the correlations do *not* necessarily mean that by providing people with additional knowledge about rape, they will change their attitudes toward the offense. These data do suggest, however, that an experimental public education program aimed toward changing people's attitudes concerning rape may be worthwhile.

From the data presented in this chapter, it would appear that rape attitudes are an important consideration in conducting research on the law as it relates to rape. Certainly, such research efforts may take on many forms. For example, one interesting application of the ATR described which may hold some promise is in voir dire hearings involving the selection of jurors for a rape trial. It might be hypothesized that to the extent juries and judges differ in their decisions concerning a case, the greater the probability that variables, such as jury members' attitudes, extraneous to the case may have influenced jurors' decisions. Kalven and Zeisel (1966, p. 56) reported that in rape cases where there was no violence, only one assailant, or no prior acquaintance between the victim and the defendant, the judges and juries would have reached the same decision only 40 percent of the time. Brownmiller (1975a) suggested that juries tend to be allies of rape defendants and enemies of female complainants since juries are composed of citizens, many of whom believe the myths about rape. Using the attitudinal dimensions described earlier and one of the experimental methodologies described by Harris, Bray, and Holt (in press), a study might be designed to test the hypothesis that rape attitudes are predictive of jurors' verdicts. If so, questions similar to those on the ATR may be used in screening jurors for a rape trial (Kairys, Schulman, and Harring 1975; Shulman, Shaver, Colman, Emrich, and Christie 1973). The next chapter will provide some information relative to this issue by examining, among other variables, the relations between jurors' attitudes toward rape and their verdicts in a rape trial.

Summary

Several research questions were addressed in this chapter: namely, how do people view rape? Are selected background characteristics of people predictive of their views? Do different groups of respondents differ in their attitudes toward rape? How much do people know about rape? Can this knowledge be predicted from the characteristics of the respondents?

Using a battery of questionnaires, data were collected from 1,448 respondents including citizens ($n = 1,056$); patrol police officers ($n = 254$); convicted rapists ($n = 20$); and rape crisis center counselors ($n = 118$). Results reported in this chapter were derived primarily from the responses by these groups to two of the instruments, that is, the Attitudes toward Rape (ATR) questionnaire and the Rape Knowledge Test (RKT).

A factor analysis of the ATR was made in order to determine *how* the respondents perceived rape. The results showed that eight major dimensions of rape perceptions were used: *woman's responsibility in rape prevention, sex as motivation for rape, severe punishment for rape, victim precipitation of rape, normality of rapists, power as motivation for rape, favorable perception of a woman after rape*, and *resistance as woman's role during rape*. These same dimensions were found for the citizens, patrol police officers, and rape crisis counselors. Due to a small sample size, this analysis could not be conducted for the rapists.

Although similarities were found among three of the respondent groups in the dimensions of rape perceptions, further analyses revealed highly significant differences among the four respondent groups on the dimensions of rape attitudes. Rape crisis counselors were quite different from police officers, citizens, and rapists in their perceptions of rape while citizens and police were most similar. No differences were found between the police and the rapists on half of the eight attitudinal dimensions.

Correlations were computed between various respondent background characteristics and the eight attitudinal dimensions to see if attitudes toward rape might be predicted for the total sample. The correlations suggested that sex, race, and marital status were the most important respondent characteristics for predicting the dimensions of rape attitudes. However, within the four respondent subgroups, other characteristics (such as the respondents' attitudes toward women and their roles in society) were found to be equally as important.

In terms of knowledge about rape, scores on the RKT showed that, in general, most people knew very little about the facts regarding rape. The average score of the respondents on the fourteen-item test was less than four items correct. Rape crisis counselors scored significantly higher than any of the other groups. No differences were found among the citizens and the police. The rapists scored significantly lower than any of the remaining groups.

Correlations were also made between background characteristics of the respondents and their knowledge about rape. For the rape crisis counselors, police officers, and rapists few correlates of rape knowledge were found, which implies that rape knowledge could not be predicted, at least by these respondent characteristics. For the citizens, however, several variables were found to relate to five of these attitudinal dimensions. In general, men scored higher on knowledge about rape than women, whites knew more about rape than blacks, and those individuals with more years of education did better than those having fewer years of education. Such correlations suggest that citizens' attitudes about rape might be modified by providing them with information on the factual aspects of rape.

Notes

1. The proportion of people agreeing with a particular item on the ATR was based on the number of people answering strongly agree, agree, or slightly agree on the response scale.

2. Earlier, sex and race differences were examined in terms of the proportion of people agreeing with each of the ATR items. For descriptive purposes, percentages are useful for summarizing results. These analyses, however, involved the collapsing of the three agreement points on the six-point rating scale resulting in rather gross comparisons among the groups. Correlations between these characteristics and the dimensions of rape attitudes provide a more sensitive, interpretable analysis since data from the full rating scale are used. This section discusses the results from the correlational analyses.

3. In testing the significance of the reported correlations, the following degrees of freedom were used for the four respondent groups: citizens (df = 1,054); rapists (df = 18); patrol police officers (df = 252); and rape crisis counselors (df = 116).

4. Sex differences for the citizen sample with respect to each of the ATR items are summarized in table 3-1.

5. Race differences for the citizen sample with respect to each of the ATR items are summarized in table 3-1.

6. As indicated in table 3-1, sex of the respondent was a good predictor of rape attitudes. Race of the respondent was an even more powerful predictor of differences in rape attitudes.

7. These are acts categorized by Amir (1971) as being humiliating. However, his classification scheme does not provide for the insertion of objects (for example, bottles) into a victim's vagina. Several states have included such acts in their rape and sex offense laws. These state laws are reviewed in chapter 5.

8. In several states (see chapter 5), the law notes that the victim's uncorroborated testimony is sufficient; penetration is required but does not have to be corroborated. However, though the law may not require corroboration, such evidence may be implicitly required by some jurors.

9. Brutal beatings of the victim include such forms of physical violence as kicking or hitting with a closed fist or weapon (Amir 1971, p. 155).

References

Aitken, J. Rape prosecutions. *Women Lawyers Journal* 60 (1974):192-198.

Amir, M. *Patterns of forcible rape*. Chicago: University of Chicago Press, 1971.

Barber, R. Judge and jury attitudes to rape. *Australian and New Zealand Journal of Criminology* 7 (1974):157-172.

Barker, N. She felt like a defendant. *Washington Post*, December 2, 1972, E1.

Blitman, N., and Green, R. Inez Garcia on trial. *Ms.* 3 (May 1975):49-54.

Bohmer, C. Judicial attitudes toward rape victims. *Judicature* 57 (1974):303-307.

Bohmer, C., and Blumberg, A. Twice traumatized: The rape victim and the court. *Judicature* 58 (1975):390-399.

Brown, B. Crime against women alone. Memphis Police Department Sex Crime Squad, May 18, 1974 (mimeograph).

Brownmiller, S. *Against our will: Rape, women, and men*. New York: Simon and Schuster, 1975a.

————. Heroic rapist, *Mademoiselle* 81 (September 1975b):128-129, 196-197, 198.

Burgess, A., and Holmstrom, L. Coping behavior of the rape victim. *American Journal of Psychiatry* 133 (1976):413-418.

Calvert, C. Is rape what women really want? *Mademoiselle* 78 (March 1974):134-135, 187-189, 191, 193-194.

Cattell, R. The screen test for the number of facts. *Multivariate Behavioral Research* 1 (1966):245-276.

Chappell, D. Forcible rape: A national survey of the response by prosecutors (research report). Seattle: Battelle Human Affairs Research Center, Law and Justice Study Center, November 1975*a*.

_____ . Forcible rape: A national survey of the response by police (research report). Seattle: Battelle Human Affairs Research Center, Law and Justice Study Center, November 1975*b*.

Comrey, A. *A first course in factor analysis*. New York: Addison-Wesley, 1973.

Curtis, L. Victim precipitation and violent crime. *Social Problems* 21 (1974):594-605.

Dawes, R. *Fundamentals of attitude measurement*. New York: John Wiley, 1972.

Gager, N., and Schurr, C. *Sexual assault: Confronting rape in America*. New York: Grosset and Dunlap, 1976.

Galton, E. Police processing of rape complaints: A case study. *American Journal of Criminal Law* 4 (1976):15-30.

Goldner, N. Rape as a heinous but understudied offense. *Journal of Criminal Law, Criminology, and Police Science* 63 (1972):402-407.

Gump, J. Comparative analysis of black women's and white women's sex-role attitudes. *Journal of Consulting and Clinical Psychology* 43 (1975):858-863.

Hale, M. *History of the pleas of the Crown*. Philadelphia: R.H. Small, 1847.

Harman, H. *Modern factor analysis*. Chicago: University of Chicago Press, 1967.

Harris, J.; Bray, R.; and Holt, R. The empirical study of social decision processes in juries. In J. Tapp, ed., *Law, justice and the individual in society: Psychological and legal issues*. New York: Holt, Rinehart, and Winston, in press.

Heinz, G. Time for a change in this nation's rape laws. *Congressional Record* 120 (May 2, 1974):E2709.

Hibey, R. The trial of a rape case: An advocate's analysis of corroboration, consent, and character. *The American Criminal Law Review* 11 (1973):309-334.

Holmstron, L., and Burgess, A. Rape: The victim goes on trial. In I. Drapkin and E. Viano, eds., *Victimology: A new focus*. Lexington, Mass.: Lexington Books, D.C. Heath, 1975.

Kairys, D.; Shulman, J.; and Harring, S. *The jury system: New methods for reducing prejudice*. Philadelphia: National Jury Project, 1975.

Kaiser, H. The varimax criterion for analytic rotation in factor analysis. *Psychometrika* 23 (1958):187-200.

Kalven, H., and Zeisel, H. *The American jury*. Boston: Little, Brown, 1966.

Keefe, M., and O'Reilly, H. Changing perspectives in sex crimes investigation. In M. Walker and S. Brodsky, eds., *Sexual assault*. Lexington, Mass.: Lexington Books, D.C. Heath, 1976.

Lake, A. What women are doing about the ugliest crime. *Good Housekeeping* 179 (August 1974):84-85, 133-137.

Landau, S. Rape: The victim as defendant. *Trial* 10 (July-August 1974): 19-21, 32.

Lebourdais, E. Rape victims: The unpopular patients. *Dimensions of Health Services* 53 (March 1976):12-14.

LeGrand, C. Rape and rape laws: Sexism in society and law. *California Law Review* 63 (1973):919-941.

Leurs, N. The behind-the-scenes story of the unanimous repeal bill victory. *Majority Report* 3 (March 23, 1974):6-7.

MacKellar, J. *Rape: The bait and the trap*. New York: Crown, 1975.

Mathiasen, S. The rape victim: A victim of society and the law. *Wilamette Law Journal* 11 (1974):36-55.

McGuire, C., and Stern, D. Survey of incidence of and physician's attitudes toward sexual assault. *Public Health Services* 91 (1976):103-109.

Medea, A., and Thompson, K. *Against rape*. New York: Farrar, Straus, and Giroux, 1974.

National Commission on the Causes and Prevention of Violence. Washington: U.S. Government Printing Office, 1969.

Nie, N.; Hull, C.; Jenkins, J.; Seinbrenner, K.; and Brent, D. *Statistical package for the social sciences*. New York: McGraw-Hill, 1975.

Rape: Does justice turn its head? *Los Angeles Times*, March 12, 1972, E1.

Salerno, E. Violence, not sex: What rapists really want. *New York Magazine* 8 (June 23, 1975):36-49.

Sasko, H., and Sesek, D. Rape reform legislation: Is it the solution? *Cleveland State Law Review* 24 (1975):463-503.

Schulman, J.; Shaver, P.; Colman, R.; Emrich, B.; and Christie, R. Recipe for a jury. *Psychology Today* 7 (May 1973):37-44, 77-84.

Schwendinger, J., and Schwendinger, H. Rape myths: In legal, theoretical, and everyday practice. *Crime and Social Justice* 1 (1974):18-26.

Sherman, J. Power in the sexes: Rape. Women's Research Institute of Wisconsin, Madison, Wisconsin, 1975.

Steinem, G. But what do we do with our rage? *Ms.* 3 (May 1975):51.

Symonds, M. Victims of violence: Psychological effects and after effects. *The American Journal of Psychoanalysis* 35 (1975):19-26.

Taylor, J., and Parker, H. Graphic ratings and attitude measurement: A comparison of research tactics. *Journal of Applied Psychology* 48 (1964):37-42.

Uniform Crime Reports for the United States. Federal Bureau of Investigation, Department of Justice. Washington: U.S. Government Printing Office, 1975.

Welkowitz, J.; Ewen, R.; and Cohen, J. *Introductory statistics for the behavioral sciences.* New York: Academic Press, 1971.

Winer, B. *Statistical principles in experimental design.* New York: McGraw-Hill, 1971.

Wood, P. The victim in a forcible rape case: A feminist view. *The American Criminal Law Review* 11 (1973):335-354.

Juror Decision-Making in Rape Trials

The study of the effects of variables extraneous to a trial on juror deliberations and jury verdicts has had a long history among researchers interested in social behavior. Table 4-1 summarizes many of the major investigations which have examined the influence of selected victim, defendant, juror, and crime characteristics on trial outcomes. We will not synthesize the results of these studies since comprehensive reviews of the jury research literature have been made (Bray 1976; Davis, Bray, and Holt 1977; Gerbasi, Zuckerman, and Reis 1977; Stephan 1975). However, an examination of the reported research as well as the writings of legal scholars leaves little doubt that there are a number of extra-evidential factors which affect trial outcomes.

From a similar perspective, legal writers and individuals concerned with the prosecution of rapists have pointed out that it is factors such as those in table 4-1 which have made it difficult to obtain convictions in rape cases. An examination of conviction rates reported in table 4-2 of defendants accused of rape relative to defendants convicted of other violent crimes seems to support the supposition that various factors lead to an inordinate number of acquittals in these cases.

Moreover, the data show that of the four violent crimes, rape has the *highest* rate of acquittal or dismissal and the *lowest* rate of conviction for the offense charged. Further, based upon recent crime statistics, an individual who commits rape has only about 4 chances in 100 of being arrested, prosecuted, and found guilty of any offense. With the comparatively good opportunity for acquittal, individuals charged with rape may be less likely to waive their right to a trial by jury than defendants in other criminal cases. Seemingly, the low conviction-low trial waiver rates for rape can be attributed to at least three important factors: the current writing of state rape laws and statutes; the nature and procedural aspects of rape trials; and the characteristics of a specific rape case brought to trial, including characteristics of the defendant, victim, jury members, and the particular offense. A review of current rape laws and their impact on jury trials will be made in detail in chapter 5. For the purpose of better understanding the research results reported here, the nature of the two remaining factors will be briefly discussed.

Table 4-1
Variables Suggested as Having Discriminatory Effects in Jury Trials

Juror Characteristics

Age
(Chappell 1977*; Mathiasen 1974*; Sealy and Cornish 1973*)

Attitudes toward sex and sexuality
(Brownmiller 1975*; LeGrand 1973*; Mathiasen 1974*)

Attitudes toward women
(LeGrand 1973*; Mathiasen 1974*; Wood 1973*)

Authoritarianism
(Berg & Vidmar 1975; Boehm 1968; Bray 1974; Crossen 1966; Jurow 1971; Kirby & Lamberth 1974; Mitchell & Byrne 1973)

Belief in the death penalty
(Jurow 1971)

Belief in a just world
(Gerbasi & Zuckerman 1975; Lerner 1970; Zuckerman & Gerbasi 1973)

Birthplace
(Reed 1965)

Empathy with defendant
(Archer & Aderman 1974)

Intelligence

Victim Characteristics

Age
(Barber 1974*)

Behavior before the offense
(Hibey 1973*)

Character (respectability)
(Barber 1974*; Brooks, Doob & Krishenbaum 1975; Eisenbud 1975*; Feldman-Summers & Lindner 1976*; Griffin 1971*; Washburn 1975*)

Demeanor of the victim after the offense (emotional condition)
(Brownmiller 1975*)

Dress or clothing
(Hibey 1973*; Scroggs 1976*)

Marital status
(Feldman-Summers & Lindner 1976*; Jones & Aronson 1973*)

Physical appearance after the offense (bruises, cuts, disheveled appearance)
(Hendrick & Shaffer 1975; Scroggs 1976*)

Physical attractiveness (includes physical appearance after offense)

Defendant Characteristics

Age
(Barber 1974*; Chappell 1977*; Reynolds & Sanders 1975)

Ambiguity of guilt
(Phares & Wilson 1972)

Character (respectibility)
(Barnett & Feild, in press*; Berg & Vidmar 1975; Byrne & Clore 1970; Fishman & Izzett 1974; Frederick & Luginbuhl 1976*; Izzett & Leginaski, in press; Jones & Aronson 1973*; Kaplan & Kemmerick 1974; Landy & Aronson 1969; Mitchell & Byrne 1972; Nemeth & Sosis 1973)

Description by peers versus those given by psychologists
(Dowdle, Gillen, & Miller 1974)

Physical attractiveness
(Byrne & Clore 1970; Efran 1974; Nemeth & Sosis 1973; Sigall & Ostrove 1975)

Previous criminal convictions
(Barber 1974*; Chappell 1977*; Doob & Kirshenbaum 1972; Hans & Doob 1976; Kalven & Zeisel 1966)

Trial Characteristics

Adversary versus inquisitorial presentation of evidence
(Thibaut, Walker, & Lind 1972)

Appeal by defense attorney
(Archer & Aderman 1974)

Decision rules
(Kerr, Atkin, Stasser, Meek, Holt, & Davis 1976)

Instructions given to the jury
(Archer & Aderman 1974; Dodson 1973*; Green 1967; Hoibert & Stires 1973*; Kline & Jess 1966; Mitchell & Byrne 1972; Sealy & Cornish 1973; Simon, 1967, 1968; Sue, Smith, & Caldwell, in press; Sue, Smith, & Gilbert 1974)

Juror decision alternatives (number and severity)
(Child 1975*; Frederick & Luginbuhl 1967*; Kaplan & Simon 1972; Larntz 1975; Vidmar 1972)

Location
(Chappell 1977*)

Mandatory sentence for the offense

(Hoiberg & Stires 1973*)

Internal-external locus of control

(Phares & Wilson 1972; Sosis 1974)

Level of education

(Sealy & Cornish 1973*; Simon 1967, 1968)

Occupation

(Harrington & Dempsey 1969; Hermann 1970; Sealy & Cornish 1973*; Simon 1967)

Perceived similarity-dissimilarity with defendant

(Byrne 1971; Byrne, Erwin, & Lambert 1970; Gerbasi & Zuckerman 1975; Griffitt & Jackson 1973)

Perceptions of rape

(LeGrand 1973*; Mathiasen 1974; Wood 1973*)

Previous service on a jury

(Reed 1965; Sealy & Cornish 1973*)

Race

(If She Consented Once, She Consented Again, 1976*; Simon 1967)

Religion

(Becker, Hildum, & Bateman 1965; Harrington & Dempsey 1969)

(Brownmiller 1975*; Does Justice Turn its Head? 1972*; Fishman & Izzett 1974; Landy & Aronson 1969; Luginbuhl 1975*; Luginbuhl & Mullin 1976*)

Prior sexual history with defendant and others

(Barber 1974*; Cann, Calhoun, & Selby 1977*; Eisenbud 1975*; Mathiasen 1974*)

Occupation

(Brownmiller 1975*)

Race

(Chappell 1977*; Hibey 1973*; Kaplan & Simon 1972)

Relation to the offender (friend, lover)

(Barber 1974*; Chappell 1977*; Calhoun, Selby, & Warring 1976*)

Resistance by the victim

(Chappell 1977*; Scroggs 1976*; Washburn 1975*; Wood 1973*)

Severity of the outcome (degree of force)

(Barber 1974*; Chappell 1977*; Hoiberg & Stires 1973*; Phares & Wilson 1972)

Use of alcohol or drugs

(LeGrand 1973*)

Race

(Barnett & Feild, in press*; Bullock 1961*; Chappell 1977*; Hibey 1973*; Nemeth & Sosis 1973)

Social class

(Gordon & Jacobs 1969; Rose & Prell 1955; Landy & Aronson 1969)

Suffering before, during, or after crime

(Austin, Walster, & Utne 1976; Sigall & Landy 1972)

Use of a weapon by offender

(Chappell 1977*)

Use of alcohol

(Barber 1974*; Chappell 1977*)

(Child 1975)

Nonverbal behavior of judges

(Greenbaum 1975)

Number of defense and prosecution arguments

(Calder, Insko, & Yandell 1974)

Number of jurors

(Davis, Kerr, Atkin, Holt, & Meek 1975*; Gordon 1968; Kerr, Atkin, Stasser, Meek, Holt, & Davis 1976*)

Order of presentation of defense and prosecuting attorney's arguments

(Lawson 1968; Stone 1969; Walker, Thiabaut, Andreoli 1972)

Perceptions of rape by judge

(Blitman & Green 1975; Bohmer 1974*; LeGrand 1973*; Blitman & Green 1975; Bohmer & Blumberg 1975*)

Precipitory versus forcible

(Dodson 1975*)

Prestige of defense attorney

(Kalven & Zeisel 1966)

Pretrial publicity

(Hoiberg & Stires 1973*; Padawer-Singer & Barton 1975; Simon 1968)

Table 4-1 (continued)

Juror Characteristics	Victim Characteristics	Defendant Characteristics	Trial Characteristics
Sex (Bray 1974*; Brownmiller 1975*; Calhoun, Selby, & Warring 1976*; Cann, Calhoun, Selby 1977; Davis, Kerr, Atkin, Holt, & Meek 1975*; East 1972; Efran 1974; Feldman-Summers & Lindner 1976*; Griffitt & Jackson 1973; Hoiberg & Stires 1973*; Jones & Aronson 1973*; Landy & Aronson 1969; Laughlin & Izzett 1973; Mathiasen 1974*; Medea & Thompson 1974*; Richey & Fichter 1969; Sealy & Cornish 1973*; Selby, Calhoun, & Brock 1973*; Sue, Smith, & Gilbert 1977*; Wood 1973*) Socioeconomic status (Adler 1973; Nemeth & Sosis 1973; Reed 1965)			Race of attorneys (D'Agostino & Brown 1975) Religion of judge (Barber 1974*) Sex of defense attorney (Brownmiller 1975*) Strength of evidence (Kaplan & Simon 1972; Sue, Smith, & Caldwell, in press) Testimony of an "expert" witness (Centers, Shomer, & Rodrigues 1970) Type of crime committed (Barnett & Feild, in press*; Feldman-Summers & Linder 1976*; Sigall & Ostrove 1975) Type (familiar versus novel) of arguments presented by defense and prosecuting attorneys (Sears & Freedman 1965) Verbal behavior of lawyers (Lind & O'Barr 1977) Witnesses (Chappell 1977*)

Note: The variables and sources listed are not exhaustive. The citations represent major variables and key references frequently cited in the literature on juror/duty selection and deliberation. The sources included are those which have cited empirical data or opinions as to variables found or thought to be important in predicting the outcome of jury trials. Those references followed by an asterisk (*) concern variables found or thought to be influential in jurors' verdicts in rape trials.

Table 4-2
Disposition of Reported Violent Crimes for Adults

| | Violent Crime | | | |
| | | | Aggravated | Armed |
Treatment of Crime[a]	Rape	Murder	Assault	Robbery
Percent of crimes not reported to the police	75[b]	5[c]	45[d]	47[d]
Of those crimes reported				
Percent of crimes cleared by arrest	51	78	64	27
Percent of arrested that were prosecuted	58	55	68	58
Percent of arrested found guilty on original offense	42	54	47	55
Percent of arrested found guilty on lesser charge	12	14	12	9
Percent of charged ending in acquittal or dismissal	46	32	41	36
Probability of committing crime and not being arrested, prosecuted, and found guilty of any offense	.96	.72	.86	.95

[a]Data on the treatment of criminal offenses were obtained from the *Uniform Crime Reports*, 1975.

[b]The percentage of unreported rapes is based upon the frequently cited estimate of 75 percent (Brownmiller 1975; Curtis 1974).

[c]No published data are available apparently on the percentage of murders unreported to the police. However, 5 percent would appear to be a reasonable estimate.

[d]These estimates are based on data reported in *Criminal Victimization in the United States*, 1977, pp. 32-33.

Nature and Procedural Aspects of Rape Trials

The common-law definition of rape plays a major part in determining the victim's role in a rape trial. In general, most state statutes define rape as being sexual intercourse with a woman, not the wife of the perpetrator, which is against her will. Given this definition, Gager and Schurr (1976) noted that, by law, rape is classified as a crime against the state. Thus the role of the victim in a trial is that of a witness; she is not a plaintiff and may not choose the attorney to prosecute the case. She has no legal standing other than that given to other witnesses appearing at the trial. In effect, she simply serves as a witness to the offense.

Furthermore, rape has been viewed historically by the courts as being a charge which is easy to make, hard to prove, and even harder to defend (Hale 1847). This philosophy of the courts has created some of the prosecutorial difficulties encountered in rape trials. But there are other explanations for these problems. Because of the assumption that jurors are likely to feel sympathy for the victim and because rape is quite often a "private crime," with the victim and the defendant the only witnesses, the law on rape has been written and administered in court for the protection of the accused from a "fabricated" charge of rape. As a consequence, the law has offered greater protection to the rape defendant than to other criminal defendants by permitting a more careful examination of the rape victim than of plaintiffs or witnesses in other criminal cases. This careful examination of the rape victim's testimony in a routine manner implies that she is less credible than other witnesses.

To gain a more complete understanding of how the procedural aspects of a rape trial may influence its outcome, it may be helpful to provide an overview of the evidential requirements of a rape case. More specific detail on the various elements of rape laws and their role in rape trials will be presented later.

Given the common-law definition of rape, the prosecution of a rape case has three major points which must be addressed and proven: identification of the defendant as the offender, penetration or sexual intercourse with the victim by the defendant, and intercourse without the victim's consent. Since verbal testimony by the victim may be "false," many jurisdictions have indicated that a defendant may not be prosecuted for rape on the basis of victim testimony alone; evidence which corroborates her testimony must be presented.[1] Yet her testimony must be supported by evidence in a crime which frequently occurs in covert circumstances. Thus numerous writers (Dodson 1975; Mathiasen 1974; Wood 1973) have argued that this evidentiary burden (that is, the corroboration requirement) borne by the prosecution is greater than that required in other criminal cases.

Once accused of rape, the defendant has two major defensive options; denial that he was the assailant, and admission that intercourrse took place but with the woman's consent. This latter option is most frequently cited when a rape case is brought to trial.

The nature and quantity of evidence necessary to corroborate a charge of rape depends upon the "danger of falsification" by the victim as well as the nature of the defendant's defense. Where the sole issue in a rape case is the *identification* of the defendant as the offender (that is, it has been established that a rape occurred, but the defendant denies he was the offender), the only evidence that may be required of the prosecution is showing that the victim had an opportunity to observe the rapist. Proof of identification may consist of a police lineup, photographic identification, fingerprints, hair, or other physical elements associated with the defendant. Similarly, when *penetration* is at issue (that is, it is established that the defendant was with the victim at the time and place of the alleged assault, but he denies penetration through intercourse), the prosecution may use such forms of evidence as a medical examination of the victim, physical ex-amination of the defendant, eyewitness testimony, or the results of scien-tific tests on items, such as the clothing of the victim or the defendant, as proof.

Under the defense that the defendant was not the offender, the defense may attempt to show the victim's lack of credibility as a witness by in-troducing character evidence as to the victim's reputation for chastity. Although some jurisdictions may not admit descriptions of the victim's *specific* sexual activities, her *general* reputation for chastity may be presented. Evidence of the victim's unchastity may be admitted to demonstrate her lack of credibility as a witness. Thus, upon admission, it is assumed that a woman of immoral character is also one who would not tell the truth; an unchaste woman is thought to be more likely to fabricate a charge of rape than a chaste woman.

Rather than denial of the offense, the defendant may also claim victim consent. It is interesting to note that rape is the *only* crime in which victim consent is treated as a critical component in evaluating whether the offense occurred or not. For example, a victim of robbery is not required to prove that consent was not given to being robbed. Because consent plays a crucial role in the determination of a rape case, the victim must prove that she resisted the assault, or physical threats were made against her if she did not comply.

It is the consent defense which has resulted in some of the more con-troversial aspects of rape trials. Under this defensive strategy, the defendant concedes the elements of time and place of the incident, the persons in-volved, and sexual intercourse with the complaining witness. However, the defendant argues that intercourse took place with the consent of the woman, not against her will as she has alleged.

In addition to other evidence including the physical condition of the vic-tim and location of the alleged rape, the defendant, under a consent defense, may also investigate the chastity of the woman by examining her life-style and general reputation for chastity to prove consent. Some courts will permit the introduction of evidence as it relates to the victim's sexual activities with men other than the defendant; most courts will not. Some courts will permit evidence to be introduced that relates to any acquaintance or sexual activity the victim may have had with the defendant prior to the assault. Evidence of the victim's consensual sex activities, including those with third parties, may be permitted by the court under the assumption that an unchaste woman is more likely to consent to intercourse than a chaste one.

Naturally, the prosecution will attempt to limit the admission of evidence on the victim's sexual activities since such evidence may prejudice the jury against their case. The prosecution may argue that previous consensual sex activities do not characterize a woman who will consent to intercourse on all occasions or necessarily on the specific occasion in question. The defense may counter this argument in noting that the jury must be knowledgeable of prior consensual intercourse in order to evaluate the act on trial which is claimed to be forcible. It is up to the judge to rule on the admission of such evidence. Regarding this decision, Mathiasen (1974) pointed out that a higher court may reverse a lower-court decision if it is found that the defendant did not have an ample opportunity to fully cross-examine the victim and her testimony. Therefore, judges may feel that it is safer and easier to permit evidence on the victim's sexual reputation to be admitted as evidence. The state may not appeal an acquittal, though the defendant may appeal a conviction. Thus the judge does not have to worry about a reversal of his decision for admitting too much evidence concerning the sexual reputation of the victim.

Characteristics of a Rape Case Brought to Trial

Hibey (1973, p. 310) noted that experience with rape trials has shown that the presence or absence of corroboration, consent, or character evidence does not ensure the predictability of the verdict because the jury's assessment of the evidence is not always rational. It would appear when jurors are dealing with the lives of individuals associated with an emotion-laden issue such as rape, characteristics of the defendant, victim, jury member, or the offense itself may also influence the outcome of the trial. Clearly, the factors potentially affecting rape trials are numerous. Yet relative to other crimes (table 4-1), little information, obtained through empirical research, appears to be available on the impacts of these variables on trial outcomes. On the other hand, there is no lack of speculation about the variables thought to produce such influences. These variables and their speculated effects include but are not limited to the following factors.

1. Race of the defendant: according to Brownmiller (1975), race of the defendant represents one of the most influential variables affecting the outcome of a rape trial. Research studies (Partington 1965; Wolfgang and Cohen 1976) have shown that blacks have been punished more severely than whites for rape. Based upon these survey results, it might be predicted that a defendant's race would serve as a discriminatory variable in sentencing rape defendants.

2. Race of the victim: rather than predict racial differences in sentencing solely on the basis of the defendant's race, the race of the victim would also appear to be an important consideration. Even though statistical tests have not been made among the various victim-defendant racial combinations for defendant sentencing, several investigations (Howard 1975; Wolfgang and Riedel 1975) reported harsher sentences for the rape of white women than for black women. These conclusions, however, have been based on judges' decisions; no comparable research has apparently been

conducted with jurors. Thus the effect of victim race on jurors' verdicts remains an unresolved issue.

3. Physical attractiveness of the victim: the connection between victim attractiveness and precipitation of rape has been developed so explicitly by our communications media that we are inclined to conclude that rape is a crime of passion caused by feminine beauty. Due to the belief that attractiveness precipitates rape, the effect of victim attractiveness on juror decisions might work in one of several ways. For an attractive victim, a juror might conclude that "the poor guy was so overcome with passion, he just couldn't help himself." On the other hand, a juror may also reason for an unattractive victim, "she's so homely, who would want to rape her?" (for such an example see Rape: Does justice turn its head? 1972). Such reasoning may produce more lenient treatment of rape defendants than deserved. Unfortunately, no previous research has been undertaken on victim attractiveness in rape trials to help us determine the effects of this seemingly important variable.

4. Moral character of the victim: perhaps no single variable is thought to produce more discriminatory effects in rape trials as the introduction of the victim's sexual reputation or moral character as evidence. Drawing from the many writings of feminists as well as legal scholars, a rape defendant could be expected to be treated more leniently by a jury when the victim is characterized in court as being unchaste than when she is presented as being chaste. For an unchaste victim, the jury may feel that if she has consented once to intercourse, she quite likely consented to intercourse on the occasion in question; she got what she was asking for or deserved; or one who has had immoral sexual experiences is not a credible witness; she may be making a false charge of rape.

5. Type of rape: conceptually speaking, there are two major types of rape: precipitory where actions or appearance of the victim could be interpreted as the woman "asking" to be raped, or nonprecipitory where the victim's behavior or appearance could not be judged as "suggestive." Using such categorical definitions, it might be hypothesized that an offender in a precipitory rape case would be treated more leniently than a defendant in a nonprecipitory case since in a precipitory case, the defendant "simply gave the woman what she was asking for." Judging from anecdotal evidence, there seems to be some support for this hypothesis. Police and prosecuting attorneys seem likely to conclude that in a precipitory rape case, there is not enough evidence to prosecute an offender; thus these types of cases will probably be dismissed (Brownmiller 1975; Chappel 1977; Galton 1976). However, no objective study of the effects of the type of rape on rape trials has been made.

6. Strength of evidence in the case: although not considered as a factor having discriminatory effects in rape trials, the strength of evidence presented

by the prosecution has been discussed as an important variable affecting rape convictions (Harris 1976; Hibey 1974). Based upon these discussions, it could be hypothesized that the greater the strength of evidence in a case, the greater the probability of a rape conviction. Assuming impartiality in rape trials, it would be expected that the evidence given would be more important in explaining jurors' decisions concerning a rape defendant than factors such as race of the victim or defendant, attractiveness of the victim, or some other extra-evidential factor.

7. Juror characteristics: as given in table 4-1, various juror characteristics, such as age, education, and sex, have been found to correlate with or influence jurors' decisions in trials. With the exception of a study by Scroggs (1976) and one by Sealy and Cornish (1973), little empirical research has been published on the relationships among juror characteristics and juror decision making in rape trials. Nevertheless, given the emotional aspects of a rape case, it would appear that juror background characteristics such as age, education, and sex as well as variables such as attitudes toward women or rape (see chapter 3) would be important considerations in studying factors thought to affect the outcome of these trials.

8. Interactions among victim, defendant, case, and juror characteristics: if single variables have an influence on jurors' decisions, it might be expected that combinations of variables may also produce these effects. However, research studying systematically the influence of victim, defendant, case, and juror characteristic *interactions* has been practically nonexistent. Some limited survey data, however, on differences among victim-defendant racial combinations in terms of defendant sentencing point to the importance of considering interactions among different variables. Brownmiller (1975, p. 237) reported that sentencing for rape in Baltimore was approximately four times harsher for black men raping white women than for any other victim-defendant racial combination. Clearly, more research is needed which considers these possible variable interactions.

The lack of empirical research has left many questions on the effects of factors such as those listed unanswered. But data on such effects are needed if modifications in state rape statutes or rape trial procedures are to be considered and, possibly, implemented. Experimental research may provide some of this needed evidence.

Using the six defendant, victim, and rape case characteristics described in chapter 2 and listed above as a basis (that is, defendant race, victim race, victim physical attractiveness, victim moral character, type of rape, and strength of evidence), the purpose of the present chapter is to determine how these factors, in addition to selected juror characteristics, influence jurors' verdicts in rape trials. These variables will be examined both independently and in combination. Given this purpose, three important questions need to be addressed.

1. Do defendant, victim, and rape case characteristics, singly or in combination, have any effect on jurors' verdicts in rape trials?
2. Are jurors' attitudes toward rape and toward women as well as selected background characteristics predictive of their decisions in such trials?
3. Do characteristics of jurors seem to combine in unique ways with defendant, victim, and rape case characteristics to influence jurors' verdicts?

Application of the Legal Rape Case

Chapter 2 provided a detailed description of the Legal Rape Case (LRC) which served as the principal vehicle for collecting the data reported in the present chapter. Before discussing each of the research questions, a brief review of the LRC will help to clarify the reported findings.

Recall for a moment that the LRC consisted of a detailed, narrative description of a rape case which had been brought to trial. Within the instrument, the factors of race of the victim (black or white), physical attractiveness of the victim (attractive or unattractive), moral character of the victim (sexually experienced or sexually inexperienced), race of the defendant (black or white), type of rape (precipitory or nonprecipitory), and strength of the evidence (strong or weak) presented at the trial were systematically varied such that all possible combinations were represented in one of the sixty-four versions given to the jurors in the study. By using all combinations of the variables, it would then be possible to determine the effects of these variables (singly or in combination) on jurors' decisions in a case.

Following their reading of the case, the jurors were asked to decide on the guilt or innocence of the defendant; to rate how confident they were of their verdict; and if they found the defendant guilty, to sentence the defendant to a prison term from one to ninety-nine years (if the defendant was found innocent, he was given a score of 0 years). Correlations computed among each of these three variables showed them to be highly interrelated. Since the three variables appeared to be measuring the same construct, it was decided to select one of them to serve as a measure of the jurors' decisions in the trial. Based on research by Berg and Vidmar (1975), Efran (1974), Landy and Aronson (1969), and Sigall and Ostrove (1975), the assigned prison term given to the defendant was chosen for evaluating the jurors' decisions as it would provide a more sensitive measure of their decisions than would their verdicts of guilt or innocence.

The LRC was administered to 1,056 black and white jurors. Each of the sixty-four versions was given randomly to fourteen white jurors (seven women and seven men) resulting in a total of 896 white jurors. However, due to the smaller number of black citizens in the population, it was possible to use only sixteen versions of the LRC incorporating all possible combinations of four factors: (1) race of the defendant, (2) race of the victim, (3) moral character of the victim, and (4) strength of the evidence. These sixteen versions were presented at random to 160 black jurors so that ten black jurors (five women and five men) responded to each of the sixteen cases.

Effects of Defendant, Victim, and Rape Case Characteristics on Juror Decision Making

To investigate the effects of the defendant, victim, and rape case characteristics on the jurors' decisions, a six-way factorial analysis of variance involving the six characteristics discussed previously was computed for the white jurors and a four-way factorial analysis of variance using four of these factors was computed for the black jurors. Since all possible combinations of the factors were represented in the cases, these analyses determined how these factors, separately as well as jointly, influenced the jurors' decisions in the trial. Table 4-3 summarizes the results of these analyses for the white and black jurors.

White Jurors

Four of the six factors (that is, the main effects) manipulated in the cases were found to influence the white jurors' decisions. For race of the defendant, the black offender ($M = 17.67$) as compared to the white offender ($M = 11.47$) was given a significantly harsher sentence ($p < .001$).[2] Similarly, race of the victim also had an effect. The offender who had raped the black victim ($M = 12.16$) received a significantly lighter sentence ($p < .001$) than the defendant who had assaulted the white woman ($M = 16.98$). When the jurors were asked to sentence the defendant based on the type of rape, the offender in the precipitory rape situation ($M = 8.59$) was treated more leniently ($p < .001$) than the individual charged with the nonprecipitory offense ($M = 20.55$). Finally, the jurors were also found to have considered the nature of the evidence presented. Where the evidence was strong ($M = 17.20$), the defendant received a longer prison term ($p < .01$) than when the evidence was weak ($M = 11.95$).

However, since several of the interactions or combinations of these six factors were significant, the differences on the main effects should be interpreted with caution. Rather than based simply on one factor, these significant interactions indicate that the assigned prison sentence to the defendant depends upon the joint effect of two or more of the six victim, defendant, or rape case characteristics.

The interaction between the race of the defendant and the race of the victim was found to be significant, indicating that the jurors treated the defendant differently depending upon the race of the defendant and the race of the victim involved. A plot of the mean prison sentences assigned to the defendant for different victim-defendant racial combinations (figure 4-1) and tests on the simple effects showed that the black and white offenders were treated *no* differently when a black woman was the victim. Differences were found to occur, however, when the victim was white. A black offender ($M = 22.15$) who assaulted a white woman received a longer sentence ($p < .05$) than a black ($M = 13.20$) or white ($M = 11.13$) man assaulting a black woman, or a white man ($M = 11.81$) accused of raping a white woman.

The significant interaction of victim attractiveness, the race of the defendant, and the race of the victim suggested that defendant-victim racial differences in recommended sentencing may depend, at least in part, on the attractiveness of the victim. As in figure 4-1, figure 4-2 depicts the black defendant as being treated more harshly ($p < .05$) than the white one for raping a white woman, regardless of her physical beauty. In addition, for the attractive victim, a black assailant ($M = 23.55$) who had raped a white woman was punished more severely ($p < .05$) than a black man ($M = 10.21$) who had raped a black woman. No such difference was apparent for the white defendant. On the other hand, when the victim was physically unattractive, no difference in sentencing was found for the black defendant regardless of the victim's race. This same result was also true for the white defendant.

The sexual experience of the victim in combination with her attractiveness and the defendant's race was also found to influence the jurors' recommended sentences. A plot of the means for this interaction (figure 4-3) showed that there was no difference in the sentences of the black and white defendants accused of raping a sexually experienced victim regardless of her attractiveness. Additionally, there were no racial differences in defendant sentencing when an attractive, sexually inexperienced woman had been assaulted. But when the sexually inexperienced victim was unattractive, the black man ($M = 20.76$) received a longer prison term ($p < .05$) than did the white man ($M = 10.37$).

A significant interaction (graphed in figure 4-4) between the type of rape and the strength of evidence revealed that a defendant accused of a nonprecipitory rape was recommended a heavier prison term ($p < .05$) than a defendant in a precipitory case, irrespective of the strength of the evidence presented at the trial. The strength of evidence presented also showed no effects in the precipitory offense; the jurors treated the defendant in the strong evidence case no differently from the one in the weak evidence case. On the other hand, in the trial involving the nonprecipitory offense, the

Table 4-3

Summary of the Effects of Defendant, Victim, and Rape Case Characteristics on Jurors' Recommended Prison Sentences for a Rape Defendant

	White Jurors (N = 896)			Black Jurors (N = 160)		
Factor	df	MS	F	df	MS	F
Race of the defendant (A)	1	8625.45	14.02****	1	888.31	1.41
Race of the victim (B)	1	5197.50	8.45***	1	4.56	.93
Victim physical attractiveness (C)	1	115.72	.19	1		
Victim sexual experience (D)	1	617.79	1.00	1	29.76	.05
Strength of evidence (E)	1	6184.50	10.04**	1	6877.51	10.91***
Type of rape (F)	1	32064.29	52.10****	1		
A × B	1	3836.29	6.23**	1	28.06	.04
A × C	1	1193.25	1.94			
A × D	1	412.57	.67	1	869.56	1.38
A × E	1	1067.50	1.74	1	684.76	1.09
A × F	1	611.16	.99			
B × C	1	546.88	.89			
B × D	1	238.22	.39	1	500.56	.79
B × E	1	58.02	.09	1	218.56	.35
B × F	1	15.54	.03			
C × D	1	255.00	.41			
C × E	1	1197.88	1.95			
C × F	1	218.04	.35			
D × E	1	242.36	.39	1	425.76	.68
D × F	1	2004.02	3.26*			
E × F	1	2921.79	4.75**			
A × B × C	1	1771.88	2.88*			
A × B × D	1	218.04	.35	1	995.01	1.58
A × B × E	1	157.79	.26	1	154.06	.24
A × B × F	1	426.25	.69			
A × C × D	1	2385.54	3.88*			
A × C × E	1	236.16	.38			
A × C × F	1	61.11	.10			
A × D × E	1	8.25	.01	1	124.26	.20
A × D × F	1	2619.45	4.26*			
A × E × F	1	495.04	.80			
B × C × D	1	445.79	.72			
B × C × E	1	187.61	.31			
B × C × F	1	1.79	.01			
B × D × E	1	80.16	.13	1	5028.81	7.98**
B × D × F	1	136.72	.22			
B × E × F	1	204.45	.33			
C × D × E	1	350.00	.57			
C × D × F	1	101.79	.17			
C × E × F	1	144.64	.24			
D × E × F	1	9.04	.02			
A × B × C × D	1	315.88	.51			
A × B × C × E	1	169.75	.28			
A × B × C × F	1	23.14	.04			
A × B × D × E	1	1161.16	1.89	1	29.76	.05
A × B × D × F	1	313.50	.51			
A × B × E × F	1	20.64	.03			
A × C × D × E	1	4.03	.01			
A × C × D × F	1	562.61	.91			

Table 4-3 *(continued)*

Factor	White Jurors (N = 896)			Black Jurors (N = 160)		
	df	*MS*	*F*	*df*	*MS*	*F*
A × C × E × F	1	617.79	1.00			
A × D × E × F	1	1527.79	2.48			
B × C × D × E	1	8.25	.01			
B × C × D × F	1	370.29	.60			
B × C × E × F	1	323.04	.53			
B × D × E × F	1	1011.50	1.64			
C × D × E × F	1	151.14	.25			
A × B × C × D × E	1	180.36	.29			
A × B × C × D × F	1	85.02	.14			
A × B × C × E × F	1	88.75	.14			
A × B × D × E × F	1	103.14	.17			
A × C × D × E × F	1	4.02	.01			
B × C × D × E × F	1	1538.25	2.50			
A × B × C × D × E × F	1	3.25	.01			
Residual	832	615.43		144	630.27	

*$p < .05$. **$p < .01$. ***$p < .001$. ****$p \leq .0001$.

defendant in the weak evidence condition ($M = 16.12$) was administered a lighter sentence ($p < .05$) than his counterpart in the strong evidence condition ($M = 24.99$).

Type of rape in conjunction with the victim's sexual experience (figure 4-5) was found to affect the sentencing of the defendant. In general, the defendant was more likely to receive a less severe sentence ($p < .05$) when accused of a precipitory rape than when accused of a nonprecipitory assault. This difference proved to be consistent across both the sexually experienced and the sexually inexperienced victim conditions.

Figure 4-6 summarizes the final significant interaction between type of rape, sexual experience of the victim, and race of the defendant. Although there were no racial differences in the sentencing of the defendants charged with assaulting a sexually experienced victim in a nonprecipitory rape situation, the black defendant ($M = 27.84$) received a higher sentence ($p < .05$) than the white defendant ($M = 17.92$) when the victim had no previous sexual experience. In the precipitory rape, this same racial difference (black $M = 13.92$; white $M = 4.59$) emerged when the victim was sexually experienced while none was evident for a sexually inexperienced victim. For the nonprecipitory offense, the black man tended to receive a higher sentence ($p < .05$) when the assault was against a sexually inexperienced victim ($M = 27.84$) than when against an experienced one ($M = 21.13$); no such difference was found for the white man accused of a nonprecipitory rape or for black or white defendants brought to trial for a precipitory one.

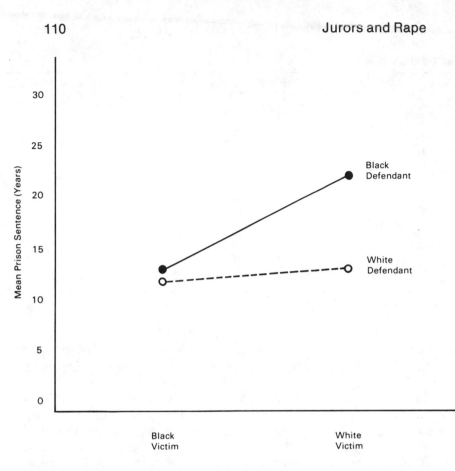

Figure 4-1. Mean Juror Recommended Prison Sentence for Rape Defendants as a Function of Race of the Defendant and Race of the
Victim

Black Jurors

Of the four main effects or factors thought to influence black jurors' decisions, only the strength of the evidence presented at the trial had any significant effect. The defendant in the strong evidence case ($M = 23.18$) received
a significantly longer sentence ($p < .05$) than the accused in the weak
evidence case ($M = 10.06$).

Over and above the strength of evidence presented, there was a statistically significant race of the victim × sexual experience of the victim ×
strength of evidence interaction. A plot of the means in the interaction (figure
4-7) and tests made on the simple effects revealed some interesting results.

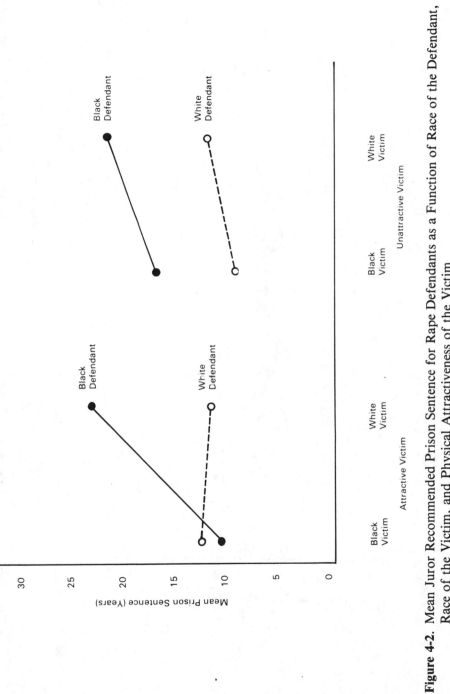

Figure 4-2. Mean Juror Recommended Prison Sentence for Rape Defendants as a Function of Race of the Defendant, Race of the Victim, and Physical Attractiveness of the Victim

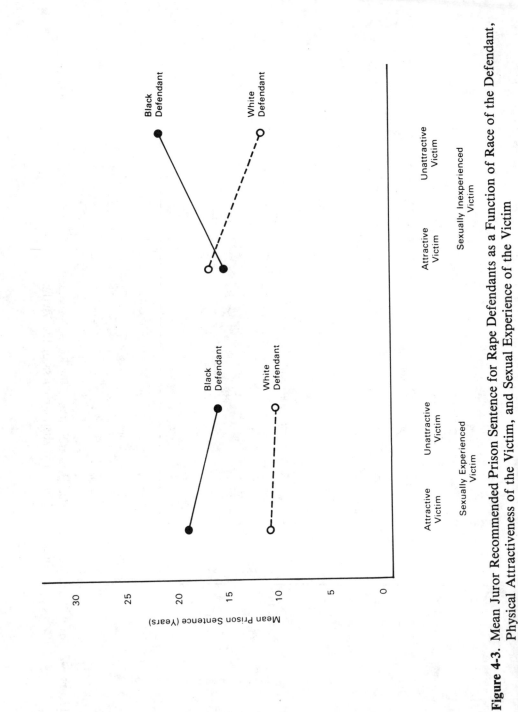

Figure 4-3. Mean Juror Recommended Prison Sentence for Rape Defendants as a Function of Race of the Defendant, Physical Attractiveness of the Victim, and Sexual Experience of the Victim

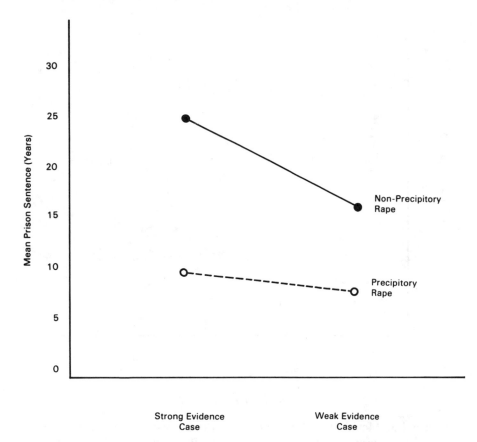

Figure 4-4. Mean Juror Recommended Prison Sentence for Rape Defendants as a Function of Type of Rape and Strength of Evidence in the Case

In the strong evidence situation involving a sexually experienced victim, the defendant who had assaulted a black victim ($M = 30.75$) was given a greater sentence ($p < .05$) than the one who had attacked a white victim ($M = 18.00$). Conversely, when the woman was sexually inexperienced, the offender who had assaulted a white woman ($M = 30.35$) was assigned a longer prison term ($p < .05$) than the defendant raping a black woman ($M = 13.60$).

When little evidence was available concerning the guilt of the defendant, results almost completely opposite of those reported in the strong

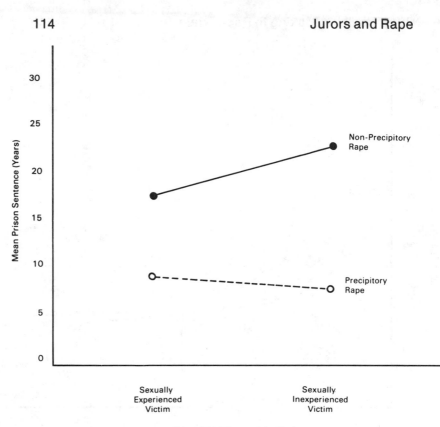

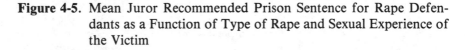

Figure 4-5. Mean Juror Recommended Prison Sentence for Rape Defendants as a Function of Type of Rape and Sexual Experience of the Victim

evidence condition were found. The assailant of a white, sexually experienced victim *tended* to receive a longer prison term than the offender of a black woman. This difference in the assigned terms, however, was not statistically significant. When the victim was sexually inexperienced, the defendant raping a black woman (M = 17.30) was given more years in prison than the one attacking a white woman (M = 6.95).

Discussion of the Results

If extra-evidential factors had no impact on juror decision making in the rape cases, no significant effects of defendant, victim, or rape case characteristics would be expected. However, significant effects were found

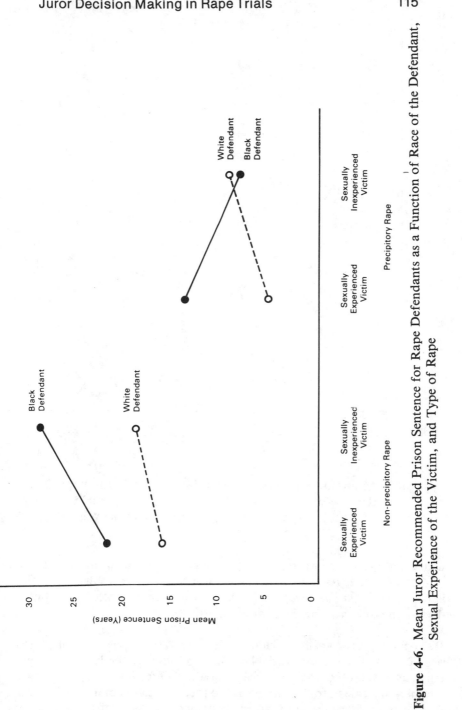

Figure 4-6. Mean Juror Recommended Prison Sentence for Rape Defendants as a Function of Race of the Defendant, Sexual Experience of the Victim, and Type of Rape

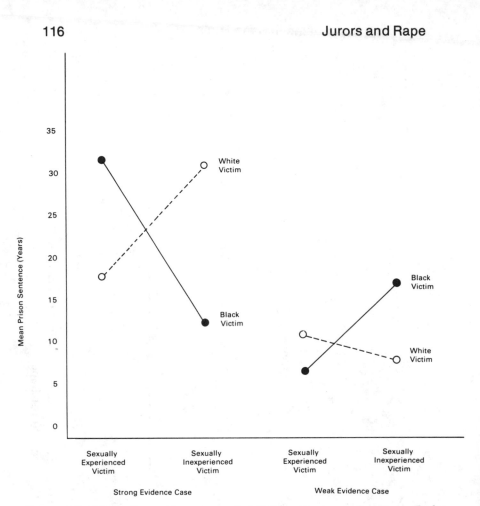

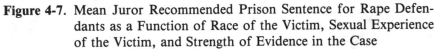

Figure 4-7. Mean Juror Recommended Prison Sentence for Rape Defendants as a Function of Race of the Victim, Sexual Experience of the Victim, and Strength of Evidence in the Case

indicating that some of these factors played a role in the jurors' sentencing of the defendant. As some writers have suspected, these results imply that issues *other than the evidence* in the case determined, to a significant degree, the treatment of the accused rapist.

Defendant Characteristics. Undoubtedly, the race of the defendant was one of the most important variables found to influence the jurors' sentencing decisions. Of the seven significant variable interactions, the defendant's race played a role in four. With regard to race, our data point to two rather significant findings: the jurors generally treated the black defendant harsher than the white defendant, and the specific treatment of the defendant depended not only upon his race but *whom* he assaulted as well.

Although racial differences in assessed penalties seem to vary for the type of crime committed, surveys of defendant sentences have generally shown blacks to be treated more severely than whites. For example, Vines and Jacobs (1963) reported that blacks received harsher treatment in the courts than whites in 70 percent of the case categories (including rape) they investigated. Statistics from the Justice Department (National Prisoner Statistics 1971) indicated that of the executions for rape since 1930, 89 percent have involved black men. Thus from data reported in studies such as these, the differential treatment of black and white men appears to be a historical fact.

Looking at the results for race of the defendant, the question might be raised as to why race played such a significant role in the white jurors' decisions. Our data do not permit us to give a definitive answer to the question, but some speculations can be made. If it can be assumed that white jurors are more likely to perceive a white defendant as more socially attractive than a black one, previous research on the social attractiveness of defendants and sentencing might be used to account for racial differences. For instance, research by Nemeth and Sosis (1973) showed that defendants with less socially desirable characteristics were seen as being less morally responsible and were attributed by the jurors other social undesirable traits. Using our assumption of racial differences in social attractiveness, this same stereotyping could have occurred in the present research with the jurors attaching negative characteristics to the black (unattractive) defendant and positive ones to the white (attractive) defendant. Similarly, the jurors may have perceived the crime to be more serious when committed by an unattractive defendant. The attractive defendant was probably viewed as being less prone to recidivism and as having greater potential worth. This perceptual process has been supported for *physically* attractive defendants (Sigall and Ostrove 1975) and quite possibly occurred in the present study where jurors were confronted with social rather than physical attractiveness. Thus the findings of Sigall and Ostrove *suggest* that the jurors perceived the socially attractive or white defendant as having more potential worth, more opportunities for improvement, and therefore deserving of more lenient treatment.

Victim Characteristics. Even though the race of the defendant had a major impact on the jurors, they were also inclined to allow certain victim characteristics (namely, race, physical attractiveness, and sexual experience) in combination with the defendant's race to influence their decisions. In this sense, defendant sentencing was determined by not only the race of the defendant but who was raped as well. For example, in terms of victim race, when the victim was black, the black and white defendants were treated similarly. However, when the victim was white, the black defendant received more severe punishment. These results are consistent with those of Wolfgang and Riedel's (1973) survey of racial differences in the imposition of the death penalty for rape. They reported that blacks convicted of raping white women were more likely to be executed than any other defendant-victim racial combination. Sentencing outcomes for rape such as those reported by Wolfgang and Riedel led Brownmiller (1975) to conclude that differential punishment of black and white men for rape is based primarily upon the desire to protect white women from black men. In the present study, the absence of sentencing differences between the white and black defendants assaulting the black woman and the presence of such differences for the white victim lends some support to her thesis. It would appear that her idea is a plausible explanation as to why sentencing differences were found among the victim-defendant racial groupings.

In addition to race of the victim, the reinforcement-affect model of interpersonal perception suggests that beauty having positive reinforcement value would lead to more positive affect responses to an attractive person. Therefore, in this study, it could be hypothesized that more severe punishment would be given to a defendant assaulting an attractive victim. Some support for this hypothesis was found for the reinforcement-affect model as there was a trend for the assailant of the unattractive woman generally to receive a more lenient sentence than the assailant of the attractive victim. However, the difference in sentencing was not statistically significant. It should not be concluded that physical attractiveness has no effect on juror decisions. When physical attractiveness was considered in conjunction with other variables (such as race of the victim, race of the defendant, sexual experience of the victim), significant effects were found.

The issue concerning the introduction of information on the victim's sexual experience has been a major focal point for those individuals interested in rape law reform. As explained earlier in the chapter, reformers have argued that the presentation of such information in court only serves to prejudice the jury. Along with race of the defendant, sexual experience of the victim proved to have important effects on juror decision making as it was involved in four of the seven significant interactions. Support for the reformers' sentiments concerning the elimination of evidence regarding third-party sexual relations is indicated by the presence of these interactions. However, the effects of information on the victim's sexual experiences are more complex than some writers have thought. For example, such information may not only prejudice the jurors against the victim but may also influence their sentences for different races of defendants (figure 4-6). The jurors in the present research tended to focus on the sexual experience of the victim in combination with other characteristics of the case such as race of the defendant, race of the victim, and the type of rape committed. Given these results, it would appear that the absence of a victim's sexual experience at the trial alone will not eliminate the prejudicial outcomes of such trials. As discussed in the next chapter, more wide-sweeping reforms will clearly be needed.

Case Characteristics. Other than intercourse, the law regarding rape deals only with the issue of consent by the woman at the time of intercourse. Jurors in rape trials frequently use broad definitions of consent to determine some degree of willingness on the part of the woman to have had intercourse with the defendant. When the jurors perceive that the woman has precipitated or encouraged the assault by her appearance or behavior, they are likely to apply the "assumption of risk" criterion. Under these conditions, the jurors are likely to be lenient with the defendant.

In the present research, the assailant in the nonprecipitory assault was given a more severe sentence than the offender in the precipitory case indicating that the jurors appeared to attribute blame to the victim when contributory behavior was implied. Several writers (Frederick and Luginbuhl 1976; Jones and Aronson 1973; Landy and Aronson 1969) have documented similar effects. Brooks, Doob, and Kirshenbaum (1975) found that jurors were more likely to convict a defendant accused of raping a woman with a chaste reputation than an identical defendant charged with assaulting a prostitute. Information on the "good" or "bad" character of the victim appears to affect the decisions of the jurors, and the definitions of good or bad are likely to be broadly defined.

Although the jurors tended to render harsher sentences to the defendant when the amount of evidence was high indicating some degree of rationality, the present research showed that the processing of case-related information may be influenced by extra-evidential factors. Numerous victim, defendant, and case characteristics were found to influence jurors' verdicts in the rape trial. Since jurors typically lack the discipline of a judge and since the court has little control over the jury's verdict in a criminal case, the jury maintains a certain degree of discretion and autonomy. To this extent, the jury may disregard the facts in a rape case and rule on the basis of extraneous information. As Hibey (1973, p. 310) noted, experience on both sides of a rape case shows that a ruling of guilty beyond a reasonable doubt or an acquittal is not always predictable since jurors' treatment of the evidence is not always rational.

Background and Attitudinal Correlates
of Juror Decision Making

The results reported in the previous section showed that selected victim, defendant, and rape case characteristics influenced jurors' decisions in the trials. Given such results, it would seem important to determine if jurors' decisions might be predicted from their background and attitudinal characteristics. If significant correlations between juror characteristics and decisions are identified, it could be argued that such variables are important considerations for defense and prosecuting attorneys involved in the selection of jurors for a rape trial.

Using data obtained from the jurors' responses to the Personal Data Sheet, Attitudes toward Rape questionnaire, Attitudes toward Woman questionnaire, Rape Knowledge Test, and jurors' recommended prison sentences for the rape defendant, two different analyses were made. First, simple correlations were computed for the juror background and attitudinal characteristics to determine how individual variables may be related to juror decison making. Following these analyses, multiple correlations were computed for the juror background and attitudinal *sets* of characteristics. These correlations were made to see if a number of variables might be combined to predict these decisions. Statistical tests could then be made to determine which set of variables (background or attitudinal characteristics) contributed most to the prediction of juror decision making.

Predicting Jurors' Decisions

Table 4-4 summarizes the simple correlations calculated between selected juror characteristics and the jurors' recommended prison sentences for the rape defendant.[3] As can be seen, these correlations are reported separately for the white and black jurors.

White Jurors. Of the simple correlations computed between the seven background characteristics and the white jurors' recommended length of prison sentence, only two significant, but weak, correlations were identified for age and education. The negative correlation between age and sentence length indicated that older jurors tended to assign lighter sentences to the defendant than did younger ones ($r = -.11$, $p < .001$). In addition, the negative correlation of years of education with the recommended prison term showed that more-educated jurors gave more lenient sentences than less-educated jurors ($r = .11$, $p < .001$). Sex, marital status, previous service on a jury, and personal knowledge of a raped woman were found to be uncorrelated with sentence length.

With regard to the attitudinal variables, four of the nine simple correlations were significant. White jurors assigning lenient sentences to the rape defendant tended to believe that women should be held responsible for preventing rape ($r = -.18$, $p < .001$); punishment for rape should not be severe ($r = .37$, $p < .001$); women precipitate rape through their appearance or behavior ($r = -.12$, $p < .001$); and rapists are normal men ($r = -.10$, $p < .01$).

Table 4-4
Correlations between Black and White Juror Characteristics and Recommended Prison Sentence Length for Rape Defendants

Predictor Variables	Black Jurors (N = 160)	White Jurors (N = 896)
Rape case characteristics		
Race of the defendant[a]	.09	−.12***
Race of the victim[a]	−.01	.09*
Victim physical attractiveness[a]	—[b]	−.01
Victim sexual experience[a]	.02	.03
Strength of evidence[a]	−.25**	−.10**
Type of rape[a]	—	−.23***
Juror background variables		
Sex (1 = female; 2 = male)[a]	−.01	−.04
Marital status (1 = single; 2 = married)[a]	.10	−.02
Age	.02	−.11***
Years of education	−.17*	−.11***
Personally know a raped woman? (1 = yes; 2 = no)[a]	.07	−.05
Served on a jury? (1 = yes; 2 = no)[a]	−.22**	.02
Occupational prestige	−.13	−.08
Juror attitudinal variables		
Attitudes toward women	−.11	.00
Woman's responsibility in rape prevention	−.41***	−.18***
Sex as motivation for rape	−.35***	−.04
Severe punishment for rape	.24**	.37***
Victim precipitation of rape	−.09	−.12***
Normality of rapists	.01	−.10**
Power as motivation for rape	.08	.01
Favorable perception of a woman after rape	−.13	−.05
Resistance as woman's role	.06	.06

[a]point-biserial correlation.
[b]These case characteristics were not presented to the black jurors.
*$p < .05$. **$p < .01$. ***$p < .001$.

Black Jurors. As with the white jurors, two of the background variables were statistically significant, with one, years of education, being common to both juror racial groups. Here again, more-educated jurors gave significantly lighter sentences than less-educated ones ($r = -.17$, $p < .05$). Contrary to whites, black jurors' service at a previous trial was also associated with sentencing. Black jurors who had served previously on a jury gave harsher sentences than individuals who had not ($r = -.22$, $p < .01$).

For the attitudinal variables, three dimensions of the ATR were associated with defendant sentencing by the black jurors. Of these three, correlations with two of the factors (*woman's responsibility in rape prevention* and *severe punishment for rape*) exhibited patterns similar to those of the white jurors. With respect to the attitudinal variables, black jurors giving lenient sentences felt that women are responsible for rape prevention ($r = -.41, p < .001$); rapists are not motivated by a need for sex ($r = -.35, p < .001$); and punishment for rape should not be harsh ($r = .24, p < .01$). As with the white jurors, attitudes toward women were uncorrelated with juror sentencing.

Contribution of Background and Attitudinal Variables to Predicting Jurors' Decisions

The simple correlations reported in table 4-4 suggested that *individual* juror characteristics are important for predicting jurors' decisions in a rape trial. However, it may be possible that combinations or sets of variables may be combined to enhance our ability to predict their decisions. To explore further the predictability of juror decision making in a rape trial, multiple correlations were used for two major purposes: to determine how well *sets* of juror characteristics (that is, the juror background and attitudinal variables listed in table 4-4) might relate to or predict jurors' decisions, and to determine which of these sets is most important in predicting these decisions.

For the white jurors, both the juror background characteristics ($R = .15, p < .05$) and attitudinal variables ($R = .43, p < .001$) were found to be associated with recommended sentencing of the defendant (table 4-5). However, only the attitudinal variables proved to be significant for the black jurors ($R = .58, p < .001$). Given the relative magnitudes of the correlations, these results suggest that attitudinal variables account for more of the differences among jurors' decisions than do background characteristics of the jurors.

To test more specifically the supposition that attitudinal variables offer more utility than background characteristics in predicting juror decision making, several additional steps were taken. Multiple correlations were computed initially between the jurors' recommended sentences and their background and attitudinal characteristics. Then tests (Cohen 1968) were made for the relative amount of variance in recommended sentences explained by the sets of variables entering into the regressions. For a set of variables to be useful in predicting juror decision making, the set should account for a significant amount of variability in juror sentencing left *unexplained* by the other set of variables. Table 4-5 summarizes the results of these tests.

Of the the two sets of variables, only the attitudinal ones were significantly associated with both the black ($R = .58$) and white ($R = .43$) jurors' recommended sentences for the defendant. Additional evidence on the importance of attitudinal variables may also be seen by comparing their contribution to predicting jurors' recommended prison sentences *over and above* that accounted for by the background variables. For both the black

Table 4-5
Contribution of Juror Background and Juror Attitudinal Variables in Predicting Jurors' Decisions in Rape Trials

Predictor Sets	Black Jurors (N = 160)			White Jurors (N = 896)		
	R	R^2	Increase in R^2	R	R^2	Increase in R^2
Rape case characteristics[a]	.27*	.07	—[d]	.30**	.09	—
Juror background characteristics[b]	.32	.10	—	.15*	.02	—
Juror attitudinal variables[c]	.58***	.33	—	.43***	.18	—
Case characteristics	.27*	.07	—	.30***	.09	—
Case + background characteristics	.41	.17	.10*	.33***	.11	.02
Case + background + attitudinal variables	.66**	.44	.27***	.52***	.27	.16***
Case characteristics	.27*	.07	—	.30***	.09	—
Case + attitudinal variables	.62***	.38	.31***	.51***	.26	.17***
Case + attitudinal + background variables	.66**	.44	.06*	.52***	.27	.01

[a]Case characteristics include the following variables presented in the rape cases: race of the victim, race of the defendant, attractiveness of the victim, sexual experience of the victim, strength of evidence, and type of rape.
[b]Background characteristics of the jurors include sex, years of education, age, occupational prestige, personal knowledge of a rape victim, previous service on a jury, and marital status.
[c]Attitudinal variables of the jurors include woman's responsibility in rape prevention, sex as motivation for rape, severe punishment for rape, victim precipitation of rape, normality of rapists, power as motivation for rape, favorable perception of a woman after rape, resistance as woman's role during rape, and attitudes toward women.
[d]Where one set of variables is not added to another set, an increase in the R^2 cannot be calculated.
*$p < .05$. **$p < .01$. ***$p < .001$.

(27 percent) and white (16 percent) jurors, the explanation of the variability in jurors' decisions was significantly ($p < .001$) improved when the attitudinal variables were added to the background characteristics. Conversely, when the background variables were added to the attitudinal ones, the prediction of jurors' sentences improved only 6 percent for the black and 1 percent for the white jurors. These results supported rather conclusively the supposition that attitudinal variables are more important in predicting jurors' recommended sentences of the defendant than are background characteristics.

Discussion of the Results

Many lawyers have acknowledged that numerous trials are won or lost even before the first piece of evidence is presented to the jury (D'Agostino and

Brown 1975, p. 199). They have recognized that *who* is sitting on the jury is one of the most important determinants of the outcome of a trial. As a consequence, practicing attorneys at rape and other criminal trials have been interested in identifying and selecting those persons for the jury who will be most favorable to their case. In choosing those individuals, lawyers have relied traditionally upon subjective impressions of candidates during voir dire (that is, the process of questioning prospective jurors prior to the trial to determine if they are prejudiced or sympathetic to their client). Lawyers have used most often clinical impressions of jurors based on a number of background characteristics (such as occupational status, race, education, sex, age) to make their predictions (Harrington and Dempsey 1969; Hermann 1970). During the past ten years, however, social scientists have been employed to aid in the jury selection process. Rather than using background information on prospective jurors in a clinical way, they have incorporated various psychological characteristics of jurors (such as attitudinal variables) and statistical procedures to predict juror decisions (Schulman, Shaver, Colman, Emrich, and Christie 1973). Judging from the application of such techniques in several recent, widely publicized cases (D'Agostino and Brown 1975; Van Dyke 1977), it would seem that the isolation of those juror characteristics predictive of juror decision making in rape trials would be important to prosecuting and defense attorneys.

In studying juror characteristics in this research, analyses of the juror background and attitudinal variables revealed several interesting findings: (1) in general, the juror characteristics which were predictive of juror decision making were different for the black and white jurors, and (2) the attitudes which the jurors held toward rape were more important in predicting their verdicts than were background characteristics. Given these findings, several points need to be made. If certain juror characteristics are to be used for selecting jurors in rape trials, our data indicate that the specific predictors to be employed should differ depending upon the race of the jurors. The jurors' race appears to moderate the relationships between the juror characteristics and their decisions in rape trials. Of the eight characteristics found to relate to juror sentencing, only three were common to both racial groups.

In addition, the correlations are far from perfect. Errors would be made in predicting any *one* decision of any *one* juror. On the average though, the ability to predict juror decision making may be enhanced by using these selected juror characteristics. Their use would appear to enhance the accuracy of juror selection decisions.

Although trial attorneys have usually incorporated background characteristics as predictors of juror decisions, our data show further that in a rape trial setting, measures of attitudes toward rape provide a better set of predictors. Measures of this type of variable would seem to offer greater utility for assessing juror decision making in rape cases than those background variables most often used by attorneys.

Effects of Juror-Rape Case Characteristic Interactions on Juror Decision Making

So far in our analyses, we have examined how both rape case and juror characteristics have been related to jurors' recommended sentences for a defendant in a rape trial. However, an argument could be made that the decisions reached in the trial may be associated with the elements of the case presented (for example, race of the defendant) *in combination* with the characteristics of the jurors (for example, their race) judging the case. The present set of analyses was designed to test this possibility by examining the significance of juror-defendant variable interactions in juror decision making. Of course, many different combinations of variables could be hypothesized as being important predictors of rape trial outcomes. Therefore, to keep the number of variables to a manageable size but to retain those variables having meaningful implications for the research, it was decided to incorporate in the analyses only those variable combinations involving one rape case and one juror characteristic. Following this strategy, eighty-eight rape case-juror characteristic interaction terms or variable combinations were created and entered as independent variables into multiple regression analysis, with the jurors' recommended prison sentence for the defendant as the dependent variable.[4] When a statistically significant interaction was found, plots and tests on the simple effects were made to clarify the nature of the interaction and its relationship to juror decision making. Table 4-6 summarizes the results of the regression analysis.

The relationships of the six single, main effect variables (such as race of the defendant) with the jurors' decisions have been discussed previously and will not be elaborated on here. Only the results of the relevant rape case-juror characteristic interactions will be presented.

Race of the Defendant Interactions

Three juror characteristics (race, personal acquaintance with a rape victim, and belief in severe punishment for rape) had a significant interaction with the race of the defendant. As shown in figure 4-8, a plot of the defendant race-juror race interaction revealed that the jurors were inclined to treat a defendant of the race *opposite* to themselves more severely than one of the *same* race. Black jurors gave the black defendant ($M = 14.26$) a lighter sentence ($p < .05$) than they gave the white one ($M = 18.98$). On the other

Table 4-6
Summary of the Effects of Rape Case Characteristics × Juror Characteristics on Jurors' Recommended Prison Sentences for a Rape Defendant

Factor	B^b	Factor	B^b
Rape case characteristics		A × L	− 4.18
Race of the defendant (A)		A × M	4.94
Race of the victim (B)		A × N	− 0.78
Victim physical attractiveness (C)		A × O	1.11
Type of rape (D)		A × P	6.24*
Victim sexual experience (E)		A × Q	− 3.53
Strength of evidence (F)		A × R	− 1.85
		A × S	− 5.28
Juror background variables		A × T	− 0.54
Race (G)		A × U	− 0.11
Sex (H)		B × G	4.65
Age (I)		B × H	0.40
Years of education (J)		B × I	− 2.66
Personal knowledge of a raped woman (K)		B × J	− 2.85
Previous service on a jury (L)		B × K	−10.11**
		B × L	− 7.28
Juror attitudinal variables		B × M	3.59
Attitudes toward women (M)		B × N	5.06
Woman's responsibility in rape prevention (N)		B × O	− 1.45
Sex as motivation for rape (O)		B × P	− 5.20
Severe punishment for rape (P)		B × Q	0.80
Victim precipitation of rape (Q)		B × R	5.24
Normality of rapists (R)		B × S	− 1.82
Power as motivation for rape (S)		B × T	− 2.95
Favorable perception of a woman after rape (T)		B × U	1.77
Resistance as woman's role during rape (U)			
		C × H	1.70
Rape case × juror characteristics[a]		C × I	− 8.19**
A × G	−13.70***	C × J	1.52
A × H	2.53	C × K	− 3.90
A × I	5.48	C × L	1.67
A × J	− 0.61	E × K	− 1.16
A × K	8.71**	E × L	6.20
C × M	− 6.32	E × M	2.27
C × N	− 7.98**	E × N	− 2.75
C × O	2.22	E × O	− 3.92
C × P	− 1.45	E × P	− 4.28
C × Q	0.64	E × Q	5.99*
C × R	− 0.87	E × R	1.83
C × S	7.40**	E × S	1.80
C × T	− 3.17	E × T	− 0.56
C × U	− 3.18	E × U	− 1.85
D × H	− 0.09	F × G	14.47***
D × I	− 1.39	F × H	1.05
D × J	− 0.45	F × I	0.77
D × K	− 7.30*	F × J	− 2.54
D × L	− 1.86	F × K	0.24
D × M	2.52	F × L	7.67
D × N	− 2.68		
D × O	0.80		

Table 4-6 *(continued)*

Factor	B^b	Factor	B^b
D × P	9.60**	F × M	2.00
D × Q	− 6.45*	F × N	− 10.42***
D × R	− 5.56	F × O	1.15
D × S	− 4.10	F × P	7.56**
D × T	7.94**	F × Q	− 5.35
D × U	− 1.91	F × R	-- 3.76
E × G	3.53	F × S	2.82
E × H	1.97	F × T	− 0.91
E × I	− 0.79	F × U	0.26
E × J	0.43		

Note: $N = 1,056$.

[a]Only the two-way interactions between the rape case characteristics and the juror characteristics are shown.

[b]Unstandardized beta weights.

*$p < .05$. **$p < .01$. ***$p < .001$. ****$p < .0001$.

hand, the white defendant ($M = 11.47$) was given fewer ($p < .05$) years in prison than the black defendant ($M = 17.67$) by the white jurors. When the defendant was black, the two juror racial groups tended to be more consistent in their decisions than when he was white.

Figure 4-9 describes the mean sentences of the black and white defendants as assigned by those jurors who had and those who had *not* personally known a woman who had been raped. No difference was found in the mean sentences decided on by these two juror groups for the white defendant. When the defendant was black, however, jurors who had known a rape victim ($M = 21.57$) recommended a longer sentence ($p < .05$) than those who had not ($M = 15.93$). In addition, jurors knowing a rape victim and judging the black defendant were harsher ($p < .05$) than either juror group sentencing the white defendant or those not knowing a rape victim and sentencing the black defendant.

Jurors who strongly believed in severe punishment for rape meted harsher prison sentences ($p < .05$) than jurors who were not as supportive of severe punishment. For this latter group of jurors, there were no racial differences in their assigned prison terms. Contrastingly, for the jurors strongly supporting severe punishment, the black defendant ($M = 25.51$) received a longer sentence ($p < .05$) than the white defendant ($M = 19.71$).

Race of the Victim Interactions

Only one of the juror characteristics had a significant interaction with the race of the victim. Figure 4-11 shows that the interaction of the jurors' personal knowledge of a rape victim and the race of the victim were related to

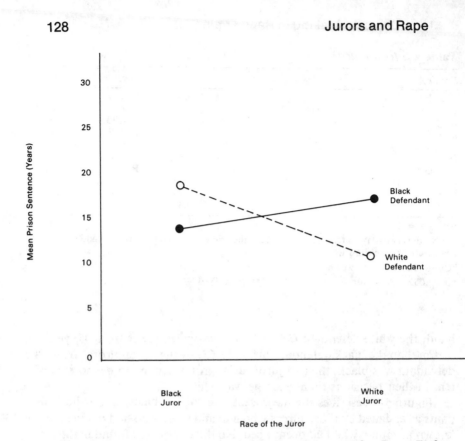

Figure 4-8. Mean Juror Recommended Prison Sentence for Rape Defendants as a Function of Race of the Defendant and Race of the
Juror

defendant sentencing. The assailant of the black victim was treated similarly
by those jurors who had known a rape victim and those who had not. Conversely, when the victim was white, jurors who had known a woman who
had been raped ($M = 21.83$) were inclined to give a defendant a longer
sentence ($p < .05$) than jurors who had not been acquainted with a rape victim ($M = 15.45$).

Victim Physical Attractiveness Interactions

When combined with juror characteristics, victim physical attractiveness
proved to be an important factor influencing juror verdicts. An examination of table 4-6 shows that the jurors' age, beliefs concerning woman's re-

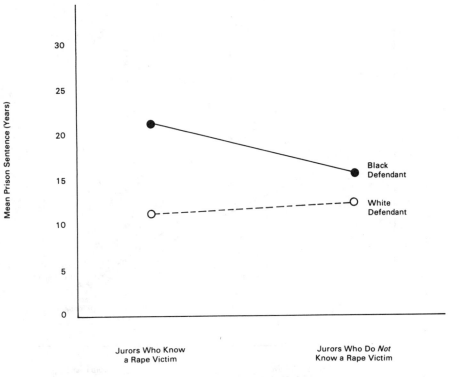

Figure 4-9. Mean Juror Recommended Prison Sentence for Rape Defendants as a Function of Race of the Defendant and Jurors' Knowledge of a Rape Victim

sponsibility in rape prevention, and beliefs concerning power as motivation for rape in combination with victim physical attractiveness were associated with the jurors' decisions in the rape cases.

Concerning juror age (figure 4-12), the physical attractiveness of the victim had no apparent effect on the decisions of jurors under the age of 30. Jurors 30 years of age or older, on the other hand, were inclined to discriminate in their sentencing decisions as the assailant of an attractive woman ($M = 15.32$) was assigned a longer sentence ($p < .05$) than the offender of an unattractive one ($M = 11.70$). In comparing between the two juror age groups, older jurors ($M = 11.70$) were more likely to decide on a lenient sentence for the offender of an unattractive victim than were younger jurors ($M = 16.93$).

The jurors' attitudes toward rape were also important considerations in evaluating the effects of victim physical appearance on defendant sentencing

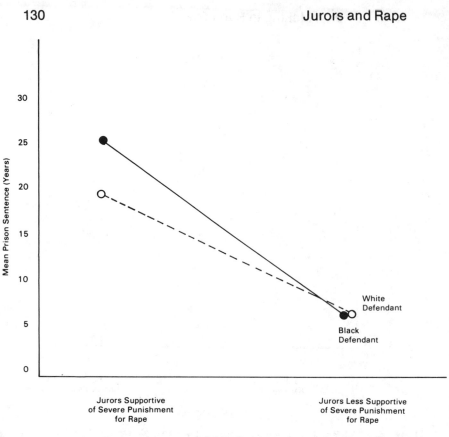

Figure 4-10. Mean Juror Recommended Prison Sentence for Rape Defendants as a Function of Race of the Defendant and Jurors' Belief that Punishment for Rape Should Be Severe

(figure 4-13). Jurors who felt that women should be held responsible for rape prevention recommended essentially the same sentence for the defendant regardless of the victim's attractiveness. However, for those jurors who did *not* strongly subscribe to this idea, if the victim was an attractive woman ($M = 22.34$), the offender received a lengthier sentence than the offender of an unattractive woman ($M = 17.23$). From a broader perspective, the sentences assigned by jurors who felt women should be responsible in rape prevention were far more lenient than the sentences prescribed by jurors who did not subscribe so strongly to this idea.

Additionally, the belief that the basic motivation for rape is power proved to have a significant influence on the jurors' decisions (figure 4-14). No differences between the sentences of the jurors who held strongly to this

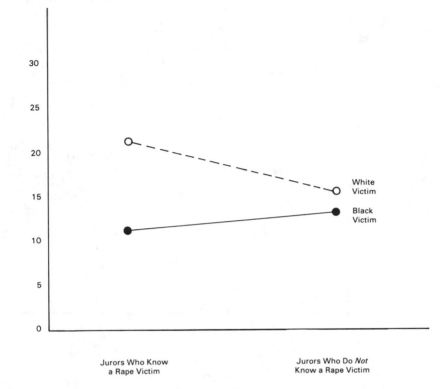

Figure 4-11. Mean Juror Recommended Prison Sentence for Rape Defendants as a Function of Race of the Victim and Jurors' Knowledge of a Rape Victim

belief versus those who did not were found for either the unattractive or the attractive victims. But *within* the group of jurors who strongly believed that rape is caused by a desire for power over women, the defendant accused of assaulting an attractive victim ($M = 16.27$) received a longer sentence ($p < .05$) than the defendant accused of attacking an unattractive woman ($M = 12.46$).

Type of Rape Interactions

In general, the defendant in the nonprecipitory rape case received a greater sentence than the one in the precipitory case. However, given the significant interaction between the jurors' personal knowledge of a rape victim and the

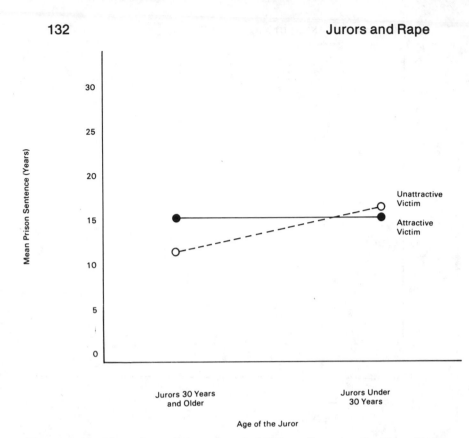

Figure 4-12. Mean Juror Recommended Prison Sentence for Rape Defendants as a Function of Physical Attractiveness of the Victim and Age of Juror

type of rape committed, it appears that the jurors' sentencing in precipitory and nonprecipitory cases may depend upon whether the jurors had personally known a raped woman. Figure 4-15 indicates that no significant differences in the mean sentences assigned by jurors who knew a rape victim versus those who did not were found for either of the two types of assault cases. Yet comparison *between* these types of cases showed some interesting results. For those jurors who did not know a rape victim, the defendant in a nonprecipitory assault ($M = 19.91$) was given a longer sentence ($p < .05$) than the individual accused of a precipitory offense ($M = 7.42$). However, when jurors personally knew a rape victim, they treated the defendant of nonprecipitory and precipitory assault cases equally as severe. No significant difference in their mean sentences for the defendants in these two cases was found.

Belief in severe punishment for rape was also associated with the decisions reached by the jurors in the two types of rape cases. For each type of

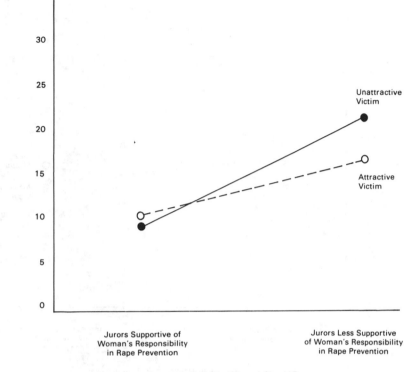

Figure 4-13. Mean Juror Recommended Prison Sentence for Rape Defendants as a Function of Physical Attractiveness of the Victim
and Jurors' Belief that Women Should Be Responsible for
Preventing Their Own Rape

case, the jurors who strongly supported severe punishment for rape tended
to administer longer sentences for the rapist than those jurors who did not
have such strong sentiments. Further evidence of the importance of this
belief may be seen by comparing the sentences of the jurors for the two
types of cases. In a rape situation which could be described as one where the
victim's appearance or behavior may have provoked the assault, one might
expect the defendant to be treated less severely than the defendant in a case
which was not victim-provoked. The present data generally support this
contention; however, the data additionally show that judgments of a defendant do not depend solely on the type of rape committed. These judgments
are also a function of the jurors' beliefs concerning punishment for rape. As
shown in figure 4-16, jurors who believed in severe punishment for rape

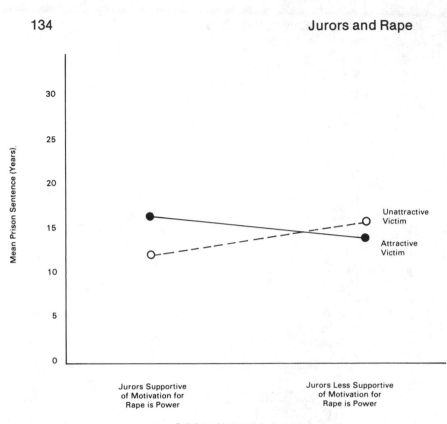

Belief that Motivation for Rape is Power

Figure 4-14. Mean Juror Recommended Prison Sentence for Rape Defendants as a Function of Physical Attractiveness of the Victim
and Jurors' Belief that Motivation for Rape Is Power

sentenced the defendant of a precipitory case to a longer prison term than
did jurors less supportive of severe punishment who were judging the defendant accused of a nonprecipitory offense.

Victim Sexual Experience Interactions

The belief that a victim precipitates or causes her rape through her appearance or behavior was identified as having a significant interaction with
the sexual experience of the victim. An examination of the interaction plot-
ted in figure 4-17 revealed no differences in the sentence of the assailant of a
sexually inexperienced victim given by jurors who believed that victims
precipitate rape and those jurors who did not have such a belief. Nevertheless, a significant difference was found when the woman was sexually experienced. In this instance, jurors who did *not* strongly believe that women

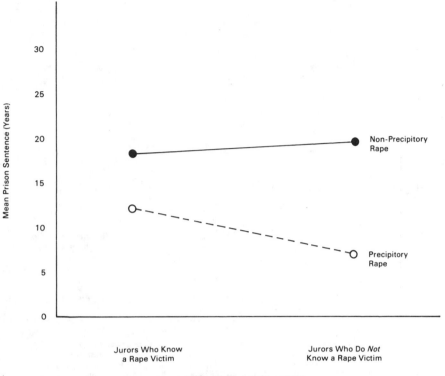

Figure 4-15. Mean Juror Recommended Prison Sentence for Rape Defendants as a Function of the Type of Rape and Jurors' Knowledge of a Rape Victim

precipitate rape (M = 17.94) gave a significantly higher sentence ($p < .05$) to an assailant of a sexually experienced woman than jurors who strongly believed in victim precipitation (M = 10.42).

Strength of Evidence Interactions

The defendant in a case characterized as having strong evidence was typically administered a more severe sentence than the defendant in a weak evidence case. The race of juror-strength of evidence interaction, shown in figure 4-18, indicated that the sentence given may depend not only on the strength of evidence presented to the jury but also on the race of the jurors evaluating the evidence. No difference in sentencing was found for the black and white jurors considering the case when the weak evidence was presented. However, in the strong evidence case, black jurors (M = 23.18)

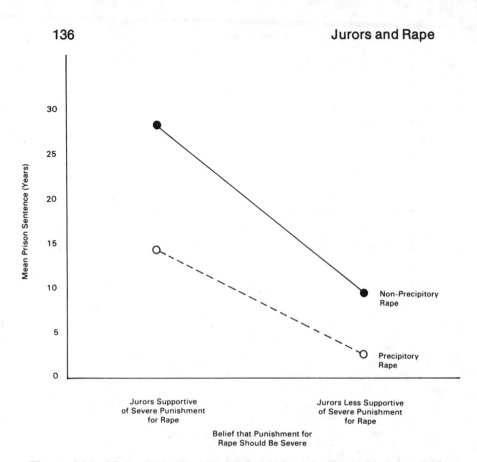

Figure 4-16. Mean Juror Recommended Prison Sentence for Rape Defendants as a Function of the Type of Rape and Jurors' Belief
that Punishment for Rape Should Be Severe

consistently gave a longer sentence than white jurors (M = 17.20) to the
defendant.

A second significant interaction with strength of evidence involved the
jurors' belief concerning woman's responsibility in preventing rape (figure
4-19). For those jurors who believed women are responsible in rape prevention, defendants in strong and weak cases were treated no differently; the
defendants generally received lenient sentences. From a contrasting point of
view, jurors who felt that women are not responsible differed in their
sentences of the defendant in the strong and weak evidence cases. The
defendant in the strong evidence case (M = 25.30) received a longer
sentence ($p < .05$) than the defendant in the weak evidence case (M =
14.32). In the weak evidence case, there was a trend for jurors less supportive of the belief that women are responsible for rape prevention to sentence

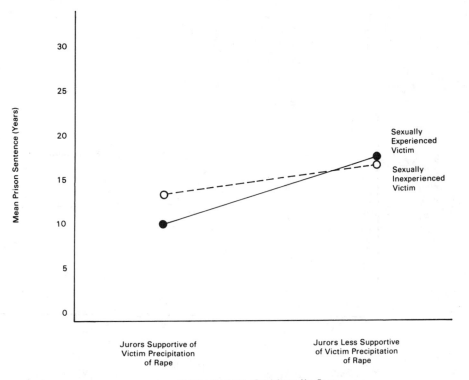

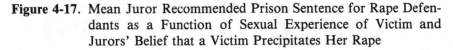

Figure 4-17. Mean Juror Recommended Prison Sentence for Rape Defendants as a Function of Sexual Experience of Victim and Jurors' Belief that a Victim Precipitates Her Rape

the defendant longer than jurors who strongly concurred with the idea; however, the sentencing difference was not significant. For the strong evidence condition, the difference in defendant sentencing was significant, with jurors who did not feel women should be responsible for rape prevention ($M = 25.30$) giving longer sentences ($p < .05$) than those supportive of this view ($M = 10.51$).

Finally, the jurors' beliefs concerning severe punishment for rape also proved to interact with the strength of evidence presented in the case. An examination of figure 4-20 indicates that jurors believing in severe punishment for rape were more punitive toward the defendant in a case where a significant amount of evidence was present ($M = 29.29$) than where the evidence presented was weak ($M = 17.19$). Conversely, when the jurors did not hold very strong beliefs regarding severe punishment, they were inclined to treat the defendants in the strong and weak evidence cases quite similarly.

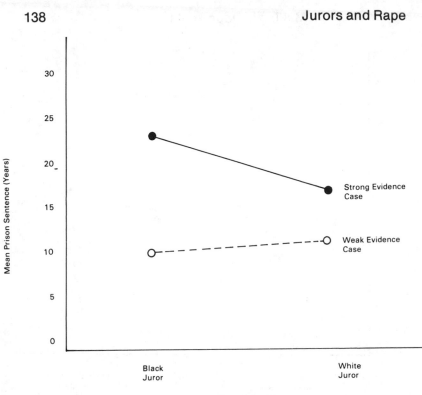

Figure 4-18. Mean Juror Recommended Prison Sentence for Rape Defendants as a Function of Strength of Evidence in the Case and Race of Jurors

Discussion of the Results

Previous research has been conducted on the factors thought to influence verdicts in rape trials, but only a few investigations have examined the effects of juror characteristics. Yet even in these few studies, the treatment of juror characteristics has only been cursory, chiefly focusing on only one or two juror background variables *independently* from other case characteristics. As evidenced here, *combinations* of juror and case characteristics are important considerations in studying or predicting juror decisions in rape trials.

The previous chapter emphasized that the attitudes of jurors toward rape are likely to be an important determinant of rape trial outcomes. Several significant correlations in our data point to their importance. However, due to the correlational nature of our research, we cannot conclude that jurors' attitudes toward rape definitely affect their decisions in a rape trial. The significant relationships between several attitudinal variables and

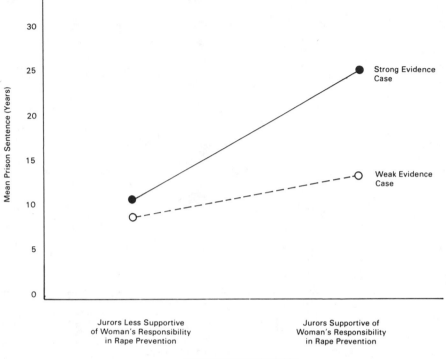

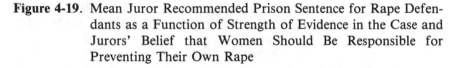

Figure 4-19. Mean Juror Recommended Prison Sentence for Rape Defendants as a Function of Strength of Evidence in the Case and Jurors' Belief that Women Should Be Responsible for Preventing Their Own Rape

defendant sentencing, however, suggest that these variables may influence jurors' decisions. Further, these correlations indicate that they may be used to predict juror decision making and, as such, may be employed by prosecuting or defense attorneys during voir dire.

The American jury system has long been an essential part of our judicial and legal institutions and yet the source of much controversy and debate. A significant amount of the controversy has centered around jurors' abilities to render fair and equitable decisions. Many legal scholars and researchers (Efran 1975; Kalven and Zeisel 1966) have argued that variables extraneous to the trial proceedings affect jurors' judgments and create what some have labeled as *the thirteenth juror*. The results reported in this study confirmed what many writers and researchers studying rape have suggested: extra-evidential factors were found to influence the outcome of the rape trials.

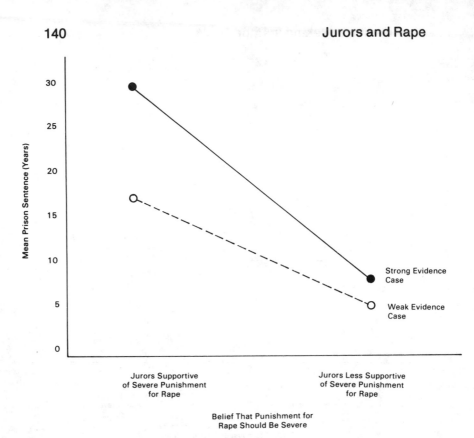

Figure 4-20. Mean Juror Recommended Prison Sentence for Rape Defendants as a Function of Strength of Evidence in the Case and
Jurors' Belief that Punishment for Rape Should Be Severe

Obviously, the law makes no distinction among rape defendants or victims based on their personal characteristics or other such variables, but our
legal system seems to be composed of some juries doing just that (Kalven
and Zeisel 1966). Knowledge of the variables affecting jurors' judgment in
rape trials is of extreme importance to our system of justice, especially today when even the principle of a trial by jury is coming into question. With
further research into the interactions between juror, victim, defendant, and
rape case characteristics and their effects on jury deliberations, significant
steps, such as through the use of scientific jury selection methods (Kairys,
Schulman, and Harring 1975), may be taken to ensure a fair trial. Only with
such research will meaning of a "trial by one's peers" take on a more
precise and meaningful definition.

Judging from the data reported in this chapter, modifications are
needed in our legal and criminal justice system as they apply to rape. Some

of these needed changes are proposed in subsequent chapters. The following chapter in part II focuses on the nature of these changes as they apply to state laws and statutes concerning rape.

Summary

Rape laws and their application in the courts have been a continuing source of controversy among legal scholars concerned with the equal protection of rape defendants and victims under the law. Recently, many writers have argued that equal protection for victims is not presently offered in the courts since the outcomes of rape trials are frequently influenced by factors other than the evidence. This chapter summarized the results of the research which was designed to assess the effects of selected extra-evidential factors (such as race of the defendant, race of the victim, sexual experience of the victim, type of rape committed, and physical attractiveness of the victim) on jurors' verdicts in rape trials.

Using simulated legal rape cases and various psychological measures, data were obtained from 1,056 citizens serving as jurors in the rape cases. These data were then used to answer the following research questions.

1. Do defendant, victim, and rape case characteristics, singly or in combination, have any effect on jurors' verdicts in rape trials?
2. Are jurors' attitudes toward rape and toward women as well as selected background characteristics predictive of their decisions in such trials?
3. Do characteristics of jurors seem to combine in unique ways with defendant, victim, and rape case characteristics to influence jurors' verdicts?

The analyses of the defendant, victim, and rape case characteristics revealed that the extra-evidential factors had discriminatory effects on the jurors' decisions. Not only were the decisions a function of who was the assailant, but they were also influenced by who the victim was as well as by how she was assaulted.

In general, the black offender was treated more harshly than the white one, while the assailant of the black woman was given a more lenient sentence than the white woman's assailant. When the victim was judged to have contributed to or precipitated the rape, the jurors were inclined to be lenient. Results also showed that combinations of the extra-evidential factors affected the jurors' decisions. More specifically, the following major effects of the variable combinations were found.

1. The jurors treated black and white offenders no differently when the black woman was raped; however, when the victim was white, the black defendant was given a longer prison sentence.

2. If the rape victim was physically unattractive, her race had no influence on the sentencing of the black defendant. When the woman was attractive, the black offender of the white woman was treated more severely than if he had attacked a black woman.

3. There were no racial differences in defendant sentencing for the sexually experienced victim regardless of her attractiveness. However, if the victim was sexually inexperienced and unattractive, the black rapist was given a longer sentence than the white one.

4. Behavior on the part of the victim which was interpreted by the jurors as being precipitory resulted in a more lenient sentence for the defendant than if the behavior was seen as being nonprecipitory.

5. When a precipitory rape had occurred, the jurors were not influenced by the strength of evidence in the case. Conversely, in the nonprecipitory case, the presence of strong evidence resulted in the jurors giving a harsher sentence than if only weak evidence was evident.

Correlations between juror characteristics and juror verdicts indicated that it was possible to predict juror decisions in rape trials. For blacks, the background characteristics of years of education and previous service on a jury were found to be related. In addition, their beliefs concerning woman's responsibility in rape prevention, sex as motivation for rape, and severity of punishment for rape also predicted their decision. Age, years of education, and beliefs concerning woman's responsibility in rape prevention, severity of punishment for rape, victim precipitation of rape, and the normality of rapists were predictors of white jurors' verdicts. Although background data have traditionally been used by laweyers to predict jurors' sentiments toward sentencing, attitudes toward rape were shown to be better predictors of defendant sentencing than background characteristics.

Further analyses of the interactions among juror characteristics and defendant, victim, as well as rape case characteristics also revealed some interesting findings. These major findings regarding the interactions of juror characteristics included the following.

1. Assailants of attractive women were given harsher sentences than assailants of unattractive women by jurors with the following characteristics: jurors who did not believe that women should be responsible for preventing rape; jurors 30 years of age or older; and jurors who believed that rape is caused by a desire for power over women.

2. Jurors were inclined to treat a defendant of the race opposite to themselves more severely than one of the same race.

3. Jurors who had personally known a woman who had been raped gave a longer sentence to the black defendant as well as the assailant of the white victim than did people without such knowledge.

4. Jurors who strongly supported severe punishment for rape sentenced defendants in both precipitory and nonprecipitory rape cases to longer sen-

tences than those without such beliefs. Similarly, individuals supportive of severe punishment for rape were likely to discriminate in defendant sentencing by giving the black defendant a longer sentence than the white one.

5. Jurors who did not strongly believe that women precipitate rape gave a significantly longer sentence to an offender of a sexually experienced woman than jurors who strongly felt that women cause rape.

Notes

1. Hibey (1973) noted that by law, many jurisdictions do *not* require corroborated testimony of the victim. However, in actual cases, proof of rape may only be obtained when victim testimony is supported by other evidence.

2. *M* refers to the mean prison sentence in years recommended by a specific group of jurors.

3. The degrees of freedom used for testing the significance of the correlations were as follows: *df* for black jurors = 158; *df* for white jurors = 894.

4. Where continuous variables were involved (such as age of the jurors), median scores were calculated in order to form a dichotomous variable consisting of a high and a low group. This dichotomous variable was then used in the subsequent analyses.

References

Adler, F. Socioeconomic factors influencing jury verdicts. *New York University Review of Law and Social Change* 3 (1973):1-10.

Archer, R., and Aderman, D. Empathy in the courtroom: The effect of an emotional appeal on the judgments of simulated jurors. Duke University, 1974.

Austin, W.; Walster, E.; and Utne, M. Equity and the law: The effect of a harmdoer's "suffering in the act" on liking and assigned punishment. In L. Berkowitz and E. Walster, eds., *Advances in experimental social psychology*. New York: Academic Press, 1976.

Barber, R. Judge and jury attitudes to rape. *Australian and New Zealand Journal of Criminology* 7 (1974):157-172.

Barnett, N., and Feild, H. Character of the defendant and defendant sentencing in rape and burglary crimes. *Journal of Social Psychology*, in press.

Becker, T.; Hildum, D.; and Bateman, K. The influence of jurors' values on their verdicts: A court and politics experiment. *Southwestern Social Science Quarterly* 45 (1965):130-140.

Berg, K., and Vidmar, N. Authoritarianism and recall of evidence about criminal behavior. *Journal of Research in Personality* 9 (1975):147-157.

Blitman, N., and Green, R. Inez Garcia on trial. *Ms.* 3 (1975):49-88.

Boehm, V. Mr. Prejudice, miss sympathy and the authoritarian personality: An application of psychological measuring techniques to the problem of jury bias. *Wisconsin Law Review* 10 (1968):734-750.

Bohmer, C., and Blumberg, A. Twice traumatized: The rape victim and the court. *Judicature* 58 (1975):390-399.

Bray, R. Decision rules, attitude similarity, and jury decision making. Doctoral diss., University of Illinois, 1974.

———— . The mock trial: Problems and prospects for jury research. Paper presented at the American Psychological Association, Washington, D.C., September 1976.

Brooks, W.; Doob, A.; and Kirshenbaum, H. Character of the victim in the trial of a case of rape. University of Toronto, 1975.

Brownmiller, S. *Against our will: Men, women, and rape.* New York: Simon and Schuster, 1975.

Bullock, H. Significance of the racial factor in the length of prison sentences. *The Journal of Criminal Law, Criminology, and Police Science* 52 (1961):411-417.

Byrne, D. *The attraction paradigm.* New York: Academic Press, 1971.

Byrne, D., and Clore, G. A reinforcement model of evaluative responses. *Personality: An International Journal* 1 (1970):103-128.

Byrne, D.; Erwin, C.; and Lamberth, J. Continuity between the experimental study of attraction and real life computer dating. *Journal of Personality and Social Psychology* 16 (1970):157-165.

Calder, B.; Insko, D.; and Yandell, B. The relation of cognitive and memorial processes to persuasion in a simulated jury trial. *Journal of Applied Social Psychology* 4 (1974):62-93.

Calhoun, L.; Selby, J.; and Warring, L. Social perception of the victim's causal role in rape: An exploratory examination of four factors. *Human Relations* 29 (1965):517-526.

Cann, A.; Calhoun, L.; and Selby, J. Sexual experience as a factor in reactions to rape victims. Paper presented at the American Psychological Association, San Francisco, August 1977.

Centers, R.; Shomer, R.; and Rodrigues, A. A field experiment in interpersonal persuasion using authoritative influence. *Journal of Personality* 38 (1970):392-402.

Chappell, D. Forcible rape: A national survey of the responses by prosecutors (research report). Seattle: Battelle Human Affairs Research Center, Law and Justice Study Center, 1977.

Child, B. Ohio's new rape law: Does it protect complainant at the expense of the rights of the accused? *Akron Law Review* 9 (1975):337-359.

Cohen, J. Multiple regression as a general data analytic system. *Psychological Bulletin* 70 (1968):426-442.

Criminal victimization in the United States. Law Enforcement Assistance Administration, Department of Justice. Washington: U.S. Government Printing Office, 1977.

Crosson, R. An investigation into certain personality variables among capital trial jurors. *Dissertation Abstracts* 27 (1967):3668B-3669B.

Curtis, L. Victim precipitation and violent crime. *Social Problems* 21 (1974):594-605.

D'Agostino, L., and Brown, J. Loaded for acquittal? Psychiatry in the jury selection process. *UWLA Law Review* 7 (1975):199-212.

Davis, J.; Bray, R.; and Holt, R. The empirical study of social decision processes in juries. In J. Tapp and F. Levine eds., *Law, justice, and the individual in society: Psychological and legal issues*. New York: Holt, Rinehart, & Winston, 1977.

Davis, J.; Kerr, N.; Atkin, R.; Holt, R.; and Meek, D. The decision processes of 6- and 12-person mock juries assigned unanimous and two-thirds majority rules. *Journal of Personality and Social Psychology* 32 (1975):1-14.

Dodson, M. People v. Rincon-Pineda: Rape trials depart the seventeenth century—farewell to Lord Hale. *Tulsa Law Journal* 11 (1975):279-290.

Doob, A., and Kirshenbaum, H. Some empirical evidence on the effect of S.12 of the Canada Evidence Act upon an accused. *Criminal Law Quarterly* 15 (1972):88-95.

Dowdell, M.; Gillen, M.; and Miller, A. Integration and attribution theories as predictors of sentencing by a simulated jury. *Personality and Social Psychology Bulletin* 1 (1974):270-272.

East, M. The effects of the sex of the defendant, the sex of the subject-juror, and the family status of the defendant on judicial decision. Master's thesis, Purdue University, 1972.

Efran, M. The effect of physical appearance on the judgment of guilt, interpersonal attraction, and severity of recommended punishment in a simulated jury task. *Journal of Research in Personality* 8 (1975):45-54.

Eisenbud, F. Limitations on the right to introduce evidence pertaining to the prior sexual history of the complaining witness in cases of forcible rape: Reflection of reality or denial of due process? *Hofstra Law Review* 3 (1975):403-426.

Feldman-Summers, S., and Linder, K. Perceptions of victims and defendants in criminal assault cases. *Criminal Justice and Behavior* 3 (1976):135-149.

Fishman, L., and Izzett, R. The influence of a defendant's attractiveness and justification for his act on sentencing tendencies of subject-jurors. Paper presented at the Midwestern Psychological Association, Chicago, 1974.

Frederick, J., and Luginbuhl, J. The accused rapist: Influence of penalty options and respectability. Paper presented at the American Psychological Association, Washington, D.C., 1976.

Gager, N., and Schurr, C. *Sexual assault: Confronting rape in America.* New York: Grossett and Dunlap, 1976.

Galton, E. Police processing of rape complaints: A case study. *American Journal of Criminal Law* 4 (1976):15-30.

Gerbasi, K., and Zuckerman, M. An experimental investigation of jury biasing factors. Paper presented at the Eastern Psychological Association, New York, 1975.

Gerbasi, K.; Zuckerman, M.; and Reis, H. Justice needs a new blindfold: A review of mock jury research. *Psychological Bulletin* 84 (1977):323-345.

Gordon, R. A study in forensic psychology: Petit jury verdicts as a function of the number of jury members. Doctoral diss., University of Oklahoma, 1968.

Gordon, R., and Jacobs, P. Forensic psychology: Perception of guilt and income. *Perpetual and Motor Skills* 28 (1969):143-146.

Green, E. The reasonable man: Legal fiction or psychosocial reality? *Law and Society Review* 2 (1967):241-257.

Greenbaum, A. Judge's nonverbal behavior in jury trials: A threat to judicial impartiality. *Virginia Law Review* 61 (1975):1266-1298.

Griffin, S. Rape: The all-American crime. *Ramparts* 10 (1971):26, 35.

Griffit, W., and Jackson, T. Simulated jury decisions: The influence of jury-defendant attitude similarity-dissimilarity. *Social Behavior and Personality* 1 (1973):1-7.

Hale, M. *History of the pleas of the Crown.* Philadelphia: R.H. Small, 1847.

Hans, V., and Doob, A. S.12 of the Canada Evidence Act and the deliberations of simulated juries. *Criminal Law Quarterly* 18 (1976):235-253.

Harrington, D., and Dempsey, J. Psychological factors in jury selection. *Tennessee Law Review* 37 (1969):173-178.

Harris L. Toward a consent standard in the law of rape. *University of Chicago Law Review* 43 (1976):613-645.

Hermann, P. Occupations of jurors as an influence on their verdicts. *Forum* 5 (1970):150-155.

Hibey, R.A. The trial of a rape case: An advocate's analysis of corroboration, consent, and character. *The American Criminal Law Review* 11 (1973):309-333.

Hoiberg, B., and Stires, L. Effects of pretrial publicity and juror traits on the guilt attributions of simulted jurors. *Journal of Applied Social Psychology* 3 (1973):267-275.

Howard, J. Racial discrimination in sentencing. *Judicature* 59 (1975): 121-125.

If she consented once, she consented again—a legal fallacy in forcible rape cases. *Valparaiso University Law Review* 10 (1976):127-167.

Izzett, R., and Leginski, W. Group discussion and the influence of defendant characteristics in a simulated jury setting. *Journal of Social Psychology*, in press.

Jones, C., and Aronson, E. Attribution of fault to a rape victim as a function of respectability of the victim. *Journal of Personality and Social Psychology* 26 (1973):415-419.

Jurow, G. New data on the effect of a death-qualified jury on the guilt determination process. *Harvard Law Review* 84 (1971):567-611.

Kairys, D.; Schulman, J.; and Harring, S., ed. *The jury system: New methods for reducing jury prejudice.* Philadelphia: National Jury Project, 1975.

Kalven, H., and Zeisel, H. *The American jury.* Boston: Little, Brown, 1966.

Kaplan, M., and Kemmerick, G. Juror judgment as information integration: Combining evidential and nonevidential information. *Journal of Personality and Social Psychology* 30 (1974):492-499.

Kaplan, K., and Simon, R. Latitude and severity of sentencing options, race of the victim and decisions of simulated jurors: Some issues arising from the Algiers Motel Trial. *Law and Society Review* 7 (1972):87-98.

Kerr, N.; Atkin, R.; Stasser, G.; Meek, D.; Holt, R.; and Davis, J. Guilt beyond a reasonable doubt: Effects of concept definition and assigned decision rule on the judgments of mock jurors. *Journal of Personality and Social Psychology*, in press.

Kirby, D., and Lamberth, J. The lawyer's dilemma: The behavior of authoritarian jurors. Paper presented at the Midwestern Psychological Association, 1974.

Kline, F., and Jess, P. Prejudicial publicity: Its effects on law school mock juries. *Journalism Quarterly* 43 (1966):113-116.

Landy, D., and Aronson, E. The influence of the character of the criminal and his victim on the decisions of simulated jurors. *Journal of Experimental Social Psychology* 5 (1969):141-152.

Larntz, K. Reanalysis of Vidmar's data on the effects of decision alternatives on verdicts of simulated jurors. *Journal of Personality and Social Psychology* 31 (1975):123-125.

Laughlin E., and Izzett, R. Deliberation and sentencing by attitudinally homogeneous juries. Paper presented at the Midwestern Psychological Association, Chicago, 1973.

Lawson, R. Order of presentation as a factor in jury persuasion. *Kentucky Law Journal* 53 (1968):523-555.

LeGrand, C. Rape and rape laws: Sexism in society and law. *California Law Review* 61 (1973):919-941.

Lenner, M. The desire for justice and reactions to victims. In J. Macaulay and L. Berkowitz, eds., *Altruism and helping behavior*. New York: Academic Press, 1970.

Lind, E., and O'Barr, W. The social significance of speech in the courtroom. Duke University, 1977.

Luginbuhl, D. Repeal of the corroboration requirement: Will it tip the scales of justice? *Drake Law Review* 24 (1975):669-682.

Luginbuhl, J., and Mullin, C. Rape and responsibility: Attribution to the victim's character, behavior, and to chance. Paper presented at the Southeastern Psychological Association, Atlanta, March 1975.

Mathiasen, S. The rape victim: A victim of society and the law. *Willamette Law Journal* 11 (1974):36-55.

Medea, A., and Thompson, K. *Against rape*. New York: Farrar, Straus, Giroux, 1974.

Mitchell, H., and Byrne, D. Minimizing the influence of irrelevant factors in the courtroom: The defendant's character, judge's instructions, and authoritarianism. Paper presented at the Midwestern Psychological Association, Cleveland, 1972.

_____ . The defendant's dilemma: Effects of jurors' attitudes and authoritarianism on judicial decisions. *Journal of Personality and Social Psychology* 25 (1973):123-129.

National prisoner statistics, Bulletin no. 46, Capital punishment. Department of Justice. Washington: U.S. Government Printing Office, August 1971.

Nemeth, C., and Sosis, R. A simulated jury study: Characteristics of defendant and the jurors. *Journal of Social Psychology* 90 (1973):221-229.

Padawer-Singer, A., and Barton, A. The impact of pretrial publicity on jurors' verdicts. In R. Simon, ed., *The jury system in America*. Beverly Hills: Sage, 1975.

Partington, D. The incidence of the death penalty for rape in Virginia. *Washington and Lee Law Review* 22 (1965):50-53.

Phares, E., and Wilson, K. Responsibility attribution: Role of outcome-severity, situational ambiguity, and internal-external control. *Journal of Personality* 40 (1972):392-406.

Rape: Does justice turn its head? *Los Angeles Times*, March 12, 1972, E1.

Reed, J. Jury deliberations, voting, and verdict trends. *Southwest Social Science Quarterly* 45 (1965):361-370.

Reynolds, D., and Sanders, M. Effects of defendant attractiveness, age, and injury on severity of sentence given by simulated jurors. *Journal of Social Psychology* 92 (1975):149-150.

Richey, M., and Fichter, J. Sex differences in moralism and punitiveness. *Psychonomic Science* 16 (1969):185-186.

Rose, A., and Prell, A. Does the punishment fit the crime? A study in social valuation. *American Journal of Sociology* 61 (1955):244-259.

Schulman, J.; Shaver, P.; Colman, R.; Emrich, B.; and Christie, R. Recipe for a jury. *Psychology Today* (May 1973):37-44, 77-84.

Scroggs, J. Penalties for rape as a function of victim provocativeness, damage, and resistance. *Journal of Applied Social Psychology* 6 (1976): 360-368.

Sealy, A., and Cornish, W. Jurors and their verdicts. *Modern Law Review* 36 (1973):496-508.

Sears, D., and Freedman, J. Effects of expected familiarity with arguments upon opinion change and selective exposure. *Journal of Personality and Social Psychology* 2 (1965):420-426.

Selby, J.; Calhoun, L.; and Brock, T. Sex differences in the social perception of rape victims. *Personality and Social Psychology Bulletin*, in press.

Sigall, H., and Landy, D. Effects of a defendant's character and suffering on juridic judgment: A replication and clarification. University of Maryland, 1972.

Sigall, H., and Ostrove, N. Beautiful but dangerous: Effects of offender attractiveness and nature of the crime on juridic judgment. *Journal of Personality and Social Psychology* 31 (1975):410-414.

Simon, R. *The jury and the defense of insanity*. Boston: Little, Brown, 1967.

————. The effects of newpapers on the verdicts of potential jurors. In R. Simon, ed., *The Sociology of Law*. San Francisco: Chandler, 1968.

Sosis, R. Internal-external control and the perception of responsibility of another for an accident. *Journal of Personality and Social Psychology* 30 (1974):393-399.

Stephen, C. Selective characteristics of jurors and litigants: Their influences on juries' verdicts. In R. Simon, ed., *The jury system in America*. Beverly Hills: Sage, 1975.

Stone, V. A primacy effect in decision making by jurors. *The Journal of Communication* 19 (1969):239-247.

Sue, S.; Smith, R.; and Caldwell, C. Effects of inadmissible evidence on the decisions of simulated jurors: A moral dilemma. *Journal of Applied Social Psychology*, in press.

Sue, S.; Smith, R.; and Gilbert, R. Biasing effects of pretrial publicity on judicial decision. University of Washington, cited in *Psychology Today* (May 1974):86-90.

Thibaut, J.; Walker, L.; and Lind, E. Adversary presentation and bias in legal decision making. *Harvard Law Review* 86 (1972):386-401.

Uniform Crime Reports for the United States. Federal Bureau of Investigation, Department of Justice. Washington: U.S. Government Printing Office, 1975.

Van Dyke, J. *Jury selection procedures*. Cambridge: Ballinger Publishing Company, 1977.

Vidmar, N. Effects of decision alternatives on the verdict and social perceptions of simulated jurors. *Journal of Personality and Social Psychology* 22 (1972):211-218.

Vines, N., and Jacobs, M. Studies in judicial politics. *Tulane Studies in Political Science* 8 (1963):77-98.

Walker, L.; Thibaut, J.; and Andreoli, V. Order of presentation at trial. *Yale Law Journal* 82 (1972):216-266.

Washburn, R. Rape law: The need for reform. *New Mexico Law Review* 5 (1975):279-309.

Wolfgang, M., and Cohen, B. *Crime and rape*. New York: Institute of Human Relations Press, 1976.

Wolfgang, M., and Riedel, M. Race and the death penalty. *Annals of the Academy of Political and Social Science* 407 (1973):119-133.

Wood, P. The victim in a forcible rape case: A feminist view. *The American Criminal Law Review* 11 (1973):335-354.

Zuckerman, M., and Gerbasi, K. Belief in a just world and derogation of victims. University of Rochester, 1973.

Part II
Rape Laws: The Accomplishments of Legislative Reform

Recent Developments in Rape Reform Legislation

Introduction

By 1980, almost every state will have passed some form of rape reform legislation.[1] As of 1979, only a few states had not made some substantive or procedural amendments to their rape laws. Rape reform legislation has usually been lobbied through state legislatures by a coalition of feminists and law and order groups. The articulated purpose of the new laws is to increase the number of rape convictions and ensure that the interests of victims are respected in the criminal justice process. The passage of new laws, the reform process, and the socialization efforts directed at professionals, educators, and police has generated an enormous literature.[2] This literature and public and popular discussion of the issues has increased pressure for further reform. As the pressure to enact rape reform legislation becomes cumulative and as an increasing number of states adopt rape reform legislation, there is a greater likelihood of additional states following suit.

Rape reform legislation is still controversial. It does not sail through the state legislative bodies without a considerable lobbying effort.[3] Legislators are still overwhelmingly male, and the legislative committees where the amending process takes place are often if not always exclusively composed of older conservative men.[4] In comparison to the slow progress in the passage of rape reform legislation note the number of states which in 1978 passed legislation regarding the pornographic exploitation of children.[5] Most of these statutes were adopted after highly publicized congressional hearings were held on the subject of pornographic exploitation of children. Model legislation was drafted at the federal level, and many state legislatures adopted statutes modeled on the federal legislation without serious opposition. The states enacted statutes simply in response to publicity and activity at the federal level. Rape reform legislation, on the other hand, has been a grass-roots lobbying effort in the state legislatures, with varying degrees of national coordination from the NOW National Task Force on Rape. Local women have made it their business to become familiar with the voting records of the state legislators in their districts, and the lobbying effort has been similar to lobbying efforts conducted by special-interest groups in other areas. Feminists sought support from traditional political organizations such as the League of Women Voters and the American Civil Liberties Union. The support and presence of such groups was probably critical to success. In every state which has passed rape reform legislation, the particular compromise and agreements between legislators and lobbyists reflect the balance between the political pressure exerted by reformers and the legislature's perceptions of the popularity or desirability of reform. In some states, reform efforts were demonstrably more successful.[6] In spite of the variety of new statutes, however, certain national trends are discernible.

National Trends in Rape Reform Legislation

During the 1976, 1977, and 1978 legislative sessions, an enormous amount of legislation affecting rape has been passed at the state level.[7] Thirty-three states have amended their rape statutes or the laws governing sex offenses in the period.[8] Some states have only passed technical amendments or made minor changes.[9] Many states have entirely rewritten their laws governing rape.[10]

Trends visible in 1976 continued. The Michigan Sexual Conduct Statute enacted in 1975[11] continued to be the model for reform in a number of states. Most states, however, did not follow Michigan in adopting a rape evidence statute which totally precluded the admissibility of evidence regarding the sexual conduct of the victim with third parties.[12] The trend toward the enactment of sex-neutral provisions continued. Also continuing was the trend toward redefining the prohibited conduct as both more than and less than what would have constituted rape under former law. Sexual penetration in reform statutes includes acts other than vaginal intercourse. Most states formerly had rape statutes derived from the English common-law definition of rape as carnal knowledge of a woman by force or against her will. Carnal knowledge was only penile-vaginal intercourse. The emphasis upon "penetration" however, is a carry-over from the traditional definition.

A common pattern in rape reform statutes continued to be the replacement of the single crime of rape, or the two crimes of rape and statutory rape, by a series of graded offenses, including lesser offenses with minor penalties. Many states defined offenses in terms of degrees in order to establish gradations of penalties for various prohibited acts.[13] Some states, however, preferred to accomplish a similar result by defining aggravating circumstances.[14] Redefinition of the offense in specific terms remained a primary reform objective. Defining the offense in terms of objective circumstances was intended to move the focus of trial away from the victim's behavior and character. This goal is unlikely to be achieved by any redefinition of the offense or by any mere change in statutory language.

Rape reform statutes continued to replace the term *rape* by a reformulation of the offense in terms of sexual assault[15], sexual battery[16], or criminal sexual conduct.[17] Twenty-nine jurisdictions, however, including some which passed reform legislation, continue to define a crime called rape.[18] The District of Columbia does not mention the word rape in the title of the offense.[19] Several states now define rape in a way which would be incompatible with the traditional definition of the offense under British common law.[20] Homosexual assaults, attacks upon male victims, sexual assaults with an object, the inclusion of sexual assaults upon some categories of spouses would all fall outside the traditional common-law definition of rape in England and outside the statutory definitions of rape common in most states prior to 1975.

Since 1976, the American Law Institute's Model Penal Code (MPC) has been adopted in a number of states.[21] This statute has influenced the passage of rape reform legislation in several important ways. First, the impetus toward criminal code reform generally has in some instances helped those lobbying for rape reform legislation.[22] At the same time the comments to the 1962 MPC, which is the version currently in use pending publication of the revised comments, make a series of remarks about the necessity of protecting men from false complaints and the responsibility of women for provoking sexual assaults, which directly contradict the arguments made by feminists lobbying for rape reform legislation.[23] Most of these comments date from the mid-1950s, and they express attitudes which are inappropriate for the 1970s. If the MPC rape provisions had been published without some of the blatantly sexist comments, it might have been more difficult for feminists to argue against the MPC rape statute.[24] Both the epidemic of offenses and recent increases in public awareness generally made it relatively easy to argue against adoption of the MPC formulation of rape in the late 1970s. Many states, including New Jersey, passed comprehensive criminal code reform modeled upon the MPC with sexual assault provisions, or rape provisions, which were drafted independently.[25] Some states, however, did simply adopt the MPC rape statute when they adopted a revised criminal code based upon the MPC.[26]

Several aspects of the MPC rape statute differ significantly from rape reform statutes drafted after 1975. The MPC rape statute does include, however, some provisions, such as the introduction of sex neutrality for minor offenses and the definition of a series of graded offenses, which anticipated the reforms of the 1970s.[27] The statutory corroboration requirement, the mistake as to age provision, the prompt complaint requirement, and the statutory references to sexually promiscuous complainants were provisions in the MPC incompatible with the goals of feminists lobbying for rape reform legislation. Most states, however, which have adopted substantive criminal code reform following to a greater or lesser extent the MPC, have not adopted all these provisions of the MPC.[28] Several states have adopted the MPC formulation of consent[29] and one or another of the MPC definitions of the offense.[30] The MPC remains a significant influence, and those lobbying for rape reform legislation should be familiar with its provisions. In New Jersey serious ambiguities have been created by the incorporation of rape reform legislation within a reform of the substantive criminal law which is primarily based upon the MPC.[31]

New Jersey's rape reform statute offers an instructive example. The designation of the actor and victim is sex-neutral. There are four gradations of offenses, two offenses require sexual penetration, and two are offenses of sexual contact. Certain kinds of sexual activity between adults and children are proscribed. There is a special category of offenses for sexual acts between children and adults in a position of authority. Changes have been enacted regarding spouses. Special provisions have been included to cover victims who are mentally incompetent, mentally incapacitated, or physically helpless. Important changes have been introduced in the law of evidence. The impetus behind reform was to define the offense in terms of circumstances which would render irrelevant the defense of consent in many cases. The purpose was to define conduct of the actor as criminal and to move the judicial inquiry away from a focus upon the victim's prior sexual history or allegedly provocative behavior. In all these respects, the reform effort which took place in New Jersey was typical of that in a number of other states. The following history of the enactment of rape reform legislation in New Jersey is offered as both an example and an admonition to reformers in other states. Although rape reform legislation has been successfully passed in New Jersey after an enormous effort, good reasons exist to question whether the goals of reformers can ever be achieved with the new statute or with any statutory reform unaccompanied by other major changes in the criminal disposition process. The passage of rape reform legislation will not remedy the dislocations and injustices throughout the criminal process. One thing is certain, however. The 1979 New Jersey statute includes some features which provide greater protection for victims than the prior law.

The Legislative History of
Rape Reform Legislation in New Jersey

A detailed history of legislative changes in the law of rape in New Jersey prior to the enactment in 1978 of a rape reform statute to become effective in 1979 can be found in "Rape I."[32] Prior to reform, New Jersey had a carnal knowledge statute which defined three crimes: carnal knowledge of a woman over 16 by force, carnal abuse of a woman-child under 12, and carnal abuse of a woman-child over 12 and under 16.[33] The prior New Jersey law did not mention the word *rape.* There was a separate and special provision of the law addressed carnal knowledge of inmates in homes and institutions.[34] This section of the prior law was declared unconstitutional by a lower court because it totally precluded consenting sexual activity among confined populations.[35] Prior to the 1979 reform New Jersey had no prompt complaint requirement, no statutory corroboration requirement, and no common-law rule requiring Lord Hale's instruction. Carnal abuse was defined as sexual activity which was less than intercourse, and the carnal abuse section served as the statutory rape law. Carnal abuse usually encompassed forcible rape of females aged 12 to 16. Carnal knowledge was defined by case law as sexual intercourse. Common-law principles excluded spouses from prosecution for rape.

Although the New Jersey rape statute had been amended ten times before 1978, the statute in effect prior to the enactment of rape reform legislation was essentially the New Jersey statute enacted in 1796. This statute was derived from an Elizabethan statute of 1576. The ages of victim and offender had been changed, and ancillary provisions regarding drugs and women in institutions were added, but the definition of the offense and the terminology used were essentially the terms from the Elizabethan statute.

In October 1971 the New Jersey Criminal Law Revision Commission issued a Final Report and Commentary on its proposed New Jersey Penal Code.[36] The proposed New Jersey Penal Code followed the American Law Institute's MPC with respect to most substantive offenses, including rape.[37] Under the 1971 proposed New Jersey code, the crime of rape and aggravated rape was defined. Aggravated rape was sexual intercourse with a female other than one's wife when the female was forced to submit by force, threat of imminent death, serious bodily injury, extreme pain, or kidnaping, to be inflicted upon her or any other person. Rape was sexual intercourse in which the female was compelled to submit by any threat that would prevent resistance by a woman of ordinary resolution. The statutory age of consent was 12.[38] Sexual assault was defined as a minor sexual contact offense. The commission statute required corroboration, prompt complaint, excluded spousal rape, and recommended a statutory mistake as to age provision. The statute never became law in New Jersey.

Before the incorporation of rape reform legislation within the New Jersey Penal Code, a number of reform statutes had been unsuccessfully introduced in the legislature. Chapter 14 of the present New Jersey Penal Code was drafted in the spring of 1978 by a coalition of feminist groups with the assistance of the NOW Task Force on Rape. The rape reform statute was introduced into the penal code as a Senate Judiciary Committee amendment to what was essentially the 1971 draft of the penal code. After extensive public hearings in May and June 1978, the Senate Judiciary Committee made a number of important substantive amendments to the 1971 penal code, including the adoption of rape reform legislation within the code. There was public testimony on the issues, the reform statute was rewritten by the committee with important changes in sentencing, and the rape reform statute was reported out with the amended criminal code in June 1978.[39] The assembly reported out the penal code without making major changes in the sex offense chapters in June 1978.

The NOW bill which was adopted by both houses of thelegislature in 1978 without major definitional change was modeled upon the Center for Rape Concern Model Sex Offense Statute originally published in the *Women's Rights Law Reporter* in 1977.[40] The Center for Rape Concern Model statute was in turn based upon selections from statutory provisions in the Michigan Criminal Sexual Conduct law and provisions in the reform statutes passed in New Mexico, Minnesota, and Wisconsin. Prior to the enactment of the New Jersey sexual assault provisions, however, the New Jersey legislature had in 1976 enacted a relatively limited rape evidence statute which introduced restrictions upon the admissibility of evidence regarding the prior sexual conduct of the victim in rape cases.[41] The 1978 statute strengthened these evidence provisions and included further evidence reform within the code.[42] The penal code package was signed into law by the governor on August 10, 1978.[43]

The NOW sexual assault statute radically changed the New Jersey rape law. The crime of rape was replaced with a sex-neutral statute which defined two categories of sexual assault and two categories of criminal sexual contact. The spousal exception was removed; incest and sodomy were no longer designated crimes. The resistance requirement, the presumption of an actor's inability because of age, and the mistake as to age defense were all abolished by statute. Penalties were reduced, and mandatory terms for second offenders were adopted. Statutory rape was redefined, and penalties were removed for consensual sexual activity involving persons over 16. Although the crime of rape was redefined with the policy objective of providing greater protection for victims, the sentencing provisions of the code reduced ordinary terms. Rape formerly carried a maximum of thirty years. The imposition of the maximum term was mandatory if the convicted rapist was determined to be a "compulsive and repetitive" sex offender.[44] Under the code, a first conviction for aggravated sexual assault carries a penalty of from ten to twenty years. The theory behind reducing penalties was that juries would be more likely to convict if the penalties were reduced.

The 1978 version of the reform bill included no reference to consent or to the age of consent as an operative concept. The statute simply defined one category of sexual assault as an act of sexual penetration when the victim was less than 13 years old and the actor was four years older. Since the reform statute was drafted to obviate the need for proof of nonconsent in most circumstances, the concept of an age of consent was meaningless within the context of chapter 14. During the hiatus before the effective date there was an enormous outcry over the reduction of the statutory age to 13. Previously there had been publicity concerning the decriminalization of sodomy, but no amendment was passed recriminalizing consenting homosexual conduct. The outcry concerning the "repeal of the age of consent," as the topic was defined, however, produced sufficient political pressure to force the legislature to amend the age provisions in the package of 1979 amendments to the penal code. The 1979 amendments to the rape reform statute in New Jersey add an offense which is defined as sexual penetration with a victim less than 16. The term *consent* is not used, and after debate the restriction of a four-year age gap between the victim and the actor was removed.[45] An amendment to reintroduce the spousal exception and only exclude spouses who were living apart was narrowly defeated in committee during the amending process in 1979.

What has been insufficiently emphasized in the excitement following the passage of rape reform legislation, after years of failing to get such legislation passed, is that the reform of the rape laws in New Jersey is incorporated in a penal code which makes major substantive changes in the entire criminal justice system. Sentencing procedures are completely changed. Offenses are redefined. The penal code introduces new general principles of liability and justification. The sentencing provisions alone would have introduced enormous changes in the practice of criminal law in the state. It may be difficult to separate out the effect of rape reform legislation from the effect of other systemwide changes in the criminal law introduced by the Code of Criminal Justice. The success of rape reform legislation in New Jersey may well depend upon the success or failure of the implementation of the code as a comprehensive package of criminal reforms. The enactment of rape reform legislation should never be seen as taking place in a vacuum. If reforms are to be successful, they must include a realistic assessment of the existing criminal justice system and anticipate other major changes in the criminal law, such as those now taking place in the area of sentencing.

The Status of Consent under Reform Statutes

The debate continues over the status of consent as a defense in reform statutes. For strategists this is the most important, unresolved issue in the area of rape reform. Usually debate focuses upon two aspects of the question: is it possible to define *consent* in rape reform legislation so that the type of prejudice victim advocates found objectionable will be eliminated, and to what extent do prior common-law traditions regarding consent continue in effect after the enactment of rape reform legislation? There is no conclusive answer to either question, and recently enacted reform statutes indicate widely disparate approaches to the problem of dealing with the issue of consent.

The most basic distinction between reform statutes is whether or not the drafters of reform statutes have elected to use the term *consent* with or without definition. New Jersey, for example, has adopted a rape reform statute which does not use the word consent or refer to the concept of consent. One clear purpose behind the drafting of all reform legislation was the desire to eliminate what victim advocates felt to be a large loophole in the law.[46] Whether by accident or design, common-law consent had come to mean that a woman could consent to sexual intercourse with strangers and acquaintances under circumstances of brutality and degradation. The concept of consent itself focused upon the character of the victim, her previous sexual history, her "propensity to consent," and her reputation for chastity. These aspects of the consent standard in rape led women to charge that victims, not assailants, were on trial in a rape case. Given that the social issues surrounding sexual relations are generally approached with ambivalence, contradiction, and hypocrisy, it is perhaps not surprising that the development of the law of consent in American rape cases is a disreputable chapter in our jurisprudence.[47]

The principal purpose of rape reform legislation was to get rid of the sexist traditions which had grown up around the law of rape through the concept of consent. The question was: how to do it? The practical problems were enormous since as a matter of fact, an act which was done by consenting adults was not criminal, while the same act by the same people under different circumstances was criminal. Almost all reform statutes take a first step of defining prohibited acts in terms of circumstances and objective factors in order to limit the ambiguous and subjective standard of the victim's consent. For example, use of a weapon is a circumstance which *defines* sexual assault of criminal sexual conduct in most reform jurisdictions. The purpose of this provision is to say: when sexual intercourse occurs at knife point or gunpoint, we can conclusively presume the sexual acts were not entered into by choice. Similarly the circumstance of the commission of another crime, for example, a breaking and entering or a robbery, will define sexual intercourse as rape. These circumstances are intended to obviate the state's burden of proving the absence of consent.

The next step is more difficult. Reform statutes try to delineate circumstances which will define criminal sexual conduct in situations which are not as clear cut as those involving the use of a weapon or the commission of a felony. Reform statutes define other circumstances, such as family position or position of institutional authority, as inherently coercive. Some reform statutes adopt the tactic of defining force in specific detail. Again the purpose is to concentrate upon the behavior of the actor, not the victim. The problem with this strategy is the implication that any act or cir-

cumstance not included in that very precise definition is intended to fall outside of the statute. The situation is further complicated by the fact that
many states prior to reform had a common-law resistance requirement
which was similar to the consent standard insofar as it focused the fact-
finder's attention upon the victim's behavior as proof of the absence of consent.

The status of consent as defined in the former appellate case law is ambiguous after the enactment of a rape reform statute whose stated purpose
was to override certain general principles which found expression in the
common law.[48] When the drafters address a statutory section specifically to
overrule a particularly offensive case and that intent is clearly apparent
through the language or recorded legislative history, then that particular
case presumably no longer has precedential effect. Or it has no precedential
effect if the judge is informed that the status of the case has changed. As a
general rule, however, the drafters of legislation are confronting a consent
standard which is articulated in a series of unconnected statements or
remarks in a cluster of state appellate cases. After the passage of reform
legislation, what is the status of these cases? They probably are not "overruled," and a practicing attorney doing legal preparation will not find a
clear-cut indicator of the status of prior case law. The reform statutes clearly intend to overrule a great deal of the prior case law. Do they in fact do
so? An informed victim advocate can make a persuasive argument about
legislative intent, but what if there is no victim advocate to make a special
pleading? How can the statute erase that expression of judicial opinion once
it is enshrined in the printer case law?

A number of reform statutes, most importantly Michigan, have adopted a strategy of defining criminal sexual conduct without using the term
consent or resistance. The Michigan statute does define force and
coercion.[49] This approach has been criticized as allowing the defense of
common-law consent to apply to every section of the law.[50] Whether or not
in fact consent as defined by the prior common law is raised as a defense to
every section of the Michigan statute remains to be seen. Since Michigan
uses the terminology of criminal sexual conduct, it may make the status of
consent in Michigan a unique theoretical problem.

New Jersey has adopted a sexual assault formulation which borrows
heavily from the Michigan conceptualization of the circumstances defining
criminal conduct. The New Jersey statute does not mention consent. Since
New Jersey uses the terminology sexual assault, however, there is an additional implication of nonconsent. Can one consent to an assault? Is not
assault by definition something to which the victim does not consent?[51] On
the other hand, the assault formulation carries with it the tradition that an
assault is not a serious crime which should be punished severely unless permanent physical damage occurs. Absent pregnancy, disease, or serious

bodily injury such as a broken arm, the prosecution in a rape case may be confronted with old assault cases that excuse conduct which did not result in permanent physical impairment.[52]

The second strategy adopted by reformers is a strategy which retains the concept of consent, even if the term rape is removed, and attempts to legislate out those aspects of the consent standard considered to be at the root of the problem[53] The New Jersey sexual assault formulation does not define consent, but a general provision in the code, derived from the MPC, defines consent in the context of criminal prosecutions, including "consent to bodily harm."[54] New Jersey has also incorporated into its sexual assault statute the definition of criminal coercion from the MPC.[55] There is, therefore, no special definition of consent which was drafted to apply to cases of sexual assault, but the definition of coercion was taken from a part of the code which dealt with kidnaping, a different kind of crime. Clearly, these general provisions defining consent apply to the sexual assault sections, and reformers will argue that the general provisions must be interpreted consistently with the intent of chapter 14 to supersede prior law. The general rule is that prior case law which is not directly contradicted by a new statutory provision continues in effect after the enactment of a revised criminal code. New Jesey has an unusual provision which provides for the retention of all common-law defenses.[56] Rape victim advocates will argue that chapter 14 indicates a clear legislative purpose to overrule prior case law on consent. They may be unsuccessful.

An analysis of the development of the law of consent in rape demonstrates the impossibility of separating legal concepts from their social and cultural contexts. The degraded view of women which emerges from some of the case law not only indicates that the jucicial system had no respect or regard for women who were victimized. Women were to be punished and the fact of sexual assault was to be ignored or suppressed. How can the "problems" associated with the consent standard be legislated away when they came about as a consequence of deeply ingrained attitudes toward women's sexuality, independence, and adulthood? Of course, research must be addressed to whether one particular legislative strategy is more effective than another from the point of view of reform advocates, but data collection will never tell us how to challenge the hostility, hatren, and suspicion which are the cause of misogynist rules and statutes. Legislation cannot erase entrenched attitudes. Legislation may bring about some important changes, and its educative function should not be underemphasized. Legislation, however, cannot destroy the social function which the traditional rules performed. As long as large numbers of men and women believe that women are inferior and should be kept in their place through forced submission to sexual acts the law will reflect that view.

Legislative Changes in the Common-Law Spousal Exception

Under English common law, a man could not be guilty of raping his wife. The justification for what was termed either the spousal exception or the spousal exclusion was usually explained in terms of consent.[57] Given the rights of women in marriage, the notion that a woman had the right to deny her husband sexual access to her body would have been inconsistent with social expectations regarding married women which were embodied in the legal institutions of coverture, the laws of inheritance, primogeniture, spousal immunity for torts, and other doctrines which demonstrated that women were considered the physical property of their husbands. Following the English tradition, when state legislatures in the middle- and late-nineteenth century enacted statutes to codify the English common-law definitions of crimes, the spousal exclusion was commonly written into the statutory definition of rape.[58] Some states did not codify the spousal exception, however, and the common-law exception would then simply be adopted by the case law or common law of that state.[59] Prior to the late 1970s every U.S. jurisdiction had the traditional spousal exception for rape. In 1979 almost every state had codified the exception and modified it in a number of important respects.

To understand the changes which have recently taken place in the codification of the spousal exception, it is necessary to understand the form and purpose of the traditional English rule. The English rule was that a husband could not be found guilty of raping his wife because marriage, with the promise to obey, implied the right to sexual intercourse with the wife upon all occasions. The husband was entitled to sexual relations with his wife at any time or under any circumstances. Her personal consent was irrelevant. It was not the notion of the individual woman's subjective feelings on a particular occasion which was important to the English rule. The wife's refusal to have sexual intercourse was grounds for divorce. The English rule was founded upon concepts of women as the property of their husbands, as children were the property of their fathers. The purpose of marriage was procreation; there could be no sexual refusal to a husband. Therefore, notions of resistance by a wife, of the absence of the woman's consent on a particular occasion, notions of force of coercion were all utterly inappropriate to the spousal situation according to the English rule. A failure to understand the ramifications and source of the English rule has caused some confusion when the time has come to redraft spousal provisions within rape reform legislation. The English rule was unconcerned with the concept of consent insofar as that meant the subjective state of mind of an individual woman on a particular occasion. Independent of the spousal exclusion, the concept of consent to rape in American jurisprudence developed to include at least the subjective, personal consent of a woman to intercourse on a specific occasion.

With the introduction of rape reform legislation in the 1970s, the first steps were taken toward rethinking the spousal exception. It was not, however, until the late 1970s, when lobbying on behalf of battered wives became a movement of national importance, that the spousal exception began to undergo significant doctrinal change. MPC in 1973 had introduced some changes in the traditional English rule by expanding the definition of spouses to include all people living together in a consenting relationship and by excluding couples living apart under a decree of judicial separation.[60] The MPC formulation introduced a concept of personal and subjective consent by rephrasing the exclusion in terms of cohabitting members of the opposite sex. This expansion of the definition was consistent with the drafter's fear of fabricated or malicious complaints by women. The notion of expanding the spousal exception to include all cohabiting adults added a new dimension to the concept which was not present when the spousal exception was based upon a concept of wives as property. The MPC was concerned with "false complaints." Substituting a notion of permanent but subjective consent based upon cohabitation for an idea of women as property was, however, a retrogressive step in accord with the contemporaneous development of a repressive body of law concerning the "consent defense." The MPC's focus upon a hypothesized subjective or "actual" female consent as the basis of the exception was consistent with the entire formulation of the MPC which defined rape in terms of "consent" of the victim. From that point of view, however, it was logical to include common-law spouses and excluded spouses who were judicially separated. Before the national movement of reform of the rape laws, some states followed the MPC and defined spouses as persons living together and excluded persons separated by judicial decree. Irrespective of the reasoning, however, it was some small advantage for women to have separated persons removed from the shield of the spousal exception.

The first distinct national trend with respect to the spousal exception was the trend toward expanding the definition to include cohabiting couples and exclude from the definition of spouses couples who were separated or living apart.[61] The MPC limits the definition to couples who are separated pursuant to a judicial decree of separation.[62] Under this definition, if there were no formal or legal separation agreement between husband and wife, the spousal exception would continue to exempt the husband from prosecution even if the couple were living apart but refused to get a divorce for religious reasons. Most states have not adopted this approach but have rather modified the common-law spousal exception to make it inapplicable in the situation where spouses are living apart. Usually the statute is phrased to exclude either those who are legally separated or those living apart.[63] This change is clearly in response to national efforts on behalf of battered women. Public attention has been drawn to the fact that spousal assault is particularly likely to occur when a divorce is pending. Many states simply define spouses or the spousal exclusion to exclude those living apart without a specific definition of living apart.[64] The wife must move out or force her husband out to establish the absence of consent, but this standard at least begins to recognize that even a married woman might not consent to intercourse with her husband under all circumstances. Some states create an affirmative defense that the couple is living together consensually.[65] The advantage of the affirmative defense, or a presumption,[66] is that it can be disproved by contrary evidence if the circumstance should so warrant.

The common-law spousal exception was a complete defense: that is, a total bar to prosecution of a spouse. No matter how brutal the circumstances, it would not be rape if the couple was legally married. A large number of states still retain what is essentially the common-law spousal exclusion,[67] though some states codify it with a statutory formulation which is different from the common-law spousal exception. Three states with common-law rape statutes do not mention the spousal exception, though it is presumably incorporated within the state's common-law definition of rape.[68] Some states have very recently rejected the spousal exception in a piecemeal fashion. They limit the exception to certain crimes and get rid of it for forcible sexual assaults.[69] Another very interesting and relatively recent development is the abolition of the spousal exception where injury to a spouse is sustained.[70] Some states have rewritten their spousal exception to cover situations similar to the notorious English case involving spousal assault.[71]

Logically, the spousal exception has limited currency when rape is redefined as sexual assault or when rape is defined in terms which do not rely on the concept of consent. The adoption of statutes which avoid the concept of consent, however, has not necessarily meant the removal of the spousal exception.[72] Reform which is based upon the redefinition of the offense has at least partly failed when states retain the spousal exclusion. If the crime were in fact newly defined as a subcategory of assault, there would be no need for a spousal exception, just as there is no spousal exception for other assaults. There might be difficulties in getting police to answer complaints or prosecutors to charge, but that is another question. The retention of the spousal exception when rape is no longer the crime is both inconsistent and an indication that the redefinition is merely titular. On the other hand, some states have retained a rape formulation and nonetheless removed the spousal exception for rape. Only a handful of states have totally removed the spousal exception.[73]

The general trend is in the direction of defining the exception not in terms of the legal status of the marriage but in terms of cohabitation implying subjective consent. An immediate question comes to mind with regard to homosexuals in a consensual cohabiting relationship, since many of the new formulations are sex-neutral and would cover homosexual assault. If states continue to redefine rape as sexual assault or criminal sexual conduct, one would hope that legislators would realize that the spousal exception has no relevance to assault. Basically, legislators still confuse rape, an antisocial violent act, with consenting sexual relations between adults. And it is this confusion which keeps the spousal exclusion written into the statutes even when rape itself has been redefined as an assaultive crime.

Changes in Statutory Age Provisions

To understand reform efforts in the area of statutory rape, it is necessary to understand the history and development of statutory rape laws in the United States. Since the time of Elizabeth I, rape statutes have distinguished between the forcible rape of adult women and prohibited sexual relations with female children under a specific age. The statute of Elizabeth I specified 10 as the statutory age. The MPC in 1962 also recommended 10 as the statutory age. When states enacted criminal codes to codify the common law in the eighteenth and nineteenth centuries, formulations of the offense of rape characteristically followed the English law and distinguished between the rape of adult women and sexual relations between adult men and female children below a specified age. Sometimes rape was initially codified as two offenses.[74] Many states adopted 12 as the statutory age instead of 10.[75] Some statutes defined rape and carnal abuse with a child under the age of 10 or 12. Carnal abuse was then defined in the case law or assumed to be sexual activity which was not necessarily sexual intercourse. Proof of penetration was usually required for carnal abuse. As the common-law defense of consent developed in American jurisprudence, the statutory age came to be designated the "age of consent" because proof of force or the absence of consent was not an element of the crime if the female was below the age specified by statute. This was consonant with the original English formulation of carnal abuse. The terminology age of consent became confusing, however, when many states enacted two distinct forms of statutory rape: the traditional formulation prohibiting carnal abuse of children under the age of 10 or 12, and a totally different formulation which prohibited "consenting" sexual intercourse with any female either under the age of 16 or 18 or between the ages of 12 and 16. These statutes were essentially equivalent to the English common-law crime of seduction. This is what is usually referred to as "statutory rape." In the United States of the 1950s and 1960s, these so called statutory rape statutes answered a totally different social concern than the traditional prohibition against carnal abuse of girls under 10 or 12. Their purpose was not the prohibition of sexual exploitation of children or young girls but the prohibition of consenting relations with women under a specified age. Social attitudes on this subject changed dramatically in the first half of this century. The statutory rape laws originally had the purpose of "protecting virginity" and forbidding young women from engaging in sexual relations without the consent of their parents. Social attitudes toward consenting sexual relations with unmarried females under 16 were both ambivalent and hypocritical. Statutory rape laws were enforced infrequently; the penalties were low. The statutes often were used to bring about a "shotgun" marriage to a pregnant teenager who had been forbidden access to contraceptives by statute. When both carnal abuse and statutory rape were included in the same criminal formulation, the law predictably developed with contradictions and confusions. In New Jersey, for example, the former law provided more severe penalties for the forcible rape of an adult woman than for the forcible rape of a girl between 12 and 16. Social norms prohibited severe punishment for men who engaged in consenting relations with young women, but the same norms theoretically approved severe penalties for sexual imposition upon young female children.

Special defenses developed to mitigate the socially unacceptable prohibition against sexual relations with older teenaged girls and then were applied to all categories of forcible rape and the carnal abuse of children. A defense based upon the unchaste character of the prosecuting witness arguably made sense if the purpose of statutory rape law was to protect virginity. The unchaste character of the victim had no relevance to proof of a crime which was defined as a forcible attack. Corroboration rules were justified by reference to the socially unacceptable high penalties for consenting conduct. They were then applied across-the-board to all categories of forcible offenses. Once a defense was established, it came to be put forward in every case where a violation of that statute was alleged. The hypocrisy and confusion created by social attitudes, combined with the increase in constitutional protections for defendants, resulted in a situation in which it was almost impossible to convict for the rape of a young girl. In America the bugaboo of false reports was used to justify the establishment of special defenses and exceptions for forcible rape.

Reformers faced several problems when it came to the redefinition of statutory rape. Feminists generally wanted to legalize consenting or nonforcible relations between teenagers while protecting children of both genders from being preyed upon sexually by adults. For political reasons, legislators often had little sympathy with the goal of decriminalizing consenting relations among teenagers and were strongly in favor of prohibiting children from engaging in sexual relations of any sort. Reformers were not always successful in achieving either gain. Compromises perpetuated a new set of contradictions. In New Jersey the age provisions were amended in 1978 to prohibit sexual penetration with persons under 16 and sexual contact between persons aged 13 to 16 and persons four years older. The reform statute in New Jersey, however, now only provides for the most severe penalty for sexual penetration with a person between 13 and 16 when the actor is related to the victim, has supervisory power over the victim, or stands in loco parentis. In a gang-rape situation involving teenagers between the ages of 13 and 16, the most serious penalties are invoked only if the state proves both the presence of aiders and abettors and either that the actor actually used physical force or coercion or the victim was physically helpless or mentally defective or incapacitated. The threat of force or the mere presence of a gang and restricted surroundings is not sufficient for a conviction for aggravated sexual assault. The statute as passed provides the same penalty for a gang-rape situation in which it was not possible to prove the actual use of physical force, as opposed to the threat of force, as it does for consenting relations between two 15-year-olds. On the other hand, the amended age provisions which were passed in response to political pressures provide relatively serious penalties (three to five years) for a sexual contact offense between a person aged 13 to 16 and a person four years older. Sexual contact can even be the actor touching himself in the view of the victim. Nor did the reform statutes always remove what were sometimes regarded as abuses under the prior law. Legislators who made no objection to a radical redefinition of the offense would not vote for the repeal of a statutory age of consent.

The term *age of consent* referred to the fact that under both formulations of statutory rape consent of the victim was no defense. Force was not an element of the crime of statutory rape. The crime was defined as sexual intercourse or sexual activity with all females under a certain age.[76] The age of consent was usually set at 16, though in some states it was as low as 12 and in other states, as high as 18.

Given that the age provisions in most statutes encompassed situations in which the society in fact tolerated a wide range of consenting heterosexual behavior, including sexual intercourse with under-age females, special defenses to statutory rape developed to circumvent the inclusiveness of the definition of the crime. The two most noteworthy special defenses which developed were the mistake as to age defense, and a special defense to statutory rape predicated upon the prior sexual history of the complainant. The latter defense was based upon the fact that a number of statutory rape statutes specifically made reference to ''chaste'' females, or unmarried females, or females of virtuous character.[77] The mistake as to age defense developed under traditional mistake theory[78] as a rule of reasonableness to excuse defendants in situations where the girl was very close to the statutory age.

The classic case from the defense point of view is *People* v. *Hernandez*[79] in which the statutory age was 18 and a young woman who was a few months under 18 was living with the defendant in a consenting relationship. In many jurisdictions, however, the mistake as to age provision came to be a standard, or boiler-plate, defense which had little to do with the theory of a reasonable mistake of fact. The mistake as to age provisions came to be another "special excuse" for statutory rape.[80] Coupled with other sexist provisions and special rules regarding rape, the mistake as to age defense was successfully used to suggest that any female teenager with developed breasts was the seducer. The jury was invited to examine the appearance of the teenaged victim and make an "Alice in Wonderland" determination about whether the defendant could have been mistaken as to whether the victim was above the age of consent. Since the trial often took place months or even over a year after the statutory rape incident, the mistake as to age defense always operated to benefit defendants. Also the mistake as to age defense could be used to introduce evidence that the victim provoked or deserved the attack by being physically developed or wearing excessive makeup or suggestive clothes. The combination of all these factors could not only influence the jury on the question of mistake as to age, but the more subtle suggestion of victim precipitation and social blameworthiness could be set before the jury.

Given the overly inclusive nature of the definition of the crime, statutory rape provisions were also used by parents to force marriages in times when birth control information was not available to teenagers. Since most statutory rape statutes specified unmarried females, marriage of the girl to anyone, but most often to the defendant, was a complete defense. Some states specified in their common law that marriage of the victim to the defendant after the offense was a complete defense to the crime. The statutory rape laws were simply used instead of seduction statutes in these cases, even though many jurisdictions also had a statutory prohibition against seduction.

With the reform of the rape laws, there was general agreement that the entire concept of statutory rape had to be reconsidered. Greater protection was needed for children who were subject to sexual assault. The notion of a blanket proscription for all consenting relations between teenagers seemed unrealistic and an invitation to disregard the law. Nonetheless, twenty-one states have, after reconsideration of the issue, retained a statutory provision which speaks in terms of an age of consent.[81] A number of legislators wanted to keep some prohibition in the penal code in order to announce a moral standard, but few states which reformed their rape laws opted to go back to laws protecting chastity or forcing marriage under threat of criminal prosecution. At the same time, some sort of age provision beyond that needed to protect young people from adults seems to be required under the present norms of our culture. Most states, including those which have adopted reform statutes, have settled upon a two- or three-tiered age structure.[82]

In the majority of reform statutes the age categories were treated in the following manner. Most states which adopted reform legislation inlcuded in the most serious category of offenses an expanded defintion of sexual penetration with a person under a specified age.[83] This crime included homosexual acts and acts by adult females against young boys since the crime had been redefined in sex-neutral terms. This new offense also prohibited ordinary sexual intercourse with females under a specified age. The definition of this crime under the reform statutes covered some segment of what was formerly covered under statutory rape, though usually the age defined for the former statutory rape was higher than the age defined as a definitional element of the most serious crime in reform statutes.[84] The offense defined by age under reform statutes usually was lower than the former age of consent, but the reform statutes prohibited a wider variety of acts than the former law. In addition, many reform statutes adopted a second age offense which was defined as acts of sexual contact between persons of certain ages[85] and a third defined offense which prohibited sexual penetration with persons of a higher age under specified circumstances which did not include heterosexual relations between consenting teenagers.[86] In other states, the policy objective of excluding consenting teenagers is achieved by introducing a three- or four-year differential between the ages of the victim and offender.[87] A number of states compromised on the age provisions and retained some of the features of statutory rape, such as a defense based upon the chastity of the victim.[88] Some states also enacted highly unusual statutory provisions in what looks like an attempt to bridge the gap between the goals of reform advocates and the policy objectives of the former law of statutory rape.[89]

Washington is unusual because a statute which incorporated a number of reform features also defined as crime called statutory rape in the first, second, and third degree. The Washington statute includes reform provisions such as the age differential in second-degree statutory rape while retaining some characteristics of the traditional statutory rape law, such as the marriage exclusion. The Washington statute is atypical of reform statutes in that it retains relatively high penalties for statutory rape. It is unusual because it includes an evidence rule which precludes the admission of evidence of the victim's past sexual history on the question of statutory rape. Also unusual is the specific statutory provision eliminating the mistake as to age defense unless the defendant is claiming to rely upon a declaration by the victim. A number of reform states have abolished or limited the mistake as to age defense by statute.[90]

Reform statutes which define the offense in circumstances which make considerations of consent irrelevant usually do not define an age of consent. The concept of an age of consent was related to traditional notions of seduction and statutory rape. The notion of an age of consent has little meaning in a statute which formulates the crime in terms of sexual assault or sexual battery. Some states have adopted the contradictory solution of both defining an age of consent and defining the crime in terms of circumstances which do not depend upon consent.[91]

The ongoing history of legislative changes in the statutory rape laws should be particularly interesting to historians and behavioral scientists. The fact that a number of states retain several features of the prior law is an indication of the continuing authority of traditional conceptions of appropriate female sexual behavior. Statutory rape offers another example of states adopting piecemeal reform. State legislators are ready to accept only some parts of rape reform legislation, even if piecemeal reforms introduce contradictions within the statutory structure. The majority of states which have amended their age provisions in the last three years have revised them in the direction of providing harsher penalties for sexual penetration offenses with very young children while narrowing the concept of what will be prohibited under the offenses which define consenting conduct among older teenagers. The principal age breaks seem to be at 12 or 16, with only a few states retaining a statutory age of 18 for prohibited consenting sexual conduct.

Recent Legislative Developments in the Area of Evidence

In 1976 twenty-two states had adopted some form of a special provision for rape limiting the admissibility of evidence concerning the victim's sexual conduct with persons other than the defendant.[92] As of 1980 more than forty states had passed rape evidence statutes. Ten jurisdictions had no special statutory provision for the admissibility of evidence concerning the prior sexual conduct of the victim in a rape trial.[93] Often evidence statutes are enacted separately from a reform of the substantive law of rape.[94] It is difficult to predict from the nature of the substantive reform whether or not the evidence statute will be strong or weak from the victim's point of view.

The evidence provisions enacted take a variety of forms. Evidence rules such as those incorporated within Michigan's Criminal Sexual Conduct statute totally exclude all evidence of the victim's prior consenting acts with persons other than the defendant.[95] Most states, however, have enacted rules or statutes which simply require a pretrial hearing on relevance before evidence regarding the victim's sexual conduct with persons other than the defendant can be admitted. The form of the evidence statute will depend in part upon whether or not the state had codified evidence rules following the model of the Federal Rules of Evidence.[96] Some states have highly individualized evidence statutes.[97] Some states had special evidence rules for rape cases prior to the national movement for rape reform legislation which began in 1975.[98] Certain states leave the question of what is admissible on the issue of credibility to be determined entirely by case law.

Generally the evidence statutes and rules fall into one of the following categories: (1) statutes which totally exclude the admissibility of evidence regarding the victim's sexual conduct with persons other than the defendant for any purpose; (2) statutes or rules which create a presumption that evidence concerning the victim's prior sexual conduct with third parties is ir-relevant to prove consent, but allow such evidence to come in after the defense makes a showing of relevance; such statutes are ususlly silent as to the admissibility of such evidence on the issue of credibility; and (3) statutes which attempt to limit the admissibility of evidence concerning the prior or present sexual conduct of the victim for purposes of impeachment or credibility. In addition as part of rape reform, a number of states have passed statutes which eliminate special corroboration requirements for rape or for-bid the judge to give special cautionary instructions for rape. Independent of the action of the legislatures, a number of state courts have invalidated special corroboration requirements and special cautionary instructions in rape cases.[99] It might be argued that even without statutes abolishing corrobora-tion requirements this reform would have come about through the case law as changing public attitudes were reflected in the evolution of the common law. Statutes eliminating the cautionary instruction are generally not regarded as a threat to the constitutional rights of defendants to a fair trial. They simply remove a special corroboration requirement in rape cases. They do not limit a defendant's offer of evidence.

The more general rape evidence provisions have no counterpart in the common law, though technically a judge during trial can always order a hear-ing on relevance on any issue where he or she considers the introduction of evidence to be prejudicial. The fact that such hearings have not been called for by judges on their own motion can be attributed to several factors: the reluctance of the judge or the prosecutor to delay adjudication by additional hearings or motions in the absence of a preceived compelling interest; the fact that the prosecutor represents the state and not the victim; the fact that pre-judice would not accrue to the defendant by the introduction of such evidence; and a concern with the constitutional right of the defendant to in-troduce all evidence which might conceivably operate in his favor. The pro-secutor does not want a conviction which will be overturned on appeal. Given these concerns, it is surprising that over forty states have enacted statutes whose purpose is to limit the admissibility of evidence regarding the victim's sexual conduct in a rape case. Most commonly, the evidence provisions limit the admissibility of evidence regarding the victim's prior sexual conduct on the issue of consent by establishing something like a statutory presumption of irrelevance.[100] Some states simply state that in order to introduce evidence regarding the victim's prior sexual conduct with third parties, there must be an in-camera offer of proof and a judicial finding of relevance.[101] The stronger versions of these statutory formulations require that the judge write out the permitted questions.[102] Usually the statutes simply require a hearing or a special judicial finding on the question of relevance.[103] Some states specifically refer to evidence introduced before the jury.[104]

The critical distinctions, however, are between those statutes which only limit the admissibility of evidence on one issue, for example, regarding the victim's prior sexual history on the issue of consent, and those statutes which limit the admissibility of only one form of evidence, for example, evidence of specific instances of conduct. The question then becomes whether or not evidence whose admissibility is limited in one form or for one purpose can be admitted for another purpose or in another form with the same prejudicial effect the statute was designed to prevent. The evaluation of the effectiveness of these statutes will depend in part upon the estimation of the harm caused by the admission of the evidence. If, for example, it is assumed that jurors or judges irrationally excuse defendants when they are confronted with victims whose sexual conduct they disapprove of, then it does not matter whether the evidence regarding prior sexual conduct comes in on the issue of consent, credibility, or to prove the circumstances of the actus res. If, on the other hand, one assumes that jurors make the causal connection between prior sexual activity and the likelihood of consent on a particular occasion, then an evidence provision limited to admissibility on the question of consent is sufficient to protect victims from societal prejudice.

A reasonable position might be that we know so little about what influences jurors that the balance should be struck on the side of excluding such evidence for any purpose unless it can be reliably demonstrated that evidence of prior sexual conduct only influences jurors on the factual issue of consent. It would be unreasonable to expect jurors to be immune to the contradictory and confusing attitudes about sexuality, and particularly female sexuality, which are common in our culture. The fundamental function of a jury is to judge in accordance with social norms and community standards. These necessarily include sexist stereotypes and repressive attitudes toward female sexuality.

No clearly articulated philosophy or policy objective has resulted in the enactment of one type of evidence statute over another. For whatever reasons, state legislatures have only exceptionally passed rape evidence statutes which in any manner limit cross-examination or the admissibility of evidence which can be introduced for impeachment purposes.[105] Some states adopt the tactic of stating that credibility of the victim in a rape case shall be determined in the same manner as in any other criminal case.[106] These provisions may as a practical matter be mere moral pronouncements. The effect of such a blanket provision is unclear since the individual judge can always rule that prior sexual conduct is in this particular instance relevant to the fact of consent or to credibility. Aside from these general categories, there is a wide variety of special provisions in the statutes. Some states have enacted a special exception for evidence concerning prior "false" complaints.[107] The presence of this language in the statutes indicates that the pronouncements of John Henry Wigmore on the subject of false complaints are still influential, in spite of the fact that his position has long been discredited in the medical and psychological literature.[108] One state passed a specific provision to deal with the issue of a reasonable but mistaken belief in consent.[109] Other states passed novel or unusual statutory provisions which seem to have been directed at particular circumstances or cases, or perhaps even in response to the objection of a particular legislator.[110] Some evidence statutes incorporate provisions regarding retroactivity whose validity is questionable in light of recent decisions of the U.S. Supreme Court.[111] The status of statutes which phrase the exclusions in terms of a presumption will also be importantly effected by recent decisions by the U.S. Supreme Court on the constitutional validity of statutory presumptions.[112]

The Effect of Statutory Changes in the Law of Evidence

Although an enormous amount of political effort has gone into lobbying evidence rules through the state legislatures, it is questionable whether or not these new statutes will have a significant effect upon rape trials or public attitudes toward victims.

The rape evidence provisions have been severely criticized in the legal literature.[113] The substance of the criticism is generally that the evidence provisions infringe upon the constitutional right of a defendant to present *any* relevant, exculpatory evidence on his behalf during the fact-finding process. After an initial period of legislation being passed with little comment, the criticism of rape reform legislation in general, and the evidence rules in particular, has significantly increased in the past year. Some commentators have classified the rape evidence statutes from the point of the relative strength of the statutory provisions, an assessment which can only be made with an understanding of the structure of the state's evidence laws. Thus a strong evidence provision, which kept out all references to the victim's prior conduct with third parties on the issue of consent, would be less forceful if there were no limitations on the admissibility of the victim's prior conduct with third parties on the issue of credibility or the propensity to lie. States have been most likely to enact evidence provisions which limit the introduction of evidence regarding the victim's prior sexual conduct with regard to third parties on the issue of consent. States have been very reluctant to limit the admissibility of evidence on the issue of credibility.[114] The strongest possible statute would be a provision which precluded the admission of evidence concerning prior sexual conduct with third parties for *any* purpose: to impeach, to prove consent, to prove propensity to consent, to show mistaken belief in consent, to show the source of pregnancy or disease, or for any other conceivable purpose. No state has taken this position. Most states simply put a procedural obstacle in the way of admitting such evidence. Some of the stronger statutes state that the judge shall write out the questions to be permitted. The effectiveness of these provisions may well depend upon whether or not the defense can get in the identical evidence on another issue without a special hearing or a finding of relevance.

If the defense thinks that this jury will make a decision on personalistic factors, that the jury will be influenced by the fact that a rape complainant had sexual intercourse with twelve different strangers on twelve different nights, by the fact that a complaining witness of 16 had consenting sexual relations with her boyfriend the same night, the defense does not care how the jury gets that information. What about the judge who is faced with the same evidence regarding the victim's prior sexual conduct with third parties? Is he likely to be influenced or prejudiced by such evidence? The judge is theoretically trained not to decide on the basis of such evidence, especially if the legislature has declared the evidence irrelevant. The judge, however, may think that evidence of prior sexual conduct is itself probative of truthfulness or fabrication. If one believes that judges tend to disapprove of female sexual activity outside marriage, one might well believe a judge would be adversely influenced by such evidence though in theory the evidence was not relevant on the substantive issue of consent. In other words, the existence of a rape shield statute which only precludes the admission of evidence for a particular purpose may not provide sufficient protection for victims irrespective of the technical wording of the statute. It may also be that given the structure of the criminal justice system, it is impossible to protect victims from this sort of societal prejudice. The entire jury system is premised upon the notion of a *societal judgment* of the accused made by his peers. By necessity, that societal judgment is going to include sexist attitudes toward the victim.[115] The jury is sitting in judgment upon the defendant and deciding his guilt or innocence, but the jury is also judging the totality of the circumstances and making a decision whether or not punishment is to be imposed. A finding of not guilty or an acquittal does not necessarily mean that the jury thought the defendant did not do the prohibited act or even that the defendant did not commit a crime. An acquittal may mean the jury believed the defendant was innocent, but an acquittal may also mean that the jury did not think there was sufficient evidence of guilt to warrant a conviciton. If the jury thinks that a defendant has had sexual intercourse without consent with a woman who regularly has sexual intercourse with consent with strangers, that jury may acquit because it believes such behavior *should* not be criminal.

The rape shield laws have another troublesome aspect from the viewpoint of protecting the victim: they are addressed to a model which assumes a trial disposition for criminal cases. Rape shield statutes may have no effect upon disposition by plea, and in many jurisdictions the majority of all rape cases are disposed of by plea.[116] Because of the fact of plea bargaining, the effect of rape shield statutes may be different than what was expected by those lobbying for the reform.

The experience in Florida is typical and instructive. The Florida sexual battery statute, enacted in 1975[117] redefined the crime of rape, introduced new elements of proof, and incorporated evidence provisions which looked as if they would protect the victim from the introduction of prejudicial evidence of prior sexual conduct in court. The effect of the Florida provisions was not as anticiapted, in part because those lobbying for the reform did not and could not regulate the informal norms of the criminal justice process.

The original version of the Florida rape evidence statute was similar to the Michigan evidence statute: it excluded all evidence of prior consensual activity between the victim and any person other than the offender.[118] This version was drastically altered in committee. What was intended as a reform of the evidence law became changed into a recodification of existing case law concerning evidence. As one commentator remarked: "In fact, the new statute is a step backward from case law."[119] The statute was considered a step backward because the former case law allowed in prior consensual activity between the victim and third parties only for the limited purpose of showing "promiscuous intercourse with men, or common prostitution."[120] The new reform statute, which was not drafted by those in fact advocating legal reform, provided that testimony concerning specific instances of prior sexual conduct could be admitted when "such activity shows such a relation to the conduct involved in the case that it tends to establish a pattern of conduct or behavior on the part of the victim which is relevant to the issue of consent."[121] The new statute which specifically stated that such conduct was always potentially relevant to the issue of consent opened the door to making prior sexual history admissible in every case where consent was a potential issue. Not only did the new statute provide less protection for victims than the prior law, but the new statute suggested that consent might be raised in all cases. And if the evidence is relevant to consent, it is relevant to a mistaken belief in consent.

The new statute provided that relevance had to be demonstrated away from the jury, but this portion of the statute merely codified the judge's existing power to order such hearings. The new statute did not give Florida judges authority they did not have before; the matter was always within their discretion. More importantly, the realities of pretrial procedures in criminal court are such that it is unlikely that the judge *would* order an extensive pretrial hearing on a routine case either before or after the enactment of the statute. The threshold showing for relevance is minimal and the predisposition is to admit *not* exclude evidence. A trial court judge is much more likely to be reversed on appeal because evidence favorable to the defense was excluded than because admitted evidence was arguably pre-judicial to the state. One problem with the rape shield statutes is that they ask a court to balance the privacy interests of the victim against the constitutional right of a defendant to a fair trial, including the right to be confronted with all evidence against him. A judge is not going to be disposed to keep out arguably relevant evidence even after a hearing. The statute then merely requires that the defense go to some trouble in order to admit the evidence. The statutes which mandate a hearing may only keep out the most outrageous or flagrant misuse of evidence concerning the victim's prior sexual activity.

Given the way decisions are reached in criminal cases, perhaps the implementation of reform objectives would be more successful if evidence statutes were always formed in terms of a presumption. Although the difference between a statutory presumption of inadmissibility and a rule which requires the defense to prove relevance before evidence can be admitted seems like a mere technicality, to practicing lawyers the difference is crucial. In the formulation of a presumption, the defense has the burden of coming forward with information to rebut a codified assumption (the presumption) that evidence of prior sexual conduct is irrelevant to the entire case.[122] The judge then is put in the position of telling the defense to reverse a policy decision on relevance made by the legislature. In practice, judges may admit the evidence on any sort of showing in spite of the presumption.[123] The defense, however, will now have to make a strategic decision whether or not the evidence they have regarding the victim is "worth getting in." Without the presumption, the motion for admissibility, or for a hearing on the relevance of proposed evidence, is without substantive prejudice. When there is no presumption to overcome, the statute simply says there must be a hearing on relevance. The defense has an easier burden. That calculation of whether or not to make the motion will be made by the defense attorney based in part upon the attorney's perception of the strength of the case as a whole, the viability of the victim as a witness irrespective of potentially damaging evidence, and the defense attorney's estimation of how sympathetic the judge or jury will be to the client.[124] The attorney may be influenced by whether or not other motions are before the judge in the same case, for example, a motion to suppress or a special series of discovery motions.

One problem with statutes, such as the Florida statute, may be that these statutes presume an adjudicative system which responds to precise statutory definitions. Statutes such as the rape evidence statutes assume a decision making model which bears little relationship to the realities of disposition in the criminal justice system. A rape evidence statute may ask too much when it asks a busy judge to make one determination of relevance on the issue of consent and a second and independent determination on the issue of credibility, while holding in mind the possibility of a defense based upon a mistaken belief in consent.

In fact, trial courts do not spend a great deal of time and effort interpreting complicated or detailed statutes.[125] In practice, trial courts may simply ignore, bypass, or circumvent a complicated or ambiguous statute which reformers thought would be a major instrument for change. An assistant attorney in Florida reported that in her experience in one particular county, the judges invariably admitted all evidence of prior sexual conduct irrespective of the 1975 statutory limitation stating that such conduct was only admissible to prove consent. The judges in practice made no distinction between cases where consent was in issue and cases where consent was not an issue.[126] From the judge's point of view, it was perhaps a waste of time to expend a pretrial hour discussing the potential admissibility of evidence at trial when the case was likely to be disposed of without trial. Even if all judges and attorneys were personally and professionally motivated to carry out the precise intention of the statute, the practicalities of the situation might make holding time-consuming hearings on the admissibility of evidence impossible. Most criminal cases are disposed of without trial. Complicated rules regarding the admissibility of evidence *at trial* may simply be irrelevant because trials almost never take place. Evidence rules may become important in the plea-bargaining situation when they significantly alter the bargaining position of one side or the other. Since most evidence reforms allow for the admission of prior sexual conduct evidence upon motion, the threat of introducing unfavorable evidence remains theoretically available to the defense in the bargaining situation even when the jurisdiction has a relatively strong evidence statute. Far too little empirical research has been conducted on the actual effect of reform statutes. What commentary there is suggests that the Florida experience is probably not unusual.[127]

The impact of legislative reform in this area may be unanticipated for another reason. If a state has enacted an evidence provision which is worded so that its constitutionality is questionable, the defense can threaten in plea-bargaining conferences to use this case to challenge the reform statute, to "take the case all the way up." Since both the prosecutor and the defense attorney know eventually there is going to be a case which challenges the statute, the threat is credible. Probably neither the defense nor the prosecutor want an elaborate trial. Both sides may feel for different reasons that this case is not the right case to test the statute, but the decision to plead will be influenced by the existence of a new statute which is subject to challenge at some point in the future. All new statutes are subject to appellate interpretation. Some statutes, however, are drafted broadly with overly inclusive categories. These statutes invite legal challenge at the earliest opportunity.

Most challenges to the rape evidence provisions have been brought by Public Defender Associations. These challenges are recent, and no rape evidence statute has yet been declared unconstitutional by the State Supreme Court.[128] Challenges are usually based upon the fifth amendment right to a fair trial in accordance with due process of law and the accused's sixth amendment right to confront the witnesses against him. The sixth amendment right of confrontation is developing in a manner which suggests that courts are becoming increasingly receptive to the idea that defendants are entitled to subject all accusing witnesses to extensive cross-examination.[129]

Cross-examination is a particularly sacred right, and statutes which impose limits upon cross-examination have not been favorably regarded by courts. At the same time, victim advocates are aware that limitations on the use of substantive evidence are meaningless if facts excluded on direct examination can come in automatically on cross-examination. Other problems are raised by the fact that the courts will weigh the interests of the state and the defendant differently in rape cases than in other cases involving confrontation rights. The typical case in which the courts have limited the scope of cross-examination have been cases involving police informants.[130] In those circumstances, the courts weigh the interests of law-enforcement agencies in getting information sufficient to indict against the defendant's interests in a fair trial. In the informer situation, police have argued that informers are absolutely necessary for law enforcement. Most courts have found this to be a suffiently strong interest to withhold identification evidence. The excluded evidence, however, rarely has any probative value for the jury with respect to questions affecting substantive guilt, while the danger to the witness-informer is immediate and apparent.

With rape victims the counterbalancing interest usually articulated is not arresting criminals or law enforcement but the personal right of the victim to privacy. This is not an interest which will be weighed favorably by a court in contrast to the defendant's right to a fair trial. The U.S. Supreme Court has held that statutes which prohibit publicity concerning rape victims are unconstituitional.[131] The constitutional challenges to rape shield statutes may be successful for this reason. Rape shield statutes have also been justified because they increase reporting. There has never been a reliable or authoritative demonstration of the connection between the enactment of a rape shield statute and an increase in the reporting of rape. If reliable, concrete data were available indicating that the evidence statutes increase reporting, or in other ways demonstrably help the prosecution, the courts could weigh that interest more favorably in the balance.

In summary, rape evidence statutes may not accomplish their stated objectives for a number of reasons. The statutes may have limited applicability in practice because of the way in which they are drafted: the statutes may only exclude evidence of one particular type of evidence introduced for one particular purpose. Second, the statutes may be ineffective because they are drafted so broadly as to be subject to viable constitutional challenge at any time. Third, the statutes may be ineffective because judges and juries rule according to irrational sexist attitudes which are highly prevalent in the society, and a simple rule of evidence will not change that fact. Fourth, evidence statutes may be ineffective because practicing lawyers and judges are uninformed or unaware of their existence. Or finally, rape evidence statutes may fail to accomplish reform because they are directed at a model of trial disposition when the vast majority of criminal cases are decided by plea agreement without a trial.

The Social Implications of Legislative Changes in the Rape Laws

It is impossible to measure whether or not legislative changes or reforms in the area of rape are themselves a reflection of changing social attitudes toward women, or whether changing the rape laws produces or causes changes in attitudes. Irrespective of causation the educative role of rape reform legislation is significant. For professionals such as police, prosecutors, investigators, court clerks, hospital personnel, and others whose job it is to carry out the society's instructions in a variety of institutional settings, changing the law means an immediate change in some behavior or practice and perhaps eventually a change in attitudes. Institutional actors may often have no choice except to implement the reform whether or not the individual agrees with the policy objective of the reform. Even if the objectives of the reform are not perfectly carried out, the reform has accomplished something if it simply announces that the law, or the legal definition of the crime, has been officially changed. It is probably inevitable that reform statutes will accomplish less than their drafters hope and expect, and it is certainly true that at the moment we have no concrete relaible data on the impact of rape reform legislation which has already been passed.[132] For example, no one has convincingly demonstrated that the new evidence statutes have increased reporting. We know that the number of rapes has dramatically increased. We know that large numbers of victims are going to rape crisis centers and that such centers formally did not exist. One of the primary goals of reformers, however, was to increase reporting. The theory was that if victims were assured they would not be harassed or humiliated at trial, then reporting would increase.[133] Perhaps the increase in the number of rapes is an increase in reporting, but perhaps it is an increase in incidence. Since most cases do not reach tr'al, perhaps a victim's hypothesized fear of what was going to happen at trial was unwarranted or unrealistic. In terms of behavior, it is not likely that victims sat down and made a careful calculation about whether or not the law had changed before they dicided to report? This seems as unlikely as the hypothesis that a criminal considers the legal status of the death penalty on appeal before he pulls the trigger in a robbery. Is not the decision to report governed by factors which have nothing to do with the statutory definition of the offense or the relative strength of the evidence provision in effect in the jurisdiction?

What is clear, however, is that victims and women generally are more aware of the fact that hospitals now have special facilities for rape victims, that hotlines and crisis counseling are available. This knowledge may well influence reporting. Social attitudes toward rape have changed to the extent that articles in the popular press, for example, treat the subject entirely differently than they did five years ago. Can this be attributed to changes in legislation? Certainly the legislative changes would not have occurred without some change in attitudes. Women who lobbied through legislative changes in the legislature were flexing their political muscle by delivering the message that women voters were no longer prepared to tolerate a legal definition of rape which said that women could consent to brutal sexual assaults, that women routinely lodged false and vindictive complaints, and that only virgins deserved protection. If nothing else, the passage of evidence statutes over in forty states makes an important political statement. If no rapist is convicted who would not have been convicted under the old law, the fact that some form or rape reform legislation has been passed in many states is itself significant. There will be a continuing national debate about the effectiveness of rape reform legislation. And it is crucial that reliable data on the impact of reform statutes be generated. The backlash which in 1980 is evident with regard to women's issues generally may well express itself in the state legislatures with a movement to reverse reforms in the area of rape.[134] Statutory reform in the area of rape has already had an important effect upon public opinion whether or not it has had any impact at all upon decision making or adjudication within the labyrinths of the criminal justice system. Unfortunately, there is every reason to think that the institutional characteristics of the criminal justice system will preclude rape reform legislation from achieving its articulated objectives.

Whether or not you call rape criminal sexual conduct, sexual assault, or sexual battery, it remains a crime. Crimes are handled by judges, prosecutors, and defense attorneys. Given that most criminal indictments are disposed of without trial, either through dismissal or by a plea-bargaining process, it is surprising that so much of the rape reform literature has been concerned with attitudes of jurors. Juries actually decide very few rape cases. Studies of jurors or prospective jurors are attractive because they lend themselves to survey research methodology. Also understanding jurors' attitudes toward rape is at the heart of the mystery surrounding attitudes toward the crime itself.[135] The suspicion is juries who will not convict are reflecting social values which reverberate in the legislature as well as throughout law-enforcement agencies and the criminal justice system. Researchers also suspect that jurors' views about rape and sex offenses are irrational, and if it were possible to understand the nature of this irrationality, it would be possible to legislate it out of the decision-making process. Several of the rape evidence statutes assume that one important societal prejudice concerns jurors' opinions about the probability of consent by a victim who has been previous sexual experiences. This assumption may be incorrect.

Most strikingly in the area of rape, the norms which purport to be upheld by the system are in fact disregarded by the system. Prior to the reforms of the 1970s the law stated that rape was a serious crime, but few offenders were convicted. The reform statutes declare sexual assault to be a serious crime; few may be convicted. The articulated goals of the criminal justice system are that a defendant is innocent until proven guilty; every defendant will be adjudged guilty or innocent at a jury trial where all issues of fact and law will be vigorously contested. The reality of the situation is that by the time a defendant has reached the stage where he is going to be tried by jury, the criminal justice system has assumed his guilt without proof. That assumption is communicated in a number of important ways. Most cases never get to trial at all, and very few cases get to jury trial. For those cases which do go to trial, almost all the participants are programmed with a set of contradictory and illogical expectations which have little to do with the definition of the offense under the statute. A person charged with rape or sexual assault is likely to be convicted of a lesser or different offense.

Reformers are often frustrated by the fact that criminal laws and institutions have little or nothing to do with victims. One reason why rape evidence provisions have been so popular is perhaps because reformers saw them as statutes which "did something for victims" in the criminal justice process. Rape reform legislation can, however, do little beyond making pronouncements about the status of victims in the criminal process. The criminal justice machinery is designed to process accusations against a defendant. He is the person with constitutionally guaranteed rights who is charged and may be convicted. What happens at trial will effect him, not the victim. Once the crime has occurred, the victim's status is not affected by anything else that happens. Her liberty is not at stake; she will not be put in jail. The victim is a relatively unimportant spectator who may or may not be called upon to testify as a witness in a formal proceeding. Rape victims and their advocates are partly responding to their shock at this discovery when they express rage at the criminal justice process.

Most defendants accept a plea bargain at a stage long before trial. Their conviction is the result of negotiation between the prosecutor and the defense attorney. The victim, if it is a rape case, will probably not even be informed of the fact of a bargained conviction, the sentence agreed upon, or the exact plea. There will be no ruling or issues of law; there will be no jury verdict. There will be no hearing on evidence. In a few jurisdictions the terms of the bargain will be made a part of record. In most states this is not even required. Legislative reform, unless it explicity addresses the practice of plea bargaining, will have no effect upon most cases. Unless rape reform legislation has a discrete impact upon sentencing, or unless it adds new offenses in a dramatic way, the fact of legislative reform will not influence the result in the majority of plea-bargained rape cases.[136] Rape reform is significantly affected by a national movement away from indeterminate sentencing.[137] Trends in sentencing which have importance for rape include the imposition of higher or different penalties when severe injury occurs,[138] mandatory custodial sentences,[139] restrictions upon parole,[140] and the definition of special or extended terms.[141] These statutory changes which were not necessarily directly tied to reform of the rape laws may be the most single significant new influence dispositions in sex offense cases.

Popular representations of trials emphasize the adversarial process. A few cases do exemplify this model. When those cases are described in the newspapers, the public is left with the misleading impression that the vast majority of criminal cases are disposed of by long jury trials. In fact, the realities of criminal justice adjudication are governed by small group dynamics.[142] The same participants face each other day after day. The most important decisions are settled in informal discussion. During the criminal disposition process prosecutors, defense attorneys, judges, defendants, witnesses, court clerks, and victims interact in a variety of situations. Operational decisions are usually made by prosecutors and defense attorneys who are themselves influenced and constrained by the other actors as well as by institutional factors beyond their control. Reformers mistakenly assume a definition in a statute will be the one determinative factor. Attorneys cannot ignore the language in the statute defining the crime, but the defense attorney and the prosecutor are also influenced by a host of other factors, including their perception of one another, the judge, the client, the victim, and other witnesses. Institutional and practical factors which have nothing to do with the individual characteristics of the case, or with the fact that the case involves sexual assault, will also be crucial. The system is one in which attorneys exercise a great deal of informal discretion. Formal rules, evidence requirements, statutory definitions of offenses, and jury instructions may be largely irrelevant to the way in which decisions are made. "In practice, an informal network of relationships is the most significant characteristic of the judicial process. Most issues are negotiated rather than adjudicated, and an atmosphere of cooperation and accommodation, rather than explicit competition, prevails. Informal relationships exert as much or more influence than formal law."[143]

In theory, each actor in the process controls only a small part of the process. The defense attorney controls the choice of defense issues or strategies;

the prosecutor controls the severity of the charge; the judge controls the formality of sentencing. In fact, each participant has a good idea of the strategic position of others. The defense attorney knows the prosecutors cannot repeatedly get away with excessive charging. The judge knows the sentence must bear some relationship to sentences given to past offenders with similar characteristics who were convicted of the same crime. Practice varies enormously from community to community. In one court, a judge may have particularly strong control. In another county or state, the public defender's office may enjoy special prestige. In some cities, the prosecutor may have a particularly large amount of political power. Whatever the particular distribution of power within the informal network, however, the actors are interested in two factors: preserving ongoing relationships and minimizing time and effort. Ongoing cooperation between prosecutors and defense attorneys is the norm, including mutual disclosure of information prior to trial, agreement to minor procedural changes such as continuances, and an avoidance of legal and factual disputes which would disrupt informal disposition. The withdrawal of cooperation is the most powerful threat within the system.

In most rape cases, the prosecutor's position is reflected in an outright offer of plea negotiation or an implied willingness to accept a plea. The decision of the prosecutor in a rape case may be governed by a variety of factors.[144] One factor the prosecutor may respond to is political pressure from the community to increase rape convictions. Whatever the particular pressures in a single case, however, the prosecutor will see this case as one of many in the office case load. If one case goes to trial, it means another case will not go to trial because all criminal institutions are committed to only taking a certain percentage of cases to trial.

The defense attorney's judgment is affected by a series of personal judgments relating to that individual attorney's overall perception of the case, the particular defense attorney's case load, the status of the law, and the defense attorney's assessment of the judge and the prosecutor. For private defense attorneys, the question is the nexus between income and efficiency of disposition. The attorney's input in a case is limited by the client's ability to pay. For public defenders, cost effectiveness concerning time and effort operates both with regard to overall case load and specific cases. Private attorneys with a significant number of criminal cases also usually conform to norms of systematic cooperation with other professionals in the criminal justice system. "Since most defendants are (or are presumed to be) provably guilty of some offense and contesting guilt may require excessive time, the focus is on obtaining either the least severe disposition possible or, at most, the normal disposition imposed on defendants in like situations."[145]

Since the crucial factor in plea bargaining is sentencing, the introduction of a new factor such as the redefinition of an offense may operate in unexpected ways. If the new definition of sexual assault is accompanied by shortened penalties and there are ambiguities in the statute, the result may simply be shorter bargained sentences until both sides decide to test the new statute at trial. Similarly, new provisions which increase the number of procedural hurdles before the defense can introduce evidence of the victim's prior sexual conduct at trial may simply make it more likely that cases will not reach trial. Bargained convictions necessarily result in shorter sentences. The enacted legislative change in the evidence laws may have a result exactly counter to what was desired or expected. Reformers may have thought the purpose of the evidence laws was to spare the victim humiliation or embarrassment at trial. The effect of the reform statute may simply be an increase in plea bargains and consequently a reduction in the amount of time served by convicted persons.

It is not uncommon for the results of a legislative change to be different from what was expected by those who initiated the reform. In the District of Columbia, the legal change affecting the corroboration requirement in rape, which most people working for reform of the rape laws would regard as a major reform goal, seemed to have no measurable effect upon case disposition or upon sentencing.[146] Factors which were significantly related to the conviction rate were factors which, with one exception, were untouched by rape reform legislation. The factors found to increase the chances of conviction were age of defendant, whether a sodomy charge was also brought, whether property or other evidence was recovered, time between an offense and arrest, and presence of other witnesses than the victim. Only the presence of a sodomy charge or the presence of other witnesses arguably would be affected by the legislative changes in the definition of rape. The fact of a sodomy charge would be changed by the redefinition of rape as sex-neutral, sexual assault in many states, and the presence of other witnesses than the complaining witness might be considered as the presence or absence of legally required corroboration. More importantly, factors which the data indicate are determinative of conviction differ markedly from the factors cited by prosecutors as being important to conviction.[147] Prosecutors cited use of force and injury to victim as the two most important factors in obtaining a conviction; but serious offenses were no more likely to result in conviction than other cases.

The fact that legislative reform is less than perfectly successful is not peculiar to rape. In a recent study of mandated procedural reforms in Denver, Colorado,[148] it was found that a reform which was intended to increase the number of pleas and speed cases to disposition actually had the effect of increasing the average elapsed time to disposition. The failure of the reform was explained in part by the fact that reform goals were set unrealistically high.

Legislative change in the area of rape has proceeded with great pace in the legislatures; it is unknown whether or not the impact of reform is what was expected by reformers. One knowledgeable commentator suggested that there is not even a consistent systemwide set of policy objectives on the part of rape victim advocates.

> But is there a shared criminal justice goal in regard to rape? If there is, what is it? To stop rape? To convict all offenders, or to convict some offenders as "examples"? To protect women? To symbolize community approbation of sexual assault? As an observer of the criminal justice institutions, I have begun to doubt that the goals are either very clear, or even shared to the extent that agencies are even functioning interdependently. The goals of organizational self-preservation appear to predominate, and often to divide the "system" into separate preserves.[149]

This same commentator characterized the overall goals of rape reform legislation as encouraging more victims to report, providing police with clear investigatory goals, increasing the proportion of reported cases which result in a criminal charge, "normalizing" the treatment of the offense, and increasing convictions. Her conclusion, however, was that "as yet no research has been conducted that would shed light on the role and value of law reform . . . We do not yet know the impact of legislated changes in sexual assault laws on the functioning of the criminal justice arena."[150]

The enactment of some sort of rape reform legislation in the majority of states is an example of both the success and the failure of the feminist movement in the United States. The mere passage of rape reform legislation through overwhelmingly male state legislative bodies dominated by regional and party concerns is a demonstration of the perceived political power of feminists. Fifteen years ago the most radical feminists would not and could not have predicted that state legislatures would be persuaded to redefine the crime of rape in a manner which reflected the concerns of victims. At the same time, it is at least arguable that the impact of rape reform legislation upon those factors which motivated feminists to lobby for legislative change has been, if not negligible, at least far short of reform goals. Ironically, the educative side effects of getting rape reform legislation passed, rather than the direct substantive impact upon the processes of the criminal justice system, may be most important. Direct educational effects can be seen in the introduction of special police training for rape cases, in the provision of mandated hospital services for victims and specially trained support staff, and in new community services and public discussions of the subject. Indirect change has come about as public opinion has been influenced by the frank and critical discussions in the press of the problems rape victims face in the criminal justice system. Perhaps the overall impact of new legislation will only be seen after several years. Even though laws take effect almost immediately, customs, attitudes, and unwritten procedures take a long time to change, if they are ever subject to change by the imposition of legislative edict.

The history of the enactment of rape reform legislation in New Jersey is an illuminating example of both the success and failure of reform efforts. The fact that rape reform legislation is incorporated within a comprehensive reform of the criminal laws may make it difficult to see the effect of the change in the rape laws. Reformers also modified goals and strategies to deal successfully with the political realities of the legislative arena, but without such adaptation, rape reform legislation would not have passed. In New Jersey the passage of rape reform legislation accompanied the adoption of a new criminal code which redefined other crimes, codified new defenses, and introduced entirely new criteria for sentencing. Over thirty states have enacted comprehensive penal code reform. The status of rape reform legislation within such codes is a subject which has not been adequately dealt with in the literature. At present, it is possible only to comment upon the intended effect of rape reform legislation and to speculate upon systemwide impact. The important empirical work which will tell us if rape reform legislation has brought about any of the goals of reformers remains to be done. When all the lobbying is finished and the statutes have been rewritten, was anything accomplished? It is going to make any difference? Have reform goals, however they are defined, been advanced?

The symbolic importance of the changes in the rape laws is not insignificant, but how much more satisfying it would be to know reform was accomplished. If the semantic changes in the definition of the offense do not necessarily accomplish the goals of reformers, legislation mandating improved services for victims cannot be dismissed as insignificant. A large number of states have passed laws requiring the state or county to pay for medical examinations in connection with a rape case.[151] Not only does this spare the victim the outrage caused by receiving expensive hospital bills for examinations required by the state, but these statutes represent an admission of responsibility by the state. A few states have even introduced statutes which use the terminology of reparations and restitution.[152] Nevada is still exceptional in requiring the state to pay for counseling for rape victims and their spouses, but a number of states now define injury to include psychological and emotional harm.[153] These reforms, though they have not taken place in the majority of states, represent an important step toward the recognition that rape is a violent, assaultive crime against women which bears no relationship to consensual sexual activity. Until society internalizes that reality, women will continue to be victims of rape on the street and in their homes and offices. Women will continue to be degraded and humiliated by our social and judicial institutions which carry the message to the victim that whatever happened to her, it was her fault. If statutory reform cannot by itself change people's attitudes toward rape or implement systemwide comprehensive change within the criminal justice system, statutory reform represents an important first step toward those goals.

Empirical research may tell us our articulated goals were not all or partly accomplished, but it does not look like the data are going to say the effort at reform has been completely futile.

Notes

1. The material in this chapter is discussed with greater emphasis upon legal issues in L. Bienen, "Rape III," *Women's Rights Law Reporter*, vol. 6 (1980). Rape "III" also includes an edited version of the state-by-state analysis of the rape laws in chapter 6. Citations in chapters 5 and 6 follow the standard legal form.

2. See H. Feild and N. Barnett, "Forcible Rape: An Updated Bibliography," *J. Crim. L. & Crimin.* 68 (1977):146. This bibliography lists 371 items. A bibliography dated 1980 would include at least double that number of items. This bibliography is especially useful for lawyers because it includes numerous references to the social science literature and to books and articles written for a general audience.

3. If feminists had not allied themselves with law and order groups, the backlash against the women's movement might have blocked the enactment of some form of rape reform legislation in many states. Piecemeal reform is the norm. (See detailed analysis in chapter 6.)

4. During 1978 and 1979 rape reform legislation was introduced in the New Jersey Senate Judiciary Committee, amended there, and then introduced and amended again in the Assembly Judiciary Committee. The membership of these two committees changed slightly in September 1978. At no time during the effective debate on this bill before either committee, however, was there a female committee member. Yet both committee chairmen were personally committed to the reform bill.

5. See Florida, L. 1978, Ch. 78-326 and Hawaii, L. 1978, Act 214.

6. Compare Colo. Rev. Stat. Ann. §18-3-401 et seq. (Supp. 1976). D.C. Code Ann. §22-2801 (1973) and Ga. Code Ann. §26-2018 (1978).

7. Compare "Rape II," *Women's Rights Law Reporter*, no. 3, 3 (1977) and "Rape I," *Women's Rights Law Reporter*, no. 2, 3 (1976) with the state by state summary in chapter 6.

8. The following states have made some legislative change in their rape laws since research on "Rape II" was completed in 1976: Alabama, Alaska, Arizona, California, Delaware, Florida, Georgia, Idaho, Illinois, Iowa, Kansas, Kentucky, Louisiana, Maryland, Massachusetts, Minnesota, Montana, Nebraska, Nevada, New Jersey, New Mexico, New York, North Carolina, North Dakota, Oregon, South Carolina, South Dakota, Tennessee, Utah, Vermont, Virginia, West Virginia, and Wyoming.

9. See Illinois, Kansas, and Minnesota.

10. South Carolina, S.C. Code Ann. §16-3-651 et seq. (Supp. 1978) and Tennessee, Tenn. Code Ann. §39-3702 et seq. (supp. 1978). California has enacted major reforms, including the abolitions of the spousal exception, by the serial addition of new offenses based upon reform principles without abolishing the traditional offense. See Cal. Penal Code §§261-189 (West 1970) and (West Supp. 1980).

11. Mich. Comp. Laws Ann. §750.520a et seq. (Supp. 1978-1979).

12. See discussion of Mich. Comp. Laws §750.520j.

13. As of 1979, the following states adopted a formulation which used the concept of degrees of offenses: Alabama, Alaska, Arkansas (but not for rape), Colorado, Connecticut, Delaware, Hawaii, Iowa, Kentucky, Maryland, Michigan, Minnesota, Nebraska, New York, North Carolina, Oregon, South Carolina, Tennessee, Virgin Islands, Washington, West Virginia, Wisconsin, and Wyoming.

14. See Del. Code Ann. tit. 11 §764 (Supp. 1978). Rape in the first degree is defined as where serious physical, mental, or emotional injury has occurred to the victim. See also Utah Code Ann. §76-5-405 (Repl. 1978) which defines aggravated sexual assault as rape or sodomy, or attempts, when the actor causes serious bodily injury or causes submission by threat of kidnapping death or serious bodily injury upon anyone. See Utah Code Ann. §76-5-405 (1978 Repl.).

15. The following states have adopted the terminology of sexual assault to define the principal crime: Alaska, Arizona, Colorado, Connecticut, Nebraska, Nevada, New Hampshire, New Jersey, Vermont, West Virginia, Wisconsin, and Wyoming.

16. Florida alone titles the principal offense sexual battery. South Carolina titles the principal crime "criminal sexual conduct" but defines it as sexual battery. See S.C. Code Ann. §16-3-651 (Supp. 1979).

17. Four states define the crime as criminal sexual conduct: Michigan, Minnesota, South Carolina, and Tennessee.

18. Twenty-nine jurisdictions have a crime called rape in their criminal codes: Alabama, Arkansas, California, Delaware, District of Columbia, Georgia, Hawaii, Idaho, Illinois, Indiana, Kansas, Louisiana, Maine, Maryland, Massachusetts, Mississippi, Missouri, New York, North Carolina, Oregon, Pennsylvania, Puerto Rico, Rhode Island, South Dakota, Texas, Utah, Virgin Islands, Virginia, and Washington.

19. See D.C. Code Ann. §22.2801 (1973). Jurisdictions which codified the English common-law offense often did not define rape or carnal knowledge. See Georgia, Ga. Code Ann. §26-2001 (1978) and the former N.J.S.A. 2A:138-1 (1969) (repealed in 1979).

20. In Kansas a female can be guilty as a principal. Delaware changes the common-law definition by adding additional acts. Indiana adds some definitions from the reform statutes to what is essentially a codification of

the common law. Maryland and California define rape as sex-neutral. South Dakota calls the crime rape but uses Michigan's definition of sexual penetration for the acts prohibited.

21. The American Law Institute is preparing revised comments to the Model Penal Code. As of spring 1979, thirty-six states had revised their criminal codes. Not all state revisions have followed the MPC on every issue. The experience in New Jersey is typical. The structure of the code and the early chapters defining intent, criminal liability, the structure of defenses, retroactivity, and jurisdiction all essentially follow the MPC. The rape provisions of the MPC were not adopted in New Jersey. The sentencing provisions are entirely new and based upon relatively recent ideas concerning determinate sentencing. See *N.J.S.* 2C: Code of Criminal Justice (1979).

22. In New Jersey once a rape reform bill was incorporated within the omnibus penal code reform bill the political pressure put upon the legislature to pass the penal code package carried rape reform legislation along with it. Feminists had lobbied unsuccessfully for rape reform legislation from 1976-1978.

23. See Comments, American Law Institute, Model Penal Code, §213.1 (proposed official draft 1962).

24. Reformers should not underestimate the continuing influence of the MPC and its commentary. The commentary is repeatedly cited by opponents of reform. The revised commentary which criticize reform statutes will also be influential. If there had been no comments and if the MPC had not included a statutory corroboration requirement, a prompt complaint requirement, and a mistake as to age provision, the MPC redefinition of the offense in sex-neutral terms might have appeared to be a reform.

25. See Legislative History of Rape Reform Legislation in New Jersey.

26. See New York, Pennsylvania, Hawaii, and Maine. But in 1979 Hawaii redefined the offense in sex-neutral terms and removed the statutory prompt complaint requirement.

27. The MPC also introduced the concept of sexual assault which it defined as a minor crime. Reformers then took this concept and used it as the basis for redefining rape in sex-neutral terms.

28. Pennsylvania adopted the MPC rape statute when it enacted a revised criminal code in 1972. In 1976 Pennsylvania repealed its MPC corroboration requirement, prompt complaint requirement, and mistake as to age provision. See Pa. Stat. Ann. tit. 18 §3102, et seq. (1973 and 1978-1979 Supp.).

29. See New York, N.Y. Penal Law §130.05 (1977). The New York formulation is the strongest provision in effect from the point of view of defendants. See also Ariz. Rev. Stat. Ann. §13-401(5)(1978). These statutes defining consent in MPC terms are in sharp contrast to victim-oriented con-

sent statutes which attempt to limit the common-law defense of consent to rape by defining consent by statute. See Washington, Wash. Rev. Code Ann. §9.79.140(6) (1977).

30. See Ky. Rev. Stat. §510.010 (1975) which essentially adopts the MPC rape provisions without adopting the other sex offense provisions of the MPC.

31. For example, the New Jersey Code of Criminal Justice includes a general definition of consent which implicity applies to the sexual assault provisions of the code. The sexual assault provisions of the code never mention the word consent, nor is consent defined specially in the section of the code dealing with sex offenses. The mandatory sentence for second offenders contradicts the general sentencing provisions of the code. The intent requirements for sexual assault are not spelled out in terms of the carefully formulated definitions of intent incorporated in the code. The interpretation of these ambiguities by courts will be critical to the success of reform goals.

32. See L. Bienen, "Legislative History of Rape Law in New Jersey," *Women's Rights Law Reporter* 3 (1976):45.

33. The former New Jersey rape law can be found in *N.J.S.A.* 2A:138-1 (1969) (Repealed in 1979).

> *Rape and Carnal abuse; penalty.* Any person who has carnal knowledge of a woman forcibly and against her will, or who, being of the age of 16 or over, unlawfully and carnally abuses a woman-child under the age of 12 years, with or without her consent, is guilty of a high misdemeanor and shall be punished by a fine of not more than $5,000, or by imprisonment for not more than 30 years, or both; or who, being the age of 16 or over, unlawfully and carnally abuses a woman-child of the age of 12 years or over, but under the age of 16 years, with or without her consent, is guilty of a high misdemeanor and shall be punished by a fine of not more than $5,000 or by imprisonment of not more than 15 years, or both.

Note: An offense against a girl between 12 and 16 carried a penalty of 15 years, and rape of an adult female carried a penalty of 30 years. Sometimes this section was interpreted to punish less severely the rape of young girls.

34. See *N.J.S.A.* 2A:138-2.

> *Carnal knowledge of inmates of homes or institutions for the feebleminded or mentally ill.* Any person who has carnal knowledge of a female inmate of any home or institution for feebleminded or mentally ill females, or of any home or training school for the feebleminded, with or without her consent, is guilty of a misdemeanor.

35. See *State* v. *Hill*, 166 N.J. Super 224 (Law Div. 1979). The court cited "Rape I" in support of its holding. The lower court holding was

reversed on appeal, and the New Jersey Supreme Court refused to hear the case.

36. See New Jersey Criminal Law Revision Commission, "The New Jersey Penal Code Vol. I: Report and Penal Code" and "The New Jersey Penal Code Vol. II: Commentary," Newark, 1971, cited hereafter as 1971 Penal Code and 1971 Commentary.

37. See chapter 14, 1971 Penal Code. The New Jersey Criminal Code enacted into law in 1978, effective 1979, adopted large chunks of the code as recommended by the Criminal Law Revision Commission in 1971.

38. The American Law Institute's MPC recommended 10 as the statutory age of consent. See A.L.I. Model Penal Code, §213. et seq. final draft 1962. This meant consent was a defense for any acts with females over 10.

39. The chairmen of the Senate and Assembly Judiciary Committees were both exceptionally sympathetic to the goals of rape reform legislation. Without their personal commitment to the passage of a reform bill, the two committees might well have adopted the 1971 commission statute. Public debate inappropriately focused upon the age of consent, though the statute did not use that term. The statutory age was raised from 13 to 15 in a package of amendments adopted in 1979.

40. See L. Bienen and L. Meyer, Philadelphia Center for Rape Concern Model Sex Offense Statute, "Rape II," *Women's Rights Law Reporter* 3 (1977):91.

41. See former *N.J.S.A.* 2A:84-32.1 to 32.3 (1978 Supp). This section was replaced by a stronger evidence provision incorporated within the sex offense section of the code.

42. See *N.J.S.* 2C:14-7 (1979). The 1979 evidence statute requires the defense to establish the relevance of the victim's sexual conduct more than one year before the date of the incident by clear and convincing proof.

43. The effective date was September 1, 1979. In 1979 there were numerous attempts to push forward the effective date, and important amendments were passed in July and August 1979.

44. See the former *N.J.S.* 2A:164-1, et seq. The reenacted sex offender statute removed the mandatory maximum term and made other significant amendments concerning offenders found to be "compulsive and repetitive" and sentenced to treatment. See *N.J.S.* 2C:47-1, et seq. (1979).

45. See amendments to code dated August 2, 1979, *N.J.S.* 2C:14-2 and 2C:14-3, as amended. Essentially, these amendments reintroduce the offense of statutory rape and create a new offense of statutory criminal sexual contact when the victim is over 13 and under 16 and the actor is over 4 years older. See *N.J.S.A.* 2C:14-3(b).

46. See "Legislative Note: Michigan's Criminal Sexual Assault Law," *U. Mich. J. L. Reform* 8 (1974-1975):127; Pitcher, "Rape and Other Sexual Offense Law Reform in Maryland, 1976-1977," *U. Balt. L. Rev.* 7

(1977-1978):151; and S. Weddington, "Rape Law in Texas: H.B. 284 and the Road to Reform," *Am. J. Crim. L.* 4 (1975-1976):1.

47. See Harris, "Toward a Consent Standard in the Law of Rape," *U. Chi. L. Rev.* 43 (1976):613.

48. For example, Nebraska had a common-law corroboration requirement prior to the enactment of rape reform legislation, including an evidence statute, to become effective in 1979. The Nebraska statute does not explicitly overrule the prior case law, but the stated legislative intent of the reform statute is directly counter to the rationale of a corroboration requirement. See State v. Garza, 187 Neb. 407, 191 N.W. 2d 154 (1972) and Nebraska, Neb. Rev. Stat. §28-317 (Supp. 1978).

49. See Mich. Comp. Laws Ann. §750.520 b (1)(f) i-iv (Supp. 1978-1979). See also the following comment: "Unfortunately, courts including in the present case a majority of this one, often tend to confuse these two elements—force and lack of consent—and to think of them as one. They are not. They mean, and require, different things." Rusk v. Maryland, Md. Ct. of Special Appeals, October 10, 1979; Wilner, J., dissenting opinion at 2. The majority found that circumstances involving "lightly choking" were not sufficient to induce reasonable fear to overcome her will to resist. See Rusk v. Maryland, majority opinion at 6:9.

50. See Battelle, *Forcible Rape: An Analysis of Legal Issues* (National Institute of Law Enforcement and Criminal Justice, March 1978), pp. 15-17.

51. In People v. Samuels, 250 Cal. App. 2d 501, 58 Cal. Rptr. 439 (1967) cert. denied 390 U.S. 1024 (1968). A California appeals court said it was common knowledge that a normal person in full possession of his faculties does not freely consent to the use, upon himself, of force likely to produce great bodily injury. The court noted consent is not generally a defense to assault and said the state had an interest in prohibiting certain conduct irrespective of the victim's personal submission or acquiescence. The circumstances involved the state's prosecution of actors who were making a sadomasochistic movie. There was no victim complainant in the case.

52. A number of reform statutes have attempted to anticipate this problem by defining harm or injury to include emotional harm. See New Jersey and Michigan.

53. Wisconsin defines consent as "words or overt actions by a person who is competent to give informed consent indicating a freely given agreement to have sexual intercourse or sexual contact . . ." See Wis. Stat. Ann. §940.225(4) (Supp. 1978-1979).

54. See *N.J.S.* 2C:2-10 (1979) providing in part:

b. Consent to bodily harm. When conduct is charged to constitute an offense because it causes or threatens bodily harm, consent to such conduct or to the infliction of such harm is a defense if: (1) The bodily harm consented to or threatened by the conduct is not serious; or (2) The conduct and the harm are reasonably foreseeable hazards of joint participation in a concerted activity of a kind not forbidden by law.

55. See *N.J.S.* 2C;14-1j (1979) incorporating sections of *N.J.S.* 2C:13-5 (1979).

56. *N.J.S.* 2C:2-5 states: "Conduct which would otherwise be an offense is excused or alleviated by reason of any defense now provided by law for which neither the code nor other statutory law defining the offense provides exceptions or defenses dealing with the specific situation involved and a legislative purpose to exclude the defense claimed *does not otherwise plainly appear.*" [Italics added.]

57. The seventeenth-century British jurist Lord Hale is usually cited for the uncontroverted assertion that a "husband cannot be guilty of rape committed by himself upon his lawful wife, for by their mutual matrimonial consent and contract the wife hath given up herself in this kind unto her husband, which she cannot retract," 1 M. Hale, in *The History of the Pleas of the Crown*, ed. S. Emlyn, 1978, p. 629. Note the language "consent and contract." Hale is also the authority for the statement that rape is "an accusation easily to be proved and hard to be defended against." As a judge, Hale sentence women to death for being witches. Scholars have found a connection between his misogynist attitudes toward rape and witchcraft. See G. Geis, "Lord Hale, Witches and Rape," *Brit. J. Law and Soc.* (January 1978):26-44. See also "Note: The marital Rape Exemption," *N.Y.U.L.* 52 (1977):306, and D. Drucker, "Comment: The Common Law Does Not Support a Marital Exception for Forcible Rape," *Woman's Rights Law Reporter* 5 (1979):181. For a more philosophical analysis, see C. Pateman, "Women and Consent," *Political Theory* 8 (1980):149.

58. See Illinois and California.

59. See Mississippi and Massachusetts.

60. See American Law Institute, Model Penal Code, proposed official draft 1962 §213.6(2).

61. See Mich. Comp. Laws Ann. §750.520(a) and Minn. Stat. Ann. §609.341 (supp. 1979).

62. A few states eliminate the spousal exception only for separated couples who have filed for divorce. See Louisiana (spousal exception excludes those judicially separated); Utah (spousal exclusion does not include those living apart pursuant to a court order); Wisconsin (prosecution will be barred if parties are living apart and one has filed for annulment or separation); and Wyoming (spousal exception excludes those separated by a decree of judicial separation).

63. See Idaho (spousal exception terminates if divorce proceeding begun or couple living apart for six months); Indiana (no spousal exclusion

if a petition for dissolution pending and spouses living apart); and New Hampshire (spousal exception excludes those who have filed for separate maintenance or divorce or those living apart).

64. The traditional spousal exception is extended to include all persons living together in the following states: Alabama (all persons cohabiting); Alaska (spousal exception excludes persons living apart); Colorado (defines spouses to include common-law spouses but excludes persons living apart even if no judicial decree is filed); Michigan (excludes those living apart when one has filed for separate maintenance or divorce); Minnesota (cohabiting adults are excluded from prosecution); Missouri (spousal exception excludes those living apart under a judicial decree); Montana (spouses are persons living together); New Mexico (spousal exception excludes those living apart); New York (spousal exception excludes those living apart pursuant to a written agreement or judicial decree); Pennsylvania (spouses excludes those living in separate residence, or in the same residence but under terms of a written separation agreement or order of a court of record. Exclusion extends to all persons living together as man and wife regardless of the legal status of the relationship); South Carolina (spousal exception excludes those living apart for first and second degree offense); West Virginia (adds to the definition of spouses those living together as man and wife).

65. Connecticut and Maine have made the spousal exclusion into an affirmative defense. Alaska makes marriage an affirmative defense unless the parties are separated or the defendant caused physical injury to the victim. Connecticut and Maine also make cohabitation of the parties an affirmative defense.

66. New Jersey abolishes the spousal exception with a negative presumption. *N.J.S.* 2C:14-5 (b) (1979). "No person shall be presumed to be incapable of committing a crime under this chapter because of age or impotency or marriage to the victim." The provision simultaneously eliminates the common-law presumption that males under the age of 14 are incapable of committing rape, the common-law defense of impotency, and the common-law spousal exclusion. The defense of impotency does not have much credence in the era of *Playboy* ethics. Illinois, for example, continues to recognize a common-law defense of impotency for rape. The logic seemed to be that anyone who would publicly plead impotency ought to be excused from a rape charge in spite of the fact that empirical studies of assaultive and violent rapists indicated they were especially likely to be impotent during the rape or in other circumstances.

67. The following jurisdictions retain the spousal exception without limitation: District of Columbia, Georgia, Illinois, Kansas, Kentucky, Puerto Rico, Vermont, Washington, and West Virginia.

68. The following states do not mention the spousal exception or use the term married or unmarried in their statutory definition. But since these

states define the crime as common-law rape, the common-law spousal exception presumably applies. See Massachusetts, Mississippi, and Texas.

North Dakota retains the spousal exception, though it is incorporated within the definition of sexual act. See N.D. Cent. Code §12.1-20-02(1) (1976 Repl.) (Supp. 1979). Arizona defines the crime as sexual assault but keeps the spousal exception. Hawaii defines the crime as three degrees of rape and includes the spousal exception by defining *female* as any female to whom the actor is not married. In 1979 Hawaii replaced female with the term *person* in the definition of rape. The status of the spousal exception is consequently unclear.

69. The piecemeal abolition of the spousal exception is a phenomenon of the past two or three years. See Arkansas (spousal exception applies only to carnal abuse, sexual misconduct, and sexual abuse in the second degree); Delaware (spousal exception eliminated for rape and sodomy, retained for sexual assault and sexual misconduct); Iowa (no spousal exclusion for sexual abuse in the first or second degree); and South Carolina (spousal exception does not apply if spouses are living apart and if the offense is an offense of the first or second degree). The variety of these statutory formulations indicates the parameters of the debate.

70. See Alaska (no spousal exception where injury to a spouse occurs in the course of sexual assault).

71. Two statutes seem to be drafted to preclude the result DDP v. Morgan (1975), 2 All E.R. 347: Montana (definition of spouses shall not preclude convictions of a spouse in an act which he or she causes another person to perform) and Nevada (a person may not be convicted of sexual assault upon a spouse unless the act is other than sexual intercourse or the person was an accomplice or accessory).

The common law usually allowed conviction of a husband as an accomplice rather than as a principal in such circumstances. The common law also allowed for the conviction of a woman for rape as an accomplice. Penalties for conviction as an accomplice were smaller, and few cases report convictions of accomplices who were husbands or females.

72. The Michigan sexual conduct statute, for example, does not mention the word *consent* and was drafted to avoid the concept of consent, yet the spousal exception remains.

73. States which have totally removed the spousal exception are New Jersey, Nebraska, and Oregon. South Dakota repealed the spousal exception in 1975 and put it back in 1977. All three states which have repealed the spousal exclusion recognize a statutory or common-law defense of consent which would allow proof of consensual cohabitation or proof of prior consenting sexual relations between the parties.

74. See chapter 6 for a detailed history of the age provisions in the rape laws. Many states changed the statutory age several times before enacting

rape reform legislation. Some states never adopted the traditional age of 10 and never adopted the traditional presumption against convicting males below a specified age, which was usually set at 14. (See former New Jersey Law: *N.J.S.* 2A:138-1.) The idea of "an age of consent" developed in the eighteenth and nineteenth centuries in the United States and is not derived from the traditional English formulation. Many states made several amendments to the statutory age for females around 1910 and in the 1950s.

75. A number of states which have kept the concept of the age of consent have set the age at 16. See Alabama, Alaska, Delaware, Illinois, Kentucky, Massachusetts, Montana, Rhode Island, and West Virginia.

76. The United States Supreme Court recently granted a *writ of certiorari* in a case which challenged on grounds of equal protection the California statutory rape law which defines the offense as sexual intercourse with a female under 18. See Michael v. Superior Court, Docket No. 79-1344, *cert. granted*, June 9, 1980.

77. Such references are still found in the statutes. See, e.g. North Carolina, Puerto Rico, Texas and Virginia. The reference to unmarried females in the traditional statutory rape statutes is a reference to chastity and should not be confused with the spousal exception or exclusion.

78. See L. Bienen, "Mistakes," *Philosophy and Public Affairs*, no. 3, 7 (1978):224-245.

79. 61 Cal. 2d 529, 393 F.2d 673 (1964). See Annot. "Mistake as to Age Defense," 8 *A.L.R.* 3d 1100 (1966).

80. For arguments in support of the defense see L. Myers, "Reasonable Mistake as to Age: A Needed Defense to Statutory Rape," *Mich. L. Rev.* 64 (1966):105. The position taken is that the criminal law should not be responsible for regulating consenting sexual behavior which is not socially harmful. The MPC and a number of states following the MPC specifically adopt this view. Many proponents of the defense, however, assume a large number of false complaints by spurious victims. There is no reliable concrete data supporting this assumption and much data refute it.

81. The following jurisdictions continue to define an age of consent: Alabama (16), Alaska (16), Arizona (15), California (18), Dealware (16), District of Columbia (16), Georgia (14), Idaho (18), Illinois (16), Kentucky (16), Massachusetts (16), Mississippi (12), Montana (16), New York (17), North Carolina (12), Oregon (18), Rhode Island (16), Utah (14), Virginia (13), West Virginia (16), and Wisconsin (15). New Jersey does not define an age of consent as such, but the practical effect of the amended age provisions is the re-enactment of a statutory offense for persons under 16. Since the statute is sex neutral, it is unclear who is the victim in a "consenting" relationship.

82. States adopting the two-tiered age structure are Alabama, Connecticut, Indiana, Maryland, Michigan, Mississippi, New Hampshire, New

Mexico, North Carolina, North Dakota, Tennessee, Virgin Islands, Wisconsin, and Wyoming. The following states adopt three basic age gradations: Kentucky, New Jersey, New York, Oregon, South Carolina, and Washington.(But see Arkansas, which has more than three statutory age classifications.)

83. See Michigan.

84. The most common age in traditional statutory rape laws was 16. Most reform states define the most serious crime in terms of sexual acts committed with a person under 12 or 13. (See New Jersey, Alaska, and Michigan.) Some confusion is introduced by the variety of language used to designate the precise age.

85. See New Jersey and Alaska.

86. See Tennessee; the offense is defined in terms of age and a relationship of authority between the victim and actor. This is common in a number of reform states.

87. Some states only adopt the age differential for some crimes; see Delaware. In addition to Delaware other states adopting a four-year age gap are Colorado, Maryland, and West Virginia. A three-year gap is adopted for some offenses in Montana, South Carolina, South Dakota, Tennessee, Utah, and Virginia. Iowa adopted a five-year age gap for some offenses. Maine has a three-year gap, a four-year gap, and a five-year gap for different offenses. Minnesota has age differentials of two, three, and four years for various offenses.

88. See Indiana; marriage of the child to anyone is an affirmative defense to child molesting. Louisiana keeps the provision regarding unmarried girls. North Carolina retains the terminology referring to a virtuous child under 12.

89. Wisconsin adopts a compromise position on the age of consent. The age of consent is set at 15. For ages 15 to 17, there is a rebuttable presumption of nonconsent. For another innovative statutory approach, see Nevada's definition of statutory sexual seduction.

90. Some states have abolished the mistake as to age defense for some offenses while retaining it for others. Connecticut, Florida, New Jersey, and Virginia have abolished the defense altogether. The following states have limited the defense by statute: Colorado (only if victim is over 15), Hawaii (defendant must be reckless with regard to knowledge of age), Louisiana (only if victim is over 12), Maine (limited to some offenses), Montana, North Dakota, Oregon, Pennsylvania, and Wyoming limit the defense to certain age categories. Washington requires the defense to be reasonable.

91. See Arizona, Delaware, and Oregon.

92. See "Rape II," *Women's Rights Law Reporter*, n. 5, p. 136.

93. The following jurisdictions had no special rape evidence statute or court rule as of 1979: Alabama, Arizona, Connecticut, District of Columbia, Kansas, Maine, Puerto Rico, Utah, Virgin Islands and Virginia.

94. See California.

95. Most states have not followed Michigan Comp. Laws §750.520j. Generally, the evidence provisions passed limit the admissibility of evidence of the victim's prior sexual conduct unless there is an independent proof of relevance by the defense. Any evidence can come in after an initial offer of proof by the defense in most states. But see South Carolina, S.C. Code Ann. §16-3-659.1 (1977).

96. See New Jersey. The New Jersey rules of evidence follow the federal rules of evidence, and special rules of evidence for rape will be interpreted in accordance with general principles enunciated in the New Jersey rules of evidence.

97. See California.

98. South Carolina in 1909 enacted special procedures for taking depositions from rape victims in camera.

99. See People v. Rincon Pineda, 14 Cal. 3d 864, 583 P. 2d 247, 123 Cal. Rptr. 119 (1975).

100. See Colo. Rev. Stat. Ann. §18-3-407 and Ga. Code Ann. §38-202.1.

101. See Md. Code Art. 27 §461A (Cum. Supp. 1978); Mont. Rev. Codes Ann. tit. 45, ch. 5 §503(5)-(7) (1978); N.M. Stat. Ann. §40A-9-26 (Supp. 1975).

102. See Tex. Penal Code §21.13(a)-(d) (Supp. 1978-1979): all forms of evidence regarding the victim's prior conduct shall be determined relevant at an in-camera hearing with the questions to be asked on cross-examination to be determined after a hearing on the record.

103. See Alaska Stat. §12.45.045 which was enacted in 1975 and amended in 1978 to strengthen the provisions for what was required to be shown in the in-camera hearing.

104. See Ark. Stat. Ann. §41-1810.4 (1977 Repl.).

105. See Cal. Evid. Code §782 (West Supp. 1978) (The Robbins Rape Evidence Law): setting out the procedures for the admissibility of evidence regarding the victim's character for purposes of impeachment; Haw. Rev. Stat. tit. 37 §707-742 (1975): concerning the admissibility of evidence regarding credibility; La. Rev. Stat. §15.498 (Supp. 1978): victim's prior sexual conduct with person other than the defendant, and reputation evidence concerning same, inadmissible for purposes of impeachment; Miss. Code Ann. §97-3-68 (Supp. 1978): if evidence regarding the victim's sexual history is offered on the issue of credibility, the defense must make an offer of proof to the court; N. Dak. Cent. Code §12.1-20-15 (1976 Repl.): evidence of prior sexual conduct offered for impeachment purposes must be proved relevant away from the jury, written motion required; Vt. Stat. Ann. tit. 13 §3255 (Supp. 1978): if evidence of the victim's prior sexual conduct with third party is relevant to credibility, court may admit the evidence on limited subjects; Wash. Rev. Code Ann. §9.79.150 (1977):

evidence of victim's prior sexual behavior inadmissible to impeach; Wis. Stat. Ann. §906.08 (Supp. 1978-1979): victim's credibility can be attacked only by opinion or reputation evidence of truthfulness.

106. See Pa. Stat. Ann. tit. 18-3106 (Supp. 1978-1979); S.D. Compiled Laws Ann. §23-44-16.2 (1978 Pamph.).

107. See Minn. Stat. Ann. §609.347 (Supp. 1979) exception for "fabricated" charge; Vt. Stat. Ann. tit. 13, 3255 (1978): exception for specific instances of past false allegations; Wis. Stat. Ann. §972.11 (Supp. 1978-1979): exception for prior untruthful allegations of sexual assault.

108. Wigmore, in his *Treatise on Evidence*, makes the unequivocal recommendation that all complaining witnesses in sex offense cases should be examined by a psychiatrist to determine if they are lying. Wigmore was one of the first legal scholars to recognize that psychiatry might have a role to play in legal determinations. It is, however, unfortunate that his dated and discredited views on this subject continue to be quoted as authoritative.

The 1934 Supplement to the second edition of John Henry Wigmore's *Treatise on Evidence* incorporated a new section, 924a, in which the author stated categorically that there should be a presumption that all women and girls who alleged they were victims of sexual assault were either lying or fabricating the charge. The "scientific" basis for this conclusion was a 1915 study of *Pathological Lying*, which has now been repudiated. In addition to the 1915 monograph, Wigmore includes as support for his position several letters from physicians which appear to have been solicited. In the 1940 edition of the *Treatise*, Wigmore reprinted as additional and independent authority for the view presented a 1937-1938 Report of the American Bar Association Committee on Improvements in the Law of Evidence. Wigmore did not mention in the *Treatise* that he himself was the chairman of that ABA committee and the author of the Report which strongly endorses the position advocated in the *Treatise*. The 1970 revised edition of the *Treatise* incorporates 924a without change. Opinions of the 1970s still quote 924a as the "modern" view. See J. Wigmore, *Treatise on Evidence* 3d ed. rev. (Chadbourn, 1970), vol. IIIa, section 924a; and vol. 63 of the American Bar Association, *Annual Reports* (Chicago, 1939).

109. See Ga. Code Ann. §38-202.1 (1978): prior sexual history of complainant admissible to prove a reasonable belief in consent. See L. Bienen, "Mistakes," *Philosophy and Public Affairs*, no. 3, vol. 7 (1978).

110. Nebraska has a highly unusual provision which prohibits the introduction of evidence of the prior sexual history of the victim or the defendant. Neb. Rev. Stat. §28-321 (Supp. 1978). New York has a special provision allowing for the admissibility of prior convictions of the complaining witness. N.Y. Crim. Proc. Law §60.42 (L. 1975). This provision is almost certainly required by the United States Constitution irrespective of the statute. Some states specifically mention that evidence regarding the victim's prior sexual history can come in if it is in rebuttal or introduced by

the prosecution. See Nev. Rev. Stat. §50.090 (1977); N.Y. Crim. Proc. Laws §60.42 (L. 1975); W.Va. Code Ann. §61-813-12 (1979 Repl.); prior sexual conduct of the complaining witness can be used to impeach credibility if the prosecution introduces the issue. South Carolina has a special provision allowing acts of adultery to be used for purposes of impeachment. S.C. Code Ann. §16-3-659.1 (Supp. 1978).

111. Vt. Stat. Ann. tit. 13 §3251 et seq. (Supp. 1978) specifically states that the section is not retroactive. But at least one court has held that if an evidence provision favorable to the defendant is enacted after the crime but before trial or retrial, that statute must be interpreted retroactively. On the other hand, Maryland has specifically made its evidence provision retroactive. Md. Ann. Code Art. 27, §461A (Supp. 1978). The Maryland retroactivity provision may be in violation of constitutional principles forbidding ex post facto laws.

112. Recently the U.S. Supreme Court made important and perhaps contradictory pronouncements concerning the constitutional issues surrounding presumptions. See Sandstrom v. Montana, 442 U.S. 510, (1979).

113. See F. Eisenbud, "Limitations on the Right to Introduce Evidence Pertaining to the Prior Sexual History of the Complaining Witness in Cases of Forcible Rape: Reflection of Reality or Denial of Due Process?" *Hofstra L. Rev.* 3 (1975):403; J. Sutherlin, "Indiana's Rape Shield Law: Conflict with the Confrontation Clause?" *Indiana L. Rev.* 9 (1976):418; P. Westen, "Confrontation and Compulsory Process: A Unified Theory of Evidence for Criminal Cases," *Harv. L. Rev.* 91 (1978):567; Comment, "Ohio's New Rape Law: Does It Protect the Complainant at the Expense of the Rights of Accused," *Akron L. Rev.* 9 (1976-1977):337; L. Herman, "What's Wrong with the Rape Reform Laws?" *The Civil Liberties Review* (December 1976/January 1977):60; and J. Tanford and A. Bocchino, "Rape Victim Shield Laws and the Sixth Amendment," *U. Pa. L. Rev.* 128 (1980):544.

114. The reluctance of state legislators to pass evidence statutes which limit cross-examination in any way may be attributable to the fact that state legislators are often lawyers with experience in trial practice. Trial lawyers have a high regard for the persuasiveness of cross-examination.

115. Particularly interesting are the rape evidence statutes which define prior sexual conduct to include general concepts such as living arrangement or life-style. See N.J. Code 2C:14-7 (Pamph. 1979): sexual conduct includes living arrangement and life-style. See also Wis. Stat. Ann. §972.11 (Supp. 1978-1979): sexual conduct includes use of contraceptives, living arrangements, and life-style. These broad definitions may result in the statutes being declared unconstitutional.

116. Cases are most likely to be disposed of by plea in urban jurisdictions where most rapes occur. See N.J. Uniform Crime Reports (1978 Preliminary Annual Release), April 1979, "Five Year Comparison—Per-

cent Changes of Index Offenses." In New Jersey in 1978, there were 1,115 forcible rapes in urban areas; 480 forcible rapes in suburban areas; and 130 forcible rapes in rural areas. In New Jersey's urban areas, approximately 80 percent of all cases are disposed of by plea agreement without a trial. Are the evidence statutes totally irrelevant to these dispositions?

117. (Fla. Stat. Ann. §794.011 et seq. L. 1975). The literature on the impact of the reform statutes is still small. A number of local law journals have published articles describing the lobbying process and the legislative history of rape reform bills. There is little systematic analysis of the actual impact of legal reform in this area.

118. "Prior consensual activity between the victim and any person other than the offender shall not be admitted into evidence in prosecutions under section 794.02" (see) Fla. H.R. 3814 §1(7) Reg. Sess. 1974, introduced by Rep. Gordon. This statute never became law in Florida.

119. "Florida's Sexual Battery Statute: Significant Reform but Bias against the Victim Still Prevails," *U. Fla. L. Rev.* 30 (1978):419, 438.

120. Rice V. State, 35 Fla. 236, 238, 17 So. 286, 287 (1895). See also Huffman v. State, 301 So. 2d 815, 816 (Fla. 2d D.C.A. 1974).

121. Fla. Stat. Ann. §794.022(2) (1975). This is the present law in Florida.

122. The commentator in the *U. of Fla. Law Review* suggests a statutory formulation which phrases the evidentiary exclusion in terms of a rebuttable presumption of irrelevance. See "Notes," *Fla. L. Rev.* 30 (1978):440.

A strong version of such a statute would state that the presumption of irrelevance or prejudice applied to such evidence when it was introduced for any purpose. These statutes could be phrased in terms of an irrebuttable presumption, but then the statute would stand a much higher chance of being declared unconstitutional. See Leary v. United States, 395 U.S. 6 (1969) (irrebuttable presumption concerning knowledge of possession of illegal contraband declared unconstitutional). As long as any evidence can come in after an initial offer of proof, the statute is unlikely to be declared unconstitutional.

123. See comments on the subject of judicial atttitudes toward rape victims in C. Bohmer, "Judicial Attitudes toward Rape Victims," *Judicature* 57 (1974):303; "The admissibility of evidence of the victim's prior sexual conduct is part of a legal tradition, established by men, that the complaining witness in a rape case is fair game for character assassination in open court. Its logical underpinnings are shaky in the extreme." Commonwelath v. Manning, 328 N.E. 2d 496, 501 (Mass. 1975) (Brancher, J. dissenting).

124. Very little information is available on what defense attorneys consider in making these choices. See comments of Nancy McKissack. "As a practical matter I don't think that [the introduction of evidence of prior sex-

ual conduct] is really important as an evidentiary matter, because an experienced defense lawyer generally would not try to impeach or attack a complaining witness in a rape case where there is definite evidence, independent of the witness herself, of some force or violence. . . . Often if the woman is battered or bruised, it would backfire upon an attorney to try and attack this woman in front of a jury as a promiscuous woman." Hearings before the Assembly Criminal Justice Committee and the California Commission on the Status of Women, Los Angeles, October 18, 1973. *Revising California Laws Relating to Rape*, p. 64.

125. When issues such as the admissibility of evidence under the fourth amendment require a great deal of subtlety in interpretation, the legal definitions are usually worked out by the appellate courts with the trial courts following relatively simple rules of thumb on admissibility.

126. In the opinion of this attorney: "That provision in the statute might as well not exist." The practice is for the defense attorney to ask questions regarding prior sexual activity on cross-examination. The state's attorney raises an objection. The objection is overruled. The evidence comes in before the jury. When attorneys attempt to have the evidence held inadmissible prior to trial, the judge characteristically responds that there is no evidence before the court, and the judge will rule during the trial. *U. Fla. L. Rev.* 30, n 152, n. 154, (1978) p. 439. (Interview with M. Jost.)

127. Idaho passed a rape shield statute in 1977. See Idaho Code §18-1605 (L. 1977). In 1979 a commentator interested in the legal arguments supporting such statutes conducted an informal survey of the trial courts in the state and "found a lamentable lack of awareness of even the very existence of the statute." C. Nicoll, "Idaho Code §18-6105: A Limitation on the Use of Evidence Relating to the Prior Sexual Conduct of the Prosecutrix in Idaho Rape Trials," *Idaho L. Rev.* 15 (1979):323, 342. One court was reported to have made a ruling directly contrary to the new statute, relying instead upon an outdated legal encyclopedia. *Idaho L. Rev.* 15 (1979):323, 342. Since 1975 the unique Ohio provision providing for independent representation of victims during evidence hearings has apparently been largely ignored or misinterpreted. See Ohio Rev. Code Ann. §2907.02E and §2907.05E (1975 Repl.) (Supp. 1979).

128. Litigation involving the Michigan rape evidence statute has been the most extensive to date. The Michigan statute totally excludes all forms of evidence concerning the victim's prior sexual conduct except conduct with the defendant or conduct which would show the source of pregnancy, disease, or other relevant physical condition of the victim. The history of the legal challenge to the Michigan statute is not complete as of this writing. The Michigan Court of Appeals declared unconstitutional that portion of the state's rape evidence statute which required notice and a hearing before the admission of evidence concerning specific instances of the victim's prior

sexual conduct with the defendant. The court also invalidated the notice requirement when applied to evidence concerning the victim and the defendant. The court found that the hearing and notice requirements were valid only with regard to evidence concerning the victim's prior sexual acts with third parties. See People v. Williams, Michigan Court of Appeals, decided January 22, 1980 released February 4, 1980. For other cases challenging the Michigan evidence statute, see People v. Oliphant, 250 N.W. 2 443 (Mich. 1976); People v. Dawsey, 267 N.W. 2d 236 (Mich. App. 1977); and People v. Patterson, 262 N.W. 2d 835 (Mich. App. 1978).

129. See P. Westen, "Confrontation and Compulsory Process: A Unified Theory of Evidence for Criminal Cases," *Harv. L. Rev.* 91 (1978):567.

130. U.S. v. Roviaro, 353 U.S. 53 (1957).

131. See Cox Broadcasting v. Cohen, 420 U.S. 469 (1975). A few states have recently enacted statutes which try to limit public accessibility to the names of victims or to hearings regarding the admissibility of evidence concerning the victim's prior sexual history with third parties. Whether or not these statutes will survive constitutional attack after Cox and subsequent first amendment cases remains to be seen. Presumably, the statutes which require an in-camera hearing on relevance present no constitutional problems. See, however, N. Car. Gen. Stat. §8-58.6 (Supp. 1977); the record of the in-camera hearing shall not be public. See also Wyo. Stat. Ann. §6-4-312 (1977): any motion submitted for the introduction of evidence regarding the prior sexual history of the victim is privileged and not to be released or available for public scrutiny. A slightly different Massachusetts provision has been upheld. See Mass. Gen. Laws Ch. 278 §16.

132. The most extensive research to date is a study of Michigan's Criminal Sexual Conduct Law conducted by the Institute for Social Research at the University of Michigan. The research project, funded by the National Center for the Prevention and Control of Rape, is attempting to assess the impact of the 1975 statutory reform in Michigan by interviewing prosecutors, police, rape crisis counselors, and others.

133. See "Legislative Note: Michigan's Sexual Assault Law," *U. Mich. J.L.* 8, Reform 217, 228 (1974-1975) and "Rape and Other Sexual Offense Law Reform in Maryland, 1976-1977," *Balt. L. Rev.* 7 (1977):150, 157.

134. In 1975 Nevada enacted a statute which mandated that the state pay for counseling and medical care for victims and their spouses. In 1977 the provisions for what had to be shown in order to qualify for counseling were made more strict. Perhaps this was in response to abuse under the former law; perhaps the change indicated a change in the attitudes of legislators. South Dakota removed the spousal exception in 1975 and put it back in 1977.

135. See H. Feild and N. Barnett, "Forcible Rape: An Updated Bibliography," *J. Crim. L. And Crimin.* 68 (1977):146. The Kalven and

Zeisel study is usually cited for the proposition that jurors will not convict in rape cases where a judge would convict. See H. Kalven and H. Zeisel, *The American Jury* (1966), p. 253. The data for that study is over fifteen years old. The meager information available on judges' attitudes does not provide much reason for thinking judges are free from bias when it comes to rape cases.

136. In a few states rape reform legislation has attempted to address this issue. Most rape statutes have introduced reduced penalties for rape on the questionable theory that reduced penalties make it more likely a jury will return a conviction. See "Rape and Other Sexual Offense Law Reform in Maryland, 1976-1977," *Balt. L. Rev.* 7 (1977):151, 164. Certainly a reduction in penalties without any other reforms will simply reduce sentences. A number of states have introduced mandatory custodial sentences and mandatory sentences for repeated offenders. See Cal. Penal Code §1205 (West Supp. 1978) and Cal. Penal Code §264.2 (West Supp. 1978) which limit probation and the imposition of suspended sentences. See also New Jersey: *N.J.S.A.* 2C:14-6 (1979).

137. See the sentencing provisions of the New Jersey Code of Criminal Justice, chapter 45, et seq. The special mandatory 5 year minimum term for second offenders in sex offense cases is counter to this general philosophy.

138. See Cal. Penal Code 264 (West Supp. 1978); Ky. Rev. Stat. §532.060 (1975); Mon. Rev. Codes Ann. tit. 45, ch. 5 §520(3) (1978); Neb. Rev. Stat. §319(1) and §320(2) (Supp. 1978); Nev. Rev. Stat. §200.355 (1977); Tenn. Code Ann. §39-3703 et seq. (supp. 1978).

139. Mass. Gen. Laws Ch. 276 §87 (Supp. 1979) and *N.J.S.A.* 2C:14-6 (1979).

140. See Fla. Stat. Ann. §794.011(2) (Supp. 1979); Idaho Code §20-223 (Supp. 1978); La. Rev. Stat. §14:42 (Supp. 1978); Neb. Rev. Stat. §200.366(a) (1977) and Nev. Rev. Stat. §200.375 (1977); Tenn. Code Ann. §39-3703 et seq. (Supp. 1978); Wash. Rev. Code Ann. §9.79.170 et seq. (1977).

141. See Haw. Rev. Stat. tit. 37 §706-661 (1975); Iowa Code Ann. §902.9 et seq. (Pamph. 1978); Mo. Rev. Stat. §558.016 (Pamph. 1979); N.M. Stat. Ann. §40A-29-29 (Supp. 1975); N.Y. Penal Law §70.02 (supp. 1978); S.D. Compiled Laws Ann. §22-1-2(8) (Supp. 1978); Wyo. Stat. Ann. §6-4-306 (1977).

142. For an analysis and discussion of courts in terms of functional analysis see Raymond T. Nimmer, *The Nature of System Change: Reform Impact in the Criminal Courts*, American Bar Foundation, Chicago, 1978, especially the discussion in chapter 2. See also George Cole, ed., *Criminal Justice: Law and Politics* (Calif., 1972) and J. Tapp and F. Levine, eds., *Law, Justice, and the Individual Society: Psychological and Legal Issues* (New York: Holt, Rinehart, 1977).

143. Nimmer, *Nature of System Change*, p. 28, footnotes omitted.

144. The Battelle prosecutor's survey asked prosecutors a number of questions about their perception of the strength of the case, the strength of the law, and so on. The Battelle analysis did not address itself to the informal aspects of judicial process except to note that the vast proportion of all rape cases were plea bargains, and that the situation was unlikely to change. See Bartelle *Prosecutor's Report*, vol. 1, table 29, p. 18.

145. Nimmer, *Nature of System Change*, p. 44.

146. See Kristen M. Williams, "The Prosecution of Sexual Assaults," Institute for Law and Social Research, Washington, D.C., 1978.

147. See Battelle, *Forcible Rape: A National Survey of the Response by Prosecutors* (Washington: U.S. Government Printing Office, 1977) table 30, titled "Most Important Factors Involved in Obtaining a Conviction of Forcible Rape, According to Prosecutor's Opinions," cited by Williams, "Prosecution of Sexual Assaults," p. 31.

148. See Institute for Court Management, "Plea Negotiations in Denver" (Institute for Court Management, University of Denver Law Center, 1972), discussed in Nimmer, *Nature of System Change*, p. 110. et seq.

149. Testimoiny of Jan BenDor, *Research into Violent Behavior: Overview and Sexual Assaults*, Hearings before the Subcommittee on Domestic and International Scientific Planning Analysis and Cooperation of the Committee on Science and Technology, House of Representatives, 95th Congr. 2d sess. January 10, 11, 12, 1979, p. 431 et seq.

150. Ibid.

151. Iowa Code Ann. §709.10 (Supp. 1978); Maryland, L. 1977, Ch. 854; Minn. Stat. Ann. §299B.03 (supp. 1979); Nev. Rev. Stat. §217.280 (1977); Wyo. Stat. Ann. §6-4-309 (1977).

152. See Minn. Stat. Ann. §299B.03 (supp. 1979) ("Reparations" includes the cost of the victim's attorney's fees.); N.M. Stat. Ann. §40A-29-18.1 (L.1977); Pa. Stat. Ann. tit. 18 §1106 (Supp. 1978-1979); S.D. Comp. Laws Ann. §22-48A1 (Pamph. 1978). New Mexico, Pennsylvania, and South Dakota speak in terms of restitution.

153. For example, see Del. Code Ann. tit. 11 §764 (Supp. 1978).

6

State-by-State Analysis of the Rape Laws

This chapter provides a state-by-state summary of the current state statutes concerning rape. As presented, each state statute is broken into six sections, each with subcategories. Thus the presentation of information relative to each state statute is organized in the following categories:

1. Derivation
    History
    Present law
2. Statutory structure
    Changes
    Offenses
    Requirements
    Principals
    Spouses
3. Terminology
    Language
    Definitions
4. Statutory age provisions
    Age of consent
    Offenses
5. Evidence provisions, defenses, and cross references
    Evidence
    Defenses
    Cross references
6. Penalties
    Terms
    Special sanctions

This chapter presents an overview of current laws concerning rape and criminal sexual conduct. Chapter 5, however, offers a summary of these statutes and analyzes specific provisions in terms of national trends.

Alabama

State Statutes

Ala. Code tit. 13A-6-60 to 70 (1977)
§60 Definitions
§61 Rape in the first degree
§62 Rape in the second degree
§63 Sodomy in the first degree
§64 Sodomy in the second degree
§65 Sexual misconduct
§66 Sexual abuse in the first degree
§67 Sexual abuse in the second degree
§70 Lack of consent

Derivation

History

First codification of common-law sex offenses was enacted in 1852; a seduction offense added in 1876; the age of consent was raised from 12 to 16 years of age in 1896; offenses of child molestation and enticing a child for immoral purposes added in 1955. Original 1852 statute recodified and renumbered without significant changes until its repeal in 1977 (effective June 1, 1979). Offense of enticing a child for immoral purposes saved from repeal.

Present Law

Model Penal Code (MPC) type revision of criminal laws, with most prior common-law sex offenses retained; enacted 1977 (effective June 1, 1979).

Statutory Structure

Changes

Common-law carnal knowledge offense essentially unchanged; resistance: element of force necessary to overcome resistance supplemented by alternative of inability to resist, see Commentary, §§61 and 62; statutory rape: liability of male under 16 for consensual acts with female less than 12 removed, see Commentary; express spousal exception added.

Offenses

Rape (two degrees; includes statutory rape); sodomy (two degrees); sexual misconduct; sexual abuse (two degrees).

Requirements

Lack of consent, §70; rape: sexual intercourse; sodomy: deviate sexual intercourse; sexual misconduct: either of three acts: (1) sexual intercourse by male actor upon female victim with proof of nonconsent by circumstances of fraud or artifice, (2) sexual intercourse by female actor upon nonconsenting male victim, (3) consensual deviate sexual intercourse; sexual abuse: sexual contact.

Principals

Rape: male actor/female victim; all other offenses: sex-neutral, actor/victim.

Spouses

Express marital exception included in new statutory definition of female as "not married to the actor," §60(4), and similarly in definitions of prohibited acts of deviate sexual intercourse, §60(2), and sexual contact, §60(3). Neither termination of marriage nor exception defined; exception extends to all persons cohabiting regardless of legal relationship, §60(4).

Terminology

Language

A male commits the crime of rape in the first degree if: (1) he engaged in sexual intercourse with a female by forcible compulsion; or (2) he engages in sexual intercourse with a female who is incapable of consent by reason of being physically helpless or mentally incapacitated. . . . §61.

Definitions

Lack of consent means forcible compulsion, incapacity to consent, or, for the offense of sexual abuse, express or implied nonacquiescence, §70. *Forc-*

cible compulsion means physical force that overcomes earnest resistance, or a threat placing person in fear of death or serious injury, §60(8). *Sexual intercourse* means any penetration, however slight, §60(1). *Sexual contact* means touching of another's sexual or intimate parts for sexual gratification of either party, §60(3). *Deviate sexual intercourse* means any act of sexual gratification involving sex organs of one person and another's mouth or anus, §60(2).

Statutory Age Provisions

Age of Consent

Age of consent is 16, §70; inability to consent depends on actor's and victim's specific ages and for second-degree rape, age disparity of participants; actor's basic liability for consenting conduct ensues at 16, exists until the victim is 16.

Offenses

First-degree rape: male 16 or older with a female less than 12, §61(a)(3); second-degree rape: male 16 or older with a female less than 16 and more than 12, but actor must be 2 years older than the female, §62(a)(1); first-degree sodomy, first-degree sexual abuse: person 16 or older with a person less than 12, §§63(a)(3), 66(a)(3); second-degree sodomy: person 16 or older with a person less than 16 and more than 12, §64(a)(1); second-degree sexual abuse: person 19 or older with a person less than 16 and more than 12, §67(a)(2).

Evidence Provisions, Defenses, and Cross References

Evidence

No statutory provisions limiting the admissibility of evidence concerning the victim's prior sexual conduct; state common law bars the defendant's use of the victim's specific sexual acts with third persons as proof of her bad character for chastity, *Carter* v. *State*, 56 Ala. App. 450, 322 So.2d 741 (1975); reputation: state common law permits the defense to introduce the victim's general reputation for chastity on the issue of probability of consent, *Brown* v. *State*, 50 Ala. App. 471. 280 So.2d 177, cert. denied 291

Ala. 774, 280 So.2d 182 (1973); corroboration: state common law does not require corroboration of the victim's testimony to obtain conviction, *Williams* v. *State*, 335 So.2d 249 (Ala. App. 1976).

Defenses

Consent: a person is deemed incapable of giving consent if less than 16, or mentally defective, mentally incapacitated, or physically helpless, §70; mistake: honest mistake as to female's age or mental defect is a statutory defense to second-degree rape, §62(a)(3), and a factor which can reduce second-degree sodomy to sexual misconduct, §64(c).

Cross References

Incest, corroboration of victim's testimony required, §13A-13-3; indecent exposure, §68; enticing child for immoral purposes, §69; consensual homosexual acts, prohibition retained by legislature over contrary recommendation by criminal code revision commission, §65.

Penalties

Terms

First-degree rape, first-degree sodomy: class A felony, §§61(b), 63(b); second-degree rape, second-degree sodomy, first-degree sexual abuse: class C felony, §§62(b), 64(b), 66(b); second-degree sexual abuse, sexual misconduct: class A misdemeanor, §§65(b), 67(b); class A felony, 10-99 years or life, §13A-5-6; class C felony, 1 year and 1 day to 10 years, §13A-5-6; class A misdemeanor, up to 1 year, §13A-5-7.

Special

Fines: class A felony, up to $20,000.00, §13A-5-11(a); class C felony, up to $5,000.00, §13A-5-12(a). Death penalty: mandatory if conviction on an indictment which stated charge was rape and intentional killing of victim with aggravation, §13A-5-31(a)(3).

Alaska

State Statutes

Alaska Stat. §§11.41.410 to .470 (1978)
§410 Sexual assault in the first degree
§420 Sexual assault in the second degree
§430 Sexual assault in the third degree
§440 Sexual abuse of minor
§445 General provisions
§470 Definitions

Derivation

History

U.S. Congressional Act of 1899 establishing penal code for Alaska Territory enacted carnal knowledge and statutory age offenses (male 16; female under 16), with victim's age a determinant of penalty based on Ohio law. Recodified without change in 1913, 1933, 1949; 1951 amendment added defendant's age to penalty determination, reducing penalty for defendants under 19. 1957 amendment eliminated all life sentences, modifying penalties according to age of victim where the victim was under 16 rather than only under 12. 1974 amendment made offense sex-neutral; 1976 change added accomplice liability and redefined carnal knowledge to include oral and anal intercourse.

Present Law

Sexual assault reform statute introduced with a revised criminal code enacted in 1978 (effective Jan. 1, 1980).

Statutory Structure

Changes

Sexual assault formulation replaces rape offense; resistance: not required to show lack of consent, §470(3)(A); spouses: express exception added.

Offenses

Sexual assault (three degrees); sexual abuse of minor.

Requirements

First degree: sexual penetration without consent, or attempted sexual penetration without consent causing serious physical injury, or sexual penetration with criminality defined by age of the parties, relation, or circumstances of legal custody; second degree: sexual contact coerced by threat or by physical injury to any person; third degree: sexual penetration where the victim has a mental defect or disorder, or is incapacitated; sexual abuse of minor: sexual penetration or sexual contact with offense defined by age of victim and actor.

Principals

Sex-neutral; person/person.

Spouses

Express marital exception: an affirmative defense that the victim was the defendant's legal spouse; marriage not defined; but the exception and defense terminate if the spouses were living apart, or if the defendant caused physical injury to victim, §445(a).

Terminology

Language

"A person commits the crime of sexual assault in the first degree if, (1) being of any age, he engages in sexual penetration without consent of that person; (2) being any age, he attempts to engage in sexual penetration with another person without consent of that person and causes serious physical injury to that person. . . ." §410.

Definitions

Without consent means (1) the victim, with or without resisting, is coerced by force used against any person or property or by express or implied threat of anyone's imminent death, physical injury, or imminent kidnaping; or (2) the victim incapacitated by the defendant's act, §470(3). *Incapacitated* means temporary inability to appraise the nature of conduct and a physical inability to express unwillingness to act, §470(1). *Threat* means express or implied, with object either anyone's imminent death, physical injury, or kidnaping, §§420(a), 470(3). *Coercion* means force, threat, or physical injury, §§420(a), 470(3).

Statutory Age Provisions

Age of Consent

There is no absolute age of consent; inability to consent depends on specific age of participants; actor's liability for consenting conduct ensues at 16, exists until the victim is 16.

Offenses

First-degree sexual assault: sexual penetration either by a person 16 or over with a person under 13, §.410(3), or by a person 18 or over with a person under 18 either entrusted to an older person's care, or the son or daughter of that person, §.410(4). Sexual abuse of minor: sexual penetration by a person 16 or over with a person under 16 but over 13; sexual contact by a person 16 or over with a person under 13, §440.

Evidence Provisions, Defenses, and Cross References

Evidence

Evidence statute enacted in 1975 and amended in 1978 limits the admissibility of evidence concerning the victim's prior sexual conduct; requires court order for admission, with application made out of the jury's presence; provides for in-camera hearing to determine relevance, with probative value weighed against potential for prejudice, confusion, and the invasion of privacy, §12.45.045(a); victim's sexual conduct more than 1 year prior to date of offense presumed inadmissible absent persuasive contrary showing, §12.45.045(b).

Defenses

Mistake: defendant's reasonable mistaken belief may be an affirmative defense to statutory age offenses unless the victim is under 13, §445(b);

marrige: marriage to victim is affirmative defense unless the spouses are living apart or the victim was physically injured, §445(a).

Cross References

Incest, separate offenses defined, §450; child pornography, new offense of unlawful exploitation of minor, §445; homosexuality, consensual acts among adults decriminalized by repeal of prior law.

Penalties

Terms

First-degree sexual assault: class A felony, §.410(b); second-degree sexual assault: class B felony, §.420(b); third-degree sexual assault, sexual abuse of minor: class C felony, §.430(b), §.440(b); class A felony, not more than 20 years, with presumptive terms of 6 years for the first felony conviction, 10 years for the second felony, and 15 years for the third felony, §12.55.125(c); class B felony, not more than 10 years, with presumptive terms of 4 years for the second felony, and 6 years for the third felony, §12.55.125(d); class C felony, not more than 5 years, with presumptive terms of 2 years for the second felony, 3 years for the third felony, §12.55.125(d).

Special

Presumptive terms subject to adjustment by factors in aggravation and mitigation, §12.55.155.

Arizona

State Statutes

Ariz. Rev. Stat. Ann. §13-1401 through 1414 (1978)
§13-1401 Definitions
§13-1404 Sexual abuse; classifications
§13-1405 Sexual conduct with a minor; classifications
§13-1406 Sexual assault; classification
§13-1410 Molestation of a child

Derivation

History

Penal code of 1901 contained a statute based upon the California code of 1872 defining rape in terms of circumstances such as lunacy rendering a victim incapable of consent or when resistance overcome or prevented, or when the female is unconscious or submits under the belief the perpetrator is her husband. Statutory age of the female defining capacity to consent was 17. Penalty was a minimum of 5 years. Code of 1913 increased the statutory age of the female to 18 and the punishment was life or a minimum of 5 years. Amendment in 1962 divided offense into first and second degree. Second-degree rape was sexual intercourse with a female under 18 under circumstances not amounting to first-degree rape. Present statute enacted in 1978 when criminal code revision based upon the Model Penal Code (MPC) was enacted.

Present Law

In 1978 rape was redefined as sex-neutral sexual assault with some reform definitions. Statutory rape redefined as sexual conduct with a minor and molestation of a child. No evidence statute enacted. Prior definitions of without consent retained.

Statutory Structure

Changes

Two degrees of rape, rape and statutory rape, replaced by a statute defining a variety of sex offenses. Principal offense defined as sexual assault. Molestation of a child carried over from prior law. New classifications based upon age, new offenses defined. New offense sex-neutral. Some modification of the traditional definition of spousal exception. No evidence statute.

Offenses

Sexual assault; sexual abuse; sexual conduct with a minor; molestation of a child.

Requirements

Sexual assault: sexual intercourse or oral sexual contact with a person not his or her spouse without consent, §13-1406; sexual abuse: sexual contact with a person not his or her spouse without consent or with any person under 15, not his or her spouse, §13-1404; sexual conduct with a minor: sexual intercourse or oral sexual contact with a person under 18 not his or her spouse, §13-1405; molestation of a child: fondling, playing with, or touching the private parts of a child under 15 or causing a child under 15 to fondle, touch, or play with his or her private parts, §13-1410.

Principals

Person/person; sex-neutral.

Spouses

Explicit spousal exception for sexual assault, sexual abuse, sexual conduct with a minor, phrased in terms of acts with "a person not his or her spouse," §13-1406; §13-1404; §13-1405; spouse means a person who is legally married and cohabiting, §13-1401(4).

Terminology

Language

"A person commits sexual assault by intentionally or knowingly engaging in sexual intercourse or oral sexual contact with any person not his or her spouse without consent of such person," §13-1406.

Definitions

Sexual intercourse means penetration into the penis, vulva, or anus by any part of the body or by any object or manual masturbatory contact with the penis or vulva, §13-1401(3). *Sexual contact* means any direct or indirect fondling or manipulating of any part of the genitals, anus, or female breast, §13-1401(2). *Oral sexual contact* means oral contact with the penis, vulva, or anus, §13-1401(1).

Statutory Age Provisions

Age of Consent

Age of consent is 18 but several offenses define conduct with a person under 15 as criminal.

Offenses

Sexual conduct with a minor: sexual intercourse or oral sexual contact with a person under 18, §13-1405; molestation of a child: fondling, touching, or playing with the private parts of a child under 15 or causing the child to fondle, play with, or touch the private parts of a person, §13-1410.

Evidence Provisions, Defenses, and Cross References

Evidence

No rape reform evidence statute. Introduction of prior acts of unchastity on cross-examination properly denied, *State* v. *Quinn*, 121 Ariz. 582, 592 P.2 778 (1979).

Defenses

Without consent means any of the following: (a) the victim is coerced by the immediate use or threatened use of force against a person or property, (b) the victim is incapable of consent by reason of mental disorder, drugs, alcohol, sleep, or any other similar impairment of cognition and such condition is known or should have reasonably been known to the defendant,

(c) the victim is intentionally deceived as to the nature of the act, (d) the victim is intentionally deceived to erroneously believe that the person is the victim's spouse, §13-1401(5); defenses: (A) that the act was done in furtherance of lawful medical practice, (B) if the victim is 15, 16, or 17, a defense that the defendant did not know and could not reasonably have known the age of the victim, (C) that the act was done in rendering emergency medical care, §13-1407.

Cross References

Incest, §13-3608; public sexual indecency, §13-1403; crime against nature, §13-1411; expenses of investigation of sexual assault, §13-1414; adultery, §13-1408 et seq.; sexual exploitation of children, §13-3551 et seq.

Penalties

Terms

Sexual assault: class 2 felony, §13-1406; sexual abuse: class 5 felony, §1404; sexual conduct with a minor: class 2 felony if minor under 15, class 6 felony if minor over 15, §13-1405; molestation of a child: class 2 felony, without eligibility for suspended sentence or commutation of sentence, probation pardon or parole, or release until two-thirds of the sentence imposed has been served, or a minimum of 5 years, §13-1410; lewd and lascivious acts: class 3 misdemeanor, §13-1412; class 2 felony, 7 years; class 5 felony, 2 years; class 6 felony, one and a half years, §13-701; class 3 misdemeanor, 30 days, §13-707.

Special

Dangerous and repetitive offenders, §13-604; diagnostic commitment, §13-605; sentencing (aggravating and mitigating circumstances), §13-702.

Arkansas

State Statutes

Ark. Stat. Ann. (1977) (1979 Sup.) §41-1801 through §41-1813
§41-1801 Definition
§41-1802 General provisions applicable to sexual offenses
§41-1803 Rape
§41-1804 Carnal abuse in the first degree
§41-1805 Carnal abuse in the second degree
§41-1806 Carnal abuse in the third degree
§41-1807 Sexual misconduct
§41-1808 Sexual abuse in the first degree
§41-1809 Sexual abuse in the second degree

Derivation

History

1823 compilation of the laws of Arkansas territory defined rape as carnal knowledge forcibly and without consent. Penalty was death. Compilation of 1838 detailed offenses of rape, sodomy, forcing to marry, administering potions, and so on. For negroes or mulattos death penalty for attempts upon a white woman. Act of 1838 added offense of carnal knowledge of a female child "under the age of puberty"; penalty was 5 to 21 years. Compilation of 1874 included proof of pentration requirement for rape and sodomy. Compilation of 1894 specified age for carnal abuse as under 16. Act of 1899 changed minimum penalty for carnal abuse to 1 year. Note to compilation of 1947 reports the definition of the offense is unchanged but specifies the penalty as death or life imprisonment. Law of 1967 changed force to forcible compulsion and added distinctions between first and second degree. Law of 1975 rewrote the section, following the New York Penal Code and Model Penal Code (MPC). Law of 1977 introduced a rape reform evidence statute.

Present Law

Redefinition of rape as sex neutral and new sex offenses included in a revision of the sex offense statutes passed in 1975. Rape reform evidence statute included in 1977. Revision modeled on New York Penal Code but with some reform features incorporated. Much of the prior law retained.

220

Statutory Structure

Changes

Rape in the first and second degree replaced by rape and three degrees of carnal abuse. 1975 revision expanded the prohibited acts to include deviate sexual intercourse under rape, made rape sex-neutral. Penalties for rape reduced and graded in 1975. Rape reform evidence statute introduced in 1977; consenting homosexual conduct recriminalized as sodomy in 1977.

Offenses

Rape; carnal abuse in the first, second, and third degree; sexual misconduct; sexual abuse in the first and second degree.

Requirements

Rape: sexual intercourse or deviate sexual activity by forcible compulsion or with person who is incapable of consent because physically helpless or less than 11, §41-1803(1); first-degree carnal abuse: person over 18 who has sexual intercourse or deviate sexual acivity with person under 14, §41-1804(1); second-degree carnal abuse: sexual intercourse or deviate sexual activity with a person who is incapable of consent because mentally defective or mentally incapacitated, §41-1805(1); third-degree carnal abuse: person over 20 who engages in sexual intercourse or deviate sexual activity with a person under 16, §41-1806(1); sexual misconduct: sexual intercourse or deviate sexual activity with a person under 16, §41-1807(1); first-degree sexual abuse: sexual contact by forcible compulsion or with a person incapable of consent because physically helpless or when person over 18 engages in sexual contact with person under 14, §41-1808; second-degree sexual abuse: sexual contact with a person incapable of consent because mentally defective or mentally incapacitated, §41-1809.

Principals

Person/person; sex-neutral.

Spouse

No specific spousal exception for rape, nor does commentary indicate if the statute assumes the common-law spousal exception applies. Commentary states the principal offense is the same as the former offense of rape. Prior law had no explicit spousal exception for rape but was a codification of the traditional offense defined as forcible carnal knowledge without consent. Explicit spousal exception for carnal abuse in the first, second, and third degree and for sexual misconduct: "with another person not his spouse," §41-1804(1), §41-1806, and §41-1807; explicit spousal exception for only one category of sexual abuse in the first degree: sexual contact with a person not his spouse who is less than 14, §41-1808; explicit spousal exception for sexual abuse in the second degree "with another person not his spouse who is incapable of consent," §41-1809; proviso: "the definition of an offense excluding conduct with a spouse shall not be construed to preclude accomplice liability of a spouse," §41-1802(1).

Terminology

Language

"A person commits rape if he engages in sexual intercourse or deviate sexual activity with another person, by forcible compulsion, or who is incapable of consent because he is physically helpless, or who is less than 11 years old," §41-1803(1).

Definitions

Sexual intercourse means penetration, however slight, of a vagina by a penis, §41-1801(9). *Sexual contact* means any act of sexual gratification involving the touching of the sex organs or anus of a person, or the breast of a female, §41-1801(8). *Deviate sexual activity* means any act of sexual gratification involving (a) the penetration, however slight, of the anus or mouth of one person by the penis of another person; or (b) the penetration, however slight, of the vagina or anus of one person by any body member or foreign instrument manipulated by another person, §41-1801(1). *Forcible compulsion* means physical force, or a threat, express or implied, of death or physical injury or kidnaping of any person, §41-1801(2). *Sexual contact* defined: "As used in this Act unless the context plainly requires otherwise, "sexual contact" means deviate sexual activity, sexual contact, or sexual intercourse as those terms are defined by Arkansas Statutes annotated," §41-1801, §41-1810.3.

Statutory Age Provisions

Age of Consent

Age of consent defined as 11 in the rape statute, §41-1803(1)(c); for other offenses the age of the victim and sometimes the age of the actor will define the offense.

Offenses

Rape: sexual intercourse or deviate sexual activity with a person under 11, §41-1803(1)(c); first-degree carnal abuse: person over 18 who engages in sexual intercourse or deviate sexual activity with a person under 14, §41-1804(1); third-degree carnal abuse: person over 20 who engages in sexual intercourse or deviate sexual activity with a person under 16, §41-1806(1); sexual misconduct: person who engages in sexual intercourse or deviate sexual activity with a person under 16, §41-1807(1); first-degree sexual abuse: a person over 18 who engages in sexual contact with a person under 14, §41-1808(1)(c).

**Evidence Provisions, Defenses, and
Cross References**

Evidence

Opinion evidence, reputation evidence, or evidence of specific instances of the victim's prior sexual conduct with the defendant or any other person is not admissible by the defendant, either on direct examination of any defense witness or through cross-examination of the victim or other prosecution witness, to attack the credibility of the victim, to prove consent or any other defense, or for any other purpose, §41-1810.1; but upon written motion the defendant may offer and the court may admit evidence of the victim's prior sexual conduct with the defendant or any other person after a finding of relevance and with a written order as to what evidence shall be admitted and the nature of the questions permitted; the victim shall be given an opportunity to review the order and both parties shall have the right to an interlocutory appeal on the issue of admissibility, §41-1810.2; reference to the victim's prior sexual conduct by counsel or defendant prohibited in the absence of an order, §41-1810.4.

Defenses

Consent is a defense to rape. No mistake as to age defense if the criminality of conduct depends upon child being under 11; but if the criminality of conduct depends upon a child being of an age other than 11, mistake as to age is an affirmative defense; an affirmative defense that the actor reasonably believed the victim was not incapable of consent by reason of being mentally defective or mentally incapacitated, §41-1802(2)-(4).

Cross References

Incest, §41-2403; wife battering in the first, second, and third degree, §41-1653 to 1655(L.1979); aggravated assault on a wife, §41-1656(L.1979); first-, second-, and third-degree assault on a wife, §41-1657 to 1659(L.1979); sexual solicitation of a child, §41-1810; sodomy, §41-1813; public sexual indecency, §41-1811; medical treatment for victims, §41-1814; types of treatment available, §41-1815; payment for treatment (by the state), §41-1816; reimbursement of medical facilities for treatment of rape victims, §41-1817; §41-1814 to 1817(L.1979).

Penalties

Terms

Rape: class A felony, §41-1803; first-degree carnal abuse: class C felony, §41-1804; second-degree carnal abuse and first-degree sexual abuse: class D felony, §41-1805 and §41-1808; third-degree carnal abuse and second-degree sexual abuse: class A misdemeanor, §41-1806 and §41-1809; sexual misconduct: class B misdemeanor, §41-1807; class A felony: minimum 5 years, maximum 50 years or life; class C felony: minimum 2 years, maximum 10 years; class D felony: maximum 5 years; class A misdemeanor: maximum 1 year; class B misdemeanor: maximum 90 days; all penalties specified in §41-901.

Special

Extended term for habitual offenders, §41-1001; fines, §41-1101; no suspended sentence or probationary sentence if the defendant pleads guilty to first-degree rape, §41-1201.

California

State Statutes

Cal. Penal Code §261 through §268, §283 through §290 (West 1970)(Supp. 1980).

§261   Rape defined
§261.5   Unlawful sexual intercourse with female under 18
§262   Rape of a spouse
§263   Rape; essentials; sufficiency of penetration
§264   Rape; rape of a spouse; unlawful sexual intercourse; sentence and punishment; recommendation of jury; discretion of court
§264.1   Rape; acting in concert by force or violence; punishment
§288   Lewd or lascivious acts upon the body of a child under 14; intent; punishment
§288a   Oral copulation; punishment
§289   Penetration of genital or anal openings by foreign object, etc. punishment

Derivation

Penal code of 1872 included a formulation of rape in terms of the female's resistance overcome or incapacity to consent because (1) the female was under 10, (2) incapable through lunacy, and so on, of consent, (3) where she resists but her resistance is overcome by force or violence, (4) where her resistance is prevented by threats of great and immediate bodily harm or by intoxicant, (5) where the female is unconscious, or (6) the female submits believing person is her husband. Presumption of inability for males under 14. Essential guilt is the outrage to the person and feelings of the female. Any penetration was sufficient to complete the crime. Punishment was a minimum of 5 years. Amendment in 1889 changed the age of the female to 14; amendment in 1897 changed the age of the female to 16. Lewd acts with children under 14 added in 1901. Code of 1913 changed the age of the female to 18 and added new offenses but left the definition of rape unchanged, except for minor changes in wording. Punishment increased in 1923 to a maximum of 50 years, except for statutory rape which could have a penalty of a maximum of 1 year. 1952 amendment changed penalties. In 1967 special provision added for acting in concert by force or violence. Law of 1970 redefined statutory rape as "unlawful sexual intercourse with female under 18" and moved the offense to a separate section. A series of reform statutes passed beginning in 1974. Penalty amended in 1976 to 3, 6, or 8 years for rape.

Present Law

Sex-neutral rape, definition of rape offense unchanged, but new offenses incorporate several reform features including the criminalization of spousal rape. Evidence statutes enacted in 1974. New offenses added in 1978 and 1979.

Statutory Structure

Changes

Law of 1974 introduced two rape reform evidence statutes. In 1976 penalties amended; restriction on probation and suspended sentence enacted in 1978 and repealed in 1979. Penalties amended for acts with children under 14 in 1978 and new offense defining forcible sexual acts with children added in 1979. Presumption of inability for males repealed in 1978; penetration with an object added in 1978. Offense of oral copulation added in 1978 and amended in 1979. Penalties amended again in 1978. Rape offense made sex-neutral and new offense of rape of a spouse added in 1979.

Offenses

Rape; unlawful sexual intercourse with female under age 18; rape of a spouse; lewd or lascivious acts upon the body of a child under 14; oral copulation; penetration of genital or anal openings by a foreign object.

Requirements

Rape: sexual intercourse under circumstances of incapacity to consent or when resistance overcome or prevented, §261; unlawful sexual intercourse with female under 18: sexual intercourse with female under 18, §261.5; rape of a spouse: sexual intercourse by a spouse when the spouse's resistance is overcome or prevented, §262; lewd or lascivious acts upon the body of a child under 14: lewd or lascivious acts with intent or such acts by force, violence, duress, menace, or threat and against the will of the victim, §288; oral copulation: acts of oral copulation under detailed circumstances defined by age of victim and offender, §288a; penetration of genital or anal openings by a foreign object: penetration by any foreign object, substance, instrument, or device by force, violence, duress, menace, or threat of great bodily harm and against the will of the victim for purpose of sexual arousal or gratification, §289.

Principals

Sex-neutral for rape as of 1979; person/person.

Spouses

New offenses criminalizing conduct between spouses added in 1979. "*Rape of a spouse*: (a) Rape of a person who is a spouse of a perpetrator is an act of sexual intercourse accomplished under either of the following circumstances: (1) where a spouse resists but the spouse's resistance is overcome by force or violence; (2) where the spouse is prevented from resisting by threats of great and immediate bodily harm, accompanied by apparent power of execution. (b) The provisions of Section 800 shall apply to this section; however, there shall be no arrest or prosecution under this section unless the violation is reported to a peace officer having the power to arrest for a violation of this section or to the district attorney of the county in which the violation occurred, within 30 days after the day of the violation," §262. Other offenses do not include a spousal exclusion.

Terminology

Language

"Rape is an act of sexual intercourse, accomplished with a person not the spouse of the perpetrator under any of the following circumstances: . . . (2) where a person resists but the person's resistance is overcome by force or violence; (3) where a person is prevented from resisting by threats of great and immediate bodily harm, accompanied by apparent power of execution, or by any intoxicating narcotic or anesthetic substance, administered by or with the privity of the accused," §261.

Definitions

Sexual intercourse is not defined by statute; spouse not defined by statute. *Oral copulation* is the act of copulating the mouth of one person with the sexual organs of another person, §288a.

Statutory Age Provisions

Age of Consent

For females the age of consent to sexual intercourse is 18, §261.5. Constitutionality challenged on grounds of equal protection, decision pending before

U.S. Supreme Court, see *Michael* v. *Superior Court*, Docket No. 79-1344, *certiorari* granted, June 9, 1980. For other offenses age of victim and offender define criminality of conduct.

Offenses

Unlawful sexual intercourse with female under 18: sexual intercourse with a female under 18, §261.5; lewd and lascivious acts with a child under 14: lewd acts upon the body of a child under 14 with requisite intent, §288; oral copulation: acts of oral copulation with person under 18, or by person over 21 with person under 16 (exempting circumstances of §288), or acts of oral copulation with person under 14 and over 10 by force, §288a.

Evidence Provisions, Defenses, and Cross References

Evidence

Two rape reform evidence statutes enacted in 1974. Statute prohibiting the introduction of evidence concerning the sexual conduct of the complaining witness to attack credibility, procedures specify offer of proof, hearing away from the jury, and a finding of relevance, §Cal. Evid. Code §782; psychiatric examination as to credibility for rape victims outlawed, L.1980, ch.   ; Lord Hale's instruction regarding likelihood of consent outlawed, Cal. Penal Code §1127(d); term *unchaste character* not to be used in jury instructions, Cal. Penal Code §1127(e).

Defenses

Consent a defense to rape and other offenses except when the offenses defined by age specify that the defense of consent is precluded.

Cross References

Incest, §285; seduction under promise of marriage, §268; acts of oral copulation by force while confined in state prison, §288(a)(e).

Penalties

Terms

Rape: 3, 6, or 8 years, §264; rape of a spouse: county jail for 1 year or state prison for 3, 6, or 8 years, §264; unlawful sexual intercourse with female under 18: imprisonment in county jail for 1 year or 1 year in state prison, §264; rape acting in concert: 5, 7, or 9 years, §264.1; lewd or lascivious acts with a child under 14: 3, 5, or 7 years, §288; oral copulation: 1 year or 3, 6, or 8 years, or if acting in concert, 5, 7, or 9 years; if in prison, 1 year; if person unconscious, 1 year, §288a.

Special

Registration of sex offenders, duty to register, penalties for violation, §290; mentally disordered sex offenders defined, §290(j); school employees; arrest for sex offense; notice to school authorities, §291 et seq.

Colorado

State Statutes

Colo. Rev. Stat. Ann. tit. 18-3-401 to 410 (1978 Repl.)
§401 Definitions
§402 Sexual assault in the first degree
§403 Sexual assault in the second degree
§404 Sexual assault in the third degree
§405 Sexual assault on a child

Derivation

History

1868 codification contained carnal knowledge statute; 1907 amendment introduced degrees and enumerated circumstances of nonconsent; recodified and renumbered with minor amendments in 1912, 1921, 1935, 1953, and 1963; major revision following Model Penal Code (MPC) in 1971; prior law repealed 1975.

Present Law

Sexual assault reform statute including rape reform evidence statute enacted in 1975; amended in 1977 to add requirement that acts prohibited must be "knowingly" committed.

Statutory Structure

Changes

Sexual assault formulation replaces rape, forcible deviate sexual intercourse, and other sex offenses redefined; new sections on threats by actor to retaliate and on aggravating factors; traditional marital exception limited; provision allowing for a reduction in the grade of offense of the victim was a voluntary social companion reduction eliminated; prompt complaint requirement repealed; statutory age offenses changed.

Offenses

Sexual assault in the first, second and third degree; sexual assault on child.

230

Requirements

First degree: sexual penetration under circumstances of force, violence, or under threat of imminent harm or force, or threats to retaliate §402; second degree: sexual penetration or sexual intrusion against the victim's will or when circumstances imply coercion (includes offenses defined by age, custody, and position of authority) §403; third degree: sexual contact without consent or in circumstances evidencing nonconsent, §404; sexual assault on child: sexual contact regardless of consent with age of actor and victim as elements, §405.

Principals

Sex-neutral; actor/victim.

Spouses

Express marital exception; applies to statutory, putative, or common-law marriage, §409(1); exception terminates where spouses live apart with intent to live apart, whether or not under a decree of judicial separation, §409(2); spouses also excluded under offense of assault on child, §405(1).

Terminology

Language

Sexual penetration; sexual intrusion; sexual contact; consent; submission against victim's will; force, violence, threat, retaliation.

Definitions

Sexual penetration means sexual intercourse, cunnilingus, fellatio, anal-ingus, or anal intercourse; emission not required, §401(6). *Sexual intrusion* means any intrusion by any object or any part of a person's body except the mouth, tongue, or penis, into a genital or anal opening if for the purpose of sexual arousal, gratification, or abuse, §401(5). *Sexual contact* means intentional touching of the victim's intimate parts by the actor, or of the actor's intimate parts by the victim, §401(4). *Threats* mean imminent or retaliatory conduct relating to death, serious bodily injury, extreme pain, or kidnaping,

§402(1)(b) and (1)(a). *Intimate parts* means any person's external genitalia, the perineum, anus, or pubes, or a female person's breast, §401(2).

Statutory Age Provisions

Age of Consent

There is no absolute age of consent; inability to consent depends on a 4-year age disparity between the participants; actor liable at any age, statutory liability for acts with a victim under 15, or if custodial circumstances with a victim under 18.

Offenses

Second-degree sexual assault: sexual penetration or intrusion with victim less than 15 by an actor at least 4 years older than the victim, or with a victim less than 18 by an actor who is the victim's guardian or a person responsible for the victim's supervision, §403(e) and (f); third-degree sexual assault: sexual contact with victim less than 18 by an actor who is the victim's guardian or responsible for the victim's supervision, §404(e); sexual assault on child: sexual contact with victim less than 15 by actor at least 4 years older than victim, §405(1).

Evidence Provisions, Defenses, and Cross References

Evidence

Rape reform evidence statute enacted in 1975 presumes certain evidence about the victim irrelevant; requires court order for admission; statute applies to evidence concerning the victim's prior or subsequent sexual conduct whether in the form of specific acts, opinion evidence, or reputation evidence; exception for prior or subsequent sexual conduct with the defendant and an exception for specific instances of sexual activity showing the source of semen, pregnancy, disease, or that the defendant did not commit the acts charged; special procedure to rebut presumption requires pretrial written motion and affidavit stating offer of proof of relevancy and materiality; provides for in-camera hearing either before or during trial; evidence must be found relevant to a material issue, §407. No statutory corroboration requirement but status of common-law requirement under prior law uncertain. Statutory prohibition of cautionary instruction in prosecutions for sexual assault, §408.

Defenses

Defendant's reasonable mistaken belief as to victim's age is a limited affirmative defense to statutory age offenses where the victim is actually 15 or over; mistake as to age defense not available when child is in fact below age 15, §406.

Cross References

Incest, separate offenses of incest and aggravated incest, §18-6-301; homosexuality, adult consensual homosexual acts decriminalized; medical exception, excepts from criminal conduct acts performed for bona fide medical purposes in a manner not inconsistent with reasonable medical practices, §410.

Penalties

Terms

First degree sexual assault: class 3 felony or class 2 felony is aggravating factors of aiders and abettors, bodily injury to victim, or actor armed, §402(2); second degree sexual assault: class 4 felony or class 3 felony if aggravating factors of force, intimidation or threat, §403(2); sexual assault on a child: class 4 felony or class 3 felony if aggravating factors or force, intimidation or threat, §405(2); third degree sexual assault: class 1 misdemeanor or class 4 felony if aggravating factors of force, intimidation or threat, §402(2); class 2 felony, minimum 10 years, maximum 50 years, §18-1-105; class 3 felony, minimum 5 years, maximum 40 years, §18-1-105; class 4 felony, minimum 1 day, maximum 10 years, §18-1-105; class 1 misdemeanor, minimum 6 months, maximum 24 months, to be served in county jail, §18-1-106.

Special

Fines an alternative sentence to a class 4 felony (§18-1-105) and class 1 misdemeanor (§18-1-106).

Connecticut

State Statutes

Conn. Gen. Stat. Ann. §53a-65 to 53a-73a (Supp. 1979).
§65   Definitions
§70   Sexual assault in the first degree
§70a   Sexual assault in the first degree with firearm
§71   Sexual assault in the second degree
§72a   Sexual assault in the third degree
§72b   Sexual assault in the third degree with firearm
§73a   Sexual assault in the fourth degree

Derivation

History

Carnal knowledge statute enacted in 1879 was based on the common-law offense; 1902 revision changed age provisions and added the offense of assault with intent to rape; 1918 revision placed statutes within category of offenses against Chastity; 1930 revision separated offenses of rape and carnal abuse (statutory age offense); 1943 law added specific reference to 16 as the age of consent; 1969 revision repealed Offenses Against Chastity (including rape offense) and enacted a new chapter for sex offenses modeled on the New York statutes and the Model Penal Code (MPC); 1975 revision redefined all sex offenses.

Present Law

Sexual assault reform statute enacted in 1975, amended in 1976 to increase statutory prompt complaint requirement from 3 months to 1 year from the date of the offense.

Statutory Structure

Changes

Sexual assault formulation replaces offenses of rape, sexual misconduct, deviate sexual intercourse, and sexual contact; corroboration requirement eliminated; prompt complaint limitation added and amended; aggravating factors added to enhance penalty; consent and mistake of age repealed as express defenses; cohabitation made an affirmative defense, offenses defined by age changed.

Offenses

Sexual assault in the first, second, third and fourth degree.

Requirements

First degree: compelled sexual intercourse by force or threat of force; second degree: sexual intercourse where the offense is defined by the victim's age, mental incapacity, or physical helplessness, or actor's the supervisory status, custodial role, or position of authority relative to victim; third degree: compelled sexual contact by force or threat of force; fourth degree: intentional sexual conduct in circumstances of a second-degree offense, or sexual contact without consent, or sexual contact with an animal or a dead body.

Principals

Sex-neutral; actor/victim.

Spouses

Express marital exception included in definitions of prohibited acts of sexual intercourse and sexual contact, §65(2); neither termination of marriage nor exception defined; separate provision makes consensual cohabitation an affirmative defense to any prosecution regardless of the legal status of relationship, §67(b).

Terminology

Language

A person is guilty of sexual assault in the first degree when such person compels another person to engage in sexual intercourse (1) by the use of force against such other person or a third person or (2) by the threat of use of force . . .'' §53a-70.

Definitions

Sexual intercourse means vaginal intercourse, anal intercourse, and fellatio with any penetration sufficient regardless of emission, or cunnilingus, §65(2). *Penetration* include's actor's manipulation of an object into the victim's genital or anal opening, §65(2). *Sexual contact* means any contact by the actor with the intimate parts of another person for the purpose of the actor's sexual gratification, §65(3). *Use of force* means the use of a dangerous instrument, actual physical force, violence, or superior physical strength, §65(7). *Intimate parts* include genital area, groin, anus, inner thighs, buttocks, or breasts, §65(8).

Statutory Age Provisions

Age of Consent

There is no absolute age of consent; inability to consent depends on specific age of victim; actor liable at any age; liability exists for acts with a victim under 15, or if custodial circumstance, with a victim under 18.

Offenses

Second degree: sexual intercourse with a person under 15, §71(a)(1), or, if the actor is the person's guardian or responsible for the person's supervision, with a person under 18, §81(a)(3); fourth degree: intentional sexual contact with same age provisions as second degree, §73(a)(1)(A) and (C).

Evidence Provisions, Defenses, and Cross References

Evidence

No rape reform evidence statute; common law silent on the introduction by the defense of the victim's prior sexual conduct, whether shown by specific acts, reputation, or opinion; corroboration: statutory requirement repealed in 1974.

Defenses

Mistake: actor's lack of knowledge of the victim's condition is an affirmative defense to a charge based on the victim's mental defect, mental incapacity, or physical helplessness, §67(a); cohabitation: living together by mutual consent at time of offense is an affirmative defense, §67(b); prompt complaint: statute requires victim's complaint to be made within 1 year of the date of offense, §69.

Cross References

Incest, separate offense continued, §53a-191; victim compensation, crime victim compensation board created, L.1978, P.A. 78-261.

Penalties

Terms

First degree: class B felony, §70(b); second degree: class C felony, §71(b); third degree: class D felony, §72a(b); fourth degree: class A misdemeanor, §73a(b); class B felony, up to 20 years, §53a-35; class C felony, up to 10 years, §53a-35; class D felony, up to 5 years, §53a-35; class A misdemeanor, up to 1 year, §55a-36.

Special

Minimum terms: generally 1 year minimum term for class B, C, and D felonies, §53a-35; assault with a firearm: first- or third-degree sexual assault accompanied by use or threat to use firearm requires 1 year custodial term, §§70a and 72b.

Delaware

State Statutes

Del. Code Ann. tit. 11 §76-773 (1975)(Supp. 1978)
§761 Sexual assault
§762 Sexual misconduct
§763 Rape in the second degree
§764 Rape in the first degree
§765 Sodomy in the second degree
§766 Sodomy in the first degree
§767 Rape, sodomy, sexual assault; definition of "without consent"
§772 Provisions generally applicable to sexual offenses
§773 Definitions generally applicable to sexual offenses

Derivation

History

1719 law made rape by assault or putting another in fear a felony; 1829 code penalized rape with death and provided for lesser offenses of assault with intent to rape and carnal knowledge of a female child under 10 years, each with 2 year prison terms; 1852 code increased maximum term for carnal abuse to 10 years and specified emission not required to establish penetration; 1874 code lowered child's age to under 7 for carnal abuse offense and incorporated offense in rape statute; death penalty made applicable; 1915 code permitted jury to recommend life term; 1949 amendment made jury's recommendation of mercy a bar to death penalty; 1958 amendment made jury's recommendation of mercy a bar to imposition of a life term.

Present Law

Model Penal Code (MPC) revision enacted in 1972 (effective 1973), amended in 1973 to add degrees, remove corroboration requirement, and delete provision for male victims in rape statute; 1975 amendment added evidence provisions; in 1975 cunnilingus added to prior definition of sexual intercourse; 1976 amendment raised the age of consent from 12 to 16.

Statutory Structure

Changes

Recent amendments modify MPC statute, add rape reform evidence provisions, raise statutory age, expand definition of sexual intercourse. Offense still defined in terms of victim's status or state of mind.

Offenses

Rape in the first and second degree; sexual assault (contact offense); sexual misconduct (statutory age offenses).

Requirements

Rape: sexual intercourse without consent, first degree: if serious physical mental or emotional injury to the victim, or the victim not the defendant's social companion, §763, §764; sexual misconduct: sexual intercourse or deviate sexual intercourse when age restrictions apply, §762; sexual assault: sexual contact when a person knows the contact is offensive or without consent, or when age restrictions apply, §761; sodomy: deviate sexual intercourse without consent, first degree: if serious physical, mental, or emotional injury or victim under 16, §765, §766.

Principals

Rape: male/female; sexual misconduct: male/female, person/person; sexual assault: person/person; sodomy: person/person, defendant/victim.

Spouse

Spousal exclusion defined as including persons living as man and wife regardless of the legal status of relationship; females and spouses may be convicted as accomplices, §772(b), "not his wife" deleted from rape statute effective 1974. "Person not his spouse" is part of the definition of victim for sexual assault, §761; "female not his wife," §762(a).

Terminology

Language

Sexual intercourse is without consent when the defendant compels the victim to submit by force or by threat of imminent death, serious physical injury, extreme pain or kidnaping. . . . §767.

Definitions

Without consent means compelling the victim to submit by force or by threat of imminent death, serious physical injury, extreme pain, or kidnaping, or any other threat which would compel a reasonable person to submit; or when the victim is unconscious, under age, deceived, or incapable of appraising conduct, §767. *First-degree exclusion* for circumstance when the victim was defendant's voluntary social companion and had permitted sexual contact, §764(2). *Sexual intercourse* means any act of coitus between male and female, including intercourse with mouth or anus, with any penetration, including cunnilingus, §873(b). *Deviate sexual intercourse* means intercourse between persons of the same sex, including by mouth or anus, §773(c). *Sexual contact* means any touching of sexual or intimate parts for the purpose of arousing or gratifying sexual desire of either party, §773(d).

Statutory Age Provisions

Age of Consent

Without consent defined as when a victim is less than 16, §767. For some offenses defendant must be 4 years older than the victim.

Offenses

Rape in the second degree: sexual intercourse with a female less than 16, §763; sodomy in the first degree: deviate sexual intercourse when victim is less than 16, §766; sexual assault: sexual contact with consent when the defendant knows the victim is less than 16 and the defendant is 4 years older, §761; sexual misconduct: sexual intercourse or deviate sexual intercourse with a person less than 16 when the defendant is 4 years older, §762.

Evidence Provisions, Defenses, and Cross References

Evidence

Rape reform evidence statute enacted in 1975 limits admissibility of evidence concerning the victim's prior sexual conduct on the issue of consent; motion required to offer evidence, court order will issue, tit. 11 §2508, 3509. Reputation for chastity admissible, *State* v. *Howard*, 55 Del. 143, 159 A.841 (Ct. Oyer and Terminer 1931). Corroboration: requirement repealed effective 1974.

Defenses

Without consent defined by statute for all offenses except sexual misconduct, §767; a defense to first-degree rape that the victim was the defendant's voluntary social companion, §764(2); mistake as to age defense limited to child over 16, §772(a); consenting conduct prohibited with person under 16.

Cross References

Incest, §771, within the exclusive jurisdiction of the family court, tit. 11-1108; sexual exploitation of a child (pornography)(L. 1977), tit. 11-9001; Crime Victim Compensation Board created in 1976.

Penalties

Terms

First-degree rape: class A felony, §764, maximum of life, tit. 11-4205; second-degree rape: class B felony, §763; first-degree sodomy: class B felony, §766; class B felony, 3 to 30 years, tit. 11-4205; second-degree sodomy: class C felony, §865; class C felony, 2 to 20 years, tit. 11-4204; sexual misconduct: class E felony, §762; class E felony, maximum 7 years or fine, tit. 11-4205; sexual assault: class A misdemeanor, §761; class A misdemeanor, possibility of 2 years or fine, tit. 11-4206.

Special

If third conviction, habitual criminal statute applies, tit. 11-4214.

District of Columbia

State Statutes

D.C. Code Ann. §22-2801 (1973)(Supp. 1978)
§22-2801 Definition and penalty

Derivation

History

Code of 1857 defined three categories of rape: rape of a daughter or a sister, "other" rape and rape of child under 12, and carnal knowledge of an insane woman. Compilation of 1894 outlawed rape without distinguishing victims, established minimum penalty of 10 years, maximum of 30 years, female under 16 for statutory age, life for second offense. In 1901 carnal knowledge statute enacted, statutory age of 16, minimum 5 year penalty, maximum 30 years, or death by hanging; 5 year minimum eliminated in 1920. In 1925 statute renumbered section and specified if death penalty, then to be by electrocution; 30 year maximum remained the ordinary term if death penalty not imposed. No change in recodifications, until 1970 removed the death penalty and established a 30 year maximum term.

Present Law

Source of present statute is law of 1901, codification of common-law carnal knowledge offense, including statutory rape offense.

Statutory Structure

Changes

No changes except changes in penalties since 1901.

Offenses

Rape: male/female, carnal knowledge of a female and "abuse" of a female child under 16; sodomy: oral-genital acts and anal penetration.

242

Requirements

Rape is forcible carnal knowledge of a female against her will, §22-2801; and penetration and force are elements of the offense. Carnal knowledge and abuse of a female child under 16 requires proof of penetration, *Wheeler v. United States*, 211 F.2d 19 (D.C. App. 1954).

Principals

Rape: male/female; carnal knowledge: male/female child under 16, female may be charged as principal if aider or abettor, *In the Matter of W.E.P.*, 318 A.2d 286 (D.C. App. 1974).

Spouses

No statutory authority for common-law spousal exception; but presumption is that common law spousal exception is in effect.

Terminology

Language

"Whoever has carnal knowledge of a female forcibly and against her will or carnally knows and abuses a female child is guilty of rape," §22-2801.

Definitions

Carnal knowledge undefined. Force can be threat of death or serious bodily harm, *J.E. Arnold* v. *United States*, 358 A.2d 335 (D.C. App. 1976). Penetration of victim's sexual organs an essential element of carnal knowledge, *J.E. Williams* v. *United States*, 357 A.2d 865 (D.C. App. 1976). Male/female oral-genital acts and anal penetration included in definition of sodomy, §22-3502.

Statutory Age Provisions

Age of Consent

Age of consent is 16, §2801; no statutory restrictions on age of actor.

Offenses

Carnal knowledge and abuse of female under 16 means sexual penetration, §2801, *Wheeler* v. *United States*, 211 F.2d 19 (D.C. App. 1954).

**Evidence Provisions, Defenses,
and Cross References**

Evidence

No statute limiting the admissibility of evidence regarding the victim's sexual conduct. Evidence of victim's sexual relations with third parties inadmissible to prove consent, *S.R. McLean*. v. *United States*, 377 A.2d 74 (D.C. App. 1977). Cross-examination of 13-year-old victim concerning prior sexual experience allowed, but third-party testimony as to victim's reputation for chastity not allowed, *In Matter of J.W.Y.*, 363 A.2d 674 (D.C. App. 1976). Corroboration: corroboration required, *R.D. Davis* v. *United States*, 370 A.2d 1337 (D.C. App. 1977), but see corroboration serves no legitimate purpose, *J.E. Arnold* v. *United States*, 358 A.2d 335 (D.C. App. 1976); and corroboration not required for every element, *United States* v. *G. Gray, Jr.*, 477 F.2d 444 (D.C. App. 1973); corroboration required for sex offense involving children, *United States* v. *D.A. Wiley*, 492 F.2d 547 (D.C. App. 1974), but may be absence of falsification, *United States* v. *C.E. Jones*, 477 F.2d 1213 (D.C. App. 1973). Jury instructions: no special instruction as to credibility or necessity of corroboration required or shall be given, *J.E. Williams* v. *United States*, 357 A.2d 865 (D.C. App. 1976).

Defenses

Common law defense of consent and other common law defenses established by case law. No statutory affirmative defenses.

Cross References

Incest, §22-1901; sodomy, §22-3502; indecent acts—children, §22-3501; assault with intent to rape, §22-501; sexual psychopath statute, §22-3504 et seq.

Penalties

Terms

Imprisonment for any term of years or life, §2801; minimum of 2 years for assault with intent to rape, §24-203(b).

Special

Minimum term for second conviction for rape is 7 years, §24-203; added penalties for offenses committed when armed, §22-3201 et seq.

Florida

State Statutes

Fla. Stat. Ann. §794.011 to §794.022 (1976)(Supp. 1979)
§794.011 Sexual battery
§794.05   Carnal intercourse with unmarried person under 18 years

Derivation

History

Prior to 1840 penalty statute specified death; 1868 statute codified common law: crime defined as whoever ravished and carnally knows a female, statutory age was 10; sentence of death or life. 1892 revision rephrased the statute but still defined rape and forcible carnal knowledge of a female over 10, by force, or carnally knows and abuses a female child under 10; penalty was death or imprisonment for life. 1906 code retained statutory age of consent as 10, enacted statutory presumption of fact that boy under 14 was incapable of the offense. 1920 codification renumbered, added new section prohibiting publication of the name of female victim. 1841 codification included two new offenses: carnal intercourse with a previously chaste unmarried person under 18 and carnal intercourse with an unmarried female idiot, for both offenses the penalty was 10 years. As of 1947, jury could recommend life or any term of years for rape. 1961 law prohibited defense to statutory rape on the basis of chaste character if the only previous intercourse was with the defendant. 1971 amendments changed penalties and defined rape as a capital felony; statutory rape and carnal intercourse with an idiot were second-degree felonies. 1974 law redefined rape as sexual battery, added rape reform evidence provisions, and redefined provisions for minors and mentally defective victims.

Present Law

Rape reform statute defining the principal offense as sexual battery enacted in 1974; carnal knowledge statute repealed; statutory rape offense retained from prior law.

Statutory Structure

Changes

L. 1974 with minor amendments to penalty section in 1975. Carnal knowledge statute replaced with an offense termed sexual battery, offense defined by circumstances of age, force, coercion, and nonconsent. Rape reform evidence statute enacted in 1974 minor amendment in 1977. Former law regarding carnal knowledge with females under 18 retained. 1974 revision abolished the common-law presumption of incapacity for males under 14; mistake as to age provisions; and the provisions regarding carnal knowledge with female idiots.

Offenses

Sexual battery (oral, anal, or vaginal penetration by a sexual organ or an object); carnal intercourse with a chaste female under 18.

Requirements

Sexual battery defined by actor's attempted act of penetration, age of victim and offender, and injury to victim, §794.011(2); by act, nonconsent, age of victim, and use or threat of force likely to cause serious personal injury, §794.011(3); or by act, nonconsent, age of victim under detailed circumstances (a) when victim helpless to resist; (b) when offender coerces victim by threat of force or violence; (c) when offender coerces victim by threat of retaliation; (d) when offender or another administers narcotic or intoxicant; (e) when offender is in position of familial, custodial, or official authority and uses authority to coerce victim; or (f) when victim mentally defective, and offender has reason to believe or know the fact, §794.011(4); or defined by act, age of victim, nonconsent, use of physical force or violence not likely to cause serious personal injury, §794.011(5). Statutory rape: carnal intercourse with unmarried person under 18, §794.05.

Principals

Sex-neutral; offender/victim for sexual battery; male/female for offense of carnal intercourse with person under 18.

Spouses

No mention of spousal exception in sexual battery statute. Spousal exception in §794.05(1) for all "married persons," not simply if victim married to offender.

Terminology

Language

"A person who commits sexual battery upon a person over 11 without that person's consent, and in the process thereof uses or threatens to use a deadly weapon or uses actual physical force likely to cause serious personal injury," §794.011(3). "A person commits sexual battery . . . when the offender coerces the victim to submit by threatening to use force or violence . . . and the victim reasonably believes the offender has the present ability to execute these threats," §794.011(4)(b). Evidence of prior sexual conduct of the victim may be admitted if "it tends to establish a pattern of conduct or behavior" relevant to the issue of consent, §794.022(2).

Definitions

Sexual battery means oral, anal, or vaginal penetration by or union with the sexual organ of another or the anal or vaginal penetration of another by any other object, §794.011(1)(f). *Consent* means intelligent, knowing, and voluntary consent and shall not be construed to include coerced submission, §794.011(1)(h). *Serious personal injury* means great bodily harm or pain, permanent disability, or permanent disfigurement, §794.011(1)(e). *Physically helpless* means that a person is unconscious, asleep, or for any other reason is physically unable to communicate unwillingness to act, §794.011(1)(d). *Retaliation* includes but is not limited to threats of future physical punishment, kidnaping, false imprisonment, or forcible confinement or extortion, §794.011(4)(c).

Statutory Age Provisions

Age of Consent

Age of consent is 18, for females of chaste character. For sexual battery, terminology without consent is used for all offenses where the age of victim is over 11. Only offenders over 18 can be convicted of capital felony, §794.011(2). Common-law presumption as to age of offender abolished, §794.02.

Offenses

Carnal intercourse with unmarried person, of previous chaste character, who is under the age of 18, §794.05. Person 18 or over who commits sexual battery or injures the sexual organ of a person 11 or younger in an attempt, commits capital felony, if the offender is under 18, life felony, §794.011(2). Sexual battery upon a person over 11 without consent, with use or threat of weapon or force, life felony, §794.011(3). Sexual battery upon a person over 11 without consent under detailed circumstances, §794.011(4), including when victim is over 11 but less than 18 and offender is in position of authority, §794.011(4)(e).

Evidence Provisions, Defenses, and Cross References

Evidence

Evidence statute enacted in 1974; minor tehcnical amendment added in 1977. Specific instances of prior consensual activity between the victim and third parties not admissible, unless consent is at issue; then relevance to consent may be proved, §794.022(2). Corroboration requirement repealed, §794.022(1). L.1979 adds provisions allowing testimony of child under 11 to be videotaped if the child will suffer severe emotional or mental strain if required to testify in open court, ch. 79-69, adding §794.022(3). No specific jury instruction required, *Pendleton* v. *State*, 348 So. 2d 1206 (Fla. App. 1977).

Defenses

Consent is a defense to sexual battery if the victim is over 11, §794.011(3) and (4). Ignorance or mistaken belief as to the victim's age abolished as a defense, §794.021. Common-law presumption as to age and inability of offender abolished, §794.02. Bona fide medical purposes exemption excludes medical treatment from definition of sexual battery, §794.011(1)(f). Lack of chastity of female is a defense if a consenting female is over 12 and under 18, §794.05.

Cross References

Incest, §826.04; provisions for hospital emergency care for rape victims, L.1975, ch. 75-182. Mentally disordered sex offenders, prior law repealed, new procedures established, L.1979, ch. 79-341; parole provisions, L.1978, ch. 78-630. Child pornography, L.1978, ch. 78-326; new child abuse provisions, L.1979, ch. 79-203.

Penalties

Terms

If offender is over 18 and victim under 12, sexual battery is a capital felony, §794.011(2), punishable by life with 25 years before parole or by death, §775.082(1) and (2). But see *Coker* v. *Georgia*, 433 U.S. 584 (1977) regarding constitutionality of death penalty for rape. If offender under 18 and victim under 12, life felony, §794.011(2), punishable by life term or any term over 30 years, §775.082(3)(a). Circumstances of force, threat of force, helplessness, incapacity or mental defect of victim, or actor in position of authority define crime as first-degree felony, §794.011(4)a-f, punishable by term of years not exceeding 30 years or life, §775.082(3)(b). If crime committed with force or violence not likely to cause serious personal injury, second-degree felony, §794.011(5), and carnal intercourse with unmarried person under 18, second-degree felony, §794.05; second-degree felony punishable by a maximum term of 15 years, §794.082(3)(d).

Special

Mandatory minimum term of 3 years for aggravated offense, §775.087; court may order defendant to make restitution, §775.089; habitual offenders and extended terms, §775.084; aggravating and mitigating circumstances for capital felonies, L.1979, ch. 79-353.

Georgia

State Statutes

Ga. Code Ann. Ch. 26-2001 to 26-2020 Sexual Offenses (1978)(Supp. 1979)
§26-2001 Rape
§26-2018 Statutory rape

Derivation

History

Codification of 1861 defined rape as carnal knowledge of a woman by force or against her will establishing a separate penalty structure for offenses against slaves and free persons of color; separate penal code for slaves. Code of 1882 left definition of crime unchanged, specified age of consent as 10. Code of 1895 specified death as statutory penalty unless jury recommended mercy. In 1918 sections renumbered, statutory rape codified as a separate offense with 14 as the statutory age, statutory corroboration requirement added, and codified marriage as a defense to statutory rape. 1933 codification only renumbered. L.1968 included statutory corroboration requirement for rape, rewrote defense of marriage as a spousal exclusion for statutory rape. Evidence provision enacted in 1976. Statutory corroboration requirement for rape removed in 1978.

Present Law

Common-law carnal knowledge statute; definition of offense unchanged since 1861; L.1968 source of law. Corroboration requirement for rape removed 1978, rape reform evidence provision added in 1976; separate offenses defined for rape and statutory rape.

Statutory Structure

Changes

1978 amendment removes provision in §2001 stating no conviction shall be had on the unsupported testimony of the female. 1976 adds provision limiting admissibility of evidence regarding the victim's prior sexual conduct.

Offenses

Rape; statutory rape; sodomy; aggravated sodomy.

Requirements

Rape: male/female, carnal knowledge, force, any penetration, absence of consent, §26-2001; statutory rape: male/female, sexual intercourse with a female under 14, §26-2018.

Principals

Male/female for rape; male/female under 14 for statutory rape; sodomy, sex-neutral.

Spouses

Under traditional common-law formulation husband cannot be principal in the rape of his wife. No statutory spousal exclusion for rape, statutory spousal exclusion for statutory rape. No statutory definition of spouses.

Terminology

Language

A person commits rape when he has carnal knowledge of a female forcibly and against her will, §26-2001. No conviction shall be had for this offense on the unsupported testimony of the female, §26-2018.

Definitions

Re evidence: "for the purpose of this section, evidence of past sexual behavior includes, but is not limited to, evidence of the complaining witness' marital history, mode of dress, general reputation for promiscuity, non-chastity, or sexual mores contrary to the community standards," §38-201.1. *Sodomy*: "any sexual act involving the sex organs of one person and the mouth or anus of another," §26-2002.

Statutory Age Provisions

Age of Consent

Age of consent is 14, §26-2018; child molestation statute defines child as under 14, §26-2019; no statutory age restrictions on male.

Offenses

Statutory rape: sexual intercourse with female under 14, male/female, corroboration required, §26-2018; child molestation: commission of any immoral or indecent act to or in the presence of or with a child under 14.

Evidence Provisions, Defenses, and Cross References

Evidence

Evidence of the past sexual behavior of the complaining witness not admissible on direct examination or cross-examination of the complaining witness or other witness unless the court finds such evidence directly involved the participation of the accused or the evidence supports an inference of a reasonable belief in consent. Court will issue an order regarding manner of admissibility, §38-202.1. Statutory corroboration requirement for rape removed in 1978, retained for statutory rape.

Defenses

No statutory defenses; consent not a defense to statutory rape; common-law defense of consent applies to rape.

Cross References

Incest, §26-2006; sodomy, aggravated sodomy, §26-2002; solicitation for sodomy, §26-2003; child molestation, §26-2019; masturbation for hire, §26-2021; crime victim compensation, §2-1413(a)(L.1978); sex offenders: examination required before parole, §77-539(L.1956); sexual exploitation of children, (pornography) §26-9943a; seduction, §26-2005; mandatory registration of sex offenders, §24-2715.

Penalties

Terms

Rape: death, life imprisonment, or minimum 1 year and maximum 20
years, §26-2001; death penalty for rape under Georgia statute vacated,
Coker v. *Georgia*, 433 U.S. 584 (1977); statutory rape: minimum 1 year,
maximum 20 years, §26-2018.

Special

Special examination before sex offenders released on parole, §77-539.

Hawaii

State Statutes

Hawaii Rev. Stat. tit. 37, Hawaii Penal Code §707-730 to 742 (1976 Repl.)(Supp. 1978)(L.1979)
§730 Rape in the first degree
§731 Rape in the second degree
§732 Rape in the third degree
§736 Sexual abuse in the first degree
§737 Sexual abuse in the second degree

Derivation

History

1905 code cited 1869 code as the source of a rape statute punishing anyone who ravishes or has carnal intercourse with any female by force or against her will with a fine of not more than $1,000 or hard labor for life or any term of years. Penalty for carnal abuse of female under 10 was death or life at the discretion of the court. 1925 code increased age for carnal abuse to 12, added corroboration requirement for carnal abuse, and removed death penalty. 1935 revision added new offense: sexual intercourse with female under 16, penalty of 10 years. Carnal abuse retained for females under 12. Penalty is death or life or term of years for carnal abuse and rape. Corroboration required for rape, sodomy, and sexual intercourse with female under 16. 1955 revision retained principal offenses but removed death penalty and added provision forbidding parole for rape. No further changes until prior law repealed as of 1973, when Hawaii adopted criminal code reform based upon the Model Penal Code (MPC) and the New York Penal Code.

Present Law

Modified MPC rape statute adopted in 1973. 1979 amendments removed prompt complaint requirement and amended rape to a gender-neutral offense. Limited evidence statute passed in 1975, amended in 1977. Special provisions for mentally defective, mentally incapacitated, and physically helpless victims.

Statutory Structure

Changes

Common-law rape statute defining rape, sexual intercourse with female under 16, and carnal abuse replaced with MPC rape provisions when MPC criminal code adopted. No prior offense equivalent to sexual abuse. 1979 amendment made rape gender-neutral and removed the statutory prompt complaint requirement. 1975 rape reform evidence provision amended in 1977 to require hearing in camera on the relevance of evidence of prior sexual conduct of the complaining witness.

Offenses

Rape in the first, second and third degree; sodomy in the first, second and third degree; sexual abuse in the first and second degree.

Requirements

First-degree rape: sexual intercourse by forcible compulsion when serious bodily injury inflicted except in a situation involving a voluntary social companion who had previously permitted sexual intercourse, §730; second-degree rape: sexual intercourse by forcible compulsion, or with a person under 14, §731; third-degree rape: sexual intercourse with a person mentally defective, mentally incapacitated, or physically helpless, §732. First-degree sexual abuse: forcible sexual contact or sexual contact with person under 14; second-degree sexual abuse: sexual contact with person mentally defective, mentally incapacitated, or physically helpless, or when a person is 14 or 15 and 4 years younger than the actor.

Principals

Person/person per Act No. 225, L.1979; formerly male/female for rape.

Spouses

Female means any female person to whom the actor is not married, §707-700(10). Married means persons legally married, but does not include spouses living apart under a judicial decree, §707-700(11). 1973 amendment to definition of married included male and female living together but not legally married, Act 136, L.1973. Status of spousal exception unclear after 1979 amendment making rape sex neutral. Technically a female as defined is no longer the "victim" of the offense. Spousal exception included in the definition of sexual contact, §707-700(9).

Terminology

Language

Rape is "sexual intercourse by forcible compulsion and . . . a person recklessly inflicts serious bodily injury." A person commits sexual abuse if he intentionally by forcible compulsion has sexual contact with another or causes another to have sexual contact with him.

Definitions

Consent (general): in any prosecution, the victim's consent to the conduct alleged, or to the result thereof, is a defense if the consent negatives an element of the offense or precludes the infliction of the harm or evil sought to be prevented by the law defining the offense, §702-233. *Bodily injury* means physical pain, illness, or any impairment of physical condition, §707-700(2). *Serious bodily injury* means bodily injury which creates a substantial risk of death or which causes serious, permanent disfigurement, or protracted loss or impairment of the function of any bodily member or organ, §707-700(3). *Sexual intercourse* means any act of coitus, it occurs upon any penetration, however slight, and emission is not required, §070-700(7). *Sexual contact* means any touching of the sexual or other intimate parts of a person not married to the actor done with the intent of gratifying the sexual desire of either party, §707-700(9).

Statutory Age Provisions

Age of Consent

Age of consent is 14, but statutory penalty of misdemeanor available for some circumstances involving 14- and 15-year-olds.

Offenses

First-degree rape: sexual intercourse with female less than 14 if serious bodily injury occurs, §707-730(1)b; second-degree rape: sexual intercourse with female less than 14, §707-731(1)b; first-degree sexual abuse: sexual contact with person less than 14, §707-736(1)b; second-degree sexual abuse: sexual contact with person 14 or 15 and 4 years younger than the actor, §707-737(1)b.

Evidence Provisions, Defenses, and Cross References

Evidence

1975 statute requires written motion, offer of proof, and court hearing and finding of relevance if evidence concerning the sexual conduct of the complaining witness with third parties is offered to attack credibility of the victim, §707-741. No restrictions on admissibility of evidence regarding consent.

Defenses

Affirmative defense to first-degree rape that person is a "voluntary social companion who had within the previous 12 months permitted the defendant sexual intercourse," §707-730(1)(a)i. Ignorance or mistake a general statutory defense, §702-218; an affirmative defense to second-degree sexual abuse, that the victim had engaged promiscuously in sexual relations with others, §707-737(3); consent (general), §702-233; consent to bodily injury, §702-234; ineffective consent, §702-235; statutory mistake as to age defense repealed in 1975.

Cross References

Incest, §707-741; promoting child abuse (child pornography), §707-750; first-, second-, and third-degree sodomy, defined as deviate sexual intercourse in circumstances parallel to rape, §707-733 to 735.

Penalties

Terms

First-degree rape and first-degree sodomy: class A felony, §707-730 and §707-733; class A felony, minimum 20 years, §706-660. Second-degree rape and second-degree sodomy: class B felony, §707-731 and §707-734; class B felony, maximum 10 years, §706-660. Third-degree rape and third-degree sodomy: class C felony, §707-732 and §707-735; first-degree sexual abuse: class C felony, §707-736; incest: class C felony, §707-741; class C felony, maximum 5 years, §706-660. Second-degree sexual abuse: misdemeanor, §707-737; misdemeanor, maximum 1 year, §706-663.

Special

Mandatory terms if firearm used, §706-660.1; extended terms, §706-661 et seq.

Idaho

State Statutes

Idaho Code §18-6101 to 6107 (1979)
§6101 Rape defined
§6104 Punishment for rape

Derivation

History

L.1874-75 contained carnal knowledge statute, statutory age of female was 12, penalty 5 years to life. Stat. 1887 redefines offense: rape is sexual intercourse with a female under 10, where the female is incapable of consent through lunacy, and so on, where resistance is prevented, where the female is unconscious, where the female believes the male is her husband; no conviction of male under 14. Penal laws of 1897 returns to carnal knowledge formulation, statutory age of 10, penalty death or life, adds statutory corroboration requirement. 1901 penal code redefines rape as sexual intercourse with a female under 18 and returns to 1887 formulation of circumstances of nonconsent, penalty 5 years to life, and no statutory corroboration requirement. Statutes of 1919 specify a minimum 5 year term. 1948 code reduces minimum term to 1 year, maximum is life. L.1977 enacts rape reform evidence provisions, exception to spousal exclusion, and provision for restitution to victims.

Present Law

Codification of traditional common-law offense with a rape reform evidence statute and limitation on the spousal exception; present formulation enacted in 1972.

Statutory Structure

Changes

Traditional definition of offense unchanged, rape reform evidence statute enacted in 1977, minor exceptions to spousal exclusion codified in 1977.

260

Offenses

Rape defined by circumstances of victim's age, status, and incapacity or inability to consent.

Requirements

Sexual intercourse, without consent, when resistance overcome or prevented, when victim unconscious, or when victim submits in belief person is husband, §6101; any penetration is sufficient, §6103.

Principals

Male/female; male under 14 presumed incapable, §6102.

Spouses

Statutory spousal exclusion, but exception terminates if spouses have initiated legal proceedings for divorce or separation or if spouses have been living apart for more than 180 days, §6107 (L.1977).

Terminology

Language

Rape is sexual intercourse with a female under circumstances of nonconsent: "where she resists but her resistance is overcome by force or violence," §6101(3); "where she is prevented from resistance by threats of immediate and great bodily harm, accompanied by an apparent power of execution," §6101(4).

Definitions

Rape is sexual intercourse defined by the absence of consent due to age, §6101(1); incapacity through lunacy, §6101(2); where the victim's resistance is overcome or prevented, §6101(3) and (4); where the victim is unconscious, §6101(5); and where the victim mistakenly is induced to believe the actor is her husband, §6101(6).

Statutory Age Provisions

Age of Consent

Age of consent is 18, §6101(1); offender under 14 presumed incapable, §6102.

Offenses

Rape is sexual intercourse where female is under 18, §6101(1), and actor over 14, §6102.

Evidence Provisions, Defenses, and Cross References

Evidence

Evidence of victim's prior sexual conduct not admissible unless found relevant after a hearing; court will limit questioning and control the admission of evidence at trial, but prior felony convictions of witnesses always admissible to impeach credibility, §6105(L.1977). No statutory corroboration requirement; no special jury instructions required.

Defenses

Consent is a defense unless the law has stated victim incapable of consent; mistake as to age not a defense, *State* v. *Guennen*, 36 Idaho 219, 209 P.1072 (1922).

Cross References

Incest, §6602; crime against nature, §6605; distribution of obscene materials to minors, §1513.

Penalties

Terms

Rape: imprisonment for a minimum of 1 year and maximum of life, at the discretion of the sentencing judge, §6104.

Special

Court may order offender to provide restitution, §6106(L.1977); mandatory minimum term of 3 years if second offense or the offender used, threatened, or attempted to use a deadly weapon, §19-2520A.

Illinois

Ill. Ann. Stat. Ch. 38 §11-1 to 11-5 (Smith-Hurd 1979)
§11-1 Rape
§11-2 Deviate sexual conduct
§11-3 Deviate sexual assault
§11-4 Indecent liberties with a child
§11-5 Contributing to the sexual delinquency of a child

Derivation

History

Code of 1833 contains Elizabethan carnal knowledge statute, statutory age of 10, minimum 1 year, maximum life. No substantive changes until 1887 when the age of the male is raised fromm 14 to 16 and the age of the female is raised from 10 to 14. Amendment in 1905 changed age of male from 16 to 17, age of female from 14 to 16, added language "not his wife" and a proviso allowing marriage to victim before conviction to preclude conviction, and rewrote language on force. Amendment in 1955 reduced age for males to 14. 1961 amendment added "not his wife" to substantive offense and used terminology of sexual intercourse. 1967 amendment raised minimum penalty to 4 years. Technical amendments to classification of offenses in 1973 and 1978; rape reform evidence statute passed in 1978.

Present Law

Traditional rape statute with some language changes enacted in 1961, amended as to penalty in 1967, 1973, and 1978. Statutory rape redefined as indecent liberties with a child and contributing to the delinquency of a child in 1961. Rape reform evidence statute in force since 1978.

Statutory Structure

Changes

No significant changes except in sentencing to statute rewritten in 1961 to replace traditional carnal knowledge statute; 1961 law intended to embody no change. Offenses divided into rape, deviate sexual assault, and two

264

categories for the former statutory rape: indecent liberties with a child and contributing to the sexual delinquency of a child. Rape reform evidence statute enacted in 1978.

Offenses

Rape; deviate sexual assault; indecent liberties with a child; contributing to the delinquency of a child.

Requirements

Rape: sexual intercourse by force and against her will including (1) where female unconscious or (2) where female mentally deranged or deficient, §11-1; deviate sexual assault: deviate sexual conduct under force or compulsion, §11-3; indecent liberties with a child: sexual intercourse or deviate sexual intercourse or lewd touching when age restrictions apply, also child pornography, §11-4; contributing to the sexual delinquency of a child: sexual intercourse, deviate sexual conduct, lewd fondling or touching, or any lewd act in the presence of the child when age restrictions apply, §11-5.

Principals

Rape (male/female), deviate sexual assault (person/person), indecent liberties with a child (person/person), contributing to the sexual delinquency of a child (person/person).

Spouses

Common-law spousal exception codified by: "female, not his wife," §11-1; no spousal exception for deviate sexual assault; marriage of the child a defense to indecent liberties with a child, §14-4(d).

Terminology

Language

Rape is sexual intercourse with a female, not his wife, by force and against her will, §11-1; any person who compels any other person to perform or submit to any act of deviate sexual conduct commits deviate sexual assault, §11-3; "any lewd fondling or touching of either the child or the person done or submitted to with the intent to arouse or to satisfy the sexual desires of either the child or the person or both," §11-4(3); "any lewd act done in the presence of the child with the intent to arouse or to satisfy the sexual desires of either the person or the child or both," §11-5.

Definitions

Sexual intercourse occurs when there is any penetration of the female sex organ by the male sex organ, §11-1(b). *Deviate sexual conduct* means any act of sexual gratification involving the sex organs of one person and the mouth or anus of another, §11-2. *Deviate sexual assault* means any forced act of deviate sexual conduct, §11-3. *Indecent liberties with a child* means sexual intercourse, deviate sexual conduct, and any lewd fondling or touching, and manufacture, solicitation, reproducing, or participation by a legal guardian in child pornography, §11-4. *Contributing to the sexual delinquency of a child* means sexual intercourse, deviate sexual conduct, any lewd fondling or touching, and any lewd act done in the presence of the child with requisite intent, §11-5.

Statutory Age Provisions

Age of Consent

No statutory age of consent, but sexual acts, including intercourse, are criminal with a child under 16, when the other person is over 17; no liability for males under 14 years old.

Offenses

Indecent liberties with a child: a person over 17, a child under 16, §11-4; contributing to the sexual delinquency of a child: person over 14, person under 18, §11-5.

Evidence, Provisions, Defenses, and Cross References

Evidence

In a prosecution for rape or deviate sexual assault 1978 evidence statute declares inadmissible the prior sexual activity or the reputation of the alleged victim, except concerning the past sexual conduct of the alleged victim with the accused; if conduct with the defendant is offered, defendant must first offer in-camera evidence to impeach witness' denial, ch. 38, §115-7. Corroboration required unless testimony clear and convincing, *People* v. *Thompson*, 14 Ill. Dec. 773, 57 Ill. App. 3d 134, 373 N.E. 2d 1052 (1978); prompt complaint is corroborative, *People* v. *Kilgore*, 39 Ill. App. 3d 1000, 350 N.E. 2d 810 (1976).

Defenses

Consent is a defense to rape and deviate sexual assault; marriage not a bar to prosecution under §11-4, §11-5, and §11-6; reasonable mistake to the child's age a defense to §11-4; no reasonable mistake as to age defense, §11-5.

Cross References

Aggravated incest, §11-10; incest, §11-11; indecent solicitation of a child (acts less than attempts when a child is under 13), §11-6; minimum requirements for hospitals providing emergency services to rape victims, ch. 111 1/2, §87-6; hospitals to furnish emergency service for rape victims, ch. 111 1/2, §87-2 (effective 1980); reimbursement to rape victims for emergency services, ch. 111 1/2, §87-6.3 (effective 1980).

Penalties

Terms

Rape: class x felony, §11-1(c); deviate sexual assault: class x felony, §11-3(b); class x felony, minimum 6 years, maximum 30 years, ch. 38 §1005-8-1(a)(3)(Supp. 1979); indecent liberties with a child: class 1 felony; class 1 felony, 4 years minimum, maximum 15 years, ch. 38 §1005-8-1(a) (4)(Supp. 1979); contributing to the sexual delinquency of a child: class A misdemeanor, §11-5(c); class A misdemeanor, less than 1 year, ch. 38 §1005-8-3(Supp. 1979).

Special

Probation, periodic imprisonment, or conditional discharge not allowed for conviction of rape, ch. 38 §1005-5.3 (Supp. 1979); see also new procedures on sentencing, ch. 38 §1005-4-1 (Supp. 1979), extended terms, ch. 38 §1005-8-2 (Supp. 1979).

Indiana

State Statutes

Ind. Ann. Stat. §35-42-4-1 to §35-42-4-3 (Supp. 1977) L.1978, L.1979
§35-42-4-1 Rape
§35-42-4-2 Criminal deviate conduct
§35-42-4-3 Child molesting

Derivation

History

1824 compilation included carnal knowledge statute, statutory age was 12, penalty was a minimum of 5 years and a maximum of 21 years; proof of penetration required. In 1843 the minimum term was reduced to 2 years. 1881 compilation raised the minimum term to 5 years and added a new category of rape: sexual intercourse with an insane female. Code of 1894 amended the statutory age to 14 and reduced the minimum term to 1 year. Code of 1908 introduced offense of carnal knowledge of female under 16, incorporated the provision for insane females within the principal statute, and added a new provision for sexual intercourse with female inmates. If female was under 12, penalty for rape was life. For other categories of rape, penalty remained a minimum of 2 years and a maximum of 21 years. No further change until 1974 when sections regarding female inmates and insane females were deleted and provisions were added forbidding a suspended sentence if crime is forcible. Rape reform evidence statute passed in 1975. New formulations of offenses enacted in 1976, effective 1977.

Present Law

Modified traditional rape law includes a reformulation of statutory rape as child molesting and a reformulation of sodomy as nonconsensual criminal deviate conduct, including penetration with an object. Rape reform evidence statute in effect since 1975, amended in 1979.

Statutory Structure

Changes

Statute effective in 1977 replaced carnal knowledge statute with rape, criminal deviate conduct, and child molesting; evidence statute enacted in 1975, amended effective 1977 as to definitions of offenses, amended in 1979 to exclude evidence of sexual conduct of a witness other than the accused and to allow the state to offer such evidence under specially established procedures, L.1979, P.L.289.

Offenses

Rape; criminal deviate conduct; child molesting.

Requirements

Rape: sexual intercourse by force or imminent threat of force, when person unaware, or when the person is so mentally disabled or deficient that consent cannot be given, §35-42-4-1; criminal deviate conduct: compelling a person to perform or submit to deviate sexual conduct or the penetration of the sex organ or anus by an object or any other means by force, imminent threat of force, when the other person is unaware, or when the other person is so mentally disabled or deficient that consent cannot be given, §35-42-4-2; child molesting: sexual intercourse or deviate sexual conduct with a child under 12 or between 12 and 16, and sexual contact offenses with child under 12 or between 12 and 16, §35-42-4-3.

Principals

Person/other person amendment making offense sex neutral effective 1977, replaces male/female designation but sexual intercourse still defended as any penetration of the female sex organ by the male sexual organ. Female can be a principal.

Spouses

Rape: spousal exclusion unless petition for dissolution of marriage is pending, §35-42-4-1(b); criminal deviate conduct: no spousal exclusion; child molesting: a defense that the child is or has ever been married to anyone, §35-42-4-3(f).

Terminology

Language

Rape: a person who knowingly or intentionally has sexual intercourse with a member of the opposite sex when (1) the other person is compelled by force or imminent threat of force; (2) the other person is unaware that the sexual intercourse is occurring; or (3) the other person is so mentally disabled or deficient that consent to sexual intercourse cannot be given, §35-42-4-1. Criminal deviate conduct includes a person who knowingly or intentionally causes penetration, by an object or any other means, of the sex organ or anus of another person under circumstances of force, §35-42-4-2(b).

Definitions

Sexual intercourse means an act that includes any penetration of the female sex organ by the male sex organ, §35-41-1-2. *Deviate sexual conduct* means an act of sexual gratification involving a sex organ of one person and the mouth or anus of another person, §35-41-1-2. A person who performs or submits to any fondling or touching of either the child or the older person with the intent to arouse or satisfy the sexual desires of either the child or the older person commits *child molesting*, §35-42-4-3.

Statutory Age Provisions

Age of Consent

Child under 12 cannot consent to sexual intercourse, deviate sexual conduct, or fondling or touching. If the child is over 12 and under 16, the child cannot consent to sexual intercourse, deviate sexual conduct, or fondling or touching if the actor is over 16.

Offenses

Detailed acts and circumstances defining child molesting replace former statutory rape provisions in 35-42-4-3: (1) sexual intercourse or deviate sexual conduct with child under 12, §3(a); (2) any fondling or touching, of either the child under 12 or the older person, with the intent to arouse or satisfy the sexual desires of either, §3(b); (3) sexual intercourse or deviate sexual conduct by a person 16 or older with a child over 12 but under 16, §3(c); and (4) a person 16 or older who with a child over 12 but under 16 performs or submits to any fondling or any touching, §3(d).

**Evidence Provisions, Defenses,
and Cross References**

Evidence

1975 evidence statute excludes evidence and reference to evidence of prior sexual conduct of the victim or any witness except the accused, excludes opinion evidence and reputation evidence. Special provisions for admitting evidence of conduct with the defendant or evidence showing that a person other than defendant committed the act. Right to impeach the complaining witness or the defendant with prior felony convictions preserved, §35-1-32.5 et seq. Technical amendment in 1979. Corroboration not required: *Loman v. State*, 265 Ind. 255, 254 N.E. 2d 205 (1976).

Defenses

Consent is a defense, but is not defined by statute; statutory defense to child molesting that the person believed the child was 16 or older, §35-42-4-3(e); statutory defense to child molesting that child is or has ever been married, §35-42-4-3(f).

Cross References

Incest, §35-46-1-3; criminal sexual deviancy, §35-11-3.1-1 et seq.: special provisions for the treatment, examination, commitment, right to counsel, and discharge of person found to fall under the definition of criminal sexual deviancy.

Penalties

Terms

Rape: class B felony, but class A felony if forcible or offender is armed, §35-42-4-1(b); criminal deviate conduct: class B felony, but class A felony if forcible or offender is armed, §35-42-4-2(b)(3); child molesting: class B felony if child under 12 and class A felony if forcible or offender is armed; sexual contact offense: class C felony and class A felony if forcible or offender armed; if child between 12 and 16, class C felony or class D felony but class A felony or class B felony if forcible or offender is armed, §35-42-4-3(a)-(d). Class A felony, fixed term of 30 years, §35-50-2-4; class B felony, fixed term of 10 years, §35-50-2-5; class C felony, fixed term of 5 years, §35-5-2-6; class D felony, fixed term of 2 years, or court may sentence for misdemeanor, §35-5-2-7.

Special

Use of threat or use of deadly force, or if offender armed with a deadly weapon raises gradation of offense for every category of rape, criminal deviate conduct, and child molesting. No bail pending appeal if class A felony, L.1979, P.L. 292. Habitual offenders, §35-50-2-8; all terms may be increased or decreased by aggravating and mitigating circumstances, §35-50-2-4, et seq.; criteria for sentencing defined, §35-8-1A-7.

Iowa

Iowa Code Ann. §709.1 to 709.10 (Pamph. 1979)
§709.1 Sexual abuse defined
§709.2 Sexual abuse in the first degree
§709.3 Sexual abuse in the second degree
§709.4 Sexual abuse in the third degree
§709.8 Lascivious acts with a child

Derivation

History

1850 code included carnal knowledge statute, statutory age of female was 10; penalty was life or any term of years. Separate provision for carnal knowledge after administering substance which includes stupor. Revision of 1888 raised statutory age to 13 and rewrote section concerning administering drug to proscribe carnal knowledge with an idiot. 1897 code increased statutory age to 15. Code of 1919 rewrote the statutes but substantive offenses unchanged. In the 1923 compilation the statutory age was increased to 16, distinction made between offenders over 25 and under 25. If actor over 25, statutory age of female was 17, otherwise statutory age was 16; penalty unchanged. 1927 compilation reworded statute and added minimum penalty of 5 years and that the term may be less than maximum. No further amendments until modified Model Penal Code (MPC) criminal code including redefinition of sex offenses enacted in 1976, effective 1978. Traditional sodomy statute repealed. Incest redefined. Repeal of statutory corroboration requirement under prior law. Reformulation of offense retains basic classifications of prohibited conduct under prior law, but defines new crimes and reformulates offense. 1977 amendment deleted provision for sexual abuse in the fourth degree. Amended in 1978 as to terminology and statutory age offense added.

Present Law

Rape redefined as sexual abuse within modified MPC criminal code; rape reform evidence statute and statutory prohibition against special jury instructions included in reform package.

Statutory Structure

Changes

Traditional carnal knowledge statute with two statutory age offenses replaced by statute defining three degrees of criminal sexual abuse. Prior classifications of age, mental incapacity, and force retained, but definition of prohibited sexual conduct expanded. New sexual contact offense. Age restrictions set at 12, 14, 15, and 18. Rape reform evidence statute, and former corroboration requirement repealed.

Offenses

Sexual abuse in the first, second and third degree; lascivious acts with a child.

Requirements

Sexual abuse defined as sexual act by force, or when the participant mentally defective, and so on, or when the participant is a child. First degree is when a person causes another serious injury, §709.2; second degree is when weapon displayed or use or threat of force creating risk of death or serious injury, participant under 12, or aiders and abettors and force, §709.3; third degree is force, mental defect of participant, participant under 14, or participant 14 or 15 and special familiar relationship, person in position of authority, member of same household, or age disparity of over 6 years, §709.4; lascivious acts with a child: fondling, touching, soliciting by a person over 18 with a child under 14, §709.8.

Principals

Person/person; sex act defined in sex-neutral terms, §702.17.

Spouses

Statutory spousal exclusion only specified for third-degree sexual abuse; excluded class is "persons who are not at the time cohabiting as husband and wife," §709.4. Statutory spousal exclusion for lascivious acts with a child, "unless married to each other," §709.8; no spousal exclusion for first and second degree sexual abuse.

Terminology

Language

"Any sex act between persons is sexual abuse by either of the participants when the act is performed . . . in any of the following circumstances . . .," §709.1; sexual abuse is when . . . "such other participant is suffering from a mental defect or in a capacity which precludes giving consent, or lacks the mental capacity to know the right and wrong of conduct in sexual matters," §709.1(2).

Definitions

Sexual abuse is "any sex act between persons by either participant when the act is . . . done by force, or consent or acquiescence is procured by threats of violence, or participant is suffering from mental defect or incapacity which precludes consent or lacks mental capacity . . ., or participant is a child," §709.1. *Sex act* means any sexual contact by penetration of the penis into the vagina or anus, by contact between the mouth and genitalia, or by contact between the genitalia of one person and the genitalia or anus of another person, or by use of artificial sex organs or substitutes therefore in contact with the genitalia or anus, §702.17. *Serious injury* means disabling mental illness, or bodily injury which creates substantial risk of death or which causes permanent disfigurement, or protracted loss or impairment of the function of any bodily member or organ, §702.18. *Lascivious acts with a child* includes fondling, touching, soliciting, and the infliction of pain or discomfort, §709.8.

Statutory Age Provisions

Age of Consent

Child is any person under 14, §702.15; sexual abuse defined as any sexual act when the other participant is a child, §709.1(3); in addition, several offenses specify ages for both participants.

Offenses

Second-degree sexual abuse: when the other participant is under 12, §709.3(2); third-degree sexual abuse: any sex act when the other participant is a child, §709.4(3), or when the participant is 14 or 15 and the other participant has a family relationship or is in a position of authority, §709.4(4), or when a participant is 14 or 15 and the other person is over 6 years older, §707.4(5) (L. 1978); lascivious acts with a child: person over 18 with a child, §709.8.

Evidence Provisions, Defenses, and Cross References

Evidence

Evidence rule provides for special procedures for the admission of evidence of the prosecuting witness' previous sexual conduct. In-camera hearing, court to control admission of evidence, no evidence of conduct more than 1 year prior to crime except conduct with the defendant. Prior felony conviction excepted, §813.2, Rule 20(5). Evidence that victim consented to intercourse with one person irrelevant to issue of consent with another, *State* v. *Ball*, 262 N.W. 2d 278 (1978). Corroboration not required, former law required corroboration; cautionary jury instruction prohibited, §709.6.

Defenses

Consent: sexual abuse defined in part as when "such act is done by force or against the will of the other. In any case where the consent or acquiescence of the other is procured by threats of violence toward any person, the act is done against the will of the other," 703.1(1); statutory defense of ignorance or mistake, §701.6; proof of resistance not required, §709.5.

Cross References

Incest, §726.2; pornographic sexual exploitation of children, senate file no. 2205, L.1978; in cases of sexual abuse cost of medical examination for evidence and cost of treatment for prevention of venereal disease to be borne by state, §709.10; reasonable force, §704.1; deadly force, §704.2.

Penalties

Terms

First-degree sexual abuse: class A felony, §709.2; class A felony, life and no suspended sentence or deferred sentence or reconsideration of sentence, no parole unless governor commutes to term of years, §902.1; second-degree sexual abuse: class B felony, §709.3; class B felony, maximum of 25 years, §902.9; third-degree sexual abuse: class C felony, §709.4; class C felony, maximum 10 years; lascivious acts with a child: class D felony, §709.8; class D felony, maximum 5 years, §902.9.

Special

Every 5 years record of person convicted class A felony reviewed, §902.2; special provisions for habitual offenders, §902.9; minimum sentences for habitual offenders, §902.8; minimum sentence if use of a firearm, §902.7; provision for reconsideration of sentence, §902.4.

Kansas

State Statutes

Kan. Stat. Ann. §21-3501 to §21-3508 (1974) (Supp. 1975)(Supp. 1978)
§21-3501 Definitions
§21-3502 Rape
§21-3503 Indecent liberties with a child
§21-3504 Indecent liberties with a ward
§21-3505 Sodomy
§21-3506 Aggravated sodomy

Derivation

History

Compilation of 1855 defined rape as unlawful carnal knowledge of a female under 12 or the forcible ravishment of a woman over 10; punishment was hard labor for at least 5 years. Carnal knowledge of woman after administering drugs preventing resistance also rape. Negro or mulatto who raped or attempted rape of a white woman punished by castration at the expense of defendant. Law of 1862 changed statutory age to 10, maximum penalty of 21 years. In 1889 statutory age changed to 18. Compilation of 1930 included minimum penalty of 5 years. 1963 provision specified penalty of 6 months or $1,000 fine if guardian raped his ward. Prior to 1968 common-law rape statute did not define offense. Law of 1969 defined and codified all sex offenses. Rape defined as sexual intercourse under specified circumstances of nonconsent: when resistance overcome, when woman unconscious or powerless, when woman mentally deficient, and when resistance prevented. Law of 1969 included codified spousal exception. Statutory rape defined as indecent liberties with a child. Law of 1978 increased gradation of offense to class B felony.

Present Law

Codification of traditional definition of rape, prohibited conduct defined by statute in terms of victim's resistance and incapacity or inability to consent. Present law incorporates no reform features, continues prior definition including special definition of statutory rape.

278

Statutory Structure

Changes

Rape statute amended in 1978 only to upgrade classification of offense. No change in definition of offense. L.1969 intended to codify the common-law offenses.

Offenses

Rape; indecent liberties with a child; indecent liberties with a ward.

Requirements

Rape: sexual intercourse without consent a) when a woman's resistance overcome; or b) when woman is unconscious or powerless to resist; or c) when woman is incapable of consent due to mental deficiency or disease; or d) when woman's resistance is prevented by alcohol, narcotic, and so on, §21-3502. Indecent liberties: sexual intercourse or any fondling or touching of a child or ward, §21-3503.

Principals

Male/female (definition of rape and sexual intercourse); "woman" means any female human being, §21-3501(3); offenses involving children, sex-neutral.

Spouses

Statutory spousal exception for all offenses. Rape is an act committed by a man with a woman not his wife, §21-3502; indecent liberties are acts with a child not the spouse of the offender, §21-3503; sodomy includes spousal exception, §21-3505.

Terminology

Language

"Rape is the act of sexual intercourse committed by a man with a woman not his wife, and without her consent . . . (a) when a woman's resistance is overcome by force or fear; or (b) when the woman is unconscious or physically powerless to resist; or (c) when the woman is incapable of giving her consent because of mental deficiency or disease, which condition was known by the man or reasonably apparent to him; or (d) when the woman's resistance is prevented by the effect of any alcoholic liquor, and so on," §21-3502.

Definitions

Sexual intercourse means any penetration of the female sex organ by the male sex organ, §21-3501(1). *Unlawful sexual act* means any rape, indecent liberties with a child, sodomy, aggravated sodomy, or lewd and lascivious behavior, §21-3501(2). *Sodomy* is oral or anal copulation between persons who are not husband and wife or consenting adult members of the opposite sex, §21-3505. *Indecent liberties* includes any lewd fondling or touching of the person of either the child or the offender done or submitted to with the intent to arouse or to satisfy the sexual desires of either the child or the offender, or both, §21-3503 and §21-3504. *Indecent liberties with a ward* include acts by any guardian, proprietor, or employee of any foster home, orphanage, or other public or private institution for the care and custody of minor children, to whose charge such child has been committed, under color of law, §21-3504.

Statutory Age Provisions

Age of Consent

Statutory age of consent is 16; sexual intercourse with person under 16 defined as indecent liberties with a child, §21-3503.

Offenses

Indecent liberties with a child or ward; sexual intercourse or fondling of a child under 16, §21-3503 and §21-3504; aggravated sodomy; sodomy with a child under 16, §21-3506.

Evidence Provisions, Defenses, and Cross References

Evidence

No rape evidence statute; corroboration not required, *State* v. *Brown*, 85 Kan. 418, 116 P. 508 (1911).

Defenses

Common-law defenses of marriage, absence of resistance, consent, and capacity to consent, all available.

Cross References

Incest, §21-3602; aggravated incest, §21-3603; sexual exploitation of a child (pornography), §21-3516 (L.1978); enticement of a child, §21-3509; protection from abuse act, civil remedies for sexual abuse among family members or persons who reside together, ch. 92, L.1979.

Penalties

Terms

Rape: class B felony, §21-3502; indecent liberties with a ward: class B felony, §21-3504; class B felony, minimum term between 5 and 15 years and maximum term between 20 years and life, §21-4501(b); indecent liberties with a child: class C felony, §21-3503; class C felony, minimum term between 1 year and 3 years, maximum term between 10 and 20 years, §21-4501(c).

Special

Minimum and maximum terms for second offenders, §21-4504; fines, §21-4503.

Kentucky

State Statutes

Ky. Rev. Stat. §510.010 to §510.150 (1975 Repl.) (Supp. 1978)
§510.010 Definitions
§510.010 Lack of consent
§510.040 Rape in the first degree
§510.050 Rape in the second degree
§510.060 Rape in the third degree
§510.070 Sodomy in the first degree
§510.080 Sodomy in the second degree
§510.090 Sodomy in the third degree
§510.100 Sodomy in the fourth degree
§510.110 Sexual abuse in the first degree
§510.120 Sexual abuse in the second degree
§510.130 Sexual abuse in the third degree
§510.140 Sexual misconduct

Derivation

History

Laws of 1798 punished rape with a minimum term of 4 years and a maximum term of 21 years. In 1799 the minimum penalty was increased to 10 years, and the law delineated the offense as carnal knowledge and specified 10 as the statutory age. 1802 code specified that this penalty was applicable to whites only. Law of 1813 punished slaves who attempted rape of a white woman with death. Law of 1913 provided death penalty for rape of an infant under 12. In 1852 rape was defined as carnal knowledge of any white woman against her will, or by force, or when she was insensible; penalty was 10 to 20 years. Separate offense with the same penalty prohibited carnal knowledge of a white girl under 10. Codification of 1860 punished rape of an infant under 12 with death and added to section punishing rape of white girl under 12, prohibition against carnal knowledge of an idiot. Law of 1866 equalized criminal penalties for whites and negroes except in the area of rape. Codification of 1873 punished rape of an infant under 12 with death or life imprisonment, at the discretion of the jury. Attempted rape of a female under 12 was punishable by a minimum term of 5 years and a maximum term of 20 years. Carnal knowledge by force or while a woman was insensible, punishable by 10 to 20 years or death. A new offense, carnal

282

knowledge of a female under 12 or an idiot, carried a minimum term of 10 years and a maximum term of 20 years. Law of 1906 changed statutory age to 16 in carnal knowledge statute. Law of 1922 rewrote statutory rape law to raise statutory age to 18, phrases "with consent" "or an idiot" removed, penalty structure based upon age of female. If female under 12, minimum 20 years, maximum 50 years or death; if female over 12 and under 16, minimum 5, maximum 20; if female over 16 and under 18, minimum 2, maximum 10. Other age restrictions on male defined the offense as a juvenile offense or allowed for mitigation of penalty. Law of 1944 changed penalty for rape of child under 12 to death, or life without parole, or life, or minimum 10 years and maximum 20 years. Former law repealed in 1974, effective 1975, when revised criminal code enacted.

Present Law

Model Penal Code (MPC) formulation codifying the traditional definition of the offense and adding less serious, sex-neutral offenses. Rape reform evidence statute in effect since 1976.

Statutory Structure

Changes

Traditional carnal knowledge rape statute with precise gradations of statutory rape based upon the age of the female and male repealed in 1974, effective 1975, and replaced by MPC rape statute. Rape evidence statute enacted in 1976.

Offenses

Rape in the first, second and third degree; sodomy in the first, second, third and fourth degree; sexual abuse in the first, second and third degree; sexual misconduct.

Requirements

First-degree rape: sexual intercourse by forcible compulsion or when person incapable of consent because physically helpless or under 12; second-degree rape: sexual intercourse when the actor is over 18 and the other person is under 14; third-degree rape: sexual intercourse with a person incapable of consent because mentally defective or mentally incapacitated, or a person over 12 with person under 16. First-, second-, and third-degree sodomy: deviate sexual intercourse under circumstances of first-, second-, and third-degree rape; fourth-degree sodomy: deviate sexual intercourse with another person of the same sex (lack of consent no defense). First-degree sexual abuse: sexual contact under circumstances of first-degree rape; second-degree abuse: sexual contact with person mentally defective or mentally incapacitated or with a person under 14; third-degree sexual abuse: sexual contact without consent, a defense that the person is over 14 and under 16 and the actor is less than 5 years older. Sexual misconduct: sexual intercourse or deviate sexual intercourse without consent.

Principals

Rape: male/female. Sexual intercourse means sexual intercourse in its ordinary sense, §510.010(8); other offenses sex-neutral: person/person.

Spouses

Statutory spousal exception for rape and sodomy. Marriage means persons living together as man and wife regardless of the legal status of their relationship. Spouses living apart under a decree of judicial separation are not married to one another for purposes of this chapter, §510.010(3), and sexual intercourse is limited to sexual intercourse between persons not married to each other, §510.010(8). Deviate sexual intercourse means "any act . . . between persons not married to each other," §510.010(1).

Terminology

Language

A person is guilty of rape in the first degree when he engages in sexual intercourse with another person by forcible compulsion or . . . with another person who is incapable of consent because he is physically helpless, §510.040. Lack of consent results from forcible compulsion or incapacity to consent; if the offense charged is sexual abuse, any circumstances in addition to forcible compulsion or incapacity to consent in which the victim does not expressly or impliedly acquiesce in the actor's conduct, §510.020.

Definitions

Lack of consent defined by force and incapacity to consent due to age, person mentally defective, mentally incapacitated, or physically helpless, §510.020. *Sexual intercourse* means "sexual intercourse in its ordinary sense . . . any penetration, however slight, emission is not required," §510.010(8). *Deviate sexual intercourse* means any act of sexual gratification between persons not married to each other involving the sex organs of one person and the mouth or anus of another, §510.010(1). *Sexual contact* means any touching of the sexual or other intimate parts of a person not married to the actor done for the prupose of gratifying the sexual desire of either party, §510.010(7). *Forcible compulsion* means physical force that overcomes earnest resistance by placing a person in fear of immediate death or physical injury to himself or another person or in fear that he or another person will be immediately kidnaped, §510.010(2).

Statutory Age Provisions

Age of Consent

Age of consent is 16, incapacity to consent defined in part by age of less than 16, §510.020(3)a; in addition, several offenses define criminal conduct in terms of age of one or both participants.

Offenses

First-degree rape: sexual intercourse with a person under 12, §510.040(1)(b) (2); second-degree rape: sexual intercourse by a person over 18 with a person under 14, §510.050(1); third-degree rape: sexual intercourse by a person over 21 with a person under 16, §510.060; first-degree sodomy: deviate sexual intercourse with a person under 12, §510.070(1)(b)(2); second-degree sodomy: deviate sexual intercourse by a person over 18 with a person under 14, §510.080(1); third-degree sodomy: deviate sexual intercourse by a person over 21 with a person under 16, §510.090(1)(b); first-degree sexual abuse: sexual contact with a person under 12, §510.110(1) (b)(2); second-degree sexual abuse: sexual contact with a person under 14, §510.120(1)(b); a defense to third-degree sexual abuse that the person was over 14 and under 16 and the actor was less than 5 years older, §510.130 (1)(b).

Evidence Provisions, Defenses, and Cross References

Evidence

Rape reform evidence statute enacted in 1976 excludes evidence of the victim's prior sexual conduct or habits in the form of reputation evidence or specific instances of prior conduct, except evidence of conduct with the defendant or evidence pertaining to the act on which prosecution is based, §510.145; corroboration not required, *Hogue* v. *Commonwealth*, 305 Ky. 298, 203 S.W. 2d (1947).

Defenses

"Whether or not specifically stated, it is an element of every offense defined in this chapter that the sexual act was committed without consent of the victim," §510.020(1); but consent not a defense to fourth-degree sodomy, §510.100(2); ignorance or mistake a defense if it negates the existence of a culpable mental state, §510.070; for all crimes based upon incapacity to consent, including age, defendant may prove in exculpation that he did not know of the facts or conditions responsible for such incapacity to consent, §510.030.

Cross References

Incest, §530.020; sexual exploitation of minors (pornography), §531.300 (L.1978).

Penalties

Terms

Jury determines penalty in addition to finding degree of offense, Ky. R. Crim. Proc. 9.84 (1972). First-degree rape and sodomy: class B felony, unless the victim is under 12 or receives serious physical injury, then class A felony, §510.040, §510.070; second-degree rape and sodomy: class C felony, §510.050, §510.080; third-degree rape and sodomy: class D felony, §510.060, §510.090. First-degree sexual abuse: class D felony, §510.110; all other offenses misdemeanors. Class A felony, minimum 20 years, maximum life; class B felony, minimum 10 years, maximum 20 years; class C felony, minimum 5 years, maximum 10 years; class D felony, minimum 1 year, maximum 5 years, §532.060.

Special

Persistent felony offender sentencing, §532.080; special procedures where death penalty might be imposed, include detailed aggravating and mitigating circumstances, §532.025 et seq.; court may modify jury sentence within statutory limits, §532.070.

Louisiana

State Statutes

La. Rev. Stat. §14:41 to 43 (Supp. 1979) §14:80 (Supp. 1979)
§41 Rape; defined
§42 Aggravated rape
§42.1 Forcible rape
§43 Simple rape
§43.1 Sexual battery
§80 Carnal knowledge of a juvenile

Derivation

History

1833 code included unusual carnal knowledge statute defining rape as carnal knowledge under detailed circumstances of force, menace, or fraud, with factors subjective to the victim considered; age of consent was 11. 1852 code simply provided death penalty for rape without definition of acts or offense. 1915 code set age of consent at 12, and no presumption that male under 14 was incapable. 1932 incorporated special provisions for carnal knowledge of insane or feebleminded woman and prohibited sexual intercourse with a female over 12 and under 18. 1943 code reduced age of consent to 17, raised age of male to over 17, prohibited mistake as to age offense, penalty of 5 years for statutory rape. 1943 code divided rape into simple rape and aggravated rape, death penalty for aggravated rape. Spousal exclusion in definition of rape, statutory age of 12 for aggravated rape continued prior rule. 1951 code simplified formulation of simple and aggravated rape. In 1975 offense was reformulated as homosexual rape and heterosexual rape; this statute was repealed in 1978 and new classifications of offenses were defined.

Present Law

Unique formulation enacted in 1978, replaced unusual formulation of homosexual rape and heterosexual rape enacted in 1975. 1978 statute returns to earlier classification of rape and aggravated rape for principal offense and adds new offenses.

288

Statutory Structure

Changes

1975 act rewrote rape statute to define heterosexual rape, homosexual rape, and forcible rape. 1978 act redefined offenses, retained forcible rape, increased penalty for simple rape, added sexual battery, and reinstated categories of aggravated rape and simple rape existing prior to 1975. Definition of rape amended to include anal intercourse with a male or female; oral and anal intercourse added to offenses affecting minors. L.1979 redefined aggravated sodomy to parallel definitions of nonconsent in aggravated rape.

Offenses

Aggravated rape; forcible rape; simple rape; sexual battery; carnal knowledge of a juvenile.

Requirements

Aggravated rape: anal or vaginal sexual intercourse without consent because (1) the victim resists and resistance overcome; (2) the victim is prevented from resisting by acts or threats of great and immediate bodily harm; or (3) the victim is under 12, §42. Forcible rape: anal or vaginal sexual intercourse because the victim is prevented from resisting by force or threat or violence, §42.1. Simple rape: anal or vaginal sexual intercourse without consent because (1) the victim is incapacitated by drug or abnormality; (2) the victim is incapable of understanding the act; or (3) the female is induced to believe the male is her husband, §43. Sexual battery: genital acts short of intercourse and oral-genital acts under compulsion, §43.1. Carnal knowledge of a juvenile: sexual intercourse, anal or oral sexual intercourse, with consent, when age restrictions apply, §80.

Principals

Rape: male offender with male or female victim, §41; sexual battery: offender/person; carnal knowledge of a juvenile: male/female, or person/person, §80.

Spouses

Spousal exclusion for all categories of rape defined in §41; spousal exclusion for sexual battery, §43.1; for carnal knowledge of a juvenile, female means unmarried female, §80. Spouses: a person shall not be considered to be a spouse if a judgment of separation from bed and board has been rendered, §41.

Terminology

"Where the victim resists the act to utmost, but whose resistance is overcome by force; or where the victim is prevented from resisting by threats of great and immedite bodily harm, accompanied by apparent power of execution," §42; "when the victim is prevented from resisting the act by force or threats of physical violence under circumstances where the victim reasonably believes that such resistance would not prevent rape," §42.1. "Sexual battery is . . . where the offender compels the other person to submit by placing the other person in fear of receiving bodily harm," §43.1.

Definitions

Rape is the act of anal or vaginal sexual intercourse committed without the person's lawful consent, §42. *Without lawful consent* defined by the victim is resistance and the age of victim, §42, by the victim's resistance being prevented by force or the threat of physical violence, §42.1, by the victim's incapacity caused by intoxicant, stupor, or abnormality, unsoundness of mind, or when the victim is deceived, §43. *Sexual battery*: the intentional engaging in a sexual act by compulsion. *Sexual act* means contact between the penis and vulva, penis and anus, mouth or tongue and penis, or the mouth or tongue and vulva, §43.1.

Statutory Age Provisions

Age of Consent

No statutory age of consent. Presumption of nonconsent if victim under 12, §42. Females can consent to sexual intercourse at 17, or between the ages of 12 and 17, if the male is not 2 years older. Persons can consent to anal or oral sexual intercourse at 17, or between the ages of 12 and 17, if the age difference is less than 2 years. No liability for consenting persons between

12 and 17 if no 2 year age difference. No liability for females who have sexual intercourse with males over 12 and under 17.

Offenses

Anal or vaginal sexual intercourse with a victim under 12, §42; male over 17 with a female over 12 and under 17, with consent, when age difference of more than 2 years, §80(1).

Evidence Provisions, Defenses, and Cross References

Evidence

1975 evidence statute precludes admissibility of evidence of the victim's prior sexual conduct and reputation for chastity in prosecutions for rape or carnal knowledge, except "incidents arising out of the victim's relationship with the accused," §15:498.

Defenses

Lack of knowledge of victim's age is no defense, §42; lack of knowledge of juvenile's age is no defense, §80; marriage of the female a defense, §80; consent a defense to all categories of rape, but the absence of consent "deemed" when resistance is overcome or prevented, when the victim is under 12, §42; when force or threat of violence, §42.1; or when the victim is incapacitated or deceived, §43. Consent not a defense under §80.

Cross References

Incest, §78; indecent behavior with juveniles, §81; pornography involving juveniles, §81.1; prostitution, §82 et seq.; crime against nature, §89; aggravated crime against nature, §89.1 (amended L.1979).

Penalties

Terms

Aggravated rape: life, §42; forcible rape: minimum 2 years, maximum 40 years, §42.1; simple rape: maximum of 25 years, §43; sexual battery: maximum of 10 years, §43.1; carnal knowledge of a juvenile: maximum of 10 years, §80.

Special

Life imprisonment is at hard labor without benefit of parole, probation, or suspension of sentence, §42. Former mandatory death penalty declared unconstitutional, *State* v. *Williams*, 340 So. 2d 1382 (La. 1976); forcible rape term at hard labor and 2 year minimum without benefit of probation, parole, or suspension of sentence, §42.1.

Maine

State Statutes

Me. Rev. Stat. Ann. tit. 17-A §251 to §255 (Pamphlet 1979)
§251 Definitions and general provisions
§252 Rape
§253 Gross sexual misconduct
§254 Sexual abuse of minors
§255 Unlawful sexual contact

Derivation

History

1822 compilation defined rape as carnal knowledge of any woman by force or against her will, statutory age was 10, penalty was death. 1831 compilation changed penalty to life. 1842 code reworded the offense in terms of ravish and carnally knows by force. 1857 code added carnally knows and abuses a child under 10 and a section on abduction to compel mariage. 1884 compilation changed penalty to any term of years. 1904 code added offense of carnal knowledge of an unmarried female child between 14 and 16 by a male over 12, with a penalty of a fine or a maximum term of 2 years. Term for rape remained at any term of years. 1916 code put statutory rape in crimes against children, offense unchanged. 1930 compilation reduced age of male to 18. No change until carnal knowledge formulation repealed, effective 1976, when Model Penal Code (MPC) criminal code reform enacted sex offenses based upon MPC, prior law, and proposed Massachusetts criminal code and proposed federal criminal code.

Present Law

MPC rape statute: new offense of gross sexual misconduct based upon proposed federal code and proposed Massachusetts criminal code; sexual abuse of minors essentially the former statutory rape broadened to include sexual acts other than intercourse; unlawful sexual contact new, based upon proposed Massachusetts criminal code and proposed federal criminal code.

Statutory Structure

Changes

Traditional carnal knowledge statute defining rape and carnal knowledge of girls 14 to 16 replaced by four offenses: MPC rape statute, two categories of gross sexual misconduct, sexual abuse of minors, and unlawful sexual contact.

Offenses

Rape; gross sexual misconduct; sexual abuse of minors; unlawful sexual contact.

Requirements

Rape: sexual intercourse with a person under 14 or when a person is compelled to submit by force, threat of death or serious bodily injury or kidnaping, §252; gross sexual misconduct: sexual act by force or threat of death, serious bodily injury or kidnaping or with a person under 14 and sexual intercourse or sexual act under circumstances in which nonconsent is presumed, §253; sexual abuse of minors: sexual intercourse and sexual acts with person over 14 and under 16 and actor 5 years older, §254; unlawful sexual contact: sexual contact, without acquiescence; when a person is unconscious or incapable of resisting and has not consented; or with a person under 14 and when the actor is 3 years older; when a person suffers from a mental disease; or when a person is in official custody and the actor has supervisory power, §255.

Principals

Person/person but definition of sexual intercourse is any penetration of the female sex organ by the male sex organ; rape is therefore male/female. All other crimes sex-neutral.

Spouses

Common-law spousal exception assumed, see Comment (1975) to chapter 11, Sex Offenses (*Maine Criminal Code*, 1979 Pamphlet, p. 99). "Spouse means a person legally married to the actor, but does not include a legally married person living apart from the actor under a de facto separation," §251(1)(A); an affirmative defense that defendant and victim were living together as man and wife at the time of the crime, §252(2) and §253(4).

Terminology

Language

Rape is sexual intercourse when submission compelled . . . "by threat that death, serious bodily injury, or kidnaping will be imminently inflicted on the person or any other human being," §252(1)(B)(2); gross sexual misconduct is . . . "when he has substantially impaired the other person's power to appraise or control his sex acts by administering or employing drugs, intoxicants, or other similar means . . . or the other person is unconscious or otherwise physically incapable of resisting and has not consented to such sexual intercourse or sexual act," §253(2)(A)(1); "a person is guilty of unlawful sexual contact if he intentionally subjects another person, not his spouse, to any sexual contact, and the other person has not expressly or impliedly acquiesced in such sexual contact," §255(1)(A).

Definitions

Sexual act means any act of sexual gratification between two persons involving direct physical contact between the sex organs of one and the mouth or anus of the other or direct physical contact between the sex organs of one and the sex organs of the other, or direct physical contact between the sex organs of one and an instrument or device manipulated by the other. A sexual act may be proved without allegation or proof of penetration, §251(1)(C). *Sexual contact* means any touching of the genitals, directly or through clothing, other than as would constitute a sexual act, for the purpose of arousing or gratifying sexual desire, §251(1)(D). *Person in official custody* means as a probationer or a parolee, or detained in a hospital, prison or other institution and the actor has supervisory or disciplinary authority over such other person, §253(2)(E).

Statutory Age Provisions

Age of Consent

Statutory age of 14 retained from prior law for most offenses, including rape; sexual abuse of minors includes persons under 16; no prosecution of person under 18, §53.

Offenses

Rape: sexual intercourse with any person who has not in fact attained his 14th birthday, §252(1)(A); a gross sexual misconduct: sexual act when other person is under 14, §253(1)(B); sexual abuse of minors: sexual intercourse or sexual act by person over 19 with a person over 14 and under 16; unlawful sexual contact: sexual contact when person under 14 and the actor is 3 years older.

Evidence Provisions, Defenses, and Cross References

Evidence

No evidence statute; corroboration not required, *State* v. *Wheeler*, 150 Me. 332, 110 A.2d 578 (1955); no prompt complaint requirement.

Defenses

Rape statute does not use terminology of consent, but consent a defense to MPC rape statute and to common-law rape. MPC consent formulation not adopted. If the victim was a voluntary social companion who had permitted sexual contact, gradation of crime will be reduced, §252(3) and §253(4); mistake as to age a defense to sexual abuse of minors, §254(2); ignorance and mistake as a defense, generally, §52.

Cross References

Incest, §556; sexual exploitation of minors, §2921.

Penalties

Terms

Rape: class A crime unless the victim falls within the exception for a voluntary social companion, then class B crime, §252(3); gross sexual misconduct: if forced sexual act or person under 14, class A crime unless the victim falls within the exception for a voluntary social companion, then class B crime, §252(4); if person is incapable because of mental illness or defect or an administered intoxicant or a person in custody, class B crime; if a person is unconscious or physically incapable or compelled by threat, class C crime, §253(5); sexual abuse of minors: class D crime, §254(3); unlawful sexual contact: if a person subjected to sexual contact and the person has not acquiesced, class C crime; all other forms of unlawful sexual contact a class D crime, §255(2). Class A crime, definite term not to exceed 20 years; class B crime, definite term not to exceed 10 years; class C crime, definite term not to exceed 5 years; class D crime, definite term less than 1 year, §1252.

Special

Grade of crime increased if dangerous weapon used, §1252(4); minimum custodial term if offense committed with firearm, §1252(5); authorized fines, §1301.

Maryland

State Statutes

Md. Ann. Code art. 27 §461 to §465 (Supp. 1979)

§461	Definitions
§462	First-degree rape
§463	Second-degree rape
§464	First-degree sexual offense
§464A	Second-degree sexual offense
§464B	Third-degree sexual offense
§464C	Fourth-degree sexual offense

Derivation

History

1809 statute penalized rape (undefined) by death or a minimum term of 18 months to a maximum term of 21 years, proof of penetration required. Carnal abuse had the same penalty; statutory age of female was 10. Recodification in 1860, no change until code of 1914 changed statutory age to 14, added provision regarding sexual intercourse with mentally incompetent woman or imbecile. Sodomy statute enacted in 1916. Compilation of 1924 made no change to rape or carnal abuse but added new crime (L.1924), carnal knowledge of any female between 14 and 16, a misdemeanor. Prohibition against prosecution of male under 18. 1951 Added jury instruction stating if not death penalty, then the maximum was 21 years. In 1976 these penalty statutes with no statutory definition of the offense were replaced by a statute defining two degrees of rape and four degrees of sexual offenses. Carnal knowledge of male under 14 by female over 18 repealed in 1976; sodomy and perverted practices not repealed. Rape reform evidence statute passed in 1976, coverage expanded in 1977. Gradation of statutory rape of person under 14 downgraded to second degree in 1977.

Present Law

Rape reform legislation passed in 1976, including an evidence statute. Act of rape defined in traditional terms with specific circumstances of violence and force delineating degrees; sexual offenses defined in accordance with reform definitions of sexual act and sexual contact. Traditional crime of statutory rape retained.

Statutory Structure

Changes

Common-law rape and penalty statute replaced in 1976 by reform statute defining two degrees of rape and sexual offenses in the first, second, third, and fourth degree. Common-law sodomy statute not repealed; offenses overlap. Rape reform evidence statute enacted in 1976 and strengthened in 1977.

Offenses

Rape in the first and second degree; first, second, third and fourth degree sexual offense.

Requirements

First-degree rape: vaginal intercourse by force and without consent and (1) weapon, or (2) a person inflicts suffocation, strangulation, disfigurement, or serious physical injury upon the person or anyone else, or (3) threatens or places the victim in fear of imminent death, suffocation, strangulation, disfigurement, serious physical injury, or kidnaping, or (4) aiders and abettors, art. 27 §462. Second-degree rape: vaginal intercourse (1) by force or threat of force against the will and without consent, or (2) with a person mentally defective, mentally incapacitated, or physically helpless and the other person knows of the condition, or (3) with a person under 14 when the other person is 4 years older, art. 27 §463. First-degree sexual offense: sexual offense: sexual act under circumstances defining first-degree rape or by force or threat of force, art. 27 §464. Second-degree sexual offense: sexual act under circumstances of second-degree rape, art. 27 §464. Third-degree sexual offense: sexual contact by force and (1) weapon or (2) infliction of suffocation, and so on, art. 27 §464B. Fourth-degree sexual offense: (1) sexual contact without consent or (2) sexual act with a person 14 or 15 when the actor is 4 years older, or (3) vaginal intercourse with person 14 or 15 when the actor is 4 years older, art. 27 §464C.

Principals

Rape is male/female; sexual offenses refer to person/person.

Spouses

Statutory spousal exception creates a complete defense to all offenses involving legal spouses unless the parties are living apart pursuant to a decree of divorce, art. 27 §464D; special provisions require the police to aid in cases of spousal assault and provide immunity from civil liability for police acting in good faith, art. 27 §11F (L.1979).

Terminology

Language

First-degree rape is vaginal intercourse by force and against her will and without consent, art. 27 §462; second-degree rape is vaginal intercourse by force or threat of force against the will and without the consent of the other person or with a person who is mentally defective, mentally incapacitated, or physically helpless and person knows or should know of other person's condition, art. 27 §462.

Definitions

Vaginal intercourse has its ordinary meaning of genital copulation. Penetration, however slight, is evidence of vaginal intercourse; emission of semen not required, art. 27 §461(g). *Sexual act* "means cunnilingus, fellatio, analingus, or anal intercourse, but does not include vaginal intercourse . . .[it] also means the penetration, however slight, by any object into the genital or anal opening of another person's body if the penetration can be reasonbaly construed as being for the prupose of sexual arousal or gratification or for abuse of either party . . . [medical exception]," art. 27 §461(e). *Sexual contact* "means the intentional touching of any part of the victim's or actor's anal or genital areas or other intimate parts for the purposes of sexual arousal or gratification or for abuse . . . and includes penetration by any part of a person's body other than the penis, mouth, or tongue, into the genital or anal opening," art. 27 §461(f). *Sexual abuse*, for the purposes of prosecution under the child-abuse statute, shall mean any act or acts involving sexual molestation or exploitation, including but not limited to incest, rape, or sexual offense in any degree, by any parent or person with custody, art. 27 §35A.

Statutory Age Provisions

Age of Consent

Age of consent is 14, unchanged from prior law; requirement that actor must be 4 years older for all statutory age offenses added in 1976.

Offenses

Second-degree rape: vaginal intercourse with person under 14 when the other person is at least 4 years older, art. 27 §463a(3); second-degree sexual offense: sexual act with a person under 14 and the other person is 4 years older, art 27 §464a(3); third-degree sexual offense: sexual contact with a person under 14 and the other person is 4 years older, art. 27 §464Ba(3); fourth-degree sexual offense: sexual act or vaginal intercourse with a person 14 or 15 and the other person is 4 years older, art 27 §464Ca(1) and (2).

**Evidence Provisions, Defenses,
and Cross References**

Evidence

1976 evidence statute prohibits admission of reputation and opinion evidence concerning victim's chastity; specific incidents of prior conduct may be admitted if the judge finds relevance and the evidence concerns (1) conduct with defendant, (2) source or origin of semen, pregnancy, disease, or trauma, (3) supports claims of ulterior motive, or (4) for the purpose of impeachment when the prosecutor puts the victim's prior sexual conduct in issue; in-camera hearing required, art. 27 §461A.

Defenses

Common-law defense of consent retained for crimes involving persons over 14; spousal exception a complete defense; defendant entitled to bill of particulars, art. 27 §461B.

Cross References

Incest, art. 27 §335; sodomy, art. 27 §553; unnatural or perverted sexual practices, art. 27 §554; previous common-law constructions retained unless express contrary intention, art. 27 §464E; victims of rape and sexual offenses not to be charged for medical exam, L.1977, ch. 854; police training on rape mandated, L.1977, ch. 293; causing abuse to child under 18, art. 27 §35A et seq.; restitution for crimes, art. 27 §640.

Penalties

Terms

First-degree rape: maximum life term, art. 27 §462(b); second-degree rape: maximum 20 years, art. 27 §463(b); first-degre sexual offense: maximum of life, art. 27 §464(b); second-degree sexual offense: maximum 20 years, art. 27 §464A(b); third-degree sexual offense: maximum of 10 years, art. 27 §464B(b); fourth-degree sexual offense: maximum of 1 year and/or $1,000 fine, art. 27 §464C(b).

Special

Mandatory sentences for crimes of violence, including rape, and first- and second-degree sexual offense, are a mandatory life term without the possibility of parole for fourth offense, mandatory minimum term of 25 years without parole or a suspended sentence for third offense, art. 27 §643B; provisions for restitution, art. 27 §640.

Massachusetts

State Statutes

Mass. Gen. Laws Ch. 265 §22-23 (Supp. 1979) (L.1979)
§22   Rape in general; punishment
§22A   Rape of a child; use of force
§23   Rape and abuse of a child

Derivation

History

Laws of 1649 define rape as to ravish any maid or single woman, by force of against her will, that is above the age of 10, punishable by death or some other grievous punishment. Compilation of 1672 added carnal copulation with child under 10, punishable by death. Code of 1836 contained traditional, single carnal knowledge rape statute, including carnal knowledge and abuse of any female child under 10. No change in 1861 but penalty changed to life or any term. Act of 1886 increased statutory age to over 13, carnal abuse was of a female under 13. Compilation of 1890 added carnal knowledge of female in an institution or sexual intercourse with a female under 18 in addition to rape statute. L.1893 raised age of consent to 16 for rape. Code of 1902 kept carnal knowledge statute, statutory age of 16, penalty was life or any term of years. Code of 1921 recodified law in two sections. No change until 1956 when offenders over 21 received a mandatory minimum term of 5 years. Law of 1955 distinguished between forceful rape of a child and rape and carnal abuse of a child; statutory age of 16 for both. 1966 amendment as to punishment for second offense. 1973 amendment reduced age of actor to 18 for second offender status. Law of 1974 redefined all categories of rape in sex-neutral terms as forcible sexual intercourse or unnatural sexual intercourse. Rape reform evidence statute passed in 1977. 1979 amendment to section on carnal knowledge of mentally disabled persons.

Present Law

Sex-neutral rape statute prohibits forcible sexual intercourse and unnatural sexual intercourse; two categories of sex-neutral rape of a child, forcible and nonforcible; rape reform evidence statute.

Statutory Structure

Changes

Traditional carnal knowledge statute with two categories of rape and carnal abuse of a child. 1974 revision made offense sex-neutral and redefined prohibited acts for all offenses as sexual intercourse and unnatural sexual intercourse. Rape reform evidence statute passed in 1977.

Offenses

Rape; forcible rape of a child; rape and abuse of a child (statutory rape).

Requirements

Rape: sexual intercourse or unnatural sexual intercourse, by force or against his will, §22; rape of a child: sexual intercourse or unnatural sexual intercourse with child under 16, by force and against his will, §22A; rape and abuse of a child: sexual intercourse or unnatural sexual intercourse and abuse of a child under 16, §23.

Principals

Person/person; sex-neutral.

Spouses

No statutory spousal exception for rape or rape of a child, common-law spousal exception may be presumed to continue. Specific spousal exception in rape and abuse of a child; "whoever *unlawfully* has sexual intercourse . . . ," §23. Prior law did not have explicit spousal exception.

Terminology

Language

"Whoever . . . compels such person to submit by force and against his will, or compels such person to submit by threat of bodily injury . . .," §23,

§22A. "Whoever has unlawful sexual intercourse with a person who is feebleminded, an idiot or imbecile, or insane, under circumstances which do not constitute rape, shall if such person has reasonable cause to believe such other person was feebleminded . . .," ch. 272 §5.

Definitions

For all forms of rape and abuse, prohibited acts are sexual intercourse and unnatural sexual intercourse; mentally disabled person defined as person who is feebleminded, an idiot or imbecile, or insane person, ch. 272 §5 (L.1979 ch. 305).

Statutory Age Provisions

Age of Consent

Age of consent is 16. Two offenses for rape of person under 16, forcible and nonforcible; offender must be over 18 for second offender status.

Offenses

Statutory rape: sexual intercourse, unnatural sexual intercourse, and abuse of child under 16, §23; forcible rape of a child: sexual intercourse by force of a child under 16, §22A; inducing person under 18 to have sexual intercourse, ch. 272, §4 (seduction statute).

Evidence Provisions, Defenses, and Cross References

Evidence

1977 statute prohibits the introduction of reputation evidence of the victim's sexual conduct and evidence of specific instances of the victim's sexual conduct, except conduct with the defendant or as alleged cause of physical feature, characteristics or condition of victim, then hearing and written findings required, ch. 233, §21B. Exclusion of public from trial for sex offenses involving persons under 18, ch. 278, §16A; constitutionality upheld, *Ottaway Newspapers, Inc.* v. *Appeals Court*, 372 Mass. 539, 362 N.E. 2d 1189 (Mass. 1977).

Defenses

Common-law consent a defense to rape and forcible rape of a child.

Cross References

Incest, ch. 272, §17; drugging persons for sexual intercourse, ch. 272, §3; inducing person under 18 to have sexual intercourse, ch. 272, §4; carnal knowledge of mentally disabled persons, ch. 272, §5 (amended L.1979); standardization of preservation of evidence in rape cases, ch. 217, L.1979; adultery, ch. 272, §14; child pornography, ch. 272, §29A et seq.; venue may be changed for sex offenses, ch. 265, §24A.

Penalties

Terms

Life or any term of years, §22; life or any term of years, but minimum of 5 years for second offense, §22A, 23.

Special

Five-year mandatory term without parole or probation if second offense ch. 267, §87; no suspended sentence if life term or death penalty, ch. 279, §1 et seq.

Michigan

State Statutes

Mich. Comp. Laws Ann. §750.520a-§750.5201 [Mich. Stat. Ann. §28.788(1)-§28.788(12)] (Supp. 1979-1980)
§750.520a   Definitions
§750.520b   Criminal sexual conduct in the first degree
§750.520c   Criminal sexual conduct in the second degree
§750.520d   Criminal sexual conduct in the third degree
§750.520e   Criminal sexual conduct in the fourth degree

Derivation

History

Law of 1808 included carnal knowledge rape statute and defined statutory rape as carnal knowledge and abuse of a female child under 11. Penalty was $1,000 or hard labor for life. Law of 1816 specified age of consent as 14, and age for statutory rape reduced to 10. Penalty reduced for both rape and statutory rape to a fine or a maximum of 15 years at hard labor. In 1820 the penalty was changed to a maximum fine of $300 or a maximum of 2 years in prison. In 1827 the penalty was increased to a maximum of $1,000 or solitary confinement for up to 20 years. Law of 1830 specified 10 as the age of consent, and the punishment was changed to life or any term of years. In 1897 the age of consent was raised to 16. Law of 1913 added provision allowing for prosecution of man who marries a woman he rapes and then deserts her without good cause. Law of 1913 limited prosecution for statutory rape to males over 14 who had sexual intercourse with females between 14 and 16. Penalty was maximum of 5 years or 1 year, and 1 year statute of limitations on prosecutions. Law of 1913 added specific provision regarding female patients in mental institutions. 1915 statute authorized punishment for person who represented that sexual intercourse was part of treatment. 1929 law prohibited rape of female under 18 by guardian or employer, penalty was 10 years or $1,000 fine. Sex offender statute enacted in 1948. In 1952 the penalty for rape was changed to an indeterminate term with a maximum of life. Rape reform legislation including rape reform evidence statute and redefinition of the offense passed in 1974, effective 1975.

Present Law

One of the earliest rape reform statutes which became the model for legislation in many other states.

Statutory Structure

Changes

Traditional carnal knowledge statute defining rape and statutory rape replaced by a statute defining four degrees of sex-neutral criminal sexual conduct in terms of circumstances of offense. Reform statute drafted to avoid common-law definition of consent. Rape reform evidence statute totally prohibited the introduction of evidence concerning the victim's prior sexual conduct with third parties.

Offenses

Criminal sexual conduct in the first, second, third and fourth degree.

Requirements

First-degree criminal sexual conduct: sexual penetration when (1) the person is under 13; (2) person over 13 and under 16 and the actor is a member of the household, relative, or in a position of authority; (3) during the commission of a felony; (4) when the actor is aided, and either the victim is mentally defective, mentally incapacitated, or physically helpless, or the actor uses force; (5) the actor is armed; (6) personal injury to victim and force; (7) personal injury to victim and the actor knows the victim is mentally defective, mentally incapacitated, or physically helpless, §750.520(b); second-degree criminal sexual conduct: sexual contact under circumstances of first degree, §750.520c; third-degree criminal sexual conduct: sexual penetration when (1) person over 13 and under 16; (2) force or coercion used; (3) actor knows the victim is mentally defective, mentally incapacitated, or physically helpless, §750.520d; fourth-degree criminal sexual conduct: sexual contact when (1) force or coercion used or (2) actor knows victim is mentally defective, mentally incapacitated, or physically helpless, §750.520e.

Principals

Person/person and actor/victim; sex-neutral.

Spouses

Statutory spousal exception excludes couples living apart when one has filed for separate maintenance or divorce, §750.520e.

Terminology

Language

"Force or coercion includes but is not limited to . . .(i) when the actor overcomes the victim through the actual application of physical force or physical violence, (ii) when the actor coerces the victim to submit by threatening to use force or violence on the victim, and the victim believes that the actor has the present ability to execute these threats, (iii) when the actor causes the victim to submit by threatening to retaliate in the future against the victim, or any other person, and the victim believes that the actor has the ability to execute this threat as used in this subdivision; 'to retaliate' includes threats of physical punishment, kidnaping, or extortion, (iv) when the actor engages in the medical treatment or examination of the victim in a manner or for purposes which are medically recognized as unethical or unacceptable," §750.520b(1)(f).

Definitions

Sexual penetration means sexual intercourse, cunnilingus, fellatio, anal intercourse, or any other intrusion, however slight, of any part of a person's body or of any object into the genital or anal opening of another person's body, but emission of semen not required, §750.520h. *Sexual contact* includes the intentional touching of the victim's or actor's intimate parts or the intentional touching of the clothing covering the immediate area of the victim's or actor's intimate parts, if that intentional touching can reasonably be construed as being for the purpose of sexual arousal or gratification, §750.520g. *Personal injury* means bodily injury, disfigurement, mental anguish, chronic pain, pregnancy, disease, or loss of impairment of a sexual or reproductive organ, §750.520f.

Statutory Age Provisions

Age of Consent

No statutory age of consent, traditional statutory rape statute repealed, several offenses defined by sexual penetration or sexual contact and age of victim.

Offenses

First-degree criminal sexual conduct: sexual penetration with a person under 13 and with a person over 13 and under 16 when the actor is a member of the household, a relative, or in a position of authority, §750.520(b)(1) and (2); second-degree criminal sexual conduct: sexual contact with a person under 13 or with a person over 13 and under 16 when the actor is a member of the household, a relative, or in a position of authority, §750.520(c)(1) and (2).

**Evidence Provisions, Defenses,
and Cross References**

Evidence

Rape reform statute which became effective in 1975 included an evidence provision which totally prohibits the admission of specific instances of victim's prior sexual conduct, opinion evidence, and reputation evidence of victim's sexual conduct unless the judge finds in camera the following evidence is material: past sexual conduct with the defendant or evidence of specific instances of sexual activity showing the source or origin of semen, pregnancy, or disease, §750.520j; corroboration not required, §750.520h; resistance not required, §750.520i.

Defenses

Statute drafted to limit the application of the prior common-law defense of consent, but the absence of force or coercion a defense to those offenses where force or coercion is an element of the offense. No statutory defenses and no specific statutory repeal of other common-law defenses.

Cross References

Incest, former incest statute repealed in 1974; first-degree criminal sexual conduct defined in part as sexual penetration with a person over 13 but under 16 when the actor is a member of the same household or related by blood or affinity to the fourth degree, §750.520b(1)(b); suppression of names of victim or actor upon request pending adjudication, §750.520k; child-abusive commercial activity (prostitution and assault with intent), §750.520g.

Penalties

Terms

First-degree criminal sexual conduct, felony punishable by life or any term of years, §750.520b(2); second-degree criminal sexual conduct, felony punishable by a maximum of 15 years, §750.520c(2); third-degree criminal sexual conduct, felony punishable by a maximum of 15 years, §750.520d(2); fourth-degree criminal sexual conduct, misdemeanor punishable by a maximum of 2 years or $500 fine, §750.520e.

Special

Mandatory minimum of 5 years for second conviction for first-, second-, or third-degree criminal sexual conduct, §750.520f.

Minnesota

State Statutes

Minn. Stat. Ann. §609.341 to §609.351 (Supp. 1980) (L. 1980, _____)
§609.341 Definitions
§609.342 Criminal sexual conduct in the first degree
§609.343 Criminal sexual conduct in the second degree
§609.344 Criminal sexual conduct in the third degree
§609.345 Criminal sexual conduct in the fourth degree

Deriviation

History

Law of 1851 punished rape and carnal knowledge of females over 10 with a penalty of from 10 to 30 years imprisonment. Statutory exception provided for a penalty of only 1 year if the female was a common prostitute. Proof of penetration requirement added in 1866. In 1891 rape was redefined as sexual intercourse without consent, including when female unable to consent through unsoundness of mind, when resistance overcome, when resistance overcome by fear of immediate and great bodily harm, when resistance prevented by narcotic, and so on, and when female unconscious. Statutory age unchanged. Term of punishment was 5 to 35 years. Penetration requirement changed to "any penetration, however slight." In 1894 statutory age was increased to 14, and the maximum term was reduced to 30 years. Statutory rape divided into three categories: carnal knowledge of girls between 14 and 16 was punishable with 1 to 7 years in state prison or 3 months to 1 year in county jail; carnal knowledge of girls between 10 and 14 was punishable with 7 to 30 years in prison; and carnal knowledge of a girl under 10 was punishable by a life term. In 1905 the statutory age of consent for rape was decreased to 10, but other offenses remained unchanged. In 1909 the age limit for carnal knowledge of girls was raised from 14 to 18, but no minimum sentence was set for carnal knowledge of girls between 14 and 18. A 1961 law requiring the presentence examination of sex offenders was repealed in 1979. Model Penal Code (MPC) rape statute proposed by advisory committee in 1963 but not adopted. Former rape and carnal knowledge of children statutes renumbered and included in criminal code of 1963. Law of 1967 rewrote the section and defined rape and aggravated rape in traditional terms. 1973 deleted category of statutory rape of female over 16 and under 18. 1980 amendment removed spousal exception for offenses involving adults.

Present Law

Rape reform statute modeled upon Michigan statute passed in 1974, effective 1975. Evidence statute does not strictly follow the Michigan model 1978 amendment as to technical definition of legal separation. 1979 amendment made other minor technical changes.

Statutory Structure

Changes

Prior to 1975 a traditional formulation of rape prohibited sexual intercourse without consent and defined four specific categories of nonconsent based upon the status of female and defined three separate statutory rape offenses. Rape reform statute which became effective in 1975 redefined the offense, including an expanded definition of sexual penetration, reduced penalties, provided minimum term for second offenders, added rape reform evidence statute, and excluded separated spouses from a statutory spousal exception. Common-law rape would be classified as third-degree criminal sexual conduct under this formulation. Unlike Michigan statute this statute includes a statutory definition of consent. 1980 amendment removed spousal exception for offenses involving adults.

Offenses

Criminal sexual conduct in the first, second, third and fourth degree. First and third degree are sexual penetration offenses; second and fourth degree are sexual contact offenses.

Requirements

First-degree criminal sexual conduct: sexual penetration when the complainant is under 13 and the actor is over 3 years older; or when the complainant is between 13 and 16 and the actor is in a position of authority; or when the complainant fears imminent great bodily harm; or when the actor is armed; or when the actor causes personal injury and force or coercion or the complainant is mentally defective, mentally incapacitated, or physically helpless; or the actor is aided and abetted and an accomplice uses force or coercion or an accomplice is armed, §609.342; second-degree criminal sexual conduct: sexual contact under circumstances defining first-degree criminal sexual contact, §609.343; third-degree criminal sexual conduct:

sexual penetration when the complainant is under 13 and the actor is less than 3 years older, or when the complainant is between 13 and 16 and the actor is 2 years older, §609.344; fourth-degree criminal sexual conduct: sexual contact under circumstances defining third-degree criminal sexual conduct, §609.345.

Principals

Actor/complainant; sex-neutral for all offenses.

Spouses

1980 amendment removed the spousal exception, but spousal exception retained in cases of statutory rape and where the victim is mentally or physically disabled. See §609.349 as amended by L. 1980, _____.

Terminology

Language

"A person is guilty of criminal sexual conduct in the first degree . . . if he engages in sexual penetration with another person and if any of the following circumstances exist: . . .(a) if the actor causes personal injury to the complainant, and either of the following circumstances exist: (i) the actor uses force or coercion to accomplish sexual penetration, or (ii) the actor knows or has reason to know that the complainant is mentally defective, mentally incapacitated or physically helpless," §609.342.

Definitions

Sexual penetration means sexual intercourse, cunnilingus, fellatio, anal intercourse, or any intrusion, however slight, into the genital or anal openings of the complainant's body of any part of the actor's body or any object used by the actor for this purpose, where the act is committed without the complainant's consent, except in those cases where consent is not a defense; emission of semen is not a defense, §609.341 subd. 12. *Sexual contact* includes any of the following acts committed without the complainant's consent, if the acts can be reasonably construed as being for the purpose of satisfying the actor's sexual or aggressive impulses, except in those cases where consent is not a defense: (i) the intentional touching by the actor of the complainant's intimate parts, or (ii) the coerced touching by the complainant of the actor's, the complainant's, or another's intimate parts, or (iii) the coerced touching by another of the complainant's intimate parts, or (iv) in any of the cases above, of the clothing covering the immediate area of the intimate parts, §609.341 subd. 11. *Consent* means a voluntary, uncoerced manifestation of a present agreement to perform a particular sexual act, §609.341 subd. 4. *Intimate parts* include the primary genital area, groin, inner thigh, buttocks, or breast of a human being, §609.341 subd. 5.

Statutory Age Provisions

Age of Consent

Consent is not a defense to penetration or contact offenses when the complainant is under 13 and the actor is 3 years older or when the complainant is over 13 and under 16 and the actor is 4 years older, §609.342, 609.343.

Offenses

First-degree criminal sexual conduct: sexual penetration when the complainant is under 13 and actor 3 years older and when complainant is over 13 and under 16 and actor 4 years older and actor in position of authority, §609.342; second-degree criminal sexual conduct: sexual contact under age and status restrictions of first-degree offense, §609.343; third-degree criminal sexual conduct: sexual penetration when the complainant is under 13 and the actor less than 3 years older or when complainant is over 13 and under 16 and actor is over 2 years older, §609.344; fourth-degree criminal sexual conduct: sexual contact when the complainant is under 13 and the actor is 3 years older or when the complainant is over 13 and under 16 and the actor is 4 years older, §609.345.

Evidence Provisions, Defenses, and Cross References

Evidence

1975 rape reform evidence statute provided that evidence of the complainant's previous sexual conduct shall not be admitted nor reference made to such conduct. Exception for evidence showing source of semen, pregnancy, and so on, past conduct with the defendant, evidence relevant to consent or fabrication, and evidence offered to impeach, then motion and offer of proof required by the defense, and the court shall issue an order as to admissibility, §609.347; corroboration and proof of resistance not required, §609.347 subd. (1) and (2); Lord Hale's instruction prohibited, §609.347 subd. 5 (c) and (d). Jury instructions as to probative value of previous sexual conduct prohibited, §609.347 subd. 5 (a) and (b).

Defenses

Consent as defined a defense, unless section precludes defense of consent, see §609.341 subd. 4 and §609.342(a) and (b), §609.343(a) and (b), §609.344 (a) and (b), and §609.345(a). Mistake as to age an affirmative defense to third- and fourth-degree criminal sexual conduct when the complainant is over 13 and under 16, §609.344(b) and §609.345(b). Exclusion for acts done for a bona fide medical purpose, §609.348.

Cross References

Incest, §609.365; position of authority defined to include parent and any person acting in the place of a parent and charged with any of a parent's rights, duties, or responsibilities for a child, §609.341 subd. 10; new domestic abuse statute includes criminal sexual conduct committed against minors by family or household members, §518B.01; child pornography, §617.246 et seq. Cost of medical exam for evidence to be paid by county where offense occurred, §609.35; program to aid victims of sexual attacks includes mandatory reporting requirement, §241.51 et seq.; victim's reparations act includes payment for psychiatric services, definition of injury from crime includes pregnancy, §299B.02 et seq.; sexual abuse of persons in institutions, §626.556; special provision for bail and release of those accused of assaulting a spouse or individual with whom he resides, §629.72.

Penalties

Terms

First-degree criminal sexual conduct, maximum penalty of 20 years, §609.342; second-degree criminal sexual conduct, maximum penalty of 15 years, §609.343; third-degree criminal sexual conduct, maximum penalty of 10 years, §609.344; fourth-degree criminal sexual conduct, maximum penalty of 5 years, §609.345.

Special

Restrictions on parole eligibility and minimum terms for second and subsequent offenders, §609.346; statute requiring presentence examination of sex offenders (former §609.116) repealed in 1979.

Mississippi

State Statutes

Miss. Code Ann. §97-3-65 through §97-3-71 (1972) (Supp. 1979)

§97-3-65   Rape:—carnal knowledge of female under 12 years of age, or, being over 12, against her will

§97-3-67   Rape:—carnal knowledge of chaste female over 12 and under 18 years of age

Derivation

History

Compilation of 1816 provided that every person who is convicted of rape shall suffer death. Revised code of 1924 contained the same provision and punished any slave who attempted rape of a free white woman with death. Law of 1839 prohibited carnal knowledge of a female under 10 or forcibly ravishing any woman 10 or more; minimum penalty was 10 years. Carnal knowledge of female over 10 by administering substance producing stupor, and so on, punishable by a maximum of 5 years in prison. Statue of 1857 punished a slave who raped or attempted carnal connection with a white female under 14 with or without her consent with death. Punishment for rape changed to life, and for administering drug, minimum 20 years. Law of 1906 added that where the female is under 10 it is not necessary to prove penetration of the female's private parts where it is shown they have been lacerated or torn in the attempt to have carnal knowledge. Law of 1917 changed statutory age of female to 12. Law of 1942 added new offense: carnal knowledge of an unmarried female of previously chaste character younger than himself and between 12 and 18. Punishment to be fixed by the jury. Burden is upon the defendant to prove the female was not previously chaste. Corroboration required by statute. Amendment in 1974 made minor changes in language. Evidence statute passed in 1977, but corroboration requirement and chaste-character provision remain in effect for statutory rape.

Present Law

Traditional formulation of rape and two statutory rape offenses: rape of females under 12 and carnal knowledge of chaste females over 12 and under 18. Rape reform evidence statute passed in 1977.

318

Statutory Structure

Changes

Evidence statute enacted in 1977, some minor changes in wording introduced in 1974, but substantive offense unchanged from traditional offense. Chaste-character provision and corroboration requirement remain, as does death penalty for rape of a female under 12.

Offenses

Three categories of rape: carnal knowledge of a female under 12, carnal knowledge of a female over 12 against her will, and carnal knowledge of chaste females over 12 and under 18.

Requirements

Carnal knowledge of a female under 12: proof of penetration not required "where it is shown the private parts of the female have been lacerated or torn in the attempt to have carnal knowledge of her"; and carnal knowledge of female over 12: forcible ravishment, or carnal knowledge by administration of substance producing "stupor" or "imbecility" or "weakness or body as to prevent effectual resistance," §97-3-65; carnal knowledge of chaste females over 12 and under 16: carnal knowledge of unmarried female person of "chaste character" younger than himself, §97-3-67.

Principals

Terminology is person/female, but the principals are male/female by the definition of the act constituting the offense.

Spouses

No statutory spousal exception, but traditional formulation in terms of "unlawful" carnal knowledge implies traditional common-law spousal exception. Reference to unmarried females in chaste-character provision not a spousal exception.

Terminology

Language

"Every person who shall forcibly ravish any female of the age of twelve (12) years or upward, or who shall have been convicted of having carnal knowledge of any female above the age of twelve (12) years without her consent by administering to her any substance or liquid which shall produce such stupor or such imbecility of mind or weakness of body as to prevent effectual resistance . . .," §97-3-65.

Definitions

Statutory rape: any male person who shall have carnal knowledge of any unmarried female person of previously chaste character younger than himself, and over 12 and under 18 years of age shall be punished, §97-3-67.

Statutory Age Provisions

Age of Consent

Age of consent for chaste female is 18; male must be older than female. Rape is carnal knowledge of female under 12. Age of offender determines penalty imposed; if the offender is between 13 and 18, the penalty may be life or a term of years if the female is under 12; if the offender is over 18 and the female is under 12, penalty is death.

Offenses

Rape: carnally and unlawfully knowing a female under 12, §97-3-65; rape: carnal knowledge of chaste female over 12 and under 18, §97-3-67.

Evidence Provisions, Defenses, and Cross References

Evidence

1977 rape reform evidence statute provided that opinion evidence, reputation evidence, and evidence of specific instances of complaining witness' sexual conduct, or any of such evidence, is not admissible by the defendant to prove consent. Exception for conduct with the defendant, for cross-examination of prosecution witnesses, including the complaining witness, or for evidence as to cause of pregnancy, disease, or source of semen, and special general exception if the court finds after a hearing the evidence is relevant and admissible in the interests of justice, §97-3-70. Evidence of sexual conduct may be introduced to attack credibility after a finding of relevance, §97-3-68; chaste character presumed uncorroborated testimony of victim over 12 and under 18 insufficient, §97-3-69.

Defenses

Consent a defense to rape and statutory rape; unchaste character of the "injured" female a defense if the female is over 12 and under 18, and prior sexual history of any complaining witness may be offered to impeach if the judge makes a finding of relevance; corroboration required if female over 12 and under 18.

Cross References

Incest, §97-29-27; restitution to victims, §97-37-1 et seq. (L. 1978); touching, handling, fondling a child for lustful purposes, §97-5-23; seduction of female child under age 18, §97-5-21; exploitation of children (child pornography), §97-5-31 (L.1979); unlawful to cohabit with feebleminded, §41-21-45; provision in Mississippi Constitution allows judge to exclude the public from the courtroom, Miss. Const. art. 3 §26; father or mother may bring action for seduction, §11-7-11.

Penalties

Terms

Death penalty for rape of a female under 12 by an offender over 18. Rape by carnal knowledge of female under 12, punishable by death or life imprisonment, but person over 13 and under 18 may be sentenced to a discretionary term by the court, §97-3-65; rape of female over 12, life, if the jury so provides, or a term of imprisonment as the court may determine, §97-3-65; carnal knowledge of chaste female over 12 and under 18, either a fine not exceeding $500 or imprisonment in the county jail for 6 months, or by imprisonment up to 5 years, such punishment being fixed by the jury, §97-3-67.

Special

Jury determines length and form of punishment, §97-3-67. Habitual criminals sentenced to life imprisonment, §99-19-83; jury to determine punishment in capital cases in separate sentencing procedure, after consideration of aggravating and mitigating circumstances, §99-19-101; examination by psychiatrist before person convicted of a sex crime may be released on parole, §48-7-3.

Missouri

State Statutes

Mo. Rev. Stat. §566.010 through §566.130 (1979)
§566.010 Chapter definitions
§566.030 Rape
§566.040 Sexual assault in the first degree
§566.050 Sexual assault in the second degree
§566.060 Sodomy
§566.070 Deviate sexual assault in the first degree
§566.080 Deviate sexual assault in the second degree
§566.090 Sexual misconduct
§566.100 Sexual abuse in the first degree
§566.110 Sexual abuse in the second degree
§566.120 Sexual abuse in the third degree

Derivation

History

Statute of 1825 punished rape by castration at cost to the defendant or to the state if the defendant could not pay. Carnal knowledge and abuse of a female under 10 constituted rape. Law of 1835 punished rape, either as unlawful carnal knowledge of a female under 10 or forcibly ravishing a female over 10 with a minimum of 5 years. Rape also defined as carnal knowledge by administering drugs, and so on. Castration was the penalty for rape or attempted rape by a negro or mulatto. Law of 1856 raised the statutory age of the female to 12. Law of 1879 changed the penalty to death or a minimum of 5 years for all rape at the discretion of the jury. Law of 1889 raised the age of consent to 14. Law of 1899 added a statutory rape provision: any person who had carnal knowledge of a female of previous chaste character between 14 and 18 will be punished by 2 years in prison, or a fine, or a county jail term of a minimum of 1 month and a maximum of 6 months. Law of 1919 raised the age of consent to 15 and defined statutory rape as carnal knowledge of a female over 15 and under 18, punishable by a minimum of 2 years or a maximum of 5 years. Law of 1929 raised the age of consent to 16, punishment was death or a minimum of 2 years; carnal knowledge of females between 16 and 18, then became the statutory rape offense. Law of 1939 changed the age of offender to 17. For rape of a woman by administering drugs, and so on, statutory age remained at 14. No further change until 1975 when the death penalty was removed. This law repealed in 1977 and replaced, effective 1979.

Present Law

Formulation based upon Model Penal Code (MPC) and New York Penal Code incorporates some reform features, retains much of the prior law, adds new crimes. Rape reform evidence statute enacted in 1977.

Statutory Structure

Changes

Offenses restructured but few reform features incorporated. Rape reform evidence statute passed in 1977. Common-law concept of rape as sexual intercourse by forcible compulsion without consent essentially retained. Other offenses detail age differences and distinguish between sexual intercourse, deviate sexual intercourse, and sexual contact.

Offenses

Rape; sexual assault in the first and second degree; sodomy; deviate sexual assault in the first and second degree; sexual misconduct; sexual abuse in the first, second, and third degree.

Requirements

Rape: sexual intercourse without consent by the use of forcible compulsion, or when a person is less than 14, §566.030(1); first-degree sexual assault: sexual intercourse with a person who is incapacitated or who is 14 or 15 years old, §566.040(1); second-degree sexual assault: a person over 17 who has sexual intercourse with a person 16, §566.050(1); sodomy: deviate sexual intercourse by forcible compulsion or with a person under 14, §566.060(1); first-degree deviate sexual assault: deviate sexual intercourse with a person who is incapacitated or 14 or 15 years old, §566.070(1); second-degree deviate sexual assault: deviate sexual intercourse with a person 16, §566.080(1); sexual misconduct: a person under 17 who has sexual intercourse with a person 14 or 15, or deviate sexual intercourse with another person under 17, or deviate sexual intercourse with a person of the same sex, §566.090; first-degree sexual abuse: sexual contact without consent by forcible compulsion, or with a person under 12, §566.100; second-degree sexual abuse: sexual contact with a person who is incapcitated or 12 or 13 years old, §566.110; third-degree sexual abuse: sexual contact without consent, §566.120.

Principals

Male/female for definition of sexual intercourse, though commentary states a female can be guilty of rape and the sex of the victim is immaterial.

Spouses

All crimes defined in terms of sexual intercourse, deviate sexual intercourse, or sexual contact with another person to whom he is not married; "spouses living apart pursuant to a judgment of legal separation are not married to each other for the purposes of this chapter," §566.010(2).

Terminology

Language

"When conduct is charged to constitute an offense because it causes or threatens physical injury, consent to that conduct or to the infliction of injury is a defense only if (1) the physical injury consented to or threatened by the conduct is not serious physical injury; or (2) the conduct and the harm are reasonably foreseeable hazards of (a) the victim's occupation or profession; or (b) joint participation in a lawful athletic contest or competitive sport; or (3) the consent establishes a justification for the conduct under ch. 563 of this code. The defendant shall have the burden of injecting the issue of consent," §565.080.

Definitions

Sexual intercourse means any penetration, however slight, of the female organ by the male organ, whether or not an emission results, §566.010(1). *Sexual contact* means touching of the genitals or anus of any person, or the breast of any female person, or any such touching through clothing, for the purpose of arousing or gratifying the sexual desire of any person, §566.010(2). *Deviate sexual intercourse* means any sexual act involving the genitals of one person and the mouth, tongue, hand, or anus of another person, §566.010(2).

Statutory Age Provisions

Age of Consent

No specified age of consent. Age of both victim and offender an element of several crimes.

Offenses

Rape: sexual intercourse with a person under 14, §566.030(2); first-degree sexual assault: sexual intercourse with a person 14 or 15, §566.040(1); second-degree sexual assault: sexual intercourse with a person 16, §566.060(1); sodomy: deviate sexual intercourse with a person under 14, §566.060(2); first-degree deviate sexual assault: deviate sexual intercourse with a person 14 or 15, §566.070(1); second-degree deviate sexual assault: deviate sexual intercourse with a person 16, §566.080(1); sexual misconduct: a person under 17 who has sexual intercourse with a person 14 or 15, or deviate sexual intercourse with a person under 17, or deviate sexual intercourse with another person of the same sex, §566.090; first-degree sexual abuse: sexual contact with a person under 12, §566.100; second-degree sexual abuse: sexual contact with a person 12 or 13, §566.110.

Evidence Provisions, Defenses, and Cross References

Evidence

1977 rape reform evidence statute provided that opinion and reputation evidence of the complaining witness' prior sexual conduct, and specific instances of the complaining witness' prior sexual conduct is inadmissible. Exceptions are specific instances (1) of sexual conduct of the witness with the defendant to prove consent, or (2) evidence showing an alternative source of semen, pregnancy, or disease, or (3) evidence of the immediate surrounding circumstances, or (4) evidence relating to the previous chastity of the complaining witness in cases where, by statute, previously chaste character is required to be proved by the prosecution. The defendant shall make an offer of proof on the record, followed by an in-camera hearing, where court shall make a finding of relevance and state its reasons on the record which shall be sealed, §491.015.

Defenses

Statutory definition of consent as justifying physical injury, §656.080; an affirmative defense that the defendant believed the victim was not incapacitated and reasonably believed that the victim consented, §566.020(1); reasonable mistake as to age an affirmative defense if the criminality of conduct depends upon a child's being 14 or 15, no defense if the criminality of conduct depends upon a child being under 14, §566.020.

Cross References

Incest, §568.020; child pornography, §568.060.

Penalties

Terms

Rape and sodomy: class B felony unless serious physical injury or deadly weapon displayed in a threatening manner, then class A felony, §566.030 and §566.060; first-degree sexual assault and first-degree deviate sexual assault: class C felony, unless the actor inflicts serious physical injury or displays a deadly weapon in a threatening manner, §566.040 and §566.070; second-degree sexual assault and second-degree deviate sexual assault: class D felony unless the actor inflicts serious physical injury or displays a deadly weapon in a threatening manner, then class C felony, §566.050 and §566.080; sexual misconduct: class A misdemeanor, §566.090; class A felony, minimum 10 years and maximum 30 years or life; class B felony, minimum 5 years and maximum 15 years; class C felony, maximum 7 years; class D felony, maximum 5 years; class A misdemeanor, maximum 1 year, §568.011(1).

Special

Authorized disposition, §57.011; criminal sexual psychopaths, §202.700, et seq.; jury to determine penalty within the range, unless the defendant requests the court to punish, §557.036; persistent offenders, §558.016; extended terms, §577.021; court may sentence a person convicted of a class C or D felony to a maximum of 1 year, §558.011(2).

Montana

State Statutes

Mont. Rev. Codes Ann. §45-5-501 through §45-5-606 (1979)
§45-5-501 Definitions
§45-5-502 Sexual assault
§45-5-503 Sexual intercourse without consent
§45-5-505 Deviate sexual conduct

Derivation

History

Code of 1895 contained a statutory definition of rape as sexual intercourse with a female not the wife of the perpetrator under the following circumstances: (1) where the female is under 16, (2) where the female is incapable of giving legal consent through lunacy, and so on, (3) where the resistance of the female is overcome by violence, (4) where the female is prevented from resisting by threats of immediate and great bodily harm accompanied by apparent power of execution, (5) where the female is unconscious, and (6) where the female submits under the belief the person is her husband and this belief is induced by artifice; minimum penalty is 5 years. 1895 code also contained a seduction statute with a chaste-character provision. An amendment in 1913 changed the statutory age of the female to 18 and changed the penalty to a minimum of 2 years and a maximum of 99 years. Law of 1913 also added lewd and lascivious acts with children. No further amendments until present law was enacted in 1973.

Present Law

Montana criminal code of 1973 redefined most crimes and added new general provisions incorporating some Model Penal Code (MPC) reforms; new crime of sexual assault. Present definition of sexual intercourse without consent comes from revision of 1973 and includes a rape evidence statute.

Statutory Structure

Changes

Rape redefined as sexual intercourse without consent in 1973. New crime of sexual assault is a sexual contact offense. General provisions regarding

328

defenses added in 1973, amended in 1975. 1977 recodification changed title and numbers of the offense. Minor technical amendment in 1977 to spousal exclusion. Law of 1977 added minimum terms. Law of 1979 added provision rendering consent ineffective if the victim is under 14 and the offender is 3 years older for sexual assault.

Offenses

Sexual assault; sexual intercourse without consent; deviate sexual conduct.

Requirements

Sexual assault: sexual contact without consent, §45-5-502(1); sexual intercourse without consent, §45-5-503(1); deviate sexual conduct: knowingly engaging in deviate sexual relations or causing another to engage in deviate sexual relations, §45-5-505

Principals

Person/person; sex-neutral but sexual intercourse is with a person of the opposite sex, §45-5-503(1).

Spouses

Definition of sexual assault and sexual intercourse without consent excludes conduct with a spouse: "A person who knowingly subjects another not his spouse," §45-5-502(1) and "A person who knowingly has sexual intercourse without consent with a person of the opposite sex not his spouse," §45-5-503(1). No spousal exclusion for deviate sexual conduct. "Whenever the definition of an offense excludes conduct with a spouse, the exclusion shall be deemed to extent to persons living as husband and wife regardless of the legal status of their relationship. The exclusion shall be inoperative as respects spouses living apart whether under a decree of judicial separation or otherwise where the definition of an offense excludes contact with a spouse; this shall not preclude conviction of a spouse in a sexual act which he or she causes another person, not within the exclusion, to perform," §45-5-506(2).

Terminology

Language

"A person who knowingly has sexual intercourse without consent with a person of the opposite sex not his spouse commits the offense of sexual intercourse without consent . . . if the offender inflicts bodily injury upon anyone in the course of committing sexual intercourse without consent, he shall be imprisoned in the state prison for any term of not less than 2 years or more than 40 years," §45-5-503.

Definitions

Without consent means (1) the victim is compelled to submit by force or by threat of imminent death, bodily injury, or kidnaping to be inflicted on anyone; or (2) the victim is incapable of consent because he is (a) mentally defective or incapacitated, (b) physically helpless, or (c) less than 16, §45-5-501; an act "in the course of committing sexual intercourse without consent," or "in the course of committing sexual assault," shall include an attempt to commit the offense or flight after the attempt or commission, §45-5-503(4) and §45-5-502(4).

Statutory Age Provisions

Age of Consent

A person is deemed incapable of consent because he is less than 16, §45-5-501(2)c; see also consent to sexual assault is ineffective if the victim is under 14 and the offender is more than 3 years older, §45-5-502(5).

Offenses

Sexual assault: "sexual contact without consent . . . if the victim is less than 16 and the offender is 3 years older," §45-5-502(3); sexual intercourse without consent: "sexual intercourse without consent with a person of the opposite sex . . . if the victim is under 16 and the offender is 3 years older," §45-5-503(3).

**Evidence Provisions, Defenses,
and Cross References**

Evidence

No evidence of the sexual conduct of the victim is admissible under a prosecution for sexual intercourse without consent except evidence of the victim's past sexual conduct with the offender, evidence of specific instances of the victim's sexual activity to show the origin of semen, pregnancy, or disease which is at issue in the prosecution, §45-5-503(5).

Defenses

Absence of consent an element of sexual assault and sexual intercourse without consent. Deviate sexual conduct defined as both with consent and without consent, §45-5-505. Mistake as to age: a reasonable mistaken belief that the victim was over 16 a defense, but "such belief shall not be deemed reasonable if the child is less than 14," §45-5-506(2).

Cross References

Incest, §45-5-613; sexual abuse of children (child pornography), §45-5-625; prostitution, §45-5-601, et seq.

Penalties

Terms

Sexual assault: fine not to exceed $500 or imprisonment in county jail for any term not to exceed 6 months, if the victim is under 16 and the offender is 3 years older or if the offender inflicts bodily injury upon anyone in the course of committing sexual assault, imprisonment for any term not to exceed 20 years, §45-5-502(2) and (3); sexual intercourse without consent: state prison for a minimum of 2 years and a maximum of 20 years or if the victim is under 16 and the offender is 3 years older or if the offender inflicts bodily injury upon anyone in the course of committing sexual intercourse without consent, imprisonment of a minimum of 2 years or a maximum of 40 years, §45-5-503(2) and (3); deviate sexual conduct: (with consent) maximum 10 years; (without consent) maximum 20 years, §45-5-505(2) and (3).

Special

Exception to mandatory minimum sentences, exception based upon age of offender, mental capacity of offender, actions under duress, if defendant was only an accomplice, or where no serious bodily injury was inflicted upon the victim, unless a weapon was used in the commission of the offense, §45-18-222 and §45-18-223; additional sentence for offenses committed with a dangerous weapon, §46-18-221; sentences that may be imposed, §46-18-201.

Nebraska

State Statutes

Neb. Rev. Stat. §28-408.01 through §28-408.05 (1975) (Law of 1977, LB 38)
§28-408.01 Legislative intent
§28-408.02 Terms defined
§28-408.03 Sexual assault; first degree, defined; penalty
§28-408.04 Sexual assault; second degree, defined; penalty

Derivation

History

Revised statutes of 1866 defined rape as carnal knowledge of a female forcibly and against her will. Every male over 14 who shall have carnal knowledge of any female child under 10 either with or without her consent shall be guilty of rape. Penalty was a minimum of 1 year or life. Compilation of 1873 defined separately rape upon a daughter or sister, forcibly against her will; penalty was imprisonment for life. Carnal knowledge of any other woman or female child forcibly, or if any male person over 17 shall carnally know and abuse any child under 10 with consent, he shall be guilty of rape. Maximum penalty was 20 years and minimum, 3 years. Law of 1873 included as rape carnal knowledge of an insane or feebleminded woman. Punishment was a maximum of 10 or a minimum of 3 years. Amendment of 1895 increased the age of the female to 18 and added a chaste-character provision for carnal knowledge of a female child under 18 and over 15 with her consent. No further changes, except renumbering and title change until law of 1975 redefined the offense as sexual assault.

Present Law

Law of 1975 introduced two degrees of sex-neutral sexual assault; sexual penetration and sexual contact follow the expanded definitions in other reform statutes. Rape reform evidence statute included in reform of 1975.

Statutory Structure

Changes

Two categories of sexual assault replace upon a daughter or sister, rape of any other woman, and carnal knowledge of a female child under 18 and over 15 of previous chaste character. Evidence statute included in 1975. 1977 amendment reclassifies offenses effective 1979 and adds mandatory term for second offense. Law of 1979 specifies procedures regarding mentally disordered sexual offenders.

Offenses

First-degree sexual assault; second-degree sexual assault.

Requirements

First-degree sexual assault: sexual penetration when the victim is overcome by force, threat of force, express or implied, coercion or deception; when the actor knew or should have known the victim was mentally or physically incapable of resisting or appraising the nature of his or her conduct; or when the actor is more than 18 and the victim is less than 16, §28-408.03; second-degree sexual assault: sexual contact when the victim is overcome by force, threat of force, express or implied, coercion, or deception, or the actor knew or should have known that the victim was physically or mentally incapable of resisting or appraising the nature of his or her conduct, §28-408.04.

Principals

Actor/victim; sex-neutral.

Spouses

No reference to marriage or spouses in the statute. Status of spousal exception unclear.

Terminology

Language

"It is the intent of the legislature to enact laws dealing with sexual assault and related criminal sexual offenses which will protect the dignity of the victim at all stages of the judicial process, which will insure that the alleged offender in a criminal sexual offense case have preserved the constitutionally guaranteed due process of law procedures, and which will establish a system of investigating prosecution, punishment, and rehabilitation for the welfare and benefit of the citizens of this state," §28-408.01.

Definitions

Sexual penetration shall mean sexual intercourse in its ordinary meaning, cunnilingus, fellatio, and anal intercourse, or any intrusion, however slight, of any part of the actor's body or any object manipulated by the actor into the genital or anal opening of the victim's body; sexual penetration shall not require emission of semen, §28-408.02(5). *Sexual contact* shall mean the intentional touching of the victim's sexual or intimate parts or the intentional touching of the victim's clothing covering the immediate area of the victim's sexual or intimate parts; sexual contact shall include only such conduct which can be reasonably construed as being for the purpose of sexual arousal or gratification, §28-408.02(4).

Statutory Age Provisions

Age of Consent

Law not phrased in terms of age of consent. Statutory age of victim set at 16, actor must be over 18.

Offenses

First-degree sexual assault: sexual penetration when the actor is over 18 and the victim is less than 16, §28-408.03(1)c.

Evidence Provisions, Defenses, and Cross References

Evidence

1975 rape reform evidence statute stated that upon motion by either party the court shall hold an in-camera hearing to determine the relevance of either the victim's or the offender's past sexual conduct. Judge shall determine which relevant evidence concerning the victim's or defendant's past sexual conduct shall be admitted; specific instances of prior sexual activity between the victim and any person other than the defendant shall not be admitted unless consent by the victim is at issue, then only after a showing of relevance, §28-408.05.

Defenses

Consent a defense; no reference to mistake as to age.

Cross References

Incest, §28-905; father cohabiting with daughter, §28-906; debauching a minor, §28-805.

Penalties

Terms

First-degree sexual assault: class II felony, law of 1977, LB 38 §34(2); second-degree sexual assault: class I misdemeanor, unless the actor shall have caused serious personal injury to the victim, in which case it is a class III felony, law of 1977, LB 38, §35(2). Class II felony, maximum 55 years, minimum 1 year; class III felony, maximum 25 years, fine of $25,000, or both, and minimum 1 year; class I misdemeanor, maximum not more than 1 year, law of 1977, LB 38 §5 and 6.

Special

Provisions governing sentencing, release, and confinement of mentally disordered sex offenders, law of 1979, LB 378; repealing former provisions regarding sexual sociopath, former §29-2901 et seq.; any person found guilty of first-degree sexual assault for a second time shall be sentenced to a minimum of 25 years and shall not be eligible for parole, law of 1977, LB 38, §34(3).

Nevada

State Statutes

Nev. Rev. Stat. §200.364 through §200.375 (1977)(L.1979)
§200.364 Definitions
§200.366 Sexual assault: Definition; penalties
§200.368 Statutory sexual seduction: penalties
§200.373 Sexual assault of a spouse by spouse

Derivation

History

Complied laws of 1873 contain a rape statute passed in 1861 defining rape as carnal knowledge of a female forcibly and against her will. Punishment was a minimum of 5 years or a maximum of life. Any person over 14 who has carnal knowledge of a female child under 12 with or without her consent shall be guilty of rape. Amendment of 1889 changed the age of the male to 15 and upward and the age of the female to under 14. Compilation of 1912 placed rape with crimes against morality and decency and removed it from crimes against the person. Definition of offense unchanged but added that if the rape is accompanied by an act of extreme violence or if great bodily injury is inflicted, then the minimum penalty is 20 years or the death penalty is possible if the jury affixes the death penalty. New subcategory of rape added: any person who has carnal knowledge of any female child under 16 with or without her consent is guilty of rape. Amendment of 1919 changed the age of the female to 18. Law of 1939 added new provision: a husband may not be convicted of the rape of his wife unless he is an accomplice or an accessory to the rape of his wife by a third person. Compilation of 1963 contained new sections, though the substantive offense remained the same, added that if the victim is under 14 years, the offender may not be paroled unless there is a certification by a psychiatrist that the offender is not a menace to society. Crime of rape redefined as sexual assault in 1977.

Present Law

Rape reform statute redefining rape as sexual assault and statutory sexual seduction.

Statutory Structure

Changes

Law of 1975 required county to pay for the cost of medical examinations of victims and to provide psychological counseling and victim services. In 1977 sexual assault formulation replaced rape and statutory rape, but not modeled upon other reform statutes. Evidence statute passed in 1977. Amendments to health-care provisions and fines added to penalties in 1979. Provisions for care for victims more extensive than those of any other state.

Offenses

Sexual assault; statutory sexual seduction.

Requirements

Sexual assault: sexual penetration, against the victim's will, or when the victim is mentally or physically incapable of resisting or of understanding the nature of his conduct, §200.366; statutory sexual seduction: ordinary sexual intercourse, and intercourse, cunnilingus, or fellatio by person over 18 with a consenting person under 16, §200.368.

Principals

Perpetrator/victim; sex-neutral.

Spouses

Traditional spousal exclusion with a statutory exception for couples living apart; statutory proviso, Sexual assault of spouse by spouse: A person may not be convicted of sexual assault upon his spouse unless (1) the act committed was other than sexual intercourse in its ordinary meaning; (2) he was an accomplice or accessory to the sexual assault by a third person; or (3) at the time of the sexual assault the couple were living apart and one of them had filed an action for separate maintenance or divorce §200.373.

Terminology

Language

"A person who subjects another person to sexual penetration, or who forces another person to make sexual penetration on himself or another, or on a beast, against the victim's will or under conditions in which the perpetrator knows or should know that the victim is mentally or physically incapable of resisting or understanding the nature of his conduct, is guilty of sexual assault," §200.366(1).

Definitions

Sexual penetration means cunnilingus, fellatio, or any intrusion, however slight, of any part of a person's body, or any object manipulated or inserted by a person into the genital or anal opening of the body of another, including sexual intercourse in its ordinary meaning, §200.364(2). *Statutory sexual seduction* means ordinary sexual intercourse, and intercourse, cunnilingus, or fellatio committed by a person 18 years of age or older with a consenting person under the age of 16 years, §200.364(3). *Lewdness with child under 14 years*: Any person who willfully and lewdly commits any lewd or lascivious act, other than acts constituting the crime of sexual assault, upon or with the body, or any part or member thereof, of a child under the age of 14 years, with the intent of arousing, appealing to, or gratifying the lust or passions or sexual desires of such person or of such child, shall be punished, §201.230.

Statutory Age Provisions

Age of Consent

No specific statutory age of consent. Offense of sexual assault defined in part by acts with a victim under 14, §200.366(2)(c); person over 18 with consenting person under 16 for statutory sexual seduction, §200.364(3). If the offender is under 21, punishment is for a misdemeanor for statutory sexual seduction.

Offenses

Sexual assault: sexual penetration with a child under 14, §200.366(2)c; statutory sexual seduction: act of sexual intercourse and intercourse, cunnilingus, or fellatio by person over 18 with consenting person under 16, §200.364(3) and §200.368.

Evidence Provisions, Defenses, and Cross References

Evidence

1977 rape reform evidence statute required a special offer of proof and hearing if evidence of prior sexual conduct of the victim is offered on the issue of consent; specific instances of conduct of a witness for the purpose of attacking credibility may not be proved by extrinsic evidence, but may be inquired into at cross-examination, §49.069; accused may not present evidence of previous sexual conduct to challenge victim's credibility unless the prosecution or the victim has testified concerning such conduct, then the scope of cross-examination is limited, §50.095; reference to unchaste character prohibited in any jury instruction, §175.186; court may move to exclude victim's address and telephone number, §48.071.

Defenses

Consent and the absence of force a defense to sexual assault, but not to statutory sexual seduction.

Cross References

Incest, §201.180; crime against nature, §201.190; lewdness with child under 14 years, §201.230; crime victim compensation including reasonable attorney's fees, §217.010 et seq.; victim of sexual assault or spouse may apply to county for treatment for emotional trauma, §217.310; treatment shall be made available to victim or spouse, certification, time limits, §217.320 et seq.; county to pay for emergency medical care, §217.300.

Penalties

Terms

Sexual assault, if substantial bodily harm to the victim results: life without possibility of parole or with possibility of parole after a minimum of 10 years has been served, §200.366(2)(b); sexual assault if no substantial bodily harm to the victim results: life with the possibility of parole beginning after a minimum of 5 years has been served or by any definite term of 5 years or more, with eligibility for parole beginning when 5 years has been served, §200.366(2)(b); statutory sexual seduction: if the offender is over 21, minimum 1 year, maximum 10 years, and fine up to $10,000, if offender under 21 for a gross misdemeanor, §200.368; lewdness with a child under 14: minimum 1 year, maximum 10 years, §201.230(1).

Special

Trier of fact shall determine whether substantial bodily harm has been inflicted on the victim, and if so, the sentence to be imposed upon the perpetrator, §200.366(3); limitations on parole: no person convicted of sexual assault may be paroled unless a qualified psychiatrist certifies that the person is not a menace to the health, safety, or morals of others, §200.375; restrictions on parole and probation for a person convicted of lewdness with a child under 14, §201.230(2); registration of sex offenders, §207.151.

New Hampshire

State Statutes

N.H. Rev. Stat. §632-A:1 through §632-A:8 (Supp. 1979)
§632-A:1 Definitions
§632-A:2 Aggravated felonious sexual assault
§632-A:3 Felonious sexual assault
§632-A:4 Sexual assault

Derivation

History

Law passed in 1791 and included in the compiled laws of 1805 contained traditional common-law rape statute: if any man shall ravish or carnally know any woman committing carnal copulation by force against her will, or carnal knowledge and abuse of any woman-child under 10, he shall be guilty of rape and on conviction shall suffer death. Compilation of 1843 contained the same crime but the punishment was solitary confinement not exceeding 6 months or confinement at hard labor for life. Penalty changed in 1828. Compilation of 1867 noted that a law of 1859 changed the penalty to a minimum of 7 years and a maximum of 30 years. Law of 1887 included in the compilation of 1891 changed the age of the female child to 13. Penalty simply the 30 year maximum, no minimum. Law of 1897 included in compilation of 1901 changed the age of the female to 16. No further changes until a law passed in 1971, effective in 1973, completely rewrote the definition of the offense, apparently following the Model Penal Code (MPC). This statute rewritten and amended again in 1975 and 1979.

Present Law

Statutes incorporating several reform features frame the offense in terms of three categories of sex-neutral sexual assault; limited spousal exception; evidence statute included.

Statutory Structure

Changes

MPC formulation of rape and sexual assault replaced traditional rape statute in 1971. In 1975 offenses redefined as aggravated felonious sexual assault, felonious sexual assault, and sexual assault. 1979 amendment changed definition of sexual contact to include the victim touching the actor's sexual or intimate parts.

Offenses

Aggravated felonious sexual assault; felonious sexual assault; sexual assault.

Requirements

Aggravated felonious sexual assault: sexual penetration when the actor overcomes the victim through the actual application of physical force, physical violence, or superior physical strength; when the victim is physically helpless, when the victim submits through threat, when the victim submits under circumstances of false imprisonment, kidnaping, or extortion, when the actor has administered an intoxicant, when the actor engages in a medical examination or treatment for purposes not medically recognized or acceptable, when the actor through concealment or surprise causes sexual penetration, when the victim is over 13 and under 16 and the actor is a member of the household or related by blood or affinity, or in a position of authority, and when the victim is under 13, §632-A:2. Felonious sexual assault: sexual contact causing serious personal injury under the circumstance of aggravated felonious sexual assault, §632-A:3. Sexual asault: sexual contact under the circumstances of aggravated felonious sexual assault, §632-A:4.

Principals

Person/victim; sex-neutral.

Spouses

Statutory limitation upon traditional spousal exception: "Spousal exception to sexual assault offenses: a person does not commit a crime under this chapter if the victim is his legal spouse, unless the spouses are living apart and one of them has filed for separate maintenance or divorce," §632-A:5.

Terminology

Language

"A person is guilty . . .[of felonious sexual penetration] if he engages in sexual penetration with another person under any of the following circumstances: . . . III when the actor coerces the victim to submit by threatening to use physical force, physical violence, or superior physical strength on the victim, and the victim believes the actor has the present ability to execute these threats; IV when the actor coerces the victim to submit by threatening to retaliate against the victim, or any other person, and the victim believes that the actor has the ability to execute these threats in the future," §632-A:2.

Definitions

Sexual penetration means sexual intercourse, cunnilingus, fellatio, anal intercourse, or any intrusion, however slight, of any part of the actor's body or any object manipulated by the actor into the genital or anal opening of the victim's body; emission is not required, §632-A:1V. *Sexual contact* means the intentional touching of the victim's or actor's sexual or intimate parts, including breasts or buttocks, and the intentional touching of the victim's or actor's clothing covering the immediate area of the victim's or actor's sexual or intimate parts; sexual contact includes only that aforementioned conduct which can be reasonably construed as being for the purpose of sexual arousal or gratification, §632-A:1IV. *Serious personal injury* means extensive bodily injury or disfigurement, extreme mental anguish, or trauma, disease, or loss or impairment of a sexual or reproductive organ, §632-A:1III. *Retaliation* means threats of future physical or mental punishment, kidnaping, false imprisonment, extortion, or public humiliation or disgrace, §632-A:1II.

Statutory Age Provisions

Age of Consent

Statutory age set at 13 and 16. No age discrepancy between actor and victim required.

Offenses

Aggravated felonious sexual assault: sexual penetration when the victim is under 13, §632-A:2XI, or when the victim is over 13 and under 16 and the actor is a member of the same household, or related by blood or affinity to the victim, or is in a position of authority and the actor uses this authority to coerce the victim to submit, §632-A:2X; felonious sexual assault: sexual contact and the actor causes serious personal injury to the victim when the victim is under 13 or when the victim is over 13 and under 16 and the actor is a member of the same household, §632-A:3; sexual assault: sexual contact when the victim is under 13 or when the victim is over 13 and under 16 and the actor is a member of the same household, and so on, §632-A:4.

Evidence Provisions, Defenses, and Cross Refrences

Evidence

1975 rape reform evidence statute prohibits admissibility of evidence of prior consensual activity between the victim and any person other than the actor in any prosecution under this chapter, §632-A:6; in cases when the victim is under 16, the victim's testimony shall be heard in-camera unless good cause is shown by the defendant. The record shall not be sealed and all other testimony and evidence introduced during the proceeding shall be public, §632-A:8; corroboration not required, §632-A:6.

Defenses

Lack of consent a complete defense, *State v. Lemire*, 115 N.H. 526, 325 A.2d 906 (1975); prompt complaint requirement, no prosecution unless alleged the offense was brought to the attention of law-enforcement officers within 6 months except in those cases where the victim was under 18, §632-A:7.

Cross References

Incest among the immediate family a circumstance of aggravated felonious sexual assault, §632-A:2(X).

Penalties

Terms

Aggravated felonious sexual assault: class A felony, §632-A:2; class A felony, maximum 15 years, §651:2IIa; felonious sexual assault: class B felony, §632-A:3; class B felony, maximum 7 years, §651:2IIb; sexual assault: misdemeanor, §632-A:4; misdemeanor, maximum of 1 year, §651:2IIc.

Special

Mandatory sentence for felonious use of a firearm, not to be concurrently served, not to be suspended, and shall be imposed without eligibility, §651:2IIb; extended terms, §651:6.

New Jersey

State Statutes

N.J. Stat. Ann. tit. 2C:14-1 through 2C:14-8 (1979)
§2C:14-1 Definitions
§2C:14-2 Sexual assault
§2C:14-3 Criminal sexual contact
§2C:14-4 Lewdness

Derivation

History

Common-law rape statute included in the first codification of the laws in 1796. Offense was rape or carnal knowledge of a woman against her will and carnal knowledge and abuse of a woman-child under 10. Penalty was a maximum of 15 years. An 1820 statute provided a different penalty for slaves convicted of rape or other crimes. Law of 1887 raised the statutory age of the female to 16, and the offender was required to be over 16. Minor technical changes in wording and placement within the code were enacted in 1898. Amendments in 1905 reduced the statutory age from 16 to 12, raised the fine and increased the penalty for rape to 30 years. 1905 law also created a new offense: carnal knowledge of a woman between 12 and 16 with consent. Penalty was a fine of $2,000 or 15 years of imprisonment. 1910 amendment changed the terminology of carnal abuse to "with or without her consent." In 1921 a provision was added prohibiting carnal knowledge of female inmates of homes or institutions for the feebleminded. Penalty was a $1,000 fine or 2 years in prison. 1937 revision made no substantive change. L.1949 added the Sex Offender Act requiring the presentence examination of sex offenders and a sentence to a treatment facility for the maximum term for the offense after a clinical finding of compulsive, repetitive criminal acts. 1951 revision made minor technical changes in language, raised the fine for statutory rape, and reworded and put in a separate section the provision dealing with females in institutions. No specific penalty was set for an offense involving an institutionalized female. A 1952 amendment added a provision for women under the influence of drugs. A rape evidence statute was enacted in 1976. Rape reform legislation was included with comprehensive criminal code reform which became effective in 1979.

Present Law

Rape reform statute redefining rape and sodomy as sex-neutral aggravated sexual assault, sexual assault, aggravated criminal sexual contact, criminal sexual contact, and lewdness. Evidence statute amended and strengthened; spousal exception repealed for all offenses.

Statutory Structure

Changes

Traditional formulation of rape, statutory rape, sodomy, and incest replaced by two gradations of sexual assault and two gradations of criminal sexual contact. Common-law spousal exception repealed. Evidence statute strengthened. Acts constituting the offense redefined. Penalties generally reduced, but new provisions for second offenders.

Offenses

Aggravated sexual assault; sexual assault; aggravated criminal sexual contact; criminal sexual contact; lewdness.

Requirements

Aggravated sexual assault: sexual penetration when the victim is under 13, or when the victim is over 13 and under 16 and the actor is related to victim, in a position of authority, or in the position of a parent, or when the sexual act is committed during a felony, or when the actor is armed, or when the actor is aided or abetted and the actor uses force or coercion or the victim is physically helpless, mentally defective, or mentally incapacitated; or when the actor uses force or coercion and the victim sustains severe personal injury, 2C:14-2a; sexual assault: sexual contact with victim under 13 when the actor is 4 years older; and sexual penetrtion when the actor uses force or coercion, but the victim does not sustain severe personal injury, or when the victim was physically helpless or mentally incapacitated, when the actor is in a position of authority, when the victim is at least 16 but under 18 and the actor is member of the household, when the victim is over 13 and under 16 and the actor is 4 years older, 2C:14-2(b); aggravated criminal sexual contact: sexual contact under circumstances defining aggravated sexual assault, 2C:14-3a; criminal sexual contact: sexual contact under circumstances defining sexual assault, 2C:14-3b.

Principals

Actor/victim; sex-neutral.

Spouses

Common-law spousal exception explicitly repealed. "No actor shall be presumed to be incapable of committing a crime under this chapter because of . . . marriage to the victim," 2C:14-5(b).

Terminology

Language

An actor is guilty of aggravated sexual assault if he commits an act of sexual penetration with another person under any one of the following circumstances: the actor has supervisory or disciplinary power over the victim by virtue of the actor's legal, professional, or occupational status; or the act is committed during the commission or attempted commission, whether alone or with one or more other persons, of robbery, kidnaping, homicide, aggravated assault on another, burglary, arson, or criminal escape, 2C:14-2.

Definitions

Sexual penetration means vaginal intercourse, cunnilingus, fellatio, or anal intercourse between persons or the insertion of the hand, finger, or object into the anus or vagina either by the actor or upon the actor's instruction; the depth of the insertion shall not be relevant as to the question of commission of the crime, 2C:14-1(c). *Sexual contact* means an intentional touching by the victim or actor, either directly or through clothing, of the victim's or actor's intimate parts for the purpose of degrading or humiliating the victim or sexually arousing or gratifying the actor; sexual contact of the actor with himself must be in view of the victim whom the actor knows to be present, 2C:14-1(d). *Severe personal injury* means bodily injury, disfigurement, disease, incapacitating mental anguish, or chronic pain, 2C:14-1(f). *Sexual contact* shall mean any conduct or behavior relating to sexual activities of the victim, including but not limited to previous or subsequent experience of sexual penetration or contact, use of contraceptives, living arrangement, and life-style, 2C:14-7(c).

Statutory Age Provisions

Age of Consent

No statutory age of consent. Former law specified 16 as age of consent. 1978 amendment to code added section criminalizing sexual penetration and sexual contact, when victim is over 13 and under 16 and actor is 4 years older, 2C:14-2(c)(5) and 2C:14-3(a).

Offenses

Aggravated sexual assault: sexual penetration when the victim is less than 13 years old, 2C:14-2(a)(1), and when the victim is over 13 and under 16 and either a relationship of affinity or the actor is in a position of authority or the actor is in the position of a parent, 2C:14-2(a)(2); sexual assault: sexual contact with a victim under 13 when the actor is 4 years older, 2C:14-2(b), or sexual penetration when the victim is at least 16 but under 18 and the actor is a member of the household with superivsory or disciplinary power, 2C:14-2(c)(4), or when the victim is over 13 and under 16 and the actor is 4 years older, 2C:14-2(c)(5); aggravated criminal sexual conduct: sexual contact when the victim is over 13 and under 16 and either a relationship of affinity or the actor is in a position of authority or the actor is in the position of a parent, 2C:14-3(a); criminal sexual contact: sexual contact when the victim is over 16 but under 18 and the actor is a member of victim's household with supervisory or disciplinary power over the victim or when victim is over 13 and under 16 and the actor is 4 years older, 2C:14-3(b).

**Evidence Provisions, Defenses,
and Cross References**

Evidence

Amended 1979 evidence statute limits admission of evidence of the victim's previous sexual conduct or reference to such conduct before the jury, except under order of the court after an in-camera hearing. Presumption of irrelevancy for conduct more than 1 year before the offense. Evidence of previous sexual conduct shall not be considered relevant unless it is material to negating the element of force or coercion or to proving the source of semen, pregnancy, or disease is a person other than the defendant, 2C:14-7.

Defenses

Consent: sexual assault statute does not define or mention consent, but consent in general and consent to bodily harm are defined in the code, 2C:2-10; ignorance or mistake of law or fact a statutory defense, if reasonable, 2C:2-4; mistake as to age defense abolished, 2C:14-5(c). All common-law defenses preserved unless an explicit legislative purpose to the contrary, 2C:2-5; proof of resistance not required, 2C:14-5(a); presumption as to incapacity due to age or impotence abolished, 2C:14-5(b).

Cross References

Former incest statute repealed and replaced by code provision which defines as aggravated sexual assault, sexual penetration with a person over 13 and under 16 when actor is related to the victim by blood or affinity to the third degree, 2C:14-2(a)(2)(a); coercion for the purposes of sexual assault defined circumstances of crime of criminal coercion, 2C:13-5; sex offenders to be committed for treatment according to the amended provisions of the Sex Offender Act, 2C:47-1 et seq.

Penalties

Terms

Aggravated sexual assault: first-degree offense, 2C:14-2(a); first-degree offense, term between 10 and 20 years, 2C:43-6(a)(1). Sexual assault: second-degree offense, 2C:14-2(b); second-degree offense, term between 5 and 10 years, 2C:43-6(a)(2). Aggravated criminal sexual contact: third-degree offense, 2C:14-3(a); third-degree offense, term between 3 and 5 years, 2C:43-6(a)(3). Criminal sexual contact: fourth-degree offense, 2C:14-3(b); fourth-degree offense, maximum term of 18 months. Lewdness: disorderly persons offense, 2C:14-4; disorderly persons offense, maximum 6 months, 2C:43-8.

Special

Second or subsequent offense shall include a fixed minimum term of not less than 5 years during which the defendant shall not be eligible for parole. No suspended sentence or noncustodial sentence or second offenders, 2C:14-6;

new criteria for sentencing, 2C:44-1 et seq.; fines and restitutions, 2C:43-3; extended terms, 2C:43-7; first release of all offenders on parole, 2C:43-9.

New Mexico

State Statutes

N.M. Stat. Ann. §30-9-10 through §30-9-17 (1978) (Supp. 1979)
§30-9-10 Definitions
§30-9-11 Criminal sexual penetration
§30-9-12 Criminal sexual contact
§30-9-13 Criminal sexual contact of a minor

Derivation

History

Compilation of 1865 with statutes printed in Spanish and English included a variant of the Elizabethan rape statute. Any person who ravished or had carnal knowledge of any female over 10 by force or against her will was guilty of rape. Punishment was a maximum of 30 years and a minimum of 5 years, provided the woman was not a common prostitute. For the rape of a child under 10, punishment was life. Same statute included in the 1882 compilation under the category of "offenses against lives." Law of 1887 rewrote the definition of the offense and changed the statutory age and penalties. Rape was defined as sexual intercourse with a female under 14 or when a female was over 14 but through imbecility, unsoundness of mind, whether temporary or permanent, incapable of consent, when resistance overcome or prevented by stupor or weakness produced by intoxicant or anesthetic administered by the defendant or someone in privity with the defendant; punishment, maximum of 20 years, minimum of 5 years. Presumption of inability for male under 14. Offenses of enticing females and compelling to marry added. Carnal knowledge and abuse of female under 10 remained unchanged. Punishment was life term; law of 1897 changed presumption of incapacity for males to a statutory defense. Law of 1907 adds new offense: seduction of female student under 18 with consent, penalty is minimum 1 year and maximum 5 years. An amendment in 1915 changes the statutory age for rape to 16. Proviso concerning prostitutes remains.

Amendment of 1923 changed the penalty for rape to a minimum of 1 year and a maximum of 99 years. No further changes until a Model Penal Code (MPC) revision in 1963 rewrote the entire section, though the definition of rape was essentially retained. "Wife" excluded the legally separated and included female over 18 in a relationship of consensual cohabitation.

Rape was when a male caused a female other than his wife to engage in sexual intercourse without consent: when resistance was overcome by force, when the female was incapable of consent, or when resistance was prevented by a narcotic. Rape was a second-degree felony punishable by a minimum of 10 years and a maximum of 50 years, plus a fine. New offense of statutory rape: sexual intercourse with a female under 16. Statutory defense of reasonable mistake as to age. Offense graded by age of offender: if offender under 21, a fourth-degree felony (minimum 1 year, maximum 5 years); if the victim under 13, no mistake as to age defense. New offense: sexual assault: indecent touching of a person under 16 with a defense of mistake as to age. No further changes, until 1975 revision entirely rewrote the law.

Present Law

Rape reform statute defining criminal sexual penetration, criminal sexual contact, and criminal sexual contact of a minor. Strong evidence statute. Corroboration requirement repealed.

Statutory Structure

Changes

1975 law completely redefined the offense. Emphasis upon resistance of the victim removed. Great mental anguish included in the definition of the offense. Emphasis upon the actor's use of force and coercion and demonstrable, physical harm to the victim, rather than upon the victim's subjective consent. Evidence statute enacted in 1975. 1978 statute allows for videotaping of testimony of minors to protect privacy. 1979 amendment as to penalties and statute renumbered. Technical amendments in 1978.

Offenses

First-, second-, and third-degree criminal sexual penetration; fourth-degree criminal sexual contact; third- and fourth-degree criminal sexual contact of a minor.

Requirements

First-degree criminal sexual penetration: criminal sexual penetration on a child under 13, or by the use of force or coercion which results in great bodily harm or great mental anguish to the victim, §30-9-11A; second-degree criminal sexual penetration: criminal sexual penetration on a child over 13 and under 16 when the perpetrator is in a position of authority, by the use of force or coercion resulting in personal injury to the victim, by the use of force or coercion when the perpetrator is aided and abetted, during the commission of any other felony, or when the perpetrator is armed, §30-9-11B; third-degree criminal sexual penetration: criminal sexual penetration perpetrated through the use of force or coercion, §30-9-11C; fourth-degree sexual contact: criminal sexual contact perpetrated by force or coercion resulting in personal injury to the victim; by the use of force or coercion when the perpetrator is aided or abetted, when the perpetrator is armed, §30-9-12; third-degree criminal sexual contact of a minor: criminal sexual contact of a minor perpetrated on a child under 13, or on a child 13 to 18 when the perpetrator is in a position of authority and uses this authority to coerce the child to submit, §30-9-13A; fourth-degree criminal sexual contact of a minor: all criminal sexual contact of a child 13 to 18 perpetrated with force or coercion, §30-9-13B.

Principals

Person/person; sex-neutral.

Spouses

Spousal exception included in definition of criminal sexual penetration: "Criminal sexual penetration is the unlawful and intentional causing of a person, other than one's spouse, to engage in . . .," §30-9-11; spousal exception incuded in definition of criminal sexual contact: "Criminal sexual contact is intentionally touching . . . someone other than one's spouse or intentionally causing another . . . and someone other than one's spouse . . . ," §30-9-12; spousal exception included in definition of criminal sexual contact of a minor: "Criminal sexual contact of a minor is unlawfully and intentionally touching . . . a minor other than one's spouse or unlawfully and intentionally causing a minor other than one's spouse to touch. . . , §30-9-13. Spouse means a legal husband or wife, unless the couple is living apart or either husband or wife has filed for separate maintenance or divorce, §30-9-10E.

Terminology

Language

"Force or coercion means the use of physical force or physical violence; the use of threats to use physical violence or physical force against the victim or another when the victim believes there is a present ability to execute such threats; the use of threats, including threats of physical punishment, kidnaping, extortion, or retaliation directed against the victim or another when the victim believes that there is an ability to execute such threats; or perpetrating criminal sexual penetration or criminal sexual conduct when the perpetrator knows or has reason to know the victim is unconscious, asleep, or otherwise physically helpless, or suffers from a mental condition which rendered the victim incapable of understanding the nature or consequences of the act; physical or verbal resistance of the victim is not an element of force or coercion,'' §30-9-10A.

Definitions

Criminal sexual penetration is the unlawful and intentional causing of a person, other than one's spouse, to engage in sexual intercourse, cunnilingus, fellatio, or anal intercourse, or the causing of penetration, to any extent and with any object, of the genital or anal opening of another, whether or not there is any emission, §30-9-11. *Criminal sexual contact* is intentionally touching or applying force without consent to the unclothed intimate parts of another who has reached his 18th birthday and someone other than one's spouse, or intentionally causing another, who has reached his 18th birthday and someone other than one's spouse to touch one's intimate parts. For the purpose of this section, ''intimate parts'' means the primary genital area, groin, or anus, §30-9-12. *Criminal sexual contact of a minor* is unlawfully and intentionally touching or applying force to the intimate parts of a minor other than one's spouse or unlawfully and intentionally causing a minor other than one's spouse to touch one's intimate parts. For the purpose of this section, ''intimate parts'' means the primary genital area, groin, buttock, anus, or breast, §30-9-13. *Great mental anguish* means psychological or emotional damage that requires psychiatric or psychological treatment or care, either on an inpatient or outpatient basis, and is characterized by extreme behavioral change or severe physical symptoms, §30-9-10B. *Great bodily harm* means an injury to the person which creates a high probability of death, or which causes serious disfigurement, or which results in permanent or protracted loss or impairment of the function of any member or organ of the body, §30-1-12A. *Personal injury* means bodily injury to a lesser degree than great bodily harm and includes, but is not limited to, disfigurement, mental anguish, chronic or recurrent pain, pregnancy, or disease or injury to a sexual or reproductive organ, §30-9-10C.

Statutory Age Provisions

Age of Consent

Statute does not define age of consent; age of victim an element of several offenses. Age differential between actor and victim not an element of any offense.

Offenses

First-degree criminal sexual penetration: criminal sexual penetration perpetrated on a child under 13, §30-9-11A; second-degree criminal sexual penetration: criminal sexual penetration perpetrated on a child 13 to 16 years of age when the perpetrator is in a position of authority over the child and uses this authority to coerce the child to submit, §30-9-11B; position of authority means that position occupied by a parent, relative, household member, teacher, employer, or other person who, by reason of said position, is able to exercise undue influence over a child, §30-9-10D; criminal sexual contact: offense defined to encompass only acts committed upon or caused to be committed by a person over 18, but no restriction upon age of person committing the offense, §30-9-12; criminal sexual contact of a minor in the third degree consists of all criminal sexual contact of a minor perpetrated on a child under 13 or on a child 13 to 18 years of age when the perpetrator is in a position of authority and uses this authority to coerce the child to submit, §30-9-13A.

Evidence Provisions, Defenses, and Cross References

Evidence

1975 rape reform evidence statute provided as a matter of substantive right that evidence of the victim's past sexual conduct, opinion evidence thereof, or of reputation for past sexual conduct shall not be admitted unless the court finds it is material and not prejudicial. Defendant must file a written motion prior to trial and the court shall hear it in-camera. Court shall issue a written order stating what may be introduced by the defendant and stating specific questions to be permitted, §30-9-16; section not unconstitutional on its face, *State* v. *Herrera*, 92 N.M. 7, 582, P.2d 384 (Ct. App. 1978); testimony of any alleged victim under 16 may be videotaped, including cross-examination, and heard at trial in lieu of direct testimony of the alleged victim, §30-9-17; corroboration requirement repealed, §30-9-15; resistance not required for the proof of force or coercion, §30-9-10A.

Defenses

Absence of consent is not an element of the crime of criminal sexual penetration as defined by the legislature, *State* v. *Jiminez*, 89 N.M. 652, 556 P.2d 60 (Ct. App. 1976); absence of consent, which is not defined by statute, is an element of criminal sexual contact, §30-9-12; no mistake as to age defense for offenses where age of the victim is an element of the offense.

Cross References

Incest, §30-10-3; incestuous acts also included in definition of criminal sexual penetration and criminal sexual contact with a minor, §30-9-11B and §30-9-13A(2); indecent exposure, §30-9-14; indecent dancing, §30-9-14.1; indecent waitering, §30-9-14.2; victim restitution, §31-17-1.

Penalties

Terms

First-degree criminal sexual penetration: first-degree felony, §30-9-11A; second-degree criminal sexual penetration: second-degree felony, §30-9-11B; third-degree criminal sexual penetration: third-degree felony, §30-9-11C; first-degree felony, 18 years imprisonment; second-degree felony, 9 years imprisonment; third-degree felony, 3 years imprisonment; fourth-degree felony, 18 months imprisonment, §31-18-15A; fourth-degree criminal sexual contact: fourth-degree felony, §30-9-12A; criminal sexual contact is a misdemeanor when perpetrated through the use of force or coercion, §30-9-12B; third-degree criminal sexual contact of a minor: third-degree felony, §30-9-13A; fourth-degree criminal sexual contact: fourth-degree felony, §30-9-13B.

Special

Aggravating and mitigating circumstances can be used by the judge or jury to alter basic sentences, if reasons given on the record, but use of a firearm or prior felony convictions shall not be aggravating circumstances, §31-18-15.1; aggravating and mitigating circumstances, §30-21A-5 and §30-21A-6; use of a firearm results in alteration of basic sentence, §31-18-16; habitual offenders, alteration of basic sentence, §31-18-17 et seq.; all sentences to include parole term to be served after the completion of any actual time of imprisonment, §31-18-15C. Fines may be imposed in addition to term of imprisonment, §31-18-15D.

New York

State Statutes

N.Y. Penal Law §1300 through §1300.65 (1977) (Supp. 1979)
§130.00 Sex offenses; definitions of terms
§130.05 Sex offenses; lack of consent
§130.10 Sex offenses; defenses
§130.16 Sex offenses; corroboration
§130.20 Sexual misconduct
§130.25 Rape in the third degree
§130.30 Rape in the second degree
§130.35 Rape in the first degree
§130.55 Sexual abuse in the third degree
§130.60 Sexual abuse in the second degree
§130.65 Sexual abuse in the first degree

Derivation

History

Revised statutes of 1829 defined rape as carnally and unlawfully knowing any female child under 10 or forcibly ravishing any woman over 10. Punishment was a minimum of 10 years. Carnal knowledge of a woman over 10 without consent by administering a liquid or other stupor-producing substance was punishable by a maximum of 5 years. Compelling a girl to marry, and so on, punishable by a minimum of 10 years. Compilation of 1836 adds a new offense: taking away a female under 14, punishment is up to 3 years or 1 year. Statute of 1848 introduces offense of seduction with a chaste-character provision, and a statutory corroboration requirement. Offense is misdemeanor with a maximum penalty of 5 years or 1 year. Indictment must be founded within 2 years of the offense, and subsequent marriage of the parties was a bar to prosecution. Neither these provisos nor the chaste-character provision or the corroboration requirement applied to the offense of forcible rape or to the offense of carnal knowledge of a female child under 10. No further changes until all of these statutes were repealed by a law of 1886. Penal code of 1909 redefines rape as sexual intercourse with a female not his wife against her will or without consent or where the female does not resist through idiocy, where resistance is overcome, where resistance is prevented by fear or by stupor, and so on, when the female is unconscious or in the custody of the law or in any place of lawful detention. These circumstances are rape in the first degree. All other sexual inter-course with a female under 18 are rape in the second degree. New statutory corroboration requirement applies to both forms of rape. Source listed as law of 1886. Corroboration requirement is then interpreted by case law to apply to every material fact essential to the crime. Subsequent interpretations turn the requirement into the strictest of any state. Penalty for first-degree rape is a maximum term of 10 years. Law of 1950 leaves the substantive offense and corroboration requirement unchanged. Rape in the first degree is a maximum of 20 years or an indeterminate term with a minimum of 1 day or a maximum of life. For rape in the second degree, amendment requires the offender to be over 12. Penalty is a maximum of 10 years. New offense added a misdemeanor later termed statutory rape, if the circumstances are neither rape in the first or second degree. Law of 1965 completely redefines all sex offenses following the Model Penal Code (MPC).

Present Law

MPC-type statute defines three degrees of rape, sodomy, and sexual abuse. Emphasis remains upon the victim's demonstration of resistance or inability or incapacity to consent. Rape evidence statute added in 1975. Modifications of corroboration requirement in 1972 and 1974. Amendments to spousal exception and to definition of force and resistance in 1978.

Statutory Structure

Changes

Many features of prior law retained after 1965. Although the unusually harsh character of the New York corroboration statute has been modified, the present law incorporates few of the features of reform legislation; corroboration requirement remains in force, see State v. Fuller, 66 A.D. 2d 27, 412 N.Y. Supp. 2d 703 (3d Dept. 1979). First amendment to the corroboration requirement in 1972 mitigated some effects. More important amendments to the corroboration requirement in 1974 removed the requirement for forcible rape, sodomy, and sexual abuse. Amendment of 1978 added new offense of aggravated sexual abuse, defined as penetration with an object. Amendment to the definition of force in 1977 removed the requirement of utmost resistance. Law of 1979 changes sentencing procedures and terms.

Offenses

Rape in the first, second, and third degree; sexual misconduct; sexual abuse in the first, second, and third degree.

Requirements

First-degree rape: sexual intercourse by forcible compulsion, when female is physically helpless, or with a female under 11, §130.35; second-degree rape: sexual intercourse with a female under 14, §130.30; third-degree rape: sexual intercourse with a female incapable of consent by some other factor than being under 17, or a male over 21 who engages in sexual intercourse with a female under 17, §130.25; sexual misconduct: sexual intercourse with a female without consent or deviate sexual intercourse with another person without consent, or sexual conduct with an animal or a dead body, §130.20; first-degree sexual abuse: sexual contact by forcible compulsion, or when the other person is incapable of consent because physically helpless, or when the other person is under 11, §130.65; second-degree sexual abuse: sexual contact with a person incapable of consent for reasons other than being under 17, or when the other person is under 14, §130.60; third-degree sexual abuse: sexual contact without consent.

Principals

Male/female for rape; male perpetrator for sexual misconduct; sex-neutral for sexual abuse.

Spouses

Statutory limitation on the traditional spousal exception. "For the purposes of this artcle "not married" means (a) the lack of an existing relationship of husband and wife between the female and the actor which is recognized by law or (b) the existence of the relationship of husband and wife between the actor and the female which is recognized by law at the time the actor commits an offense proscribed by this article by means of forcible compulsion against the female, and the female and the actor are living apart at such time pursuant to a valid and effective (i) order issued by a court of competent jurisdiction which by its terms or in its effect requires such living apart, or (ii) decree or judgment of separation, or (iii) written agreement of separation subscribed by them and acknowledged in the form required to entitle a deed to be recorded which contains provisions specifically indicating that the actor may be guilty of the commission of a crime for engaging in conduct which constitutes an offense proscribed by this article against and without the consent of the female," §130.00(4).

Terminology

Language

"Forcible compulsion means physical force which is capable of overcoming earnest resistance; or a threat, expressed or implied, that places a person in fear of immediate death or serious physical injury to himself or another person, or in fear that he or another person will immediately be kidnaped. Earnest resistance means resistance of a type reasonably to be expected from a person who genuinely refuses to participate in sexual intercourse, deviate sexual intercourse, or sexual contact, under all the attendant circumstances. Earnest resistance does not mean utmost resistance," §130.00(8), as amended by law of 1977, ch. 692.

Definitions

Lack of consent results from forcible compulsion or incapacity to consent or where the offense charged is sexual abuse, any circumstances in addition to forcible compulsion or incapacity to consent, in which the victim does not expressly or impliedly acquiesce to the actor's conduct. A person is deemed incapable of consent when he is less than 17 years old, or mentally defective, or mentally incapacitated, or physically helpless, §130.05. *Sexual intercourse* has its ordinary meaning and occurs upon any penetration, however slight, §130.00(1). *Sexual contact* means any touching of the sexual or other intimate parts of a person not married to the actor for the purpose of gratifying the sexual desire of either party, §130.00(3).

Statutory Age Provisions

Age of Consent

"A person is deemed incapable of consent when he is less than 17 years old," §130.05(3)a. Statutory age offenses set at 11, 14, and 17. Age differential between persons is an element of some offenses.

Offenses

First-degree rape: sexual intercourse with a female under 11, §130.35(3); second-degree rape: male over 18 who engages in sexual intercourse with female under 14, §130.30; third-degree rape: male over 21 who engages in sexual intercourse with a female under 17, §130.25; first-degree sexual abuse: sexual contact with person under 11, §130.65(3); second-degree sexual abuse: sexual contact with a person under 14, §130.60(2); third-degree sexual abuse: sexual contact without consent but an affirmative defense that person under 17 and over 14 and defendant less than 5 years older, §130.55.

Evidence Provisions, Defenses, and Cross References

Evidence

Law of 1975 limits admissibility of evidence of the victim's sexual conduct unless: it proves specific instances of conduct with the accused, it proves the victim has been convicted as a prostitute, the evidence rebuts evidence introduced by the prosecution, or it proves the accused is the source of semen, pregnancy, or disease, or the evidence is determined relevant and admissible after a hearing and an offer of proof by the accused, N.Y. Crim. Proc. L. §60.42. Statutory corroboration requirement limited by amendments in 1972 and 1974 but still in force, §130.16; resistance requirement limited by 1977 amendment but still in force, §130.00(8).

Defenses

"Whether or not specifically stated it is an element of every offense defined in this article, except the defense of consensual sodomy, that the sexual act was committed without consent of the victim," §130.05; an affirmative defense that the defendant did not know the victim was incapable of consent because mentally defective, mentally incapacitated, or physically helpless, §130.10; age difference between actor and victim under 17 and over 14 an affirmative defense to third-degree sexual abuse, §130.55.

Cross References

Incest, §255.25; first-degree sodomy, §130.50; second-degree sodomy, §130.45; third-degree sodomy, §130.40; consensual sodomy, §130.38.

Penalties

Terms

First-degree rape: class B felony, §130.35; aggravated sexual abuse: class B felony, §130.70; class B felony, maximum 25 years, §70.00(2)(b); second-degree rape: class D felony, §130.30; first-degree sexual abuses: class D felony, §130.65; class D felony, maximum 7 years, §70.00(2)(d); third-degree rapes: class E felony, §130.25; class E felony, maximum 4 years, §70.00(2)(e); sexual misconduct: class A misdemeanor, §130.20; second-degree sexual abuse: class A misdemeanor, §130.60; third-degree sexual abuse: class B misdemeanor, §1130.55; class A and B misdemeanors, maximum 1 year, §55.05(2) and §55.10.

Special

Class B violent felonies: includes first-degree rape and first-degree sodomy, §70.02(1)a; sentence for second violence felony offender, §70.04; sentence for second offender, §70.06; sentence for persistent violent felony offenders, §70.08.

North Carolina

State Statute

N.C. Gen. Stat. §14-27.1 through §14-27.10 (Supp. 1979)

§14-27.1 Definitions
§14-27.2 First-degree rape
§14-27.3 Second-degree rape
§14-27.4 First-degree sexual offense
§14-27.5 Second-degree sexual offense
§14-27.7 Intercourse and sexual offenses with certain victims; consent no defense

Derivation

History

Law of 1818 declared the Elizabethan rape statute (18 Eliz. c.7 en. 1576) to be in force in North Carolina. Assault with intent to rape codified in 1823. Law of 1868-1869 codifies the traditional offense: every person who is convicted of ravishing and carnally knowing any female of the age of 10 years or more by force and against her will or of carnally knowing and abusing any female child under 10 shall suffer death. Law of 1881 added carnal knowledge of married woman by fraud or by impersonating her husband. No change, until an amendment in 1917 changes the statutory age of the female to 12. Law of 1917 adds a new offense: obtaining carnal knowledge of virtuous girls between 12 and 14. Case notes refer to law of 1895 as source of the statute with age limits of 10 to 14. Statute of 1917 defines offense as carnal knowledge of any female child who has never had sexual intercourse with any person. Compilation of 1943 notes that in 1923 the age provisions were amended to include females over 12 and under 16. Proviso added: if the offenders shall be married, such marriage shall be a total bar to prosecution; if male is under 18, offense shall be misdemeanor. Law of 1949 adds proviso stating that if jury recommends punishment, it shall be life imprisonment, not death evidence statute passed in 1977. Essentially the traditional definition of rape with a penalty of death, and a statutory rape offense defined as carnal knowledge of virtuous girls between 12 and 16 remained in effect until 1979.

Present Law

Legislation passed in 1979 incorporated some reform features, retained many aspects of the prior law, divided offenses into two degrees and changed some of the definitions, added new offenses, and modified the spousal exception. Rape evidence statute passed in 1977, effective 1978.

Statutory Structure

Changes

Almost no legislative changes except for the three changes in the age provisions from the codification of the Elizabethan statute in 1868-1869 until the passage of a weak rape evidence statute in 1977 and the passage of the present law in 1979.

Offenses

First-degree rape; second-degree rape; first-degree sexual offense; second-degree sexual offense; intercourse and sexual offense with certain victims.

Requirements

First-degree rape: vaginal intercourse with another person by force and against the will and where person employs or displays a dangerous or deadly weapon or an article believed to be a dangerous or deadly weapon, when person inflicts serious personal injury upon the victim or another person, or when person is aided or abetted by one or more persons, or when victim is a child under 12 and defendant is 4 years older, §14-27.2; second-degree rape: vaginal intercourse by force and against the will, or where person is mentally defective, mentally incapacitated, or physically helpless, and person knows or should know of same, §14-27.3; first-degree sexual offense: sexual act under circumstances of first-degree rape, §14-27.4; second-degree sexual offense: sexual act under circumstances of second-degree rape, §14-27.5; intercourse and sexual offenses with certain victims: vaginal intercourse or sexual act between minor victim and parent, person in position of parent, or person having custody of a victim of any age, §14-27.7.

Principals

Male/female for both degrees of rape; sex-neutral for two degrees of sexual offense.

Spouses

Spousal exception excludes those living apart: "A person may not be prosecuted under this article if the victim is the person's legal spouse at the time of the commission of the alleged rape or sexual offense unless the parties are living apart pursuant to a written agreement or a judicial decree," §14-27.8.

Terminology

Language

Resistance by the victim included in definition of mentally defective, mentally incapacitated, and physically helpless: "mentally defective means a victim [who is substantially incapable] of resisting the act of vaginal intercourse or a sexual act," §14-27.1;" mentally incapacitated means a victim [who is substantially incapable of] resisting the act of vaginal intercourse or a sexual act," §14-27.1;" physically helpless means a victim who . . . is physically unable to resist . . .," §14-27.1(3)

Definitions

Sexual act means cunnilingus, fellatio, analingus, or anal intercourse, but does not include vaginal intercourse. Sexual act also means the penetration, however slight, by any object into the genital or anal opening of another person's body. Provided that it shall be an affirmative defense that the penetration was for accepted medical purposes, §14-27.1(4). *Mentally defective* means (i) a victim who suffers from mental retardation, or (ii) a victim who suffers from a mental disorder, either of which temporarily or permanently renders the victim substantially incapable of appraising the nature of his or her conduct, or of resisting the act of vaginal intercourse or a sexual act, or of communicating unwillingness to submit to the act of vaginal intercourse or a sexual act, §14-27.1(1). Intercourse and sexual offenses with certain victims, consent no defense: if a defendant who has assumed the position of a parent in the home of a minor victim engages in vaginal intercourse or a sexual act with a victim who is a minor residing in the home, or if a person having custody of a victim of any age or a person who is an agent or employee of any person or institution, whether such institution is private, charitable, or governmental, having custody of a victim of any age engages in vaginal intercourse or a sexual act with such victim, the defendant is guilty of a felony; consent is not a defense to a charge under this section, §14-27.7. *Sexual behavior* means sexual activity of the complainant other than the sexual act which is at issue in the indictment on trial, §8-58.6(a).

Statutory Age Provisions

Age of Consent

Age of consent is 13, defendant must be 4 years older, §14-27.2a(2) and §14-27.4a(2).

Offenses

First-degree rape: vaginal intercourse and the victim is a child of the age 12 years or less ant the defendant is 4 or more years older than the victim, §14-27.2a(2); first-degree sexual offense: sexual act and the victim is a child of the age of 12 years or less and the defendant is 4 or more years older than the victim, §14-27.4a(2).

Evidence Provisions, Defenses, and Cross References

Evidence

Evidence statute enacted in 1977 provides that "the sexual behavior of the complainant is irrelevant to any issue unless such behavior was (1) between the complainant and the defendant; or (2) is evidence of specific instances of sexual behavior offered for the purpose of showing that the act or acts charged were not committed by the defendant; or is evidence of a pattern of sexual behavior so distinctive and so closely resembling the defendant's version of the alleged encounter as to tend to prove that such compainant consented . . . or behaved in such a manner as to lead the defendant reasonably to believe that the complainant consented; or (3) is evidence offered as the basis of psychological or psychiatric opinion that the complainant fantasized or invented the act or acts charged . . . in-camera hearing on the record which shall be closed," §8-58.6; penetration required, emission not required, §14-27.10.

Defenses

Consent is not a defense if the defendant is in the position of a parent or has custodial authority over the victim, §14-27.7; for other offenses consent is a defense. Presumption as to incapacity due to age abolished, §14-27.9.

Cross References

Incest between certain near-relatives, §14-178; crime against nature, §14-177.

Penalties

Terms

First-degree rape: life, §14-27.2(b); second-degree rape: maximum of 40 years, §14-27.3(b); first-degree sexual offense: life, §14-27.4(b); second-degree sexual offense: maximum of 40 years, §14-27.5(b). Intercourse and sexual offense with certain victims: minimum 2 years, maximum 15 years, §14-27.7.

Special

Punishment for second or subsequent offenses , §14-2.1; maximum punishment for felonies including fines, §14-1.1.

North Dakota

State Statutes

N.D. Cent. Code §12.1-20-07 through §12.1-20-15 (1976 Repl.)(Supp. 1979)
§12.1-20-01 General provisions
§12.1-20-02 Definitions
§12.1-20-03 Gross sexual imposition
§12.1-20-04 Sexual imposition
§12.1-20-05 Corruption or solicitation of minors
§12.1-20-06 Sexual abuse of wards
§12.1-20-07 Sexual assault

Derivation

History

First penal code adopted in 1863, repealed in 1865. Code based upon New York code adopted in its place. Penal code of 1877 defined rape as sexual intercourse with a female not the wife of the perpetrator where the female is under 16, incapable through lunacy of giving consent, where resistance is overcome, where resistance is prevented by threats of immediate and great bodily harm, where resistance is prevented by intoxication, where female submits under the belief that the defendant is her husband. Presumption of incapacity for males under 14; essential guilt consists of outrage to the person and feelings of the female. Rape in the first degree is where female is under 10 or incapable by lunacy or where accomplished by force. Rape in the second degree is all other categories. Punishment: first degree, a minimum of 10 years; second-degree, a minimum of 5 years. Proviso: no conviction if female is over 10 and male is under 20, and it appears to the satisfaction of the jury the female was sufficiently matured and informed to understand the nature of the act and consented thereto. Law of 1903 raises the statutory age of the female to 18. Law of 1909 adds sexual intercourse with a female dependant or ward, including a female in a penal institution. Penalty of 1 year to 15 years added in 1911. Amendment of 1909 changes age of female to 16 for first degree and prohibits defense of consent for female under 16 for second degree. Penalties changed: first degree a minimum of 5 years; second degree a minimum of 5 years and a maximum of 15. Law of 1915 rewrites the section, and grades offense according to age of offender. Rape is if offender is over 24 and circumstances of prior law except age of female changed to under 20. Second degree is circumstances of prior law when offender is over 17 and under 20 and other cases in which the female is under 18 and offender is over 20 and under 24. Rape in the first degree: minimum of 1 year; rape in the second degree: minimum of 1 year or if defendant is a minor, commitment to reform school. New offense of rape in the third degree added by law of 1915; rape in the third degree is by person under 20 under circumstances of rape but with apparent consent of female under 18. Punishment is reform school for a minimum of 1 year and a maximum of 3 years. 1917 amendment changes the age of the offender to under 17. Law of 1953 adds indecent liberties with any individual under 18 and a provision for psychiatric treatment for persons convicted of rape. Law of 1973 rewrites entire section and redefines offenses.

Present Law

MPC-type statute incorporating some features of reform statutes enacted in 1973. Evidence statute enacted in 1975. Amendments in 1977 add penetration by an object, add new sexual contact offenses, and amend age provisions.

Statutory Structure

Changes

1973 revisions replace offense of rape with a sex-neutral offense of gross sexual imposition and sexual imposition. Sexual assault is a sexual contact offense, a misdemeanor. Statutory age changed from under 18 for females to under 15. Sexual act redefined to encompass more than sexual intercourse. Evidence statute introduced in 1975. Amendments in 1977 added penetration or contact with an object to prohibited acts. Amendment of 1977 also graded sexual contact with a victim under 15 or by force or threat as gross sexual imposition. Grading changed for sexual assault in 1977. Amendment in 1979 added solicitation of minors.

Offenses

Gross sexual imposition: sexual imposition; corruption or solicitation of minors; sexual assault.

Requirements

Gross sexual imposition: sexual act when victim compelled to submit by force or threat; when victim's power to appraise or control conduct impaired; when victim unaware; when victim under 15; or when victim mentally incapable of understanding his or her conduct; or sexual contact when victim is under 15 or when victim compelled to submit by force or threats, §12.1-20-03; sexual imposition: sexual act or sexual contact when person compelled to submit by any threat that would render a person of reasonable firmness incapable of resisting, §12.1-20-04; sexual assault: sexual contact which is offensive to the other person; when other person suffers from mental disease or defect which renders him incapable of understanding; when person's control impaired by intoxicant or other means of preventing resistance; when person is in official custody or detained in a hospital, prison, or other institution and the actor has supervisory or disciplinary power over him or her; when person is a minor and actor is parent or guardian; when other person is a minor and the actor is an adult, §12.1-21-07.

Principals

Person/person; sex-neutral.

Spouses

Definition of acts excludes parties who are husband and wife: "sexual act means sexual contact between human beings who are not husband and wife . . .," §12.1-20-02(1). Spouse defined: "in sections 12.1-20-03 through 12.1-20-09, an offense excludes conduct with an actor's spouse. The exclusion shall be inoperative as respects spouses living apart under a decree of judicial separation. Where an offense excludes conduct with a spouse, this shall not preclude conviction of a spouse as an accomplice in an offense which he causes another person to perform" §12.1-20-01(2).

Terminology

Language

"A person who engages in a sexual act with another, or who causes another to engage in a sexual act, is guilty of an offense if he compels the victim to submit by force or by threat of imminent death, serious bodily injury, or kidnaping, to be inflicted on any human being; he or someone with his knowledge has substantially impaired the victim's power to appraise or control his or her conduct by administering or employing without his or her knowledge intoxicants or other means with intent to prevent resistance . . .," §12.1-20-03.

Definitions

Sexual act means sexual contact between human beings who are not husband and wife consisting of contact between the penis and the vulva, the penis and the anus, the mouth and the penis, or the mouth and the vulva. For the purposes of this subsection, sexual contact between the penis and the vulva, or between the penis and the anus, occurs upon penetration, however slight. Emission is not required, §12.1-20-02(1). *Sexual contact* means any touching of the sexual or other intimate parts of the person for the purpose of arousing or gratifying sexual desire, §12.1-20-02(2).

Statutory Age Provisions

Age of Consent

Age of consent is not defined by statute, but age of victim is set at 15 for several offenses. Other offenses defined in terms of acts between minors and adults. Minors are persons under 18, §14-10-01.

Offenses

Gross sexual imposition: sexual act if the victim is less than 15 or sexual contact if the victim is less than 15, §12.1-20-03(1)d and §12.1-20-03(2)a; corruption or solicitation of minors: an adult who engages in a sexual act or causes another to engage in a sexual act with a minor over 15, or an adult who solicits a person under 15 to engage in a sexual act or sexual contact, §12.1-20-05; sexual assault: a person who knowingly has sexual contact with another or who causes such other person to have sexual contact with him . . . if the other person is a minor over 15 and the actor is a parent, guardian, or otherwise responsible for general supervision of the other person's welfare; or the other person is a minor over 15 and the actor is an adult, §12.1-20-07(1)e and §12.1-20-07(1)f.

Evidence Provisions, Defenses, and Cross References

Evidence

Opinion evidence, reputation evidence, and evidence of specific instances of the complaining witness' sexual conduct not admissible by the defendant to prove consent to gross sexual imposition or sexual imposition; if the prosecution offers such evidence, defendant may cross-examine witness and offer rebuttal evidence, §12.1-20-14; separate provision states procedures for offer of proof and in-camera hearing if sexual conduct of the complaining witness is offered by the defense to attack credibility, §12.1-20-15; constitutionality upheld, *State* v. *Peper*, 261 N.W. 2d 650 (N.D. 1977).

Defenses

No mistake as to age defense if offense involves conduct with child under 15, mistake as to age defense allowed for offenses involving minors (under 18), §12.1-20-01(1); mistake of law, §12.1-05-09; excuse (mistake of fact), §12.1-05-08; prompt complaint requirement: 3 months for adults, within 3 months after parent or guardian learned of offense for minors or incompetents, §12.1-20-01(3).

Cross References

Incest, §12.1-20-11; fornication, §12.1-20-08; adultery, §12.1-20-09; unlawful cohabitation, §12.1-20-10; deviate sexual act, §12.1-20-12.

Penalties

Terms

Gross sexual imposition: class A felony if actor inflicts serious bodily injury upon the victim or if the victim is less than 15, or if the victim is not a voluntary social companion of the actor and has not previously permitted him sexual liberties, otherwise the offense is a class B felony, §12.1-20-03; sexual imposition: class C felony, §12.1-20-04; corruption or solicitation of minors: class A misdemeanor, §12.1-20-05; sexual assault: class A misdemeanor if person is a minor over 15 and the actor is a parent, guardian, or otherwise responsible for supervision or person is a minor over 15 and the actor is an adult, otherwise class B misdemeanor, §12.1-20-07; class A felony, maximum 20 years; class B felony, maximum 10 years, class C felony, maximum 5 years; class A misdemeanor, maximum 1 year; class B misdemeanor, maximum 30 days, §12.1-32-01.

Special

Dangerous special offenders, extended sentences, §12.1-32-09; provision for restitution to victim as a condition of probation, §12.1-32-07(e); mandatory parole component of sentencing, §12.1-32-10; minimum prison term for armed offenders, §12.1-32-02.1 Fines in addition to prison terms, §12.1-32-01.

Ohio

State Statutes

Ohio Rev. Code Ann. §2907.01 through §2907.12 (Page 1975 Repl.) (Supp. 1979)
§2907.01 Definitions
§2907.02 Rape
§2907.03 Sexual battery
§2907.04 Corruption of a minor
§2907.05 Gross sexual imposition
§2907.06 Sexual imposition
§2907.12 Felonious sexual penetration

Derivation

History

Revised statutes of 1833 contained carnal knowledge rape statute passed in 1808-1809. If any person shall carnally know any woman-child with force and against her consent or shall carnally know any woman-child under the age of 10 with or without her consent, such person shall be deemed guilty of rape and on conviction shall suffer death. Statutes of 1841 contain a provision passed in 1835 defining as rape carnal knowledge of a daughter or sister forcibly and against her will. Punishment is hard labor for life. Statute also prohibits carnal knowledge of any other woman or female child, forcibly, or any male over 17 who carnally knows and abuses any female child under 10 with her consent. Punishment is imprisonment for a minimum of 3 years and a maximum of 20 years. New provision added for carnal knowledge of an insane woman; offense is a misdemeanor with a maximum penalty of 10 years and a minimum penalty of 3 years. Statutes of 1880 include provision that male must be over 17 for carnal knowledge of female child under 10. Rape upon a daughter, sister, or female child under 12 shall be punishable by life. On any other female a maximum of 20 years and a minimum of 3 years. Revised statutes of 1868 note a miscegenation statute was passed in 1861. Law of 1887 changes age of male to over 18 an age of female child to 14. Compilation of 1912 changes age of female to under 16 with consent. Minimum of 1 year and a maximum of 20 years or 6 months in county jail. Court is authorized to hear testimony on aggravation and mitigation. Forcible rape of daughter, sister, or child under 12 still punishable with life; any other female minimum 3 years, maximum 20. Revision effective 1953 renumbers and rewords sections but leaves major categories unchanged. 1961 law changes age of female to under 14 and adds new offense: forcible rape of a female person under 14 by person over 18; penalty: minimum 5 years, maximum 20 years. All these statutes repealed and replaced with rape reform legislation in 1974.

Present Law

One of the earliest and most comprehensive reform statutes. Several offenses included under title of sexual assault. Forcible rape redefined to include homosexual assaults. New offenses of sexual imposition and sexual battery defined. Offense specific evidence statute. New categories based upon age and status of victim and offender. All sex offenses, prostitution, and pornography included in revised chapter.

Statutory Structure

Changes

Present statute passed in 1972, effective 1974. Amendment in 1975 adds evidence statute, new definition of spouse, and new offenses. Prohibited conduct changed; age provisions changed. Mistake as to age defense limited. Penetration with an object included. Mandatory sentence to prison for second offenders. Rape evidence statute includes provision for victim to be independently represented at state expense if necessary at all in-camera proceedings concerning the admissibility of evidence of prior sexual conduct. Former incest statute repealed, effective 1974. Domestic violence act passed in 1978.

Offenses

Rape; sexual battery; corruption of a minor; gross sexual imposition; sexual imposition; felonious sexual penetration.

Requirements

Rape: sexual conduct when the offender purposely compels the person to submit by force or threat of force; or when the offender substantially impairs the other person's judgment by administering a drug or an intoxicant surreptitiously or by force, threat of force, or deception; when the other person is under 13 whether or not the offender knows the age of such person, §2907.02A; sexual battery: sexual conduct when the offender knowingly coerces the other person to submit by any means that would prevent resistance by a person of ordinary resolution; when the offender knows the other person's ability to appraise or control his conduct is substantially impaired; when the other person submits because unaware the act is being committed; when the other person mistakenly identifies the offender as his or her spouse; when the offender is the other person's natural or adoptive parent, stepparent, guardian, custodian, or person in loco parentis; when the other person is in custody of law or a patient in a hospital or other institution, and the offender has supervisory or disciplinary authority, §2907.03A; corruption of a minor: sexual conduct by a person over 18 who knows or is reckless regarding the other person being over 12 and under 15, §2907.04A; gross sexual impostion: sexual contact under circumstances of rape, §2907.05A; sexual imposition: sexual contact which is known to be offensive to the other person; when the other person's ability to appraise or control the defendant's conduct is impaired; when the other person is unaware; when other person is over 12 and under 15 and the offender is over 18 and 4 years older, §2907.06A; felonious sexual penetration: penetration with an object under circumstances of rape, §2907.12A.

Principals

Person/person; sex-neutral.

Spouses

Definition of each offense phrased in terms of sexual conduct with another, not the spouse of the offender (§2907.02A, §2907.03A, §2907.04A) or sexual contact with another, not the spouse of the offender (§2907.05A or §2907.06A) or sexual penetration with an object with a person not the spouse of the offender (§2907.12A). "Spouse means a person married to an offender at the time of an alleged offense, except that such person shall not be considered the spouse when any of the following apply: (1) when the parties have entered into a written separation agreement authorized by section 3101.06 of the revised code; (2) during the pendency of an action between the parties for annulment, divorce, dissolution of marriage, or alimony; or (3) in the case of an action for alimony, after the effective date of the judgment for alimony, "§2907.01L.

Terminology

Language

Rape: no person shall engage in sexual conduct with another, not the spouse of the offender, when any of the following apply: (1) the offender purposely compels the other person to submit by force or threat of force, (2) for the purpose of preventing resistance, the offender substantially impairs the other person's judgment or control by administering any drug or intoxicant to the other person, surreptitiously or by force, threat of force, or deception. . . . §2907.02A.

Definitions

Sexual conduct means vaginal intercourse between a male and female, and anal intercourse, fellatio, and cunnilingus between persons regardless of sex. Penetration, however slight, is sufficient to complete vaginal or anal intercourse, §2907.01A. *Sexual contact* means any touching of an erogenous zone of another including without limitation the thigh, genitals, buttocks, pubic region, or, if the person is a female, a breast for the purpose of sexually arousing or gratifying either person, §2907.01B. *Gross sexual imposition*: "no person shall have sexual contact with another not the spouse of the offender; cause another, not the spouse of the offender, to have sexual contact with the offender; or cause two or more other persons to have sexual contact when . . .," §2907.05A. *Felonious sexual penetration*: "no person without privilege to do so shall insert any instrument, apparatus, or other object into the vaginal or anal cavity of another, not the spouse of the offender, when . . .," §2907.12A. *Sexual activity* means sexual conduct or sexual contact, or both, §2907.01C.

Statutory Age Provisions

Age of Consent

No specific age of consent. Victim's age of 13 and 15 define several offenses. Age difference of 4 years between offender over 18 and victim for corruption of a minor and sexual imposition, §2907.04A and §2907.06A(4).

Offenses

Rape: "sexual conduct . . . when the other person is less than 13, whether or not the offender knows the age of such person," §2907.02A(3); corruption of a minor: a person over 18 engaging in sexual conduct with a person over 12 and under 15, when the offender knows such person is over 12 but not over 15 or the offender is reckless in that regard, §2907.04A; gross sexual imposition: sexual contact when the other person is under 13, whether or not the offender knows the age of such person, §2907.05A; sexual imposition: sexual contact when the other person is over 12 but under 15, whether or not the offender knows the age of such person and the offender is over 18 and 4 years older, §2907.06A(4); felonious sexual penetration: penetration with an object when the other person is less than 13, whether or not the offender knows the age of such person, §2907.12A(3).

Evidence Provisions, Defenses, and Cross References

Evidence

Restrictions on evidence apply only to crimes of rape and gross sexual imposition. Evidence of specific instances of the victim's sexual activity, opinion evidence, and reputation evidence of the same shall not be admitted unless it involves evidence of source of semen, pregnancy, or disease or past sexual activity with the offender, and then only after a finding of relevancy. Same restriction on past sexual history of the defendant. In-camera hearing prior to trial, §2907.02D-F and §2907.05D-F. Special provision allows the victim to be independently represented at hearings on admissibility of evidence. Court to appoint counsel if victim is indigent, §2907.02E and §2907.05E; corroboration requirement for sexual imposition, §2907.06B; proof of physical resistance not required for rape, §2907.02C.

Defenses

Force and the prevention of resistance part of the definition of rape and gross sexual imposition. Mistake as to age defense limited to offense of corruption of a minor, §2907.04A; no mistake as to age defense for rape, gross sexual imposition, sexual imposition, or felonious sexual penetration.

Cross References

Incest included in definition of sexual battery, §2907.03A(5); importuning, §2907.07; voyeurism, §2907.08; prostitution, §2907.21 et seq. Rule of evidence in prostitution cases, §2907.26. Names of victim or offender can be suppressed pending disposition, §2907.11; obscenity, §2907.31 et seq.

Definition of obscenity declared unconstitutional; *Soverign News Co. v. Falke*, 448 F.Supp. 306 (N.D. Ohio E.D. 1977); law manding hospital emergency services, §2907.29; cost of medical examination to be paid by county where offense committed, §2907.28; domestic violence, law of 1978, File no. 487, training programs established, sets out authority of court to act.

Penalties

Terms

Rape and felonious sexual penetration: first-degree felonies if the victim is under 13 and the offender purposely compels the victim to submit by force or threat of force, then offender shall be imprisoned for life, §2907.02B and §2907.12B; first-degree felony: minimum term of 4, 5, 6, or 7 years and maximum of 25 years, §2907.11B(1); sexual battery: third-degree felony, §2907.03B; corruption of a minor: third-degree felony, §2907.04; gross sexual imposition: third-degree felony if victim under 13, otherwise fourth-degree felony, §2907.05B; third-degree felony: minimum 1 year, 18 months, 2 or 3 years, and maximum 10 years, §2929.11B(3); fourth-degree felony: minimum 6 months, 1 year, 18 months, or 2 years, and maximum 5 years, §2929.11B(4); sexual imposition: third-degree misdemeanor, §2907.06C; penalty for misdemeanors: restitution, fine, or imprisonment up to 60 days, §2929.21 and 2929.22.

Special

Repeat offenders, §2929.01 et seq.; fines in addition to prison terms, §2929.11C; circumstances for court to consider in imposing sentence, §2929.12; person accused of rape, sexual battery, or corruption of a minor must be examined for venereal disease. Treatment to be condition of probation if accused found guilty. Results of examination not admissible, §2907.27; mentally deficient offenders, psychiatric examination, §2947.24.

Oklahoma

State Statutes

Okla. Stat. Ann. tit. 21 §1111 through §1123 (1958)
§1111 Rape defined
§1114 Rape in the first degree—second degree
§1115 Punishment for rape in first degree
§1116 Punishment for rape in second degree

Derivation

History

Statutes of 1893 list law of 1890 as the source of a statute defining rape as an act of sexual intercourse accomplished with a female not the wife of the perpetrator where the female is under 14, where she is incapable through lunacy, and so on, where resistance is overcome by force or violence, where resistance is prevented by an intoxicant, where female is unconscious, or where she believes the person is her husband. Presumption of inability due to age; essential guilt is outrage to the person and feelings of the female, and any penetration is sufficient. Rape upon a female under 10 or incapable through lunacy of consent is first-degree rape. All other offenses are rape in the second degree. First-degree rape has a minimum of 10 years; second-degree rape has a minimum of 5 years. Law of 1895 amends definition of first-degree rape to be upon a female under 14. Amendment of 1901 redefines rape as upon a female under 16, adds new circumstance defining offense: where female is over 16 and under 18 and of previous chaste character. Law of 1901 adds proviso allowing for a conviction of the husband of rape if husband is an accomplice. Revised statutes of 1910 make a minor change adding the word *virtuous* to the chaste-character provision and add to the presumption of inability a defense based upon the age difference between the offender and victim if the acts are consensual. No conviction for rape if female over 14 consents, unless offender is over 18. The statute also adds for first-degree rape, male must be over 18 and female under 14. Rape by force or threats added to definition of first degree. First-degree rape to carry a penalty of death or a minimum of 15 years at the direction of the jury. Penalty for second-degree rape is a minimum of 1 year or a maximum of 15. Code of 1921 adds to section on presumption of inability, "except with the consent of the female over 14." Penalty for rape in the first degree changed to a minimum of 5 years in 1965. Otherwise law of 1910 still in effect.

Present Law

Traditional definition of rape based upon 1910 formulation which in turn was essentially the same as the law of 1890. Chaste-character provision remains. Evidence statute passed in 1975.

Statutory Structure

Changes

Present law has undergone no significant change, except for a reduction in the minimum term in 1965, since law of 1910. Evidence statute passed in 1975.

Offenses

First-degree rape; second-degree rape.

Requirements

First-degree rape: sexual intercourse by male over 18 when female is under 14, or incapable of consent through lunacy or unsoundness of mind, or when accomplished by force overcoming resistance or by means of threats of immediate and great bodily harm accompanied by apparent power of execution, §1114; second-degree rape: sexual intercourse where female is under 16, where female is over 16 and under 18 and of previous chaste and virtuous character; where resistance is prevented by intoxicant; where female is unconscious; where female submits under the belief the defendant is her husband, §1111.

Principals

Traditional male/female designation.

Spouses

Traditional spousal exception: "Rape is an act of sexual intercourse with accomplished with a female, not the wife of the perpetrator," §1111.

But: "In all cases of collusion between the accused and the husband of the female, to accomplish such act [rape of the female when she submits believing the person is her husband] both the husband and the accused shall be deemed guilty of rape," §1111.

Terminology

Language

"Rape is an act of sexual intercourse accomplished with a female, not the wife of the perpetrator, under either of the following circumstances. . . where she is prevented from resisting by any intoxicating narcotic, or anesthetic agent, administered by or with the privity of the accused," §1111.

Definitions

Other circumstances defining rape include: "where she is incapable through lunacy or any other unsoundness of mind, whether temporary or permanent, of giving legal consent; where she resists but her resistance is overcome by force and violence; where she is prevented from resistance by threats of immediate and great bodily harm accomplished by an apparent power of execution. . . where she is at the time unconscious of the nature of the act and this is known to the accused; where she submits under the belief that the person committing the act is her husband, and this belief is induced by artifice, pretence, or concealment practiced by the accused," §1111.

Statutory Age Provisions

Age of Consent

Age of consent is 16, §1111, but no conviction for sexual intercourse with a female over 14 with her consent unless the offender is over 18. §1112; presumption of inability for males under 14, §1112.

Offenses

Rape: where the female is under the age of 16; and where the female is over the age of 16 years and under the age of 18, and of previous chaste and virtuous character, §1111.

Evidence Provisions, Defenses, and Cross References

Evidence

Evidence statute prohibits admission by the defendant of opinion evidence, reputation evidence, and evidence of specific instances of complaining witness' conduct in order to prove consent; provided, not applicable to evidence of the complaining witness' conduct with or in the presence of the defendant. Defendant may cross-examine as to any evidence offered by the prosecutor and offer relevant evidence in rebuttal, §tit.22§750; chaste character provision for statutory rape of female over 16 and under 18, §1111.

Defenses

Consent and absence of resistance a defense to rape by the definition of the offense in terms of resistance. If offender is under 18, a defense to first-degree rape, §1114; presumption as to inability due to age, §1112.

Cross References

Incest, §885; crime against nature, §886; abduction of person under 15, §1119, as amended by Law of 1976, c.155; lewd or indecent proposals or acts by an adult person as to a child under 14, §1123; seduction, §1120, and subsequent marriage as a defense, §1122; compelling woman to marry, §1117.

Penalties

Terms

First-degree rape: death or imprisonment for a minimum of 5 years, §1115; second-degree rape: minimum of 1 year or a maximum of 15 years, §1116.

Special

Jury has the discretion to fix penalty for first-degree rape, §1115; required examination of sex offenders, tit. 63 §63-1-524(b).

Oregon

State Statutes

Ore. Rev. Stat. §163.305 through §163.475 (Repl. 1977)
§163.305 Definitions
§163.315 Incapacity to consent
§163.355 Rape in the third degree
§163.365 Rape in the second degree
§163.375 Rape in the third degree
§163.415 Sexual abuse in the second degree
§163.425 Sexual abuse in the first degree
§163.435 Sexual misconduct

Derivation

History

Law of 1854 defined rape as carnally and unlawfully knowing a female child under 10 or forcibly ravishing a woman 10 or over, maximum penalty 20 years, minimum penalty 3 years, and if upon a sister or daughter, life. Law of 1864 stated that any person who carnally knows any female child under 14 or forcibly ravished any woman over 14 was guilty of rape; punishment unchanged. Offense involving rape of sister or daughter put in separate section: if a person is convicted of rape upon his sister, of the whole or half blood, or upon his daughter of his wife he shall be punished by a minimum of 20 years or life. Corroboration requirement for seduction. Amendment of 1895 raised the statutory age to 16. Law of 1905 added a new offense: carnal knowledge of a female over 16 and under 18 by a male over 18, if not rape and the person of previous moral character, then the offense was fornication with a penalty of a fine or 1 month in county jail, if rape then minimum of 1 to 5 years in prison. Compilation of 1940 includes provisions for mentally ill and sexually dangerous offenders. 1957 replacement leaves offenses unchanged but removes minimum 3 year term from both categories of offenses. Whole-scale revision in 1971.

Present Law

Traditional definition of rape, but offense defined in terms of three degrees. Separate offense of rape upon a sister or daughter retained from prior law.

Offenses of sodomy and sexual abuse redefined; sexual contact offenses introduced. 1971 revision adopted Model Penal Code (MPC) offenses; rape reform evidence statute introduced in 1975 and spousal exception removed in 1977.

Statutory Structure

Changes

Law of 1971 rewrote definition of offense, recharacterized rape in terms of three degrees, introduced offenses of sexual abuse and sexual misconduct, graded sodomy into three degrees. Law of 1975 added a rape reform evidence statute and made a minor amendment to the definition of forcible compulsion. Law of 1977 removed spousal exception and the defense of consensual cohabitation and amended the evidence provision. Minor amendments in 1979.

Offenses

Rape in the first, second, and third degree; sexual abuse in the first and second degree; sexual misconduct.

Requirements

First-degree rape: sexual intercourse by forcible compulsion, or when female under 12, or when female under 16 and is the male's sister, of the whole or half blood, his daughter or his wife's daughter, §163.375; second-degree rape: sexual intercourse when female incapable of consent by reason of mental defect, mental incapacitation, or physical helplessness or female under 14, §163.365; third-degree rape: sexual intercourse with female under 16, §163.365; first-degree sexual abuse: sexual contact when victim is under 12, when victim is subjected to forcible compulsion, §163.425; second-degree sexual abuse: sexual contact when victim does not consent, or when victim is incapable of consent, §163.415; sexual misconduct: Sexual intercourse or deviate sexual intercourse with unmarried person under 18, §163.445.

Principals

Male/female for all degrees of rape; person/person sexual abuse and sexual misconduct.

Spouses

Spousal exception removed in 1977 by removing the definition of female and by removing the statutory defense of consensual cohabitation.

Terminology

Language

"A person who has sexual intercourse with a female commits a crime of rape in the first degree if the female is subjected to forcible compulsion by the male; or . . . the female is under 16 years of age and is the male's sister, of the whole or half blood, his daughter or his wife's daughter," §163.375.

Definitions

Sexual intercourse has its ordinary meaning and occurs upon any penetration, however slight; emission is not required, §163.305(7). *Sexual contact* means any touching of the sexual or other intimate parts of a person or causing such person to touch the sexual or intimate parts of the actor for the purpose of arousing or gratifying the sexual desire of either party, §163.305(6). *Forcible compulsion* means physical force that overcomes earnest resistance; or a threat, express or implied, that places a person in fear of immediate or future death or serious physical injury to himself or another person, or in fear that he or another person will immediately or in the future be kidnaped, §163.305(2). *Deviate sexual intercourse* means sexual conduct between persons consisting of contact between the sex organs of the person and the mouth or anus of another, §163.305(1). *Mentally incapacitated* means that a person is rendered incapable of appraising or controlling his conduct at the time of the alleged offense because of the influence of a narcotic or other intoxicating substance administered to him without his consent or because of any other act committed upon him without his consent, §163.305(4).

Age of Consent

"A person is considered incapable of consenting to a sexual act if he is (1) under 18 years of age," §163.315; but see definition of rape. Defendant's age as a defense: if actor is less than 3 years older than the victim, a defense, §163.345.

Offenses

Third-degree rape: "A male commits the crime of rape in the third degree if he has sexual intercourse with a female under 16 years of age," §163.355; second-degree rape: male who has sexual intercourse with a female under 14 years of age, §163.365; first-degree rape: a person who has sexual intercourse with a female under 12 years of age, §163.375; second-degree sexual abuse: sexual contact when victim is over 14 and under 18 (amendment of 1979) and defendant is less than 4 years older, §163.415; first-degree sexual abuse: sexual contact when victim is less than 12 years of age, §163.425; sexual misconduct: sexual intercourse or deviate sexual intercourse with unmarried person under 18 years of age, §163.445.

Evidence Provisions, Defenses, and Cross References

Evidence

Evidence of the sexual character or sexual reputation of the complainant is not admissible for any purpose, and evidence of previous sexual conduct is presumed irrelevant, but the presumption may be overcome. If defendant wishes to introduce evidence of previous sexual conduct of the complainant, hearing required with a finding of relevance. Evidence of previous sexual conduct which may be relevant includes but is not limited to evidence showing motive or bias of the complainant or evidence to explain or rebut scientific or medical evidence. No restriction on impeachment by proof of prior conviction of a crime, §163.475.

Defenses

Incapacity to consent, §163.315; ignorance or mistake as a defense: mistake as to age a defense to first- and second-degree rape; ignorance as to incapacity to consent also a defense, §163.325; incapacity due to immaturity, §161.380.

Cross References

Incest, §163.525; incest also a subcategory of first-degree rape, §163.375(1)c; sodomy in the first, second, and third degree, §163.385 et seq.; child pornography, L.1979, c.706; victim compensation, §147.005 et seq.

Penalties

Terms

First-degree rape: class A felony, §163.355; class A felony, maximum 20 years, §161.605(1); second-degree rape: calss B felony, §163.365; calss B felony, maximum 10 years, §161.605(2); third-degree rape: calss C felony, §163.355; first-degree sexual abuse: class C felony, §163.425; class C felony, maximum 5 years, §161.605(3); second-degree sexual abuse: class A misdemeanor, §163.415; class A misdemeanor, maximum 1 year, §161.615(1); sexual misconduct: class C misdemeanor, §163.445; class C misdemeanor, maximum 30 days, §161.615(3).

Special

Fines for felonies, §161.625; fines for misdemeanors, §161.645; standards for sentencing of dangerous offenders, §161.725; procedure for determining whether offender is dangerous, including psychiatric examination, §161.735.

Pennsylvania

State Statutes

Pa. Stat. Ann. tit. 18 §3101 through §3126 (1973)(Supp. 1979-1980)
§3101 Definitions
§3102 Mistake as to age
§3103 Spouse relationships
§3104 Evidence of victim's sexual conduct
§3105 Prompt complaint
§3121 Rape
§3122 Statutory rape
§3123 Involuntary deviate sexual intercourse
§3124 Voluntary deviate sexual intercourse
§3126 Indecent assault

History

Codification of 1682 contained statute prohibiting rape or ravishment, that is, forcing a maid, widow, or wife. Punishment was 1 year, and for the second offense, mandatory life term and the forfeiture of property to victim, her parents, or husband. Law of 1700 changed penalty to public whipping or 1 year to 7 years. Property forfeiture now depended upon the offender's marital status, and property went to the state. For a second offense, offender castrated and branded with an R. For Negroes penalty was death if offense committed upon a white woman or maid. Penalty for attempted rape by a Negro was castration. Castration eliminated in 1705-1706 codification. White man to suffer life imprisonment, and branding still imposed. Negro offender to be branded and deported for an attempt. In 1718 new crimes code instated the Elizabethan codification. Recodification of 1794 changed penalty for rape to a minimum of 10 years and a maximum of 21 years; life for a second offense. Recodification of 1829 reduced the penalty to a minimum of 2 years and a maximum of 12 years. Code of 1860 spelled out the traditional definition. Age of 14 for offenders and 10 for females. Penalty was a fine not exceeding $1,000 and imprisonment of up to 15 years. Amendments in 1887 set statutory age of female and offender at 16. Chaste-character provisions introduced, and consent defense added for offense with female under 16; if with consent, offense was fornication. 1939 amendment increased fine to $7,000. No further changes until 1972.

Present Law

MPC-type rape statute passed in 1972, effective 1973. This formulation in effect until 1976 when statutory corroboration requirement was repealed and replaced with rape reform evidence statute. Amendments to the mistake as to age provision and spousal provisions were passed in 1976. The prompt complaint requirement was repealed in 1976; Lord Hale's cautionary instruction was prohibited in 1973. New section added in 1976 saying resistance not required. Changes in age provisions in 1976.

Statutory Structure

Changes

MPC rape statute which defined rape in terms of the absence of consent and strength of resistance replaced traditional rape statute in 1973. Corroboration requirement and cautionary instruction repealed in 1976; evidence statute passed in 1976. Definition of rape remains MPC definition.

Offenses

Rape; statutory rape; involuntary deviate sexual intercourse; voluntary deviate sexual intercourse; indecent assault.

Requirements

Rape: sexual intercourse by forcible compulsion, by threat of forcible compulsion that would prevent resistance by a person of reasonable resolution, when person is mentally deranged or deficient and incapable of consent, §3121; statutory rape: sexual intercourse with a person under 14 by person over 18, §3122; involuntary deviate sexual intercourse: deviate sexual intercourse under circumstances of rape or with a person under 16, §3123; voluntary deviate sexual intercourse: all other deviate sexual intercourse, §3124; indecent assault: sexual contact under circumstances of nonconsent, §3126.

Principals

Person/person. Definition of sexual intercourse includes more than heterosexual intercourse, but definition of deviate sexual intercourse is overlapping.

Spouses

Statutory spousal exception in definition of rape, "another person not his spouse," and statutory rape, §3121, §3122; definition of deviate sexual intercourse excludes spouses: "sexual intercourse *per os* or *per anus* between human beings who are not husband and wife," §3101; and "Spouse relationships: whenever in this chapter the definition of an offense excludes conduct with a spouse, the exclusion shall be deemed to extend to persons living as man and wife, regardless of the legal status of their relationship, provided, however, that the exclusion shall be inoperative as respects spouses living in separate residences, or in the same residence but under terms of a written separation agreement or an order of a court of record; where the definition of an offense excludes conduct with a spouse, this shall not preclude conviction of a spouse as accomplice in a sexual act which he or she causes another person, not within the exclusion to perform, §3103.

Terminology

Language

"The credibility of an alleged victim of an offense under this chapter shall be determined by the same standard as is the credibility of an alleged victim of any other crime. The testimony of a victim need not be corroborated in prosecutions under this chapter. In any prosecution before a jury for an offense under this chapter, no instructions shall be given cautioning the jury to view the alleged victim's testimony in any other way than that in which all victim's testimony is viewed." §3106.

Definitions

Sexual intercourse: in addition to its ordinary meaning, includes intercourse per os or per anus, with some penetration however slight; emission not required, §3101. *Indecent contact* is any touching of the sexual or other intimate parts of the person for the purpose of arousing or gratifying sexual desire in either person, §3101. *Deviate sexual intercourse* is sexual intercourse per os or per anus between human beings who are not husband and wife, and any form of sexual intercourse with an animal, §3101. *Indecent assault* is indecent contact if the other person is in custody of law or detained in a hospital or other institution and the actor has supervisory or disciplinary authority over him, §3126.

Statutory Age Provisions

Age of Consent

Statutory formulation for age of victim for rape is 14; other person must be over 18.

Offenses

Statutory rape: sexual intercourse with person under 14 by person over 18, §3122; involuntary deviate sexual intercourse: deviate sexual intercourse with person under 16, §3123.

Evidence Provisions, Defenses and Cross References

Evidence

1976 evidence statute prohibits introduction of all forms of evidence of the victim's past sexual conduct, except conduct with the defendant. Statute mandates proceedings to be followed if such evidence is to be admitted. Court to order in-camera hearing and make findings on the records, §3104. MPC corroboration requirement repealed and Lord Hale's instruction outlawed, §3106; statutory repeal of resistance requirement, §3107.

Defenses

Consent a defense to all offenses, except statutory rape or involuntary deviate sexual intercourse. Prompt complaint requirement repealed, §3105. Reasonable mistake as to age a statutory defense if criminality does not depend upon child being under 14, §3102.

Cross References

Incest, tit. 18 §4302; felony/rape, tit. 18 §6102.

Penalties

Terms

Rape: first-degree felony, §3121; first-degree felony, maximum 20 years, §1103; statutory rape: second degree felony, §3122; second-degree felony, maximum 10 years, §1103; involuntary deviate sexual intercourse: first-degree felony, §3123; voluntary deviate sexual intercourse: misdemeanor in the second degree, §3124; indecent assault: misdemeanor in the second degree, §3126; misdemeanor in the second degree, maximum of 2 years, §1104.

Special

Fines, §1101 et seq., and §1358; restitution, §1106; general standards for sentencing, §1321; presumption of probation, §1322; sentencing commission, §1381 et seq.

Puerto Rico

State Statutes

P.R. Laws Ann. tit. 33 §4061 through 4067 (1969) (Supp. 1978)
§4061 Rape
§4062 Essential circumstances of the crime
§4067 Lewd and indecent acts

Derivation

History

Compilation of 1909 punished rape with "reclusion temporal": a minimum term of 14 years and a maximum of 20 years with specified intermediate ranges. Rape is defined as lying with a woman by force, if the woman is deprived of reason or unconscious, or if the woman is under 12. Special offense for slave who violates a woman whose service he is in. Compilation of 1913 redefines the offense: rape is sexual intercourse with a female not the wife of the perpetrator where she is under 14, or incapable of resisting, or where resistance prevented, where resistance overcome, where woman is unconscious, or where she thinks the man is her husband. Penalty is a minimum term of 5 years. Penal code of 1937 contains same definition of the offense, but the penalty is reduced to a minimum of 1 year. Age of defendant must be over 14 unless ability is proved. Court may sentence to life. 1974 law rewrote statute but retained traditional definition of the offense. Maximum penalty reduced from life to 20 years.

Present Law

Traditional definition of rape. No evidence statute. Not sex-neutral. Statutory corroboration requirement retained but amended in 1974.

Statutory Structure

Changes

Very little change from the statutory definition of the offense included in the penal code of 1937. Presumption of incapacity due to age is repealed in

1974. Corroboration requirement amended in 1974 to apply only to cases where the defendant and victim had previous relations.

Offenses

Rape; lewd and indecent acts.

Requirements

Rape: carnal intercourse when female is under 14, where female is incapable of giving legal consent; where she is compelled by irresistible physical force or threats of great and immediate harm; where female is unaware; where female believes man is her husband, §4061; lewd and indecent acts: any indecent or lewd act with another person, where victim is under 14, where victim is compelled, or where victim is incapable of consent, §4067.

Principles

Male/female for rape; person/victim for lewd and lascivious acts.

Spouses

Explicit spousal exception for rape: "every person who has carnal intercourse with a female who is not his wife . . ." §4061.

Terminology

Language

"Every person who has carnal intercourse with a female who is not his wife . . . (b) where she is incapable, through illness or unsoundness of mind, whether temporary or permanent, to give legal consent; (c) Where she is compelled by the use of irresistible physical force or by threats of great and immediate bodily harm, accompanied by apparent power of execution; or by overcoming or diminishing substantially, without her knowledge, her capacity to resist by hypnotic means, narcotics, depressant drugs, or stimulants or similar substances or means, . . ." §4061.

Definitions

Lewd and indecent acts, undefined, §4067; no definition of consent, but both rape and lewd acts include as a defining circumstance: "where she is incapable, through illness or unsoundness of mind, whether temporary or permanent, to give legal consent," see §4061(b) and §4067(c). Additional circumstances defining rape: (b) where at the time of committing the act, she was not aware of its nature and this circumstance is know to the accused, . . . (e) where she submits under the belief that the accused is her husband, and this belief is induced by any artifice, pretense, or concealment practiced by the accused, §4061; essential circumstances of the crime: the crime of rape consists essentially in the outrage to the person and feelings of the female, §4062.

Statutory Age Provisions

Age of Consent

Statutory age of consent is 14, §4061 and §4067. Statutory age for seduction is 18, §4063.

Offenses

Rape: carnal intercourse with a female who is not his wife, where the female is under the age of 14 years, §4061(a); lewd and indecent acts: every person who without intending to have sexual intercourse commits any indecent or lewd act with another person where the victim is under 14 years of age, §4067(a).

Evidence Provisions, Defenses, and Cross References

Evidence

No rape evidence statute, absence of good moral character a defense to seduction, §4063; corroboration required, *People* v. *Diaz*, 87 P.R.R. 656 (1963); resistance an essential element of the crime, *People* v. *Rodriquez*, 66 P.R.R. 881 (1947); and reputation of offended female either before or after the crime relevant to the issue of consent and resistance, *People* v. *Espanol*, 16 P.R.R. 203 (1910); in 1974 amendment to statutory corroboration requirement added: "In trials for rape or attempts to commit it the corroborating evidence shall only be necessary when from the evidence shall arise the existence previous to the time of the alleged committing of the offense, relations of a friendly, or loving or intimate or equal nature between the accused and the aggrieved woman," tit. 34 App. II R.154.

Defenses

Traditional common-law defenses, including consent.

Cross References

Incest, §4121; seduction, §4063; extinguishment of action by marriage, §4064; dangerous sex delinquents; provisions for confinement in a proper institution for treatment, §3373; sodomy, §4065; bestiality, §4066.

Penalties

Terms

Rape: minimum term of 1 year, maximum of 25 years, §4061; rape where female is compelled by the use of irresistible force: minimum 10 years, maximum 50 years, §4061; lewd and indecent acts: minimum of 1 year, maximum of 5 years, §4067.

Special

Compulsive criminals, §3374; habitual criminals, maximum life and minimum 12 years, §3375, et seq.

Rhode Island

State Statutes

R.I. Gen. Laws Ann. §11-37-1 through §11-37-14 (Supp. 1979)
§11-37-1 Definitions
§11-37-2 Definition of guilty for first-degree sexual assault
§11-37-3 Penalty for first-degree sexual assault
§11-37-4 Definition of guilty of second-degree sexual assault
§11-37-5 Penalty for second-degree sexual assault
§11-37-6 Definition of guilty of third-degree sexual assault
§11-37-7 Penalty for third-degree sexual assault

Derivation

History

Common-law crime of rape, which is undefined, is included in statutes published in 1798. Punishment was death. Compilation of 1844 states the penalty as life or a minimum of 10 years; bail only to be allowed by the supreme court. No change through the compilations of 1857, 1872, 1882, 1896, 1909, and 1923. Law of 1938 is the source of the codification of the crime of common-law rape which is included in the code of 1956. Penalty is life or a minimum of 10 years. Penalty for carnal knowledge and abuse of a girl under 16 is a maximum of 15 years. This formulation remains in effect until the enactment of rape reform legislation in 1979. Evidence statute passed in 1975.

Present Law

Rape reform statute defining three degrees of sex-neutral sexual assault in terms of force, incapacity of victim, and age of victim. Sexual assault includes sexual penetration or sexual contact during medical treatment or examination. Evidence statute included from law of 1975. Corroboration requirement and resistance requirement repealed.

Statutory Structure

Changes

Traditional offense of common-law rape, defined as common-law rape and essentially unchanged since its enactment in 1798, replaced by modified rape reform statute which redefined the offense as three degrees of sex-neutral sexual assault.

Offenses

Sexual assault in the first, second, and third degree.

Requirements

First degree sexual assault: sexual penetration when victim is under 13; when victim is mentally incapacitated, mentally defective, or physically helpless; when actor uses force or coercion; when the actor through concealment or surprise overcomes the victim; when the actor engages in medical treatment or examination of the victim for the purpose of sexual arousal, gratification, or stimulation, §11-37-2; second-degree sexual assault: sexual contact under all circumstances of first-degree sexual assault except when actor overcomes the victim by concealment or surprise, §11-37-4; third-degree sexual assault: sexual penetration by person over 18 with person over 13 and under 16, §11-37-6.

Principals

Actor/victim; sex-neutral.

Spouses

Explicit spousal exception only for first-degree sexual assault: "A person is guilty . . . if he or she engages in sexual penetration with another person, not the spouse of the actor," §11-37-2. Spouse is defined as a person married to the actor at the time of the alleged sexual assault, except that such person shall not be considered the spouse if the couple are living apart and a decision for divorce has been granted, whether or not a final decree has been entered, §11-37-1.

Terminology

Language

Force or coercion shall mean when the actor does any of the following: (A) uses or threatens to use a weapon, or any article used or fashioned in a manner to lead the victim to reasonably believe it to be a weapon, (B) overcomes the victim through the application of physical force or physical violence, (C) coerces the victim to submit by threatening to use force or violence on the victim and the victim reasonably believes that the actor has the present ability to execute these threats, (D) coerces the victim by threatening to at some time in the future murder, inflict serious bodily injury upon or kidnap the victim or any other person and the victim reasonably believes the actor has the ability to execute this threat, §11-37-1.

Definitions

Sexual penetration means sexual intercourse, cunnilingus, fellatio, and anal intercourse, or any other intrusion, however slight, by any part of a person's body or by any object into the genital or anal opening of another person's body, but emission of semen is not required, §11-37-1. *Sexual contact* means the intentional touching of the victim's or actor's intimate parts, clothed or unclothed, if that intentional touching can be reasonably construed as intended by the actor to be for the purpose of sexual arousal, gratification, or assault, §11-37-1. *Intimate parts* include the genital or anal areas, groin, inner thigh, or buttock of any person or the breast of a female, §11-37-1.

Statutory Age Provisions

Age of Consent

Age of consent is 16, §11-37-6; actor must be over 18. Other offenses also defined by age of victim.

Offenses

First-degree sexual assault: sexual penetration when the victim is under 13, §11-37-2(A); second-degree sexual assault: sexual contact when the victim is under 13, §11-37-4(A); third-degree sexual assault: sexual penetration by a person over 18 with another person over 13 and under 16, §11-37-6.

Evidence Provisions, Defenses, and Cross References

Evidence

If the defendant wishes to introduce evidence of the victim's sexual activities with third parties, notice is required and a hearing will be held outside the hearing of jurors and spectators. Court shall rule on the admissibility of evidence after an offer of proof and arguments, §11-37-13. Corroboration not required, §11-37-11; proof of resistance not required, §11-37-12.

Defenses

No statutory definition of consent; status of prior common-law definition of consent unclear.

Cross References

Incest, §11-6-4; restitution, §12-19-32; Criminal Injuries Compensation Act, §12-25-1 et seq.

Penalties

Terms

First-degree sexual assault: minimum term of 10 years, maximum term of life, §11-37-3; second-degree sexual assault: minimum term of 3 years, maximum term of 15 years, §11-37-5; third-degree sexual assault: maximum of 5 years, §11-37-7.

Special

Subsequent offenses: sentence for a second or subsequent offense shall be not less than twice the minimum number of years for the most recent offense, §11-37-10.

South Carolina

State Statutes

S.C. Code Ann. §16-3-651 through §16-3-659.1 (Supp. 1979)
§16-3-651 Criminal sexual conduct; definitions
§16-3-652 Criminal sexual conduct in the first degree
§16-3-653 Criminal sexual conduct in the second degree
§16-3-654 Criminal sexual conduct in the third degree
§16-3-655 Criminal sexual conduct with minors

Derivation

History

Law of 1712 enacted the Elizabethan rape statute: if any person carnally know and abuse any woman-child under 10, that person shall be guilty of a felony and suffer as a felon without benefit of clergy. Law of 1869 stated offense as: whoever shall ravish a woman where she did not consent, or by consent where she did consent after, shall be guilty of rape and punished by hard labor for life or with a minimum of 10 years according to the aggravation of the offense; unlawful carnal knowledge of a woman-child under 10 is also rape and a felony. Compilation of 1882 cites law of 1879 which leaves the definition of the offense unchanged and specifies death by hanging as the punishment for both rape of a woman and carnal knowledge of a woman-child under 10. South Carolina constitution of 1895 art. 3 §33 prohibits any marriage between whites and negroes and states that no unmarried woman under the age of 14 shall legally consent to sexual intercourse. Law of 1896 leaves substantive definition of offense unchanged but increases statutory age for carnal knowledge of a woman-child to 14. New proviso added: if child over 10 (and under 14) the jury may recommend mercy, and the maximum term will be 14 years. Law of 1902 adds a new offense: abducting and deflowering of a woman under 16 without the knowledge of her father. Penalty is a fine and a maximum term of 5 years. Law of 1909 adds special statutory provisions concerning testimony to be taken in secret and makes it a misdemeanor to publish the name of the woman raped.

Law of 1921 rewrites the age provisions: offense is carnal knowledge and abuse of any woman-child under 16, provided that if the child is over 10, then the penalty is not to exceed 14 years. If the woman or child is over 14 and under 16, the maximum penalty is 5 years. Proviso added: if the defendant is under 18 and the female is over 14, the previous unchastity of the female may be defensively shown. The punishment then is not to exceed 1 year or a fine of $500. Punishment for rape changed in 1922: death or maximum 40 or minimum 5 years, at the discretion of the judge if the jury recommends mercy. Compilation of 1942 states the offense involving a defendant under 18 and a female over 14 is designated a statutory offense. Compilation of 1952 rewrites the section without changing the substance: "whoever shall ravish . . . punishment is death, or if jury recommends mercy, a maximum of 40 and a minimum of 5 years." Provisos rewritten as numbered sections. Miscegenation provision in constitution declared invalid in 1967. Death penalty removed in 1974, but offense unchanged until present statute enacted in 1977.

Present Law

Rape reform statute based upon Michigan's, defines three degrees of criminal sexual conduct. Offense is sexual battery. Reform statute includes an evidence provision.

Statutory Structure

Changes

Traditional rape statute defined offenses in terms of ravishing a woman (married, maid, or other), without consent and as carnal knowledge and abuse of a woman-child under 16. Law of 1977 rewrote the definition of the offense in terms of circumstances of force, when felony rape occurs, reduced penalties, added evidence statute, changed statutory age offenses, repealed corroboration requirement and statutory presumption of inability for males under 14, and changed the traditional definition of spouses. 1978 amendment added proviso "or is older than the victim," §16-3-655(3). Minor technical amendment in 1979.

Offenses

Criminal sexual conduct in the first, second, and third degree; criminal sexual conduct with minors.

Requirements

First-degree criminal sexual conduct: sexual battery when actor uses aggravated force; when victim is also victim of enumerated felonies, §16-3-652; second-degree criminal sexual conduct: sexual battery when the actor uses aggravated coercion, §16-3-653; third-degree criminal sexual conduct: sexual battery when actor uses force and coercion in the absence of aggravating circumstances, or when actor knows or has reason to know the victim is mentally defective, mentally incapacitated, or physically helpless, and aggravated force or aggravated coercion not used, §16-3-654; second-degree offenses defined by age of victim and actor in position of authority.

Principals

Actor/victim, or another person; sex-neutral.

Spouses

Statutory spousal exception exempts couples living apart under court order if offense is first or second degree: "A person cannot be guilty of criminal sexual conduct under §§16-3-651 to 16-3-659.1 if the victim is his legal spouse, unless the couple are (sic) living apart, by reason of court order, and the actor's conduct constitutes criminal sexual conduct in the first degree or second degree as defined by §16-3-652 and 16-3-653," §16-3-658.

Terminology

Language

"A person is guilty of criminal sexual conduct in the first degree if the actor engages in sexual battery with the victim and if any one or more of the following circumstances are proved: (a) The actor uses aggravated force to accomplish sexual battery. (b) The victim submits to sexual battery by the actor under circumstances where the victim is also the victim of forcible confinement, kidnaping, robbery, extortion, burglary, housebreaking, or any other similar offense or act," §16-3-652(1).

Definitions

Sexual battery means sexual intercourse, cunnilingus, fellatio, anal intercourse, or any intrusion, however slight, of any part of a person's body or of any object into the genital or anal opening of another person's body, except when such intrusion is accomplished for medically recognized treatment or diagnostic purposes, §16-3-651(h). *Aggravated coercion* means that the actor threatens to use force or violence of a high and aggravated nature to overcome the victim or another person, if the victim reasonably believes that the actor has the present ability to carry out the threat, or threatens to retaliate in the future by the infliction of physical harm, kidnaping, or extortion, under circumstances of aggravation against the victim or any other person, §16-3-651(b). *Aggravated force* means that the actor uses physical force of physical violence of a high and aggravated nature to overcome the victim or includes the threat of the use of a deadly weapon, §16-3-651(c). *Intimate parts* include the primary genital area, anus, groin, inner thighs, or buttocks of a male or female human being and the breasts of a female human being, §16-3-651(d). *Mentally incapacitated* means that a person is rendered temporarily incapable of appraising or controlling his or her conduct whether this condition is produced by illness, defect, the influence of a substance, or from some other cause, §16-3-651(f).

Statutory Age Provisions

Age of Consent

Conduct not defined in terms of age of consent. Gradation of offense changed if victim is under 11 or under 14, when the actor is 3 years older.

Offenses

First-degree criminal sexual conduct: sexual battery with a victim under 11 and the actor is at least 3 years older, §16-3-655(1); second-degree criminal sexual conduct: sexual battery with a victim 14 years of age or less but over 11, and actor is at least 3 years older §16-3-655(2); or sexual battery with a victim who is more than 14 but less than 16 and actor is in a position of familial, custodial, or official authority to coerce the victim to submit or is older than the victim, §16-3-655(3).

Evidence Provisions, Defenses, and Cross References

Evidence

Specific instances of victim's sexual conduct, opinion evidence, and reputation evidence of victim's sexual conduct shall not be admitted, except conduct with the defendant or conduct showing source or origin of semen, pregnancy, or disease admissible after a written motion, offer of proof, and an in-camera hearing. Specific proviso allows for admission of specific instances of sexual activity which would constitute adultery for purposes of impeachment, §16-3-659.1; common-law corroboration requirement abolished, §16-3-657.

Defenses

Definition of aggravated coercion and aggravated force would seem to preclude the traditional common-law defense of consent in first- or second-degree criminal sexual conduct. Common-law presumption as to male's inability due to age abolished, §16-3-659.

Cross References

Incest, §16-15-20; assaults with intent, §16-3-656; special procedures for taking depositions of victim outside open court enacted in 1909, §16-3-660 and 16-3-720; unlawful to publish name of victim, §16-3-730; buggery, §16-15-120.

Penalties

Terms

First degree criminal sexual conduct: maximum 30 years, §16-3-652(2); second-degree criminal sexual conduct: maximum 20 years, §16-3-653(2); third-degree criminal sexual conduct: maximum 10 years, §16-3-654(2).

Special

None.

South Dakota

State Statutes

S.D. Compiled Laws Ann. §22-22-1 through 22-22-7.1 (Special Supp. 1978)(1979)

§22-22-1   Rape defined-Degrees-felony
§22-22-2   Sexual penetration defined
§22-22-7   Sexual contact with child under 14 felony or misdemeanor
§22-22-7.1 Sexual contact defined

Derivation

History

Law of 1893 defined rape as sexual intercourse with a female not the wife of the perpetrator when the female is under 16, incapable of consent through lunacy, where resistance is overcome or prevented by threats, or resistance is prevented by intoxication, when female is unconscious, or where female believes defendant is her husband. Proof of ability required if defendant under 14. Essential guilt is outrage to person and feelings of the female. Rape in the first degree is where female is under 10 or incapable of consent through lunacy or rape by force; rape in the second degree is all other rape. Rape in the first degree received a minimum 10 years; rape in the second degree, a minimum of 5 years. Amendment of 1907 raised the age of the female to 18. Penalty for second-degree rape raised to a maximum of 20 years in 1909. Law of 1919 renumbered the sections but left the substantive offense unchanged. No additional amendments except renumbering, until a 1972 amendment reduced the statutory age of the female to 16.

Present Law

Rape reform statute introduced in 1975. Prohibited acts include more than traditional definition of the offense. Evidence statute and statute suppressing the names of the victim and defendent added in 1978.

Statutory Structure

Changes

Offense which was defined in terms of the victim's resistance replaced by an offense defined by circumstances of force and coercion and the victim's incapacity to consent. Age of consent reduced from under 16 to under 15.

410

Acts other than intercourse included in definition of the offense. Provision for psychiatric screening enacted in 1975. Amendments in 1976 rewrote the definition of sexual contact. 1977 amendment changed the age provisions. Formerly section prohibited sexual contact by a person over 18 with a person under 13. 1975 version had omitted the spousal exception, 1977 amendment put back the spousal exception. 1978 evidence statute replaced evidence statute enacted in 1975. Classifications of offenses amended in 1978.

Offenses

First-degree rape; second-degree rape; sexual contact with a child under 15.

Requirements

First-degree rape: sexual penetration under circumstances of force or where the victim is incapable of consent because of mental or physical incapacity, or under influence of drugs; second-degree rape: when victim under 15, §22-22-1; sexual contact with child under 15: defined as sexual contact with a person under 15, §22-22-7.

Principals

Actor/person; sex-neutral.

Spouses

Statutory spousal exception removed in 1975 and put back in 1977. Traditional spousal exception: "rape is an act of sexual penetration accomplished with any person other than the actor's spouse," §22-22-1; "any person . . . who knowingly engages in sexual contact with another person, other than his spouse," §22-22-7.

Terminology

Language

"Rape is an act of sexual penetration accomplished (1) through the use of force, coercion, or threats of immediate and great bodily harm against the victim or other persons within the victim's presence, accompanied by apparent power of execution; or (2) where the victim is incapable, because of physical or mental incapacity, of giving consent to such act; or (3) where the victim is incapable of giving consent because of any intoxicating, narcotic, or anesthestic agent, or because of hypnosis, administered by or with the privity of the accused,'' §22-22-1.

Definitions

Sexual penetrations means an act, however slight, of sexual intercourse, cunnilingus, fellatio, anal intercourse, or any intrusion, however slight, of a genital or of any object into the genital or anal openings of another person's body, §22-22-2. *Sexual contact* means any touching, not amounting to rape, of the breasts of a female or the genitalia of any person with the intent to arouse or gratify the sexual desire of either party, §22-22-7.1.

Statutory Age Provisions

Age of Consent

Presumption of incapacity to consent for victim under 16, *State* v. *Heisinger*, 252 N.W. 2d 899 (1977); actor must be over 15 for a sexual contact offense, and if actor less than 3 years older than other person, sexual contact offense is a misdemeanor, §22-22-7.

Offenses

Rape: an act of sexual penetration accomplished with any person, where the victim is less than 15 years of age, §22-22-1(4); sexual contact: any person, 15 years of age or older, who knowingly engages in sexual contact with another person, when such other person is under the age of 15, §22-22-7.

Evidence Provisions, Defenses, and Cross References

Evidence

Evidence of a victim's prior sexual conduct shall not be admitted nor reference made thereto before the jury unless the court has conducted a hearing to rule on relevancy, §23A-22-15; implied element of resistance, *State* v. *Havens*, 264 N.W. 2d 918 (1978). Rape victim's testimony to be treated as anybody else's, §23-44-16.2.

Defenses

Capacity to consent and the absence of force, coercion, or threats a defense. Reasonable mistaken belief as to age no defense, *State* v. *Fulks*, 83 S.D. 433, 160 N.W. 2d 418 (1968).

Cross References

Incest, §22-22-19; sexual exploitation of children, §22-22-22; the names and details in rape prosecution may be suppressed until disposition upon request of the victim or the accused, §23A-6-22; initial screening evaluation of offenders - psychiatric or psychological counseling, §22-22-5; restitution to victims of crime, §23A-28-1 et seq.; damages for seduction, §21-4-6; prostitution, downgraded to misdemeanor, pimping a felony, §22-23 et seq.

Penalties

Terms

Rape in the first degree: class 2 felony; rape in the second degree: class 4 felony, §22-22-1; class 2 felony, 25 years in prison and a possible fine of $25,000, §22-6-1(3); class 4 felony, 10 years in prison and a possible fine of $10,000, §22-6-1(5); sexual contact with a child under 15: class 3 felony if actor is over 3 years older; if actor less than 3 years older, class 1 misdemeanor, §22-22-7; class 3 felony, 15 years in prison and a possible fine of $15,000, §22-6-1(4); class 1 misdemeanor, 1 year in county jail or $1,000, or both, §22-6-2.

Special

Habitual offenders, §22-7-7 et seq.; counseling may be imposed as a condition of parole, §22-22-5; rape designated crime of violence, §22-1-2(8).

Tennessee

State Statutes

Tenn. Code Ann. §39-3701 through §39-3710 (1975 Repl.)(Supp. 1979)
§39-3702 Definitions
§39-3703 Aggravated rape
§39-3704 Aggravated sexual battery
§39-3705 Rape
§39-3706 Sexual battery

Derivation

History

1831 compilation defined rape as unlawful carnal knowledge of a woman against her will. Carnal knowledge is accomplished by commencement of sexual connection. Proof of circumstance which usually terminates it is not required. Penalty is a minimum of 10 and a maximum of 20 years. Unlawful carnal abuse of girls under 10 has the same penalty. Law of 1858 punished rape by a slave or free person of color upon a free white female with death by hanging. Forcibly added to the definition of rape and provision added concerning the admistration of any substance to prevent resistance. Law of 1871 added to the definition of rape carnal knowledge of a married woman by someone pretending to be her husband. Law of 1884 changed the punishment for rape to death by hanging, but the jury could commute the punishment to from 10 years to life. Law of 1932 specified that the death penalty should be carried out by electrocution, and the age of the female was changed to 12 years. Law of 1934 added provision prohibiting unlawful carnal knowledge of a female over 12 and under 21. Punishment was a minimum of 3 years and a maximum of 10 years. Evidence of prior chastity admissible by the defense only if the female is over 14, provided that nothing shall authorize a conviction when the female over 12 is a bawd, lewd, or kept female. Law of 1956 added statutory corroboration requirement to the section prohibiting carnal knowledge of woman between 12 and 21. 1974 amended penalties rape of a girl under 12, electrocution, rape of a girl over 12 life or a minimum of 10 years. Statutory age of female reduced to 18; penalty minimum 1 year, maximum 10 years. Rape redefined as four degrees of criminal sexual conduct in 1978. This law repealed and replaced by present statute in 1979.

414

Present Law

Rape reform statute modeled on Michigan statute passed in 1978 and repealed in 1979. Present law continues some features of prior law but also incorporates some reform features.

Statutory Structure

Changes

Limited evidence statute passed in 1975, rape reform statute passed in 1978 replaced traditional offense, carrying the death penalty, with four categories of criminal sexual conduct. This statute repealed and replaced by more a traditional formulation with some reform features in 1979. Limitation on traditional spousal exception passed in 1979.

Offenses

Aggravated rape; aggravated sexual battery; rape; sexual battery.

Requirements

Aggravated rape: sexual penetration (1) under circumstances of force, when actor is armed, or when actor causes personal injury to victim, or actor is aided or abetted; or (2) when victim is mentally defective, mentally incapacitated, or physically helpless and personal injury to victim, or when actor aided or abetted; or (3) when victim under 13; or (4) when victim is over 13 and under 16, and the actor is related to victim or in a position of authority, §39-3703; aggravated sexual battery: sexual contact under circumstances of aggravated rape, §39-3704; rape: sexual penetration by force, when the victim is mentally defective, mentally incapacitated, or physically helpless, by fraud, or when the victim is over 13 but less than 16, §39-3705; sexual battery: sexual contact under circumstances of rape, §39-3706.

Principals

Actor/victim; sex-neutral.

Texas

State Statutes

Tex. Penal Code §21.01 through §21.13 (1974) (Supp. 1980)
§21.01 Definitions
§21.02 Rape
§21.03 Aggravated rape
§21.04 Sexual abuse
§21.05 Aggravated sexual abuse
§21.09 Rape of a child
§21.10 Sexual abuse of a child
§21.11 Indecency with a child

Derivation

History

Statutes of 1845 state common law of England is in effect: "Every person who shall by force or violence have sexual connection with another contrary to the will of such person shall be deemed guilty of rape, and on conviction thereof shall suffer death." Statutes of 1866 defined rape as carnal knowledge of a woman without her consent obtained by force, threats, or fraud, or the carnal knowledge of a female under 10 with or without her consent and with or without the use of force, threats, or fraud. Threat must be such as might reasonably create a just fear of death or great bodily harm, in view of the relative condition of the parties and to health, strength of the parties, and other circumstances of the case. Presumption of inability for male under 14. Punishment was a minimum of 5 years, maximum of 15 years. Law of 1886 amended penalty section to death, life, or any term of years with a minimum of 5 years, at the discretion of the jury. Prosecution for rape must be within 1 year. Law of 1895 changed the statutory age for a female to 15. Code of 1936 contains the same provisions, but the statutory age of the female is 18, by an amendment in 1918. Also a new provision added that if the female is 15 or over, the defendant may show in consent cases that she was not of previous chaste character. 1970 revision keeps the basic definition of rape from prior law. Important amendments and additions to other sex offenses generally follow the Model Penal Code. Mistake as to age defense not adopted, some modification of the chaste-character provision of the MPC. Weak evidence statute enacted in 1975.

416

Present Law

Rape defined in terms of circumstances which prevent or overcome resistance, categories from former law. Commentary states that intercourse when a female is unaware is intended to cover intercourse performed under the pretence of making a medical examination. Present law continues to define as rape circumstance where female submits because she erroneously believes the male is her husband. 1970 revision includes significant amendments to definitions of homosexual conduct and sexual contact offenses. Age of consent reduced to 17.

Statutory Structure

Changes

A recodification of a traditional rape statute. In 1975 an evidence statute was enacted and several relatively minor amendments were incorporated into the definition of rape and rape of a child. 1979 amendment to definition of sexual contact.

Offenses

Rape; aggravated rape; sexual abuse; aggravated sexual abuse; rape of a child; sexual abuse of a child; indecency with a child.

Requirements

Rape: sexual intercourse under circumstances defined by the female's lack of consent, §21.02; aggravated rape: rape when a person causes serious body injury or attempts to cause death of a victim or another in the course of the same criminal episode or submission compelled by threat of death, serious bodily injury, or kidnaping to be inflicted on anyone, §21.03; sexual abuse: deviate sexual intercourse or compelling a person to engage in sexual intercourse or deviate sexual intercourse with a third person, or intercourse without consent as defined by circumstances of force or compulsion, or where the victim is incapacitated, §21.04; aggravated sexual abuse: sexual abuse or sexual abuse of a child when the actor causes serious bodily injury or attempts to cause death to the victim or another in the course of the same criminal episode or compels submission by threat of death, serious bodily injury, or kidnaping, §21.05; rape of a child: sexual intercourse with female under 17, §21.09; sexual abuse of a child: deviate sexual intercourse with a child, and the child is under 17, §21.10; indecency with a child: sexual contact with a child under 17 or exposure to child under 17 with specified intent, §21.11.

Principals

All categories of rape: male/female; sexual abuse: person/person.

Spouses

Expanded spousal exception. "General Provisions: The exclusion of conduct with a spouse from the definitions of offenses in sections §21.02 through §21.05 of this code (rape, aggravated rape, sexual abuse, aggravated sexual abuse) is extended to the conduct of persons while cohabiting, regardless of the legal status of their relationship and of whether they hold themselves out as husband and wife," §21.12. Specific spousal exception also included in definition of some offenses, female not his wife, §21.02 and §21.03; with the other person, not his spouse, §21.04; female not his wife, §21.09; a child not his spouse, §21.10.

Terminology

Language

"The intercourse is without the female's consent under one or more of the following circumstances: he compels her to submit or participate by force that overcomes such earnest resistance as might reasonably be expected under the circumstances; he compels her to submit or participate by any threat, communicated by actions, words, or deeds, that would prevent resistance by a woman of ordinary resolution, under the same or similar circumstances, because of a reasonable fear of harm, . . ." §21.02.

Definitions

Sexual intercourse means any penetration of the female sex organ by the male sex organ, §21.01(3). *Sexual contact* means any touching of the anus, breast, or any part of the genitals of another person with intent to arouse or gratify the sexual desire of any person, §21.01(2). *Deviate sexual intercourse* means any contact between any part of the genitals of one person and the mouth or anus of another person, §21.01(1).

Statutory Age Provisions

Age of Consent

Offenses defined by victim being aged 14 or under 17. Affirmative defense to rape of a child that actor is less than 2 years older than the victim.

Offenses

Rape of a child: sexual intercourse when female is younger than 17 and actor more than 2 years older, §21.09; sexual abuse of a child: deviate sexual intercourse when child is younger than 17 and actor more than 2 years older, §21.10; indecency with a child: acts with a child under 17, §21.11.

**Evidence Provisions, Defenses, and
Cross References**

Evidence

Specific instances of victim's sexual conduct, opinion evidence of victim's sexual conduct, and reputation evidence of victim's sexual conduct may be admitted if material and not prejudicial. Defense must give notice of such inquiry, then an in-camera hearing required on the record. Court shall make findings. Record shall be sealed for appeal. Statute does not restrict evidence of prior conviction for impeachment nor does it restrict the evidence of promiscuous sexual conduct of a child 14 or older, §21.13. Corroboration not required if victim informed any person of the offense within 6 months, code crim. proc. art. 38.07.

Defenses

Consent and absence of resistance defenses since rape defined in terms of absence of consent and resistance. Affirmative defense to rape of a child and sexual abuse of a child: that female was over 14 and had engaged promiscuously in sexual intercourse or that actor less than 2 years older than the victim, §21.09(b) and (c), and §21.10(b) and (c).

Cross Reference

Incest, §25.02; homosexual conduct: class C misdemeanor, §21.06; child pornography, L.1979 (HB 1742).

Penalties

Terms

Rape: second-degree felony, §21.02; rape of a child: second-degree felony, §21.09; sexual abuse: second-degree felony, §21.04; sexual abuse of a child: second-degree felony, §21.10; second-degree felony punishable by a minimum of 2 years or a maximum of 20 years and a possible fine of $10,000, §12.33; aggravated rape: first-degree felony, §21.03; aggravated sexual abuse: first-degree felony, §21.05; first-degree felony punishable by life or a maximum of 99 and a minimum of 5 years, and a possible fine of $10,000, §12.32; indecency with a child: third-degree felony, §21.11; third-degree felony punishable by a minimum term of 2 years and a maximum term of 10 years, §12.34.

Special

Punishment for repeat and habitual offenders, §12.42.

Utah

State Statutes

Utah Code Ann. (Repl. 1978) (Supp. 1979) §76-5-401 through §76-5-407
§76-5-401 Unlawful sexual intercourse
§76-5-402 Rape
§76-5-403 Sodomy—forcible sodomy
§76-5-404 Forcible sexual abuse
§76-5-405 Aggravated sexual assault
§76-5-406 Sexual intercourse, sodomy, or sexual abuse without consent of
　　　　　victim—circumstances

Derivation

History

Compilation of 1866 includes carnal knowledge statute, by force and against her will, also carnal knowledge and abuse of female child under 10. Penalty is minimum of 10 years and maximum of life. 1876 compilation redefines the offense as sexual intercourse when female is under 10, incapable of consent, when resistance overcome by force or violence, when resistance prevented, when female unconscious, or when female believes accused is her husband. Male must be over 14. Minimum penalty is 5 years. Age of consent raised to 13 in 1888. Compilation of 1898 adds new offense: carnal knowledge of female between 13 and 18. No changes until 1953 when penalty for offense when female is under 13 specified as maximum of 20 years to life, for all other cases minimum penalty of 10 years. This formulation repealed in 1973 when a Model Penal Code (MPC) revision of the criminal code was passed.

Present Law

MPC-type criminal code reform enacted in 1973 including MPC-type rape statute, made sex-neutral in 1979. Prompt complaint requirement repealed in 1979.

Statutory Structure

Changes

Characterization of rape as sexual intercourse defined as criminal by circumstances defined by female's resistance, inability to resist, or when

421

female deceived replaced by MPC rape formulation stressing consent of the victim. Lesser crimes of sexual abuse and sexual assault added.

Offenses

Rape; sodomy and forcible sodomy; forcible sexual abuse; aggravated sexual assault.

Requirements

Rape: sexual intercourse without consent, including when victim is under 14, §76-5-402; sodomy: oral-genital acts between persons without consent, including when victim is under 14, §76-5-403; forcible sexual abuse: touching of anus or genitals or taking indecent liberties with requisite intent and without consent, §76-5-404; aggravated sexual assault: rape or forcible sodomy, or attempted rape or forcible sodomy when actor causes serious bodily injury, or compels submission by threat of kidnaping, death, or serious bodily injury upon anyone, §76-5-405.

Principals

Person/person and actor/victim; sex-neutral.

Spouses

Statutory spousal exception excludes those living apart pursuant to a court order: "The provisions of this part shall not apply to conduct between persons married to each other; provided, however, that for purposes of this part, persons living apart pursuant to a lawful order of a court of competent jurisdiction shall not be deemed to be married," §76-5-407(1); specific spousal exception also in definition of rape: "rape [is] when the actor has sexual intercourse with another person, *not the actor's spouse*, without the victim's consent," §76-5-402. Specific spousal exception also in definition of unlawful sexual intercourse: "A person commits unlawful sexual intercourse . . . with a person, not that person's spouse, who is under 16 years of age," §76-5-401.

Terminology

Language

"An act . . . is without consent . . . when the actor compels the victim to submit or participate by force that overcomes such earnest resistance as might reasonably be expected under the circumstances; or the actor compels the victim to submit or participate by any threat that would prevent resistance by a person of ordinary resolution; or . . . the actor knows that as a result of mental disease or defect, the victim is at the time of the act incapable either of appraising the nature of the act or of resisting it,'' §76-5-406.

Definitions

Without consent defined by the following circumstances: force overcoming earnest resistance; threat preventing resistance; when actor knows victim is unconscious; unaware or physically unable to resist; when actor knows victim is incapable of appraising the nature of the act or resisting it due to mental disease or defect; when victim participates believing actor is spouse; when actor has administered any substance without victim's knowledge; when victim is under 14, §76-5-406. "In any prosecution for unlawful sexual intercourse, rape, or sodomy, any sexual penetration or, in the case of sodomy, any touching, however slight, is sufficient to constitute the offense," §76-5-407. "A person commits *forcible sexual abuse* if, under circumstances not amounting to rape or sodomy, or attempted rape or sodomy, the actor touches the anus or any part of the genitals of another, or otherwise takes indecent liberties with another, or causes another to take indecent liberties with the actor or another, with intent to cause substantial emotional or bodily paid to any person, or with the intent to arouse or gratify the sexual desire of any person without consent of the other regardless of the sex of any participant," §76-5-404(1).

Statutory Age Provisions

Age of Consent

When the victim is under 14 sexual acts are without consent, 76-5-406(7). In addition, unlawful sexual intercourse is defined as sexual intercourse with a person under 16, §76-5-401(1); if actor no more than 3 years older than the victim, unlawful sexual intercourse downgraded to a misdemeanor, §76-5-401(2).

Offenses

If the victim is under 14, gradation of offense raised from second to first degree for rape, §76-5-402, and forcible sodomy, §76-5-403. Unlawful sexual intercourse: sexual intercourse with a person under 16, §76-5-401.

**Evidence Provisions, Defenses,
and Cross References**

Evidence

No evidence statute. No statutory corroboration requirement, except for
testimony of accomplices, §77-31-18 (as amended by ch. 44, L.1979).

Defenses

Consent not a defense to unlawful sexual intercourse or to sodomy. Consent a defense to rape, forcible sodomy, and forcible sexual abuse. Ignorance or mistake a defense, §76-2-304.

Cross References

Incest, §76-7-102; court may exclude public during rape trial, §78-7-4; mental examination of sex offenders, §77-49-1.

Penalties

Terms

Rape: second-degree felony unless victim is under 14, then first-degree
felony, §76-5-402(2); sodomy: class B misdemeanor; forcible sodomy:
second-degree felony unless victim is under 14, then first-degree felony,
§76-5-403(3); unlawful sexual intercourse: third-degree felony unless actor
is no more than 3 years older than victim, then class B misdemeanor,
§76-5-401(2); forcible sexual abuse: third-degree felony, §76-5-404(2); aggravated sexual assault: first-degree felony, §76-5-405(2). First-degree
felony: minimum term of 5 years, maximum life, additional mandatory
penalty if firearm or representation of firearm used, §76-3-202(1); second-
degree felony: minimum term of 1 year, maximum term of 15 years, additional mandatory penalty if firearm or representation of firearm used,
§76-3-203(2); third-degree felony: maximum term of 5 years and discretionary additional term of up to 5 years, if firearm or representation used,
§76-3-203(3); class B misdemeanor: maximum of 6 months in jail,
§76-3-204.

Special

Life term without probation or parole for convicted sex offender with mental disorder, unless certified "recovered," §77-49-7; court may order defendant to pay restitution to victim, including "special" damages and medical expenses, §76-3-201 et seq; fines for felonies and misdemeanors, §76-3-301; mandatory minimum term for second offense involving firearm, §76-3-203(4); aggravating and mitigating circumstances in sentencing, §77-35-12.

Vermont

State Statutes

Vt. Stat. Ann. tit. 13 §3251 through §3255 (Supp. 1979)
§3251 Definitions
§3252 Sexual assault
§3253 Aggravated sexual assault
§3254 Trial procedure

Derivation

History

1779 statute punished any man who forcibly ravished any woman or maid and committed carnal copulation with her against her consent by death, provided the complaint was made forthwith upon the rape and the woman in time of her distress did make an outcry. Law of 1797 kept language of ravish or carnally know, added phrase 'woman, maid, or damsel,' and specified 11 as the statutory age. Penalty reduced to 10 years and a fine of $1,000. Separate offense for carnal knowledge of woman-child under 11 with her will or against her will. Law of 1824 added phrase "or either such punishments." Law of 1839 rewrote the section, consolidated two offenses. Operative language remained "ravish and carnally know" by force and against her will. Statutory age remained at 11; penalty unchanged. Law of 1849 added "with or without her consent" for offense against female under 11, and penalty increased to 20 years or a fine of $2,000, or both. Two minor changes in phrasing in 1862 and 1880. Law of 1886 specifies male must be over 16, female over 14. New offense created: carnal knowledge of female under 14 by male under 16 with consent. Penalty is for both parties to be sent to reform school. If forcible offense, then penalty as for rape. Law of 1898 changes statutory age of female to 16 for both offenses; institution or commitment changed. No change except offense retitled in 1918. Designation of institution for juveniles changed in 1947. In 1971 phrase "in state prison" omitted; 1977 statute redefined offense.

Present Law

Sexual assault and aggravated sexual assault have replaced prior common-law rape statute. Rape reform evidence statute and statutory definition of lack of consent.

426

Statutory Structure

Changes

In 1977 statutory formulation of sexual assault and aggravated sexual assault, including evidence statute and statutory definition of lack of consent, replaced traditional carnal knowledge statute distinguishing between rape by person over 16 and by person under 16.

Offenses

Sexual assault; aggravated sexual assault.

Requirements

Sexual assault: sexual act without consent or by threat or coercion or by placing other person in fear that any person will be harmed imminently or after administration of drug or intoxicant or the other person is under 16, 13252; aggravated sexual assault: sexual assault when person causes serious bodily injury, 3253.

Principals

Person/person; sex-neutral.

Spouses

Spousal exception written into definition of sexual assault. "A person who engages in a sexual act with another person, *other than a spouse* . . . [or] the other person is under the age of 16 and they are not married to each other," §3252.

Terminology

Language

"Lack of consent may be shown without proof of resistance; a person shall be deemed to have acted with the consent of the other person where the actor: knows that the other person is mentally incapable of understanding the nature of the sexual act; or knows that the other person is not physically capable of resisting, or declining consent to, the sexual act; or knows that the other person is unaware that a sexual act is being committed," §3254.

Definitions

Consent means words or actions by a person indicating a voluntary agreement to engage in a sexual act, §3251(3). *Sexual act* means conduct between persons consisting of contact between the penis and the vulva, the penis and the anus, the mouth and the penis, the mouth and the vulva, or any intrusion, however slight, by any part of a person's body other than the fingers or by any object into the genital or anal opening of another, §3251(1). *Serious bodily injury* means bodily injury which creates a substantial risk of death or which causes serious, permanent disfigurement, or protracted loss or impairment of the function of any bodily member or organ, §3251(4). *Sexual conduct* means any conduct or behavior relating to sexual activities of the complaining witness, including but not limited to prior experience of sexual acts, use of contraceptives, living arrangement, and mode of living, §3251(2).

Statutory Age Provisions

Age of Consent

Statutory definition of sexual assault criminalizes sexual acts with a person under 16, unless the participants are married, §3252(3).

Offenses

Sexual assault: sexual act with a person under 16, §3252(3); aggravated sexual assault: sexual assault including sexual acts with a person under 16 when serious bodily injury occurs, §3253.

Evidence Provisions, Defenses and Cross References

Evidence

1977 evidence statute totally excludes opinion and reputation evidence of the complaining witness' sexual conduct. Special corroboration no longer required. Evidence of prior sexual conduct of the complaining witness shall not be admitted, except when it is relevant to credibility and material to a fact at issue, the court may admit: past sexual conduct with the defendant, evidence showing source of semen, pregnancy, or disease, evidence of specific instance of the complaining witness' past false allegations of violations of this chapter. Written notice of motion required followed by in-camera hearing. Objections to admissibility shall be stated on the record, and court shall rule forthwith, §3255. Proof of resistance not required to demonstrate absence of consent, §3254(1).

Defenses

Consent; marriage of the two persons.

Cross References

Intermarriage or fornication by persons prohibited to marry, tit. 13 §205.

Penalties

Terms

Sexual assault: term of imprisonment for not more than 20 years or fine of $10,000, or both, §3252; aggravated sexual assault: term of imprisonment for not more than 25 years or fine of $15,000, or both, §3253.

Special

None.

Virginia

State Statutes

Va. Code Ann. §18.2-61 through §18.2-68 (1975) (Supp. 1979)

§18.2-61 Rape of female 13 years of age or older; carnal knowledge of female child under 13

§18.2-63 Carnal knowledge of female child between 13 and 15 years of age

§18.2-63.1 Death of victim

§18.2-64 Carnal knowledge of female patients or pupils of certain institutions

§18.2-64.1 Carnal knowledge of certain minors

Derivation

History

Codification of 1789 criminalized carnal knowledge and abuse of any woman-child under 10. No benefit of clergy. Law of 1792 defined rape as to ravish a woman, married, maid, or other, where she did not consent before or after, or to ravish a woman, married, maid, or other, with force, though she consented after. Penalty was death. Castration permitted of slave who attempted to ravish a white woman. Otherwise punishment was 10 to 21 years. Revised code of 1819 differentiated penalties by status of offender. Slaves: for rape, death; carnal knowledge of girl under 10, death or castration; attempt to ravish, castration. Free person: rape, 10 to 21 years; carnal knowledge of girl under 10, 1 to 10 years; accessory, 10 to 21 years. Law of 1823 specifies death by hanging if any slave, free negro or mulatto attempts to ravish a white woman. Law of 1825 adds "where she did not consent before nor after" and specifies death without benefit of clergy. Code of 1849 punished attempts by free negro by fraud or force at discretion of jury, death or 5 to 21 years. If a white person had carnal knowledge of a female over 12 against her will or by force, 10 to 21 years. Code of 1860 specified same penalty for carnal knowledge of female under 12. Code 1873 provided a penalty of death or 10 to 20 years for *any person* who had carnal knowledge of female over 12. Law of 1887 added provision prohibiting carnal knowledge of female inmate of any lunatic asylum. Same penalty as for rape of female over 12. Code of 1898 increased statutory age to 14; added provision for "female who is an inmate of deaf, dumb, or blind institution." Code of 1919 increased statutory age to 16 and added new category of carnal knowledge of female over 14 and under 16 with consent,

430

then penalty is from 5 to 20 years. If carnal knowledge with consent of female over 12 and under 16, subsequent marriage with consent of parent may bar prosecution. Code of 1930 added provision prohibiting carnal knowledge of feebleminded or epileptic persons. Penalty was death or 5 years to life. For female between 14 and 16, with consent, penalty was 1 to 20 years. Marriage a bar to prosecution with restrictions. 1977 statute added section concerning carnal knowledge of confined or detained juveniles. Law of 1978 added provision concerning order of proof when death of a victim occurs in connection with a rape.

Present Law

Traditional rape statute with two formulations of statutory rape. Special provisions for females in institutions or under custody of the Board of Corrections.

Statutory Structure

Changes

No rape reform legislation passed. No evidence statute. Present law is statutory formulation of common-law carnal knowledge statute with separate designations for special classes of victims. In 1977 special offense added prohibiting carnal knowledge with juveniles under the custody of the Board of Corrections.

Offenses

Rape; carnal knowledge of female child under 13; carnal knowledge of female child between 13 and 15; carnal knowledge of female patients or pupils of certain institutions; carnal knowledge of certain minors.

Requirements

Rape: carnal knowledge of a female over 13 against her will or by force or carnal knowledge of a female child under the age of 13, §18.2-61; carnal knowledge of female child between 13 and 15: including carnal knowledge without force, carnal knowledge with consent of such females, §18.2-63; carnal knowledge of female patients or pupils of certain institutions: carnal knowledge with a patient or pupil at an institution for the mentally ill, retarded, and so on, §18.2-64; carnal knowledge of certain minors: carnal knowledge of juveniles in the custody of the Board of Corrections, §18.2-64.1.

Principals

Common-law rape, principals are male/female, except for prohibition against intercourse with a male minor in §18.2-64.1.

Spouses

No explicit spousal exception, but traditional common-law offense did not allow for prosecution of a spouse.

Terminology

Language

"If any person carnally knows a female of 13 years of age or more against her will, by force, or carnally knows a female child under that age, he shall . . . be punished," §18.2-61.

Definitions

Carnal knowledge undefined; rape undefined; consent undefined; force undefined. Female patient or pupil defined as a female patient of any hospital, who has been adjudged mentally ill and has not been discharged as a patient from such hospital, or a female patient or pupil of an institution for mentally ill, mentally retarded, feebleminded, or epileptic persons," §18.2-64.

Statutory Age Provisions

Age of Consent

Age of consent is 13: "for purposes of this section a child under the age of 13 shall not be considered a consenting female," §18.2-63. Statutory rape offense forbids carnal knowledge with females, including consenting females, between 13 and 15, §18.2-63; if accused a minor and female 3 years or more his junior, offense a class 6 felony; if consenting female is less than 3 years his junior, accused guilty of fornication, §18.2-63.

Offenses

Rape: carnal knowledge of a female under 13, §18.2-61; carnal knowledge of female child between 13 and 15, §18.2-63.

Evidence Provisions, Defenses, and Cross References

Evidence

No evidence statute. Previous unchaste character may be shown on the issue of consent by proof of general reputation. *Wynne* v. *Commonwealth*, 216 Va. 355, 218 S.E. 2d 445 (1975). Deposition of female witness may be taken away from court and with the public excluded, defense shall have right to cross-examine, §18.2-67; if female over 14 is of bad moral repute and lewd and the carnal knowledge was with her consent, the defendant shall not be convicted of rape but of fornication or contributing to the delinquency of a minor, §18.2-65; corroboration required for seduction, §18.2-69; when the death of a victim occurs in connection with a rape, it shall be immaterial whether death occurred before or after the rape, §18.2-63.1.

Defenses

Consent an absolute bar to prosecution when the victim is over the age of consent, *Coles* v. *Peyton*, 389 F.2d 224 (4th Cir. 1968); no mistake as to age defense for offense involving females over 13 and under 15, §18.2-63; subsequent marriage of the parties a defense to carnal knowledge with consent, §18.2-66.

Cross References

Adultery and fornication by persons forbidden to marry; incest, §18.2-366; when depositions taken away from court, state shall bear expense, §18.2-67; taking indecent liberties with children, §18.2-370; crimes against nature (sodomy), §18.2-361; seduction, §18.2-68 et seq.

Penalties

Terms

Rape: life or any term not less than 5 years, §18.2-61; carnal knowledge of female between 13 and 15: class 4 felony; if accused a minor and more than 3 years younger, class 6 felony; if female less than 3 years younger, accused guilty of fornication, §18.2-63; carnal knowledge of female patients: class 3 felony, §18.2-64; carnal knowledge of certain minors: class 6 felony, unless minor less than 3 years younger, then guilty of fornication, §18.2-64.1; class 3 felony: 5 to 20 years, §18.2-10(c); class 4 felony: 2 to 10 years, §18.2-10(d); class 6 felony: 1 to 5 years, 1 year in country jail, §18.2-10(f). Punishment for misdemeanors: maximum confinement of 1 year or $1,000, §18.2-11.

Special

Age differential between accused and victim determines penalty for carnal knowledge of female over 13 and under 15, §18.2-63, and for carnal knowledge of certain minors, §18.2-64.1.

Virgin Islands

State Statutes

V.I. Code Ann. tit. 14 §1701 through §1706
§1701 Rape in the first degree
§1702 Rape in the second degree
§1703 Rape in the third degree

Derivation

History

Code of 1921 defined rape as sexual intercourse with a female not the wife under circumstances where the female was under 12, incapable of consent through lunacy, where resistance was prevented, or where resistance was overcome by force and violence; minimum penalty of 5 years. Code of 1941 rewrote the section following New York Penal Law. Statutory corroboration requirement added, proof of penetration beyond a reasonable doubt. Minimum penalty removed, male must be over 14. Statutory age formulations changed to present formulation. Law of 1964 increased age of victim from 13 to 14 for third-degree rape.

Present Law

Codification of common-law rape formulated in terms of three degrees, based upon age of female. Distinctions based upon circumstances defining rape retained.

Statutory Structure

Changes

Statutory formulation of rape in traditional terms of carnal knowledge of female without consent. Inability to consent defined by circumstances of incapacity, or when resistance overcome or prevented.

Offenses

Rape in the first, second, and third degree.

Requirements

First-degree rape: sexual intercourse when female incapable of consent
through lunacy, when resistance overcome or prevented by fear or intoxicant, when female unconscious, §1701; second-degree rape: sexual intercourse with a female under 14 under circumstances not amounting to first-
degree rape, §1702; third-degree rape: sexual intercourse with female under
16 but over 13 under circumstances not amounting to first-degree rape,
§1703.

Principals

Male/female.

Spouses

Statutory spousal exception included in the definition of rape in all three
degrees: "whoever perpetrates an act of sexual intercourse with a female
not his wife," §1701, §1702, §1703.

Terminology

Language

"Whoever perpetrates an act of sexual intercourse with a female not his
wife when through idiocy, imbecility, or any unsoundness of mind, either
temporary or permanent, she is incapable of giving consent, or by reason of
mental or physical weakness or immaturity or any bodily ailment, she does
not offer resistance," §1701.

Definitions

First-degree rape is when "her resistance is forcibly overcome; when her
resistance is prevented by fear of immediate and great bodily harm which

she has reasonable cause to believe will be inflicted upon her; when her resistance is prevented by stupor or weakness of mind produced by an intoxicating, narcotic, or anesthetic agent, or when she is known by the defendant to be in such a state of stupor or weakness of mind from any cause; or when she is, at the time, unconscious of the nature of the act and this is known to the defendant," §1701.

Statutory Age Provisions

Age of Consent

Two statutory rape offenses, neither of which allows for consent of the underage victim or requires proof of force or resistance. Rebuttable presumption that actor must be over 14 to be physically capable of sexual penetration, §1705.

Offenses

Second-degree rape: sexual intercourse with a female under 14, under circumstances not amounting to first-degree rape, §1702; third-degree rape: sexual intercourse with a female over 13 and under 16, under circumstances not amounting to first-degree rape, §1703.

Evidence Provisions, Defenses, and Cross References

Evidence

No evidence statute. Statutory corroboration requirement: "no conviction can be had for rape upon the testimony of the female defined, unsupported by other evidence," §1706; corroboration required as to fact of intercourse and lack of consent, *Virgin Islands* v. *Brooks*, 378 F.2d 338 (3d Cir. 1967). Reversible error not to instruct regarding complainant's bad reputation for chastity where consent was at issue. *Virgin Islands* v. *John*, 447 F.2d 69 (3d Cir. 1971).

Defenses

Consent a defense to all offenses except two categories of statutory rape.

Cross References

Incest, tit. 14 §961; sodomy, §2061; bestiality, §2062.

Penalties

Terms

First-degree rape: maximum 20 years, §1701; second-degree rape: maximum 15 years, §1702; third-degree rape: $200 fine and/or maximum of 1 year, §1703.

Special

None.

Washington

State Statutes

Wash. Rev. Code Ann. §9.79.140 through §9.79.220 (1977) (Supp. 1978)
(Laws of 1979)

§9.79.140 Definitions
§9.79.160 Defenses to prosecution under this chapter
§9.79.170 Rape in the first degree
§9.79.180 Rape in the second degree
§9.79.190 Rape in the third degree
§9.79.200 Statutory rape in the first degree
§9.79.210 Statutory rape in the second degree
§9.79.220 Statutory rape in the third degree

Derivation

History

Code of 1881 contained a version of the traditional Elizabethan rape statute: if any person shall ravish and carnally know any female of the age of 12 or more by force or against her will, or carnally know and abuse any female child under 12, he shall be imprisoned for life or any term of years. This statute also included carnal knowledge by administering any substance producing a stupor or carnal knowledge of an idiot; same penalty. Code also contained a seduction statute with a chaste-character provision. Law of 1909 rewrote the section to define rape as an act of sexual intercourse with a female not the wife of the perpetrator committed against her will and without her consent. Every person is guilty of rape who shall perpetrate such an act of sexual intercourse with a female of the age of 10 years or upward not his wife (1) when the female is incapable of consent through idiocy, (2) when her resistance is forcibly overcome, (3) when resistance is prevented by fear of immediate and great bodily harm, (4) when resistance is prevented by a stupor produced by an intoxicant, or (5) when the female is unconscious. Punishment is a minimum of 5 years. New statute defined carnal knowledge of children: every person who shall carnally know and abuse any female child under 18 not his wife shall be punished as follows: if the child is over 10 and under 15, by a minimum of 5 years, if the child is over 15 and under 18 and of previous chaste character, by imprisonment in the penitentiary for a maximum of 10 years or county jail for 1 year. Amendment in 1919 added that every female person who shall have sexual

439

intercourse with any male child under 18, not her husband, shall be punished. Punishment provisions unchanged but made sex-neutral. Chaste-character provision removed. Law of 1943 indicate the penalty is life if the child is under 10 and a maximum penalty of 20 years if the child is over 10 and under 15. Law of 1973 makes the rape law and the carnal knowledge of children section sex-neutral. This law was repealed in 1975.

Present Law

1975 rape reform statute redefined the offense to include acts other than sexual intercourse. Three degrees of rape delineated in terms of the amount of force and the age differential between the victim and perpetrator. Statute included an expansion of defenses and a rape evidence statute.

Statutory Structure

Changes

Unique formulation including several reform goals replaced a statutory definition of rape defined in terms of the victim's ability to resist. All former sex offenses repealed; some redefined and recodified. Three degrees of sex-neutral rape and three degrees of sex-neutral statutory rape replaced former rape and carnal knowledge of child. Expanded defenses for the accused and increased protections for the victim-witness. Amendment in 1975 adds clarifying language to section regarding parole eligibility.

Offenses

Rape in the first, second, and third degree; statutory rape in the first, second, and third degree.

Requirements

First-degree rape: sexual intercourse by forcible compulsion where the perpetrator or an accessory (a) uses or threatens to use a deadly weapon, (b) kidnaps the victim, (c) inflicts serious physical injury, or (d) feloniously enters into the building or vehicle where the victim is situated, §9.79.170; second-degree rape: sexual intercourse (a) by forcible compulsion, or (b) when victim is incapable of consent by reason of being physically helpless or mentally incapacitated, §9.79.180; third-degree rape: sexual intercourse (a) where victim did not consent and such lack of consent was clearly expressed by the victim's words or conduct or (b) where there is threat of substantial unlawful harm to the property rights of the victim, §9.79.190; first-degree statutory rape: a person over 13 who has sexual intercourse with a person under 11, §9.79.200; second-degree statutory rape: a person over 16 who has sexual intercourse with a person over 11 but under 14, §9.79.210; third-degree statutory rape: a person over 18 who has sexual intercourse with a person over 14 but under 16, §9.79.220.

Principals

Person/person; sex-neutral.

Spouses

All offenses refer to "another person, not married to the perpetrator." Married means one who is legally married to another, §9.79.140(2).

Terminology

Language

"A person is guilty of rape in the first degree when such person engages in sexual intercourse with another person not married to the perpetrator by forcible compulsion where the perpetrator or an accessory uses or threatens to use a deadly weapon, §9.79.170(1).

Definitions

Sexual intercourse (a) has its ordinary meaning and occurs upon any penetration, however slight, and (b) also means any penetration of the vagina or anus, however slight, by an object, when committed on one person by another whether such persons are of the same or opposite sex, except when such penetration is accomplished for medically recognized treatment or diagnostic purposes, and (c) also means any act of sexual contact between persons involving the sex organs of one person and the mouth or anus of another whether such persons are of the same or opposite sex, §9.79.140(1). *Consent* means that at the time of the act of sexual intercourse there are actual words or conduct indicating freely given agreement to have sexual intercourse, §9.79.140(6). *Forcible compulsion* means physical force which overcomes resistance, or a threat, express or implied, that places a person in fear of death or physical injury to herself or himself or another person, or in fear that he or she or another person will be kidnaped, §9.79.140(5). Evidence of the victim's *past sexual behavior* shall include but not be limited to the victim's marital history, divorce history, or general reputation for promiscuity, nonchastity, or sexual mores contrary to community standards, §9.79.150(2).

Statutory Age Provisions

Age of Consent

Statutory rape offenses determined by age of offender and victim. Seriousness of the offense determined only in part by age of the victim.

Offenses

First-degree statutory rape: a person over 13 who engages in sexual intercourse with a person less than 11, §9.79.200; Second-degree statutory rape: a person over 16 who engages in sexual intercourse with a person who is over 11 but under 14, §9.79.210; third-degree statutory rape: a person over 18 who engages in sexual intercourse with a person who is over 14 and under 16, §9.79.220.

Evidence Provisions, Defenses
and Cross References

Evidence

Evidence of the victim's past sexual behavior is inadmissible on the issue of credibility and inadmissible to prove consent unless the perpetrator and the victim have engaged in sexual intercourse with each other in the past. Where the past behavior is material to the issue of consent, evidence concerning past behavior between the perpetrator and the victim may be admissible on the issue of consent. Evidence of the victim's past sexual behavior inadmissible on the issue of credibility in any prosecution for rape or attempt or assault with intent. If such evidence offered to prove consent, it may be admitted only after a written offer of proof, then the court may order the evidence admitted or the victim may be cross-examined if prosecution offers evidence of the victim's prior sexual behavior, §9.79.150(2)-(4); corroboration not required, §9.79.150(1).

Defenses

Lack of consent as defined a defense to rape but not statutory rape. Statutory affirmative defense that the defendant reasonably believed the victim was not mentally incapacitated or physically helpless, §9.79.160(1); no mistake as to age defense to statutory rape, unless the defendant reasonably believed the alleged victim to be older based upon declarations as to age by the alleged victim, §9.79.170(2).

Cross References

Incest, §9A-64-020; domestic violence, 1979 laws, ch. 105; program to aid victim of sexual assault, 1979 laws, ch. 219.

Penalties

Terms

First-degree rape: minimum term of 20 years, without a deferred or suspended sentence, and a minimum 3 years confinement which shall not be reduced by credits, §9.79.170(2); second-degree rape: maximum of 10 years. §9.79.180(2); third-degree rape: maximum of 5 years, §9.79.190(2); first-degree statutory rape: minimum of 20 years, without deferred or suspended sentence, §9.79.200(2); second-degree statutory rape: maximum of 10 years, §9.79.210(2); third-degree statutory rape: maximum of 5 years, §9.79.220(2).

Special

Sexual psychopaths, §71.05.525; no parole for sexual psychopaths, §9.95.115.

West Virginia

State Statutes

W. VA. Code Ann. §61-8B-1 through §61-8B-13 (Rept. 1977) (Supp. 1979)
§61-8B-1 Definition of terms
§61-8B-2 Lack of consent
§61-8B-3 Sexual assault in the first degree
§61-8B-4 Sexual assault in the second degree
§61-8B-5 Sexual assault in the third degree
§61-8B-6 Sexual abuse in the first degree
§61-8B-7 Sexual abuse in the second degree
§61-8B-8 Sexual abuse in the third degree
§61-8B-9 Sexual misconduct

Derivation

History

Codification of 1868 prohibited carnal knowledge of a female over 12 against her will or by force or carnal knowledge of female under 12; minimum term of 5 years. Penalty changed as of 1891 compilation to include possibility of death penalty if guilty verdict returned by jury; ordinary term set at 7 to 20 years. Code of 1906 increased statutory age to 14 and added proviso that section should not apply to person under 14. Code of 1943 adds "not his wife" by male over 16 or carnal knowledge of a female of previous chaste character under age of 16. Penalty is life or death at discretion of jury, or 5 to 20 years. Proviso excludes case where male under 16 has carnal knowledge of female over 12 with her consent. Female over 16 who has carnal knowledge of any male under 16 is guilty of misdemeanor. Penalty is 2 to 6 months in jail. Sex offenders act included in 1957 Supp. 1963 Supp. adds provision regarding male over 16 who has carnal knowledge of a female under 10; penalty is death, life, or 5 to 20 years if with mercy. 1965 Supp. adds restriction on parole. Common law rape replaced in 1976 by statutory formulation of several offenses including the codification of statutory defenses.

Present Law

Model Penal Code (MPC) formulation of sex-neutral sexual assault and sexual misconduct with an evidence statute. Statutory spousal exception

444

expands common-law provision to include all persons living together. If the victim is a "voluntary social companion," offense cannot be first-degree sexual assault.

Statutory Structure

Changes

Traditional formulation of rape as carnal knowledge by force or without consent replaced by statutory formulation of lack of consent and offenses of sexual assault, sexual abuse, and sexual misconduct. Offense redefined, but emphasis on consent retained. Rape reform evidence statute included when offense redefined.

Offenses

First-, second-, and third-degree sexual assault; first-, second-, and third-degree sexual abuse; sexual misconduct.

Requirements

First-degree sexual assault: sexual intercourse by forcible compulsion and serious bodily injury, or use of a deadly weapon, or victim not a voluntary social companion or sexual intercourse with a person incapable of consent because physically helpless or victim less than 11 years old 61-8B-3; second-degree sexual assault: sexual intercourse by forcible compulsion or sexual penetration with an object by forcible compulsion 61-8B-4; third-degree sexual assault: sexual intercourse with a person incapable of consent because mentally defective or mentally incapacitated or with person incapable of consent because under 16 and 4 years younger than the defendant 61-8B-5; first-degree sexual abuse: sexual contact by forcible compulsion or when person incapable of consent because physically helpless or when person less than 11 years old 61-8B-6; second-degree sexual abuse: sexual contact when person mentally defective or incapacitated 6-8B-7; third-degree sexual abuse: sexual contact without consent when person incapable of consent because less than 16 but an affirmative defense that defendant less than 16 or less than 4 years older than victim 61-8B-8; sexual misconduct: sexual intercourse without consent or when person deceived, 61-8B-9.

Principals

Sex-neutral; "he" includes any human being, §61-8B-1(10); he/person.

Spouses

Statutory spousal exception exempts from prosecution all persons living together. "Marriage for the purposes of this article in addition to its legal meaning includes persons living together as man and wife regardless of the legal status of their relationship," §61-8B-1(2).

Terminology

Language

Forcible compulsion means physical force that overcomes such earnest resistance as might reasonably be expected under the circumstances, or threat or intimidation, express or implied, placing a person in fear of immediate death or bodily injury to himself or another person or in fear that he or another person will be kidnaped. For the purpose of this definition, resistance includes physical resistance or any clear communication of the victim's lack of consent," §61-8B-1(1).

Definitions

Sexual intercourse means any act between persons not married to each other involving penetration, however slight, of the female sex organ by the male sex organ or involving contact between the sex organs of one person and the mouth or anus of another person, §61-8B-1(7). *Sexual contact* means any touching of the anus or any part of the sex organs of another person, or the breasts of a female 11 years old or older, where the victim is not married to the actor and the touching is done for the purpose of gratifying the sexual desire of either party, §61-8B-1(6). A person is deemed *incapable of consent* when he is less than 16 years old, or mentally defective or mentally incapacitated, or physically helpless, §61-8B-2(c). *Mentally defective* means that a person suffers from a mental disease or defect which renders him incapable of appraising the nature of his conduct, §61-8B-1(3). *Mentally incapacitated* means that a person is rendered temporarily incapable of appraising or controlling his conduct as a result of the influence of a controlled or intoxicating substance administered to him without his consent or as a result of any other act committed upon him without his consent, §61-8B-1(4). *Physically helpless* means that a person is unconscious or for any other reason is physically unable to communicate on unwillingness to act, §61-8B-1(5).

Statutory Age Provisions

Age of Consent

Statutory age of consent is 16; "a person is deemed incapable of consent when he is less than 16 years old," §61-8B-2(c)(1); offender must be over 14 for first-degree sexual assault, and first-degree sexual abuse; age differential of 4 years and person under 16 and person over 16 for third-degree sexual assault, §61-8B-5a(2), and third-degree sexual abuse, §61-8B-8(b).

Offenses

First-degree sexual assault: sexual intercourse by person over 14 with another person who is incapable of consent because he is less than 11 years old, §61-8B-3(a)(3); third-degree sexual assault: sexual intercourse by person over 16 with another person who is incapable of consent because he is less than 16 and he is at least 4 years younger than defendant, §61-8B-5(a)(2); first-degree sexual abuse: sexual contact by person over 14 with another person who is incapable of consent because he is less than 11 years old, §61-8B-6(a)(3); third-degree sexual abuse: sexual contact when victim is less than 16, but affirmative defense that defendant was under 16 or less than 4 years older than the victim, §61-8B-8.

Evidence Provisions, Defenses and Cross References

Evidence

Evidence statute provides that for any offense where incapacity to consent is based upon age, evidence of specific instances of victim's sexual conduct, opinion evidence, and reputation evidence of same shall be totally excluded. In any other prosecution, the victim's prior sexual conduct with the defendant shall be admitted on the issue of consent, but a hearing away from the jury shall be required first. Prior sexual conduct with third persons shall be admitted to impeach credibility, if the prosecution introduces the issue first, §61-8B-12.

Defenses

Absence of consent an element of every offense, §61-8B-2(a); lack of consent results from forcible compulsion or incapacity to consent, §61-8B-2; that victim was a "voluntary social companion of the actor on the occasion of the crime," a defense to first-degree sexual assault, §61-8B-3(a)(1)(iii); a statutory affirmative defense that the actor did not know of the victim's incapacity to consent, including age offenses where the victim is over 11 and under 16, §61-8B-13.

Cross References

Incest, §61-8B-12; indecent exposure, §61-8B-10; public indecency, §61-8B-11; child pornography, §61-8C-1 et seq.

Penalties

Terms

First-degree sexual assault: minimum 10 and maximum 20 years and possible fine of $10,000, §61-8B-3; second-degree sexual assault: minimum 5 and maximum 10 years and possible fine of $10,000, §61-8B-4; third-degree sexual assault: minimum 1 year and maximum 5 years and possible fine of $10,000, §61-8B-5; first-degree sexual abuse: minimum 1 year and maximum 5 years and possible fine of $10,000, §61-8B-6; second-degree sexual abuse: misdemeanor, maximum term of 12 months in county jail and possible fine of $500; third-degree sexual abuse: misdemeanor, maximum of 90 days in county jail and possible fine of $500; sexual misconduct: misdemeanor, maximum of 12 months in county jail and possible fine of $500.

Special

None.

Wisconsin

State Statutes

Wis. Stat. Ann. §940.225(1) to §940.225(5) (1958) (Supp. 1979-1980)
§940.225(1)   First-degree sexual assault
§940.225(2)   Second-degree sexual assault
§940.225(3)   Third-degree sexual assault
§940.225(3M) Fourth-degree sexual assault

Derivation

History

1839 statutes included a carnal knowledge rape statute; penalty was 10 to 30 years, unless common prostitute, then penalty 1 to 7 years. Age for statutory rape set at 10, penalty was life. In 1898 the statutory age of consent was raised to 14, and the term increased to 5 to 35 years. Age of consent raised to 16 in 1921, and the minimum penalty was reduced to 1 year. Also a distinction introduced between offenders over 18 and under 18; for offenders over 18, the maximum penalty was 35 years, for offenders under 18, the maximum penalty was 10 years. In 1925 a statute was passed prohibiting the public dissemination of the names of victims of rape or sexual assault. This section was amended in 1947 to include communications by telephone and telegraph. Sex offender statute requiring presentence examination passed in 1951 and amended in 1953. Rape law rewritten in 1955, but the maximum penalty of 30 years was retained and the common-law definition of rape was retained. New offense of sexual intercourse without consent added, including when the female is incapable of resistance, mentally ill or infirm, or deceived. Maximum penalty was 15 years. Statutory rape rewritten as sexual intercourse with a child. Offenses defined were sexual intercourse with female under 18 (maximum penalty of 5 years) or if female under 16 and male over 18 (maximum penalty of 15 years) or if female under 12 and male over 18 (maximum penalty of 30 years). Rape reform legislation passed in 1975, effective 1976. Technical amendments passed in 1977 and 1979; amendment as to classification of offense in 1979.

Present Law

Offense of rape replaced by four degrees of sex-neutral sexual assault. Evidence statute and modification of spousal exception also passed in 1975.

449

Statutory Structure

Changes

Traditional rape formulation and gradations of statutory rape and statutorily defined sexual intercourse without consent replaced by four degrees of sexual assault. Most serious offense defined by sexual intercourse or sexual contact and injury to victim, force or threat of force, and age of victim.

Offenses

First-degree sexual assault; second-degree sexual assault; third-degree sexual assault; fourth-degree sexual assault.

Requirements

First-degree sexual assault: sexual contact or sexual intercourse without consent causing pregnancy or great bodily harm, or by use or threat of dangerous weapon or any article believed to be a dangerous weapon, or when person aided or abetted and use of threat or force, or with a person 12 or under, §940.225(1); second-degree sexual assault: sexual contact or sexual intercourse without consent by use or threat of force or violence, or causing injury, illness, disease, or loss or impairment of a sexual or reproductive organ, or mental anguish, or with person who suffers from a mental illness or deficiency, or with an unconscious person, or with a person over 12 and under 18 without consent, §940.225(2); third-degree sexual assault: sexual intercourse without consent, §940.225(3); fourth-degree sexual assault: sexual contact without consent, §940.225(3M).

Principals

Person/person; sex-neutral for all offenses.

Spouses

Statutory spousal exception: "no person may be prosecuted under this section if the complainant is his or her legal spouse, unless the parties are living apart and one of them has filed for an annulment, legal separation, or divorce," §940.225(6).

Terminology

Language

"Whoever . . . has sexual contact or sexual intercourse with another person without consent of that person by use or threat of use of a dangerous weapon or any article used or fashioned in a manner to lead the victim reasonably to believe it to be a dangerous weapon [or] is aided or abetted by one or more other persons and has sexual contact or sexual intercourse with another person without consent," §940.225(1).

Definitions

Consent means "words or overt actions by a person who is competent to give informed consent indicating a freely given agreement to have sexual intercourse or sexual contact. . . . The following persons are presumed incapable of consent but the presumption may be rebutted: . . . a person suffering from a mental illness or defect, . . . a person who is unconscious or for any other reason physically unable to communicate unwillingness to act," §940.225(4). *Sexual intercourse* includes (sexual intercourse) as well as cunnilingus, fellatio, anal intercourse, or any other intrusion, however slight, of any part of person's body or of any object into the genital or anal opening of another, but emission of semen is not required, §940.225(5)(c). *Sexual contact* means any intentional touching of the intimate parts, clothed or unclothed, of a person to the intimate parts, clothed or unclothed, of another, or the intentional touching by hand, mouth, or object of the intimate parts, clothed or unclothed, of another if that intentional touching can be construed as being for the purpose of sexual arousal or gratification or if such touching contains the elements of actual or attempted battery, §940.225(5)(b). *Intimate parts* means the breast, buttock, groin, scrotum, anus, penis, vagina, or pubic mound of a human being, §940.225(5)(a) (as amended by ch. 24, law of 1979). *Sexual conduct* means any conduct or behavior relating to sexual activities of the complaining witness, including but not limited to prior experience of sexual intercourse or sexual contact, use of contraceptives, living arrangement, and life-style, §972.11(2)(a).

Statutory Age Provisions

Age of Consent

Age of consent is 15. "A person under 15 years of age is incapable of consent as a matter of law," §940.225(4). A person who is 15 to 17 years of age is presumed incapable of consent as a matter of law, but the presumption may be rebutted, §940.225(4)(a).

Offenses

First-degree sexual assault: sexual contact or sexual intercourse with a person 12 years of age or younger, §940.225(1)(d); second-degree sexual assault: sexual contact or sexual intercourse with a person over 12 and under 18 without consent, §940.225(2)(e).

Evidence Provisions, Defenses, and Cross References

Evidence

"Evidence of the complaining witness' prior sexual conduct or opinions of the witness' prior sexual conduct and reputation as to prior sexual conduct, shall not be admitted, nor shall any reference to such conduct be made in the presence of the jury except . . . past conduct with the defendant, evidence of specific instances of sexual conduct showing the source of semen, pregnancy, or disease, for use in determining the degree of sexual assault or the extent of injury suffered, or evidence of prior untruthful allegations of sexual assault made by the complaining witness," §972.11. Judge may exclude all persons, except officers of the court or members of the witness' or defendant's families, from the hearing in any sex offense, §970.03(4).

Defenses

Consent a defense to all offenses unless statute creates a rebuttable or nonrebuttable presumption of nonconsent.

Cross Reference

Incest, §944.06 (amended in 1977); sex crimes law (commitment and sentencing of sex offenders), §975.01; sexual exploitation of children (child pornography) L.1977, §940.203; enticing a child for immoral purposes, §944.12.

Penalties

Terms

First-degree sexual assault: class B felony, §940.225(1); class B felony, maximum term of 20 years, §939.50(3)(b); second-degree sexual assault: class C felony, §940.225(2); class C felony, maximum term of 10 years and/or fine up to $10,000, §939.50(3)(c); third-degree sexual assault: class D felony, §940.225(3); class D felony, maximum term of 5 years and/or a fine up to $10,000, §939.50(3)(d); fourth-degree sexual assault: class A misdemeanor, §940.225(3M); class A misdemeanor, imprisonment not to exceed 9 months or a fine up to $10,000, §939.51(3)(a).

Special

Increased penalty for habitual criminals, §939.62.

Wyoming

State Statutes

Wyo. Stat. Ann. 1977 (supp. 1979) §6-4-3C1 through §6-4-314
§6-4-301 Definitions
§6-4-302 Sexual assault in the first degree
§6-4-303 Sexual assault in the second degree
§6-4-304 Sexual assault in the third degree
§6-4-305 Sexual assault in the fourth degree
§6-4-306 Penalties for sexual assault

Derivation

History

Compilation of 1876 included carnal knowledge rape statute. Male must be over 14. Offense defined as carnal knowledge of if female less than 10, irrespective of consent. Penalty was 1 year to life. Statutory age of female raised to 14 in 1887 revision. Statutory age of female raised to 18 in 1899 revision; specific reference to males deleted; term *unlawfully* added. Compilation of 1910 defines rape as the unlawful carnal knowledge of a woman forcibly and against her will, or of a female child under 18 with or without her consent; retains life as maximum penalty. No change in rape law through compilation of 1952. In 1965 rape statute rewritten to prohibit three degrees of rape: first degree (forcible rape of an adult woman or child) punishable by 1 year to life; second degree, carnal knowledge of a female under 15 with consent, punishable by a term of from 1 to 50 years; and third degree, carnal knowledge of a female from 15 to 18 with consent, punishable by 30 days or a maximum of 1 year. 1971 amendment changed the penalty for third degree to 1 year. 1978 amendment to 1977 evidence provision made a minor technical change and reduced standard of prejudice necessary to exclude evidence of prior sexual conduct. Former provision required "that its admission will create a substantial danger of undue prejudice."

Present Law

Rape reform legislation passed in 1977. Rape replaced by four degrees of sex-neutral sexual assault defined in terms of circumstances of offense and

454

status of participants. Corroboration requirement repealed; restriction on publication of names; state to pay costs of medical examination; rape evidence statute.

Statutory Structure

Changes

Traditional formulation of rape divided into degrees based upon age and consent of victim replaced by reform statute defining new crime of sexual assault in first, second, third, and fourth degree.

Offenses

Sexual assault in the first, second, third, and fourth degree.

Requirements

First-degree sexual assault: sexual penetration or sexual intrusion through actual application of force, by threat of death, injury, pain, or kidnaping, when victim physically helpless, or when victim mentally incapable, §6-4-302; second-degree sexual assault: sexual penetration or sexual intrusion when victim threatened with retaliation against self or others, when resistance prevented, when substance administered impairing victim's control, when victim erroneously believes actor is spouse, when victim is under 12 and actor 4 years older, when actor is in position of authority, or as part of treatment or examination inconsistent with reasonable medical practice, or sexual contact when actor causes serious bodily injury under circumstances of first- or second-degree sexual assault or when victim is under 12, §6-4-303; third-degree sexual assault: sexual contact under circumstances of first or second degree when circumstances do not meet the requirements of second degree; §6-4-304; fourth-degree sexual assault: sexual penetration or sexual intrusion on a victim under 16 when the actor is 4 years older, §6-4-305.

Principals

Actor/victim; sex-neutral.

Spouses

Statutory limitation on common-law spousal exception: "A person does not violate any provision of this act if the actor and victim are legally married, unless a decree of judicial separation or restraining order has been granted," § 6-4-307.

Terminology

Language

"Any actor . . . commits a sexual assault in the first degree if: the actor causes submission of the victim through the actual application, reasonably calculated to cause submission of the victim, of physical force or forcible confinement; or the actor causes submission of the victim by threat of death, serious bodily injury, extreme physical pain or kidnaping to be inflicted on anyone and the victim reasonably believes that the actor has the present ability to execute these threats," §6-4-302.

Definitions

Sexual penetration means sexual intercourse, cunnilingus, fellatio, analingus, or anal intercourse, with or without emission, §6-4-301a(ix). *Sexual intrusion* means any intrusion, however slight, by any object or any part of a person's body, except the mouth, tongue or penis, into the genital or anal opening of another person's body if that sexual intrusion can reasonably be construed as being for the purposes of sexual arousal, gratification or abuse, §6-4-301(viii). *Sexual contact* means the touching for the purposes of sexual arousal, gratification, or abuse of the victim's intimate parts by the actor, or the actor's intimate parts by the victim, or the clothing, covering the immediate area of the victim's or actor's intimate parts, §6-4-301a(vii). *Serious bodily injury* means disfigurement, miscarriage, or loss of movement or function to any part of the body, §6-4-301a(v). *Position of authority* means that position occupied by a parent, guardian, relative, household member, teacher, employer, custodian, and any other person who, by reason of his position, is able to exercise significant influence over a person, §6-4-301a(iv). *To retaliate* includes threat of kidnaping, death, serious bodily injury, or extreme physical pain, §6-4-303a(i).

Statutory Age Provisions

Age of Consent

Statutory age offenses not formulated in terms of age of consent. Statutory age of victim set at 12 for sexual assault in the second and third degree and at 16 for sexual assault in the fourth degree. Actor must be at least 4 years older for all offenses except second-degree sexual assault, defined by sexual contact with severe bodily injury upon a person under 12.

Offenses

Second-degree sexual assault: sexual penetration or sexual intrusion when victim is less than 12 and actor is 4 years older, §6-4-303a(v), or sexual contact with person under 12 and actor causes serious bodily injury to the victim, §6-4-303c; third-degree sexual assult: sexual contact when victim is less than 12 and actor is 4 years older, §6-4-304; fourth-degree sexual assault: sexual penetration or sexual intrusion on a victim under 16 when the actor is 4 years older, §6-4-305.

**Evidence Provisions, Defenses,
and Cross References**

Evidence

Evidence statute mandates procedures for admission of evidence of the prior sexual conduct of the victim, reputation evidence or opinion evidence as to the character of the victim; written motion required 10 days prior to trail, offer of proof, in-camera hearing required. Court shall order what evidence may be permitted. All such motions and affidavits are privileged and not to be made available to the public, exception for prior sexual conduct with the actor, §6-4-312; former case law requiring corroboration for rape expressly repealed by statute, §6-4-311.

Defenses

Consent or its absence not defined by statute. An affirmative defense that actor reasonably believed the victim was over 16; no defense that actor reasonably believed victim was over 12, §6-4-308.

Cross References

Incest, §6-5-102; medical examination of victim: statute specifies medical procedures, requires the presence of a witness the same sex as the victim, victim may be examined by his own doctor if no delay, cost to be paid by investigating agency, medical report not required for conviction, report must be available to actor and counsel, §6-4-309; names of alleged victim and actor not to be released prior to indictment, §6-4-310; soliciting anyone under 16, §14-3-104; reference to "employer" and "teacher" in definition of position of authority makes statute viable for prosecution of sexual harassment, see §6-4-301a(iv); exception for reasonable medical practices, §6-4-303a(vii).

Penalties

Terms

First-degree sexual assault: minimum 5 years, maximum 50 years; second-degree sexual assault: minimum 1 year, maximum 20 years; third-degree sexual assault: minimum 1 year, maximum 5 years; fourth-degree sexual assault: county jail term of not more than 1 year, §6-4-306a.

Special

Extended terms for sexual assault when two or more separate acts of sexual assault in the first or second degree, or when previous conviction of a crime containing the same or similar elements, §6-4-306b; extended terms: first-or second-degree sexual assault: minimum 5 years, maximum 10 years; fourth-degree sexual assault: minimum 1 year, maximum 5 years, §6-4-306c.

7

Conclusions and
Import of the Research

Even though legislation cannot possibly accomplish all the objectives of rape victim advocates, legislative solutions have dominated reform efforts. Women who felt themselves oppressed and misused by the laws and legal traditions surrounding rape have turned to the law for a redress of their grievances. The sheer volume of new legislation is overwhelming. Perhaps it is an indication of the effectiveness of feminist lobbying at the state level that so many states have adopted some form of rape reform legislation. The legislative solution is appealing to reformers because it implies there will be systemwide change at the stroke of a pen. Advocates for victims, however, have often learned that the impact of a marvelous new law may be far less than was anticipated. A new law may be ignored, interpreted contrary to the intention of its drafters, burdened with technical encumbrances, or drafted in such a way as to be totally ineffective.

Given institutionalized practices within the crimnal justice system, plea bargaining, manipulated delays and appearances, sentencing practices, and societal patterns which effect arrest, prosecution, and conviction, how can feminists or anyone else prevail by passing legislation on a single issue? On the other hand, no one would recommend waiting for a whole-scale reform of the criminal justice system before attempting to institute reform in the area of rape. Even if rape reform legislation cannot accomplish all its objectives because of the nature of the criminal justice system, an effort must be made to influence that system.

The national character of the reform movement is an indication of the support for feminist ideology within grass-roots political organizations. The people who lobbied through rape reform legislation did it with traditional methods. Some state legislatures were suprisingly responsive. If the legislative solution is to some extent doomed to failure because of the nature of the criminal justice process itself, this is not to condemn efforts at legislative reform. Legislative reforms which redefine the offense and limit the admissibility of potentially prejudicial evidence regarding the victim's prior sexual conduct will make some difference on some occasions. There may even be some courts, judges, prosecutors, and defense attorneys who will be strictly governed by the letter of the new law. The public may be influenced by publicity surrounding the new laws; public discussion of the issues may provide some with their first concrete information on the subject of rape. Changes in the law regarding rape may provoke discussion and education programs in schools. Young people may become sensitive to ways in which the law of rape has mirrored sex-role stereotyping and perpetuated the subjugated status of women in the culture as a whole. Even if only a tiny fraction of cases get before a jury, those jurors as citizens may have learned something about the impetus behind the reform of the rape laws.

The law leads and the law follows. Activists lobbying for reform persuade the legislators, who when they pass rape reform legislation are themselves leading public opinion in the direction of accepting the need for reform. Feminists have been able to make headway by presenting legislators with solid legal arguments and by appealing to the legislators as lawyers. Legislators have been reluctant to come down on the side of a traditional rape statute when the philosophical basis of that statute is pointed out.

Perhaps those aspects of rape reform which do not directly impact upon the guilt determination process of the criminal justice system will have the most significant practical effects: statutes which authorize public funds for rape counseling centers, statutes which require that a person whose sex is the same sex as the victim's be present during the medical examination, statutes which authorize restitution or crime victim compensation for rape, laws which require the state to pay for the medical costs of an examination. The effectiveness of these laws cannot fall within the chasms which yawn across the path from arrest to conviction. These statutes address institutions independent of the criminal justice system.

The impact of the introduction of rape evidence kits in hospital examinations is said to be enormous. A small, seemingly technical innovation, authorized, developed, and paid for by the state, has apparently made identification in many rape cases completely straightforward. Even weeks or months after the attack evidence preserved in the kit, recorded to conform with evidentiary requirements, provides unassailable evidence on the question of identity. The spousal assault laws may in some jurisdictions be hortatory. In others, women advocates will get a court order requiring the police to answer calls and write up complaints; prosecutors will be ordered to return indictments.

Attitudes toward rape and the reform of the rape laws are also important because the legal issues raised regarding rape have important implications for other areas of the law. The redefinition of rape as sexual assault has usually provided greater protection for children who are subjected to sexual abuse. As of 1978 every state had enacted child-abuse legislation, and most states included sexual abuse within the categories of offenses. Social workers and professionals who deal with juvenile prostitutes find a large proportion of juvenile prostitutes were victims of incest of sexual abuse in the home. A girl runs away from home because she is being sexually used or abused by her father. Her sexual experiences at home have produced both a degraded self-image and reinforced the idea that her body is something others want to use. A teenager on the streets is an easy prey to the pimps who are always looking for new, young money-makers in their stables. When the juvenile prostitute is then abused by her pimp, it is what she expects and her only alternative is to run away once more.

In the reform statutes incest is often included as a subcategory of rape. A few states, such as New Jersey, have repealed their former incest statutes. In the new incest laws, the offense is defined in terms of sexual assault upon a child by an older person in a position of authority. The traditional American incest laws were based upon English law, but incest, unlike rape, was an ecclesiastical offense, a crime against canon law. The traditional incest statutes simply prohibited marriage or sexual intercourse between persons within specified degrees of relationship. The harm was perceived as marriage between kin. The new statutes define the harm as emotional and psychological impairment from sexual assault or abuse of the child within the family setting. This is a major philosophical change.

The issue of sexual harassment grew out of the movement to reform the rape laws. The redefinition of force and coercion for the purposes of rape led women to redefine circumstances of sexual coercion which go beyond physical force. Issues concerning women's self-defense have been molded by developments in the area of rape as women realized only they could protect themselves from sexual assault and rape. Battered wives and their advocates and supporters looked to changes in the rape law for increased protection. Homosexuals and lesbians saw the sex-neutral provisions of the reform statutes as protecting them from assaults. Men and women who learned lobbying techniques in the passage of rape reform legislation applied these same techniques to bills designed to protect homosexuals from discrimination in housing and employment.

It was the nature of the reform statutes themselves which in part caused the reform effort to be characterized broadly. The drafters of reform legislation wanted simultaneously to decriminalize whole categories of consenting homosexual and heterosexual conduct while declaring criminal for the first time acts which were beyond the scope of the common-law definition of rape. Reformers wanted to protect children from sexual assaults which did not necessarily result in intercourse. At the same time, most reformers wanted to repeal statutory rape laws, decriminalize acts between consenting teenagers, and protect young girls from coercive or brutal attacks by their peers. Reform statutes criminalized sexual assaults with an object when the rape crisis centers reported such assaults with considerable frequency, and such assaults came to be defined among the most serious sex offenses. All these objectives were to be accomplished in a single statutory package which defined the offense in terms of prohibited circumstances and acts and not in terms of the victim's resistance, subjective consent, or her propensity to consent. How could any statute accomplish such contradictory and subtle objectives even in a criminal justice system which functioned with the precision of a machine?

Amazingly, a large proportion of the reformer's contradictory goals were often incorporated in the drafting process. Sodomy statutes, which had often been used to harass homosexuals, were simultaneously repealed when a sex-neutral definition of sexual assault was drafted. The statutory age for penetration offenses was lowered, but new categories of sexual contract offenses were introduced. Sexual assaults with an object have been criminalized in many states. Incest has in some states been redefined as sexual assault by any person in a position of family authority. Complicated provisions attempt to protect the especially vulnerable inmates of jails and mental institutions while not totally prohibiting consensual sexual activity among confined populations. There is this similarity between the old law and the reform statutes: both define broad categories of conduct as criminal and assume that generally held norms of social and cultural acceptability will determine what actually is reported as criminal to the authorities.

What began as a reform effort directed at one small segment of the law has had an impact far beyond what was expected by the earliest rape victim advocates. Women and men who argued that the status of rape victims in the court should be changed came to see themselves as arguing for an improvement in the status of all women as victims. The public became involved in reform efforts as jurors, potential jurors, legislators, lobbyists, journalists, parents, and public servants. Although it may seem that reform efforts have been unsuccessful insofar as they have not immediately transformed the criminal justice process in rape cases, reform efforts have had a far wider social impact than was ever anticipated. If for no other reason, changing the laws regarding rape should remain at the top of the political agenda.

What does the effectiveness of legal change to date imply for strategies for the future? Even if legislative reform cannot single-handedly accomplish all the goals of rape victim advocates, pressure for legislative reform must continue. Research on the effectiveness of alternative statutory provisions is indispensable if rape victim advocates are going to prevail. A societal backlash to the women's movement is already apparent in the political arena. If women have no data to counteract assertions that the new rape statutes are ineffective, counterproductive, or prejudicial, state legislatures may well erase legislative gains which were the culmination of years of effort. Rape reform legislation was passed in response to intense national and state political pressures from feminists. If women who are hostile to the goals of the feminist movement lobby for a return to the prior rape law, or for laws which define the offense in terms of the victim's behavior, feminists must be prepared to demonstrate with concrete data that the assertions of their adversaries must be rejected on grounds of public policy.

If a defense attorney asks a judge to invalidate a statute which excludes evidence concerning the prior sexual conduct of the victim, women who lobbied for the adoption of the statute should be prepared to supply the prosecutor with background information concerning the purpose of the legislation. If the attorney argues that the exclusion of evidence of the victim's prior sexual conduct is prejudicial to the particular case, rape victim advocates should be prepared with factual arguments based upon reliable research which demonstrate that in the vast proportion of cases the admission of such evidence is prejudicial to the state. Victim advocates must be prepared to argue from data either that the prejudice in this case is exceptional, in fact nonexistent, or if there is a bona fide question of prejudice to the defendant, the court should in this exceptional case admit the evidence. This argument will be stronger if women can show that in the vast majority of rape cases such evidence is completely irrelevant to the legal issues raised, and its exclusion, therefore, cannot be prejudicial to the defense. To make these arguments, someone must go look at what happens in a sizable number of cases.

Studies such as this one have, as their ultimate aim, increasing our understanding of what happens when real jurors decide real cases. We ask questions of potential jurors in hypothetical cases because we want to find out what real jurors do when they decide guilt or innocence in an actual case. Data such as that presented here must be supplemented with data concerning particular cases. Then a match between the two different sources of information can provide us with hypotheses which have predictive power. We want to know how or why jurors make decisions generally because we can then make a more reliable guess about how a particular jury will come down in a specific case.

Although the criminal justice system remains insulated from reform efforts by the nature of its own institutional practices and norms, reformers as citizens can put pressure on that system in a variety of informal ways. Judges notice when ordinary citizens start appearing in court to listen to trials. Victim advocates and counselors experienced with the special problems of rape victims, who must testify as witnesses in a open courtroom, can make an enormous difference in the progress of criminal trials, even if their intervention is unofficial. Ohio has provided for independent representation of rape victims in the guilt determination process, but even without that unusual statutory provision those who understand the problems of rape victims can provide enormous support in individual cases. When a judge makes an outrageously sexist comment about a victim and the community attempts unsuccessfully to impeach or unseat that judge, it is important that a vocal segment of the citizenry has made serious objection to such remarks. The next judge may not make such a comment, and even if impeachment efforts fail, no judge wants to have such proceedings initiated against himself.

The psychological effect of the presence of a substantial number of women in the courtroom during a rape trial cannot be overemphasized. The entire criminal justice system is still dominated by men. In most rape trials the prosecutor, the defense attorney, the court reporter, the judge, the clerk, and the sergeant-at-arms will all be male. Not only is it likely to be comforting to the victim to see female faces in the courtroom, but the judge and the attorney also look out and see those faces. The presence of women at sex offense trials makes an important symbolic statement. The presence of women as observers indicates that women see rape as an issue which effects them as a group. Women must also be sensitive to the other social and cultural realities within the criminal justice process. Just as the criminal justice system is overwhelmingly male, it is overwhelmingly white. The defendant who is black or a Chicano stands as alone as the woman. Women can protect one another in the courtroom without emphasizing or exploiting the racism and class bias which is along with sexism a large part of what is wrong with the institutions of criminal justice.

Rape is a political issue because the way rape victims have been treated is a consequence and side effect of the status of women in the society as a whole. Rape became a rallying cry for women because individual women who had no particular complaint about their own social or economic status found intolerable the expressions of hostility and suspicion which rape victims encountered in the courts and other social institutions. Women who had never been the victims of a crime could not bear to think that other women were subject to arbitrary and senseless victimization which seemed to be condoned by the society. Sexist attitudes, toward rape victims, ignorance and misinformation about the crime, all were woven into the cultural fabric. The official system of justice compounded the victim's difficulties. Police did not seem very interested in arresting offenders; they wanted to know what the victim had done to provoke the attack. Where was it reasonable to start?

Women went into hospitals and argued for changes in procedures regarding the routine treatment and examination of victims. Police officers received training on the special needs of rape victims. The early crisis centers were the real seedbeds of innovation. Change in the laws came relatively late. Feminists attempted to make prosecutors more sensitive to victims' concerns and fears. Many problems remain but real and significant gains can be seen in the attitudes of police, in the practices in hospitals, and in the fact that many states have now enacted statutes attempt to protect victims from harassment and ensure their privacy.

While significant gains have been made, let us not forget that approximately half of the states retain the traditional law of rape. The traditional view of rape remained the prevailing view in this country because it served the purposes of men who thought it more important to protect themselves against imagined false accusations than to convict offenders who had committed rape. Support for the traditional view has not disappeared. The old arguments are just couched in new language. People should never make the mistake of thinking that the traditional rape laws and the legal traditions surrounding rape evolved by accident or oversight. The protection of women from sexual assault was simply not a high priority item for most men. Individual husbands were expected to protect their wives, and women who lived alone did so at their own risk. It was not until women insisted upon changing the law and coupled that insistence with the threat of political retaliation that the law was changed. Change will not continue unless women continue to insist upon protection from sexual assault. To install such changes permanently within the legal system, women must come forward with clear policy objectives, conclusions based upon reliable research, and with data about the crime itself. We have a sense that the factual arguments are overwhelmingly in our favor, it is time now to marshal the facts to prove our case once and for all.

Index

Index

acquaintance rapes, 76-78; violence in, 76, 77

age of juror, decision making and, 129, 132

Alabama rape law, 208-211

Alaska rape law, 212-215

Arizona rape law, 216-219

Arkansas rape law, 220-224

Attitudes toward Rape (ATR), 18-19, 22; application to jury selection of, 87-88; construct validity of, 73; example of, 31-32

Attitudes toward Rape (ATR) response; of citizen sample, 54-56; described, 49-57; factor analysis of, 49, 57-62; respondent characteristics and, 62-70; by respondent group, 52-53, 70-74; by sex and race, 49, 50-51

Attitudes toward Women Scale (AWS), 19, 22; example of, 33-34

attractiveness in juror decision; physical, 13-14, 103, 107, 108, 111, 112, 118, 128-131; social, 117

battered wives, rape law protection for, 461

California rape law, 225

carnal abuse; defined, 157, 166; rape law and, 167

carnal knowledge; defined, 157; statute, 156-157

Center for Rape Concern Model Sex Offense Statute, 158

character evidence, 101-102, 103, 118-119, 167

children, sexual abuse of, 460

citizen sample, 9-10; personal data sheet for, 38; rape attitudes of, 50, 52-53, 54-57, 63, 64, 69, 73; rape knowledge of, 75-86

Colorado rape law, 230-233

Connecticut rape law, 234-237

consent defense, 101; assumption of risk criterion of, 119; degree of resistance in, 56-57; rape law reform and, 159-162; sexual behavior of victim and, 47; spousal exception and, 163-164; statutory age and, 166-167, 170-171

criminal offenses, disposition of, 99

cross-examination, limitations on, 179

defendant characteristics, effects of, 14, 96-98; race, 102, 107-109, 111, 112, 115, 116-117, 125-127

defense case; evidential requirements of, 101; in Legal Rape Case (LRC), 29; plea bargaining and, 184-185; reform statute challenges and, 178-179; for statutory rape, 168-169; strength of evidence and, 16-17. See also consent defense

defenses. See specific state law

Delaware rape law, 238-241

District of Columbia rape law, 242-245; corroboration requirement in, 185

education level, and rape knowledge, 87

evidence; of character, 101-102, 103, 118-119, 167; corroborating, 57, 100; effects of statutory changes on, 174-180; identifying, 81, 100, 460; of penetration, 81, 100-101; of prior sexual experience, 154, 171-174; strength of, 15-17, 103-104, 107, 109, 110, 113, 135-138. See also specific state law

Florida rape law, 246-250; evidence provisions in, 176-178, 249

Georgia rape law, 251-254

Hawaii rape law, 255-259
homosexual assault, 166; rape law
    reform and, 461

Idaho rape law, 260-263
identification of defendant, evidence
    in, 80-81, 100, 460
Illinois rape law, 264-267
incest law reform, 461
Indiana rape law, 268-272
Iowa rape law, 273-277

judge; instructions of, 5; prior sexual
    conduct evidence and, 175, 177, 178
juror decision; circumstantial factors
    in, 6-7; degree of resistance and,
    47-48, 56-57; evidence of prior sex-
    ual experience and, 47, 103, 107,
    108, 109, 118-119, 134-135, 137,
    175; personal knowledge of rape
    victim and, 127-128, 131-132, 135;
    in precipitory vs nonprecipitory
    rape, 103, 107-109, 113, 114, 119,
    131-134, 137; rape attitudes and,
    7-8, 46-48, 87-88, 120, 121-123, 126,
    128-140; rape punishment views
    and, 127, 130, 132-134, 136, 137;
    rapist normality and, 56; strength of
    evidence and, 103-104, 107, 109,
    110, 113, 135-138; victim attrac-
    tiveness in, 103, 107, 108, 117, 118,
    128-131; and victim-defendant racial
    combinations, 107, 108-109, 117-
    118, 141-142; victim precipitation
    factors in, 55; witness credibility
    and, 5-6
juror decision and juror characteristics,
    96-98, 104, 106-114, 117, 120-122,
    123-125, 126; attitudinal vs
    background factors in, 122-123;
    juror-rape case characteristic in-
    teractions in, 125-141, 142-143
juror decision study(s); of actual
    jurors, 4-5; administration pro-
    cedures in, 21; aims of, 463;
    hypothetical case approach to, 4, 5;
    sample groups in, 9-12; summary of

findings in, 95, 96-98. See also At-
    titudes toward Rape (ATR); At-
    tidues toward Women Scale (AWS);
    Legal Rape Case (LRC); Personal
    Data Sheet (PDS); Rape Knowledge
    Test (RKT)
jury selection, 87-88, 123-125, 140

Kansas rape law, 278-281
Kentucky rape law, 282-287

Legal Rape Case (LRC), 22, 105-106;
    crime characteristics in, 14; de-
    fendant characteristics in, 14;
    evidence in, 15-17; example of,
    27-30; victim characteristics in,
    13-14
Louisiana rape law, 288-292

Maine rape law, 293-297
Maryland rape law, 298-302
Massachusetts rape law, 303-306
medical personnel, rape attitudes of, 46
Michigan rape law, 307-311; sexual
    conduct of victim evidence and, 154,
    310; status of consent in, 161, 310
Minnesota rape law, 312-317
Mississippi rape law, 318-322
Missouri rape law, 323-327
Model Penal Code (MPC), rape provi-
    sions of, 155-156; spousal exception
    in, 164-165
Montana rape law, 328-332
moral character of victim. See sexual
    behavior of victim

Nebraska rape law, 333-336
Nevada rape law, 337-341
New Hampshire rape law, 342-346
New Jersey rape law, 347-352; age
    provisions in, 168, 350; legislative
    history of, 156-159, 187, 347-348;
    reform statutes of, 156, 348-349;
    status of consent in, 160, 161, 162,
    351
New Mexico rape law, 353-359
New York rape law, 360-365

North Carolina rape law, 366-370
North Dakota rape law, 371-376
NOW Task Force on Rape, sexual
    assault statute of, 157-158

Ohio rape law, 377-382
Oklahoma rape law, 383-386
Oregon rape law, 387-391

penalties. *See specific state law*
penetration; evidence on, 81, 100-101;
    legal definition of, 170
Pennsylvania rape law, 392-396
Personal Data Sheet (PDS) of sample
    respondents, 20-21, 22; citizens, 38;
    police officers, 39-40; rape crisis
    counselors, 41-42; rapists, 43
physical attractiveness. *See* attractive-
    ness in juror decision
plea bargaining, in rape cases, 182-183,
    184-185
police informants, cross-examination
    limitations on, 179
police officer(s), treatment of rape
    victim by, 46, 74, 77
police officer sample, 10, 11; per-
    sonnel data sheet of, 39-40; rape at-
    titudes of, 52-53, 65, 70, 73; rape
    knowledge of, 75-86
power, as motivation for rape, 56,
    58-59, 63, 72, 130-131, 134
prison sentences; extraevidential
    factors in, 106-125; plea bargained,
    184-185. *See also* juror decision
prosecution case; accommodation
    process and, 184; evidential re-
    quirements of, 80-82, 100-102; in
    Legal Rape Case (LRC), 28-29;
    strength of evidence and, 15, 17,
    103-104
Puerto Rico rape law, 397-400

race differences; in rape attitudes,
    50-51, 62, 63, 65, 67, 68, 70; in rape
    knowledge, 87
race of defendant, 79-80; interaction
    with juror characteristics, 125-127;

and trial outcome, 102, 107, 108,
    109, 111, 112, 115, 116-117, 141-142
race of juror, 124; black juror de-
    cisions, 110-114, 121-122, 135-136;
    interaction with race of defendant,
    125-127; white juror decisions,
    106-109, 117, 120-121
race of victim, 79-80; interaction with
    juror characteristics, 127-131; sexual
    humiliation and, 79; and trial out-
    come, 102-103, 107, 108, 109,
    141-142
rape(s); of acquaintance-victim *vs*
    stranger-victim, 76-78; aggravated *vs*
    simple, 55, 157; arrest rate for, 76,
    99; feminist definition of, 73;
    geographic distribution of, 84, 85;
    legal definition of, 3, 17, 29, 99,
    154-155, 160; location of, 78; for
    power over women, 56, 58-59, 63,
    72, 130-131, 134; precipitory *vs* non-
    precipitory, 14-15, 103, 107, 109,
    113, 114, 115, 131-134, 137; racial
    combinations in, 79-80; rapist
    definition of, 73; reporting of, 45,
    75-76, 179, 180-181; as sexual
    assault, 55, 58, 166, 460-461; sexu-
    ally humiliating practices in, 79
rape(s), violent; acquaintance and,
    76, 77; proportion of, 82-83
rape attitudes; individual differences
    and, 49, 54; of jurors, 7-8, 46-48,
    87-88, 120, 121-123, 126, 128-140;
    of medical personnel, 46; of police
    officers, 46, 52-53, 65, 70, 73; ques-
    tionnaire on, 31-32; rape definition
    and, 3-4; rape knowledge and, 87;
    rape law reform and, 181, 464-465;
    societal, 7-8, 47, 48; studies of,
    48-49; of victim, 45; view of women
    and, 69-70, 74. *See also* Attitudes
    toward Rape (ATR); victim
rape cases; acquittals and dismissals in,
    81, 82, 95, 99; convictions in, 99;
    corroborating evidence in, 57, 100;
    defensive strategies in, 101; evidence
    kit in, 460; plea bargaining in,

rape cases (cont.)
182-183, 184-185; prosecution requirements in, 80-82, 100-102; victim precipitation and, 54-55
rape crisis counselor sample, 10, 11;
personal data sheet for, 41-42; rape
attitudes of, 52-53, 65, 68, 69,
71-73; rape knowledge of, 75-86
Rape Knowledge Test (RKT), 19-20,
22; data collection for, 74-75; example of, 35-37; respondent characteristics and, 85-88; by respondent
group, 75-85
rape law; on consent, 119, 166-167;
equal protection under, 141; proof
requirements in, 46; societal attitude
and, 7-8, 48, 181, 464-465; statutory
age in, 166. See also specific state
law
rape law reform, 118, 140-141; consent
defense and, 158, 159-162; criminal
justice system and, 159, 182, 459,
463-464; educative role of, 180, 186;
evidence provisions in, 171-180;
feminist movement and, 186, 464;
future strategies for, 462-463; goals
of, 186, 461-462; impact of,
174-180; 185-188; incest provisions
in, 461; legal challenges to, 178-179;
legal implications of, 460-462; lobbying efforts in, 153-154, 186, 459,
460; Model Penal Code (MPC) and,
155-156, 164; piecemeal, 171; practical effects of, 460; reported rapes
and, 180-181; restitution provisions
in, 187; spousal provisions in,
163-166; statutory age provisions in,
166-171; trends in, 154-156. See also
specific state law
rape prevention, as women's responsibility, 58; 63, 65, 70-71, 72, 130,
133, 136-137
rape study(s); data collection in, 74.
See also juror decision study(s)
rape trials; accommodation process in,
183-184; effect of women spectators
on, 463-464; extraevidential factors

in, 95, 96-98, 102-105, 106-120,
139-140, 141; judge's instruction in,
5; jury selection in, 87-88, 123-125,
140; procedural aspects of, 99-102;
victim advocate and counselor
testimony in, 463. See also juror
decision
rape victim. See victim
rapists(s); age of, 83-84; motivation
of, 55-56, 58, 63, 72; normality of,
56, 58, 65, 72; race of, 79-80, 81.
See also defendant characteristics
rapist sample, 10, 12; personal data
sheet for, 43; rape attitudes of,
52-53, 63, 65, 67, 71-73; rape
knowledge of, 75-86
resistance during rape; attitudes to, 59,
69, 72; in jury decision, 47-48, 56-57
restitution statutes, 187
Rhode Island rape law, 401-404

sentences and sentencing. See prison
sentences; specific state law
sex differences; in rape attitude, 50-51,
62, 63, 64, 67, 69, 73; in rape
knowledge, 87
sexual assault; legal definition of, 158;
rape as, 55, 58, 166, 460-461
sexual behavior of victim; admissibility
of evidence on, 171-180; consent
defense and, 47, 101-102, 103, 167;
in juror decision, 107, 108-109,
112-114, 115, 118-119, 134-135, 137;
in Legal Rape Case (LRC) example,
14
sexual harassment, rape law reform
and, 461
South Carolina rape law, 405-409
South Dakota rape law, 410-413
spousal exception; for cohabiting
adults, 164; common-law, 165;
under English rule, 163; and rape
law reform, 165-166; for separation
and living apart, 164-165. See also
specific state law
statutory age, 166-167. See also specific
state law

statutory rape; defined, 168; mistake as
to age defense in, 168-169
statutory rape law; age of consent and,
166-167, 170; development of, 166;
reform of, 167-171

Tennessee rape law, 414-415
Texas rape law, 416-420
training program participation, rape
attitudes and, 65, 69

Utah rape law, 421-425

Vermont rape law, 426-429
victim; age of, 83; consent by, 101,
119, 167; identifying evidence of,
81; medical personnel attitudes
toward, 46; police treatment of, 46,
74; post-rape perception of, 59, 65,
72; precipitation by, 54-55, 65, 69,
72, 103, 134-135, 137; privacy rights
of, 179; race of, 79-80, 102-103,
107, 108, 109; rape attitudes of, 45;
rape attitudes toward, 54; resistance
by, 47-48, 56-57, 69, 72; responsibility in rape prevention of, 58,
63, 65, 70-71, 72, 130, 133, 136-137;
witness credibility of, 5-6, 99, 100
victim characteristics and juror
decision, 96-98; attractiveness,
13-14, 103, 107, 108, 111, 112, 117,
118, 128-131, 134; prior sexual experience, 14, 101-102, 103, 107, 108,
109, 112-114, 115, 118-119, 134-135,
137, 167, 175; race, 13, 102-103,
107-109, 111-114, 117-118, 127-128
Virginia rape law, 430-434
Virgin Islands rape law, 435-438

Washington rape law, 439-443;
statutory rape provisions in, 170
West Virginia rape law, 444-448
wives; battered, rape law protection
for, 461; spousal exception in rape
of, 163-166. *See also specific state
law*
Wisconsin rape law, 449-453
women, attitudes to, rape attitudes
and, 69-70, 74
Wyoming rape law, 454-458

About the Authors

Hubert S. Feild is an associate professor of psychology and management at Auburn University. He has served as a consultant to the National Center for the Prevention and Control of Rape and has written numerous articles on legal issues concerning rape. He obtained the Ph.D. in psychology from the University of Georgia.

Leigh Bienen is a criminal defense attorney specializing in the treatment and disposition of sex offenders. She is a former editor of the *Womens' Rights Law Reporter* and has taught law at Princeton University and at the University of California, Berkeley.